THE ADVANCEMENT OF LIBERTY

THE ADVANCEMENT OF LIBERTY

How American Democratic Principles Transformed the Twentieth Century

Matthew C. Price

PRAEGER SECURITY INTERNATIONAL
Westport, Connecticut • London

Library of Congress Cataloging-in-Publication Data

Price, Matthew C., 1962–
    The advancement of liberty : how American democratic principles
transformed the twentieth century / Matthew C. Price.
        p.   cm.
    Includes bibliographical references and index.
    ISBN: 978-0-313-34618-7 (alk. paper)
    1. United States—Foreign relations—20th century.   2. United States—Foreign
relations—Moral and ethical aspects.   3. National characteristics, American.
4. Democracy—History—20th century.   5. Civilization, Modern—American
influences.   6. World politics—20th century.   I. Title.
E744.P745 2008
973.91—dc22   2007036165

British Library Cataloguing in Publication Data is available.

Library of Congress Catalog Card Number: 2007036165

ISBN: 978-0-313-34618-7

First published in 2008

Praeger Security International, 88 Post Road West, Westport, CT 06881
An imprint of Greenwood Publishing Group, Inc.
www.praeger.com

Printed in the United States of America

∞™

The paper used in this book complies with the
Permanent Paper Standard issued by the National
Information Standards Organization (Z39.48-1984).

10   9   8   7   6   5   4   3   2   1

For Ted and Ramona Price

The world must be made safe for democracy. Its peace must be planted upon the tested foundations of political liberty. We have no selfish ends to serve. We desire no conquest, no dominion. We seek no indemnities for ourselves, no material compensation for the sacrifices we shall freely make.

—Woodrow Wilson

Contents

Introduction

CRITICISM IS NATURAL, inevitable, and productive. By it, government and private institutions are held to account, public figures are kept honest, public policies are reformed. However, a vision of America that is based exclusively upon flaws, real and imagined, is as distorting and misleading as an understanding of the world based entirely upon the sensational "if it bleeds, it leads" nightly newscast. It is possible to focus so exclusively upon the critical, that an accurate comprehension is precluded.

No nation is without its flaws, but greater balance is desperately needed in the American public discourse about America. In college (and increasingly even high school) government and history courses, the United States is consistently depicted as an imperialistic power, oppressive of its own people and exploitive of others, dominated by corrupt business interests. In some college courses across the country, students take a survey that includes a question on whether they agree or disagree with the statement that "America is the greatest nation in the world." If a student agrees, it is said to be an indicator of an "authoritarian personality"; if they disagree, it shows they are tolerant.

A study by the nonpartisan Albert Shanker Institute in 2003 entitled "Education for Democracy" found that American secondary school and university classes have focused so lopsidedly on America's failings that those failings have come to be regarded as the whole story, rather than a part of it. By contrast, teachers depict genuinely oppressive foreign systems with much greater sentimentality and indulgence, skimming over widespread and systematic human rights offenses, so that students come away with the perception that America is about as corrupt and repressive as most other societies in the world and in history. The report was supported by a broad range of public and education leaders, from former president Bill Clinton to the conservative Heritage Foundation. "People have been so anxious to be self-critical, probably with good intentions. But we feel that's just gone too far over in that direction," said Sandra Feldman, president of the American Federation of Teachers.[1] The Federation, along with the National Education Association, the nation's two leading education unions, both endorsed the report.[2]

Such portrayals do not convey anything like an accurate understanding of the American history or polity. Also, they are hazardous to the vitality of a free society. Ideology is a poor substitute for actual knowledge. A 2000 survey of thousands of U.S. college seniors at fifty-five of the nation's top colleges (including Harvard, Yale, Stanford, etc.) by the Center for Survey Research and Analysis found that less than half of students about to graduate from college possess "general information about American democracy and the Constitution," and most "do not know specifics about major wars the United States participated in." Eighty-one percent of the college seniors scored a D or F on basic *high school–level* questions. More were familiar with figures from MTV than with James Madison. Having majored in history gave no advantage. The report, funded by the American Council of Trustees and Alumni, was aptly titled, "Losing America's Memory: Historical Illiteracy in the 21st Century."[3]

That ignorance conduces to a stupefying relativism, in which every society, every culture, every political system is regarded to be as good as every other. I ask my students: "Should the United States prevent Kim Jung-Il's attempt to acquire nuclear weapons?" A frequent response: "Why shouldn't North Korea be able to have nuclear weapons? We have them." It is not an uncommon sentiment. The American government has flaws; the North Korean government has flaws: therefore they are essentially similar.

American power has been the greatest organized force for liberty and democracy in the history of the world. America's championing of freedom in the twentieth century is one of the great and pivotal sagas in the human story. At the beginning of the century there were six democratic nations in the world: the United States, Britain, Canada, Australia, New Zealand, and France. By century's end, most nations were democratic, and democracy was widely regarded as the sole legitimate form of polity. As historian Taylor Branch wrote at the close of the century, "Reborn from ancient Greece, democracy entered the twentieth century as a boisterous but lonely young orphan, and stands now after a blip of time as a solitary grandparent. . . . with scarcely anyone on the planet arguing for the future of a rival or descendant political order."

Few would dispute that the United States has been among the Great Powers of history. A good case can be made for it being the greatest power of all time. But in addition to being a Great Power, it has also been a *good* power, whose might and influence have been used to the incalculable benefit of humanity. The story of America in the twentieth century is the story of the world transformed. Democracy is today so widely accepted as the only legitimate form of polity that it hardly seems possible that, within the memories of many now living, democracy was everywhere under attack, and hung, as it were, by a slim cord. Liberty is not the inevitable condition of mankind. Freedom has been the exception in history, not the rule. It was not inevitable that things would turn out the way they did. At the dawn of the new millennium fascism might well have been pervasive. Totalitarianism might have taken deep root. The fact that liberty is ascendant has a great deal to do with American ideals, American will, American power. Early in the twentieth century, Woodrow Wilson said that the United States should strive to make the world safe for democracy. It did so. This is that story.

1

"We Seek No Indemnities for Ourselves"

AT THE DAWN of the twentieth century, the American disposition to steer clear of foreign entanglements seemed mere prudence. From the late 1800s, the Great Powers of Europe had built more and more powerful armies, and jockeyed for more formidable alliances, in preparation for a war that appeared increasingly inevitable. The nationalism that had taken root during the age of the French Revolution was now flourishing. The cry "This is my own, my native land" reverberated across the Continent, and teachers taught school-boys the ancient Latin maxim, "It is sweet and fitting to die for one's country."[1] In the years leading up to the First World War, one-third or more of the national budgets of the European powers went for military spending.[2] There were at that time only three democracies in all of Europe.

Amidst the growing clangor of strident nationalisms and the buildup of vast standing armies across the Continent, statesmen on both sides of the Atlantic warned of a drift toward war. In May 1899, representatives from twenty-six leading nations met at a villa in The Hague, Netherlands, to discuss world peace. Although the delegates managed to agree on the establishment of a Court of Arbitration to resolve international disputes (participation in which would be optional), and adopted declarations against poison gas, expanding bullets, and air bombardment, the arms race in preparation for the coming conflict only accelerated.

By 1914 a mood of revelry was in the air as armies across Europe mobilized for war. Here at long last was a chance for individuals and nations to prove their worth on the fields of martial glory. The relatively few wars on the Continent in the preceding century (including France against Russia in the 1850s, France against Austria in 1859, and Germany against France in 1870) had all been short-lived. Most Europeans had been spared direct personal experience with warfare. In 1914 it was still easy to idealize war. Freud said that he felt himself to be fully Austrian for the first time in thirty years. Philosophers and poets extolled war's ennobling influence upon individual and nation.

When, on June 28, 1914, a Slavic nationalist murdered an obscure Austrian archduke, Francis Ferdinand, the Austrians sprang at the opportunity and, backed by Germany, declared war on Serbia the following month. Russia, Britain, and France came to the aid of the Serbs. The Ottoman Empire sided with the Central Powers (Germany and Austria-Hungary). In every nation, declarations of war were met with spontaneous celebrations and exuberant nationalist demonstrations, with crowds gathering in the streets, cheering their troops and singing their national anthems.[3] By the time the war was over, thirty-two nations had been dragged or enticed into what would become, until that time, the most ruinous conflict in history.

It is said that you may start a war when you like, but not end it. This would prove more true in the age of industrialized nationalism than it had ever been before. The euphoria would not last long, as the horrors of technological war became known, but the nationalist zeal that gave rise to the conflict would keep nations fighting for pride long after they had lost all enthusiasm for the fight. The German drive into France did not bring the quick victory that the planners had counted on. Instead, fighting on the "Western Front" quickly became mired in a stasis of trench warfare, with the two sides virtually immobile for the next three years, battling and dying for a few miles, or a few hundred feet, amidst a scope of suffering and degradation unprecedented in military history.

German officers commanded their men to dig trenches as a defense against advancing Allied troops. French and British soldiers, unable to break through the German lines, dug their own trenches. Within a year the line of earthworks stretched hundreds of miles, with opposing sides facing off between a no-man's-land often only a few hundred feet across. From October 1914 until March 1918, none of the offensives launched from either side, consuming millions of lives, managed to move the front line so much as ten miles.[4] On the Eastern Front, the Russians quickly took the offensive, but were turned back in an attempted invasion of East Prussia in August–September 1914. Years of inconclusive fighting in Central Europe followed, inflicting around 1.8 million Russian combat deaths, another 2.8 million casualties, and over 2 million civilian deaths. The war devastated the Russian economy, created horrendous food shortages and mass starvation, and precipitated the Russian Revolution of 1917, which ultimately took Russia out of the conflict.

Rapid-fire machine guns, capable of shooting five hundred or more rounds per minute, were the characteristic weapon of the war, and determined the characteristic tactic: trench warfare. The ubiquitous companion to the machine gun was a less technologically sophisticated though no less seminal implement of war. In ranches of the American West, a simple invention—a length of steel wire containing projecting, sharp, coiled-wire barbs—had proved useful in controlling the movement of cattle. Together with the machine gun, barbed wire was proving invaluable in limiting the movement of men.

Trench warfare was not a combat of advancement so much as of attrition. The aim was not to conquer territory, but to annihilate as many of the enemy as possible. If the machine gun was the defensive weapon of choice, in a primarily defensive war, artillery was the main instrument of offense. From easily transported 20mm "mountain guns" to massive German 17-inch Krupp howitzer "siege guns," firing shells weighing over a ton each, artillery relentlessly pounded soldiers in the trenches (and even civilians in villages and cities) and ultimately took more lives than the machine gun, from which the earthworks at least provided some refuge. Trenches provided no sanctuary from poison gas, however, first used by the Germans in April 1915 and soon adopted by both sides. Ultimately mustard, chlorine, and other poison gases inflicted some 1.3 million casualties.

Other war technologies—tanks on the ground and flying machines in the air—added to the sense that a new age of warfare had arrived, but neither weapon would be militarily decisive in this war. What most characterized this first modern war was immobility: squalid life and inglorious death in the quagmire of filthy, soggy, rat-infested, disease-ridden holes dug into the ground.

From the security of their continental detachment, Americans witnessed the carnage and saw no reason to become embroiled in it. President Woodrow Wilson, whose first two years as president had focused on domestic affairs, offered to mediate between the two sides but was rebuffed. Over time, Wilson came to understand that the conflict was not simply another in a long series of geopolitical struggles among the Europeans, but that it represented a defense of imperiled democratic values against authoritarian aggression. He set about to convince the American public.

In May 1915, a German submarine sank the British Cunard passenger liner *Lusitania* off the coast of Ireland, killing 1,195 passengers, including 124 Americans. Though the sinking of the *Lusitania* and other ships aroused a languid American public, neither the American public nor the Congress wished to enter the war. When President Wilson hinted at retaliation, Secretary of State William Jennings Bryan resigned in protest,[5] and Wilson was threatened with a revolt by congressional Democrats.

By the end of 1916, after yet another calamitous year of mutual destruction, the zeal for war that had once excited the peoples of Europe was now long spent, and President Wilson hoped that the devastated belligerents were finally ready for peace. In December he sent a note to both sides, "merely proposing that soundings be taken in order that we may learn . . . how near the haven of peace may be for which all mankind longs with an intense and increasing longing." Describing himself as a "friend of all nations engaged in the present struggle," he called on the belligerents to state their war aims, as a starting point for discussions, and commit to a negotiated settlement.[6] Again, to no avail. By now both sides had suffered too much and inflicted too much suffering for the war to end any way but in the total desolation of one, or the other, or both.

———◆———

Secretary of State Robert Lansing had already favored siding with the Allies even before resumption of unrestricted submarine warfare. He believed that a German victory would be catastrophic for democracy worldwide. But he, like President Wilson, recognized the importance of public support in waging war. "If our people only realized the insatiable greed of those German autocrats in Berlin and their sinister purpose to dominate the world, we would be at war today," he wrote in a January 28 memo. "Sooner or later the die will be cast and we will be at war with Germany. It is certain to come. We must nevertheless wait patiently until the Germans do something which will arouse general indignation and make all Americans alive to the peril of German success in this war."[7]

The German naval leadership continued to argue for unrestricted submarine warfare, insisting that there was no point in abandoning a potent military tactic for fear of alienating the Americans. Though United States industrial power was enormous, the country was militarily weak, and German strategists agreed that American culture was distinctly lacking in martial virtues.[8] The secretary of state for the German navy assured the Reichstag, "America from a military point of view means nothing, and again nothing, and for a third time nothing."[9]

He may have been right. With only the seventeenth-largest army in the world, outdated weaponry, and an operational structure virtually unchanged since its last major battles more than half a century earlier, in the Civil War, the U.S. military posed no immediate threat to any European power. In January 1917, Germany resumed unrestricted submarine warfare, a decision that proved to be one of the great strategic blunders of the war. With American ships now under regular attack from German U-boats, when, on February 3, President Wilson cut off diplomatic relations with Germany, he had the support of most Americans. Only a few months earlier he had been reelected on the slogan "He kept us out of the war."

During March, German U-boats sank four clearly marked American merchant ships, killing thirty-six. Americans were reluctant combatants, but they had had enough. On the second day of April 1917, Woodrow Wilson spoke before a joint session of Congress, asking for a declaration of war against Germany. America's quarrel was not with the German people, Wilson said. "We are . . . the sincere friends of the German people, and shall desire nothing so much as the early reestablishment of intimate relations of mutual advantage between us, however hard it may be for them, for the time being, to believe that this is spoken from our hearts." Rather, America's fight was with a dictatorial regime that harkened back to an age of despotism, "when peoples were nowhere consulted by their rulers and wars were provoked and waged in the interests of dynasties or little groups of ambitious men who were accustomed to use their fellow men as pawns and tools."[10]

President Wilson did not argue for war merely on the basis of narrow national material interests at stake. There were greater issues involved. "Neutrality is no longer feasible where the peace of the world is involved and the freedom of its peoples. . . . We are glad, now that we see the facts with no veil of false pretense about them, to fight thus for the ultimate peace of the world and for the liberation of its peoples, the German people included." The Great War was to be about nothing less than what direction human history would take.

"The world must be made safe for democracy," Wilson said. "We have no selfish ends to serve. We desire no conquest, no dominion. We are but one of the champions of the rights of mankind. We shall be satisfied when those rights have been made as secure as the faith and the freedom of the nations can make them."

Wilson the politician was simply putting into practice principles that Wilson the intellectual had long espoused. As a student of government, he had come to regard America as exceptional among nations, with exceptional responsibilities. Without the fulfillment of those responsibilities, he felt, America could not fulfill its own potential. The United States could not realize its ideals at home, he had written much earlier, "if we suffer them to be hopelessly discredited amongst the peoples who have yet to see liberty and the peaceable days of order and comfortable progress. We should lose hope ourselves, did we suffer the world to lose faith in us as the champions of these things."[11] American action in the war was to be visible philosophy. Four days later, the Congress of the United States voted for a declaration of war (by a vote of 82–6 in the Senate).

In Western Europe the response to the American Congress's vote for a declaration of war was euphoric. Large crowds gathered outside the American embassy in Rome and other European capitals, singing "The Star Spangled Banner" and waving American flags. Former Italian premier Liezzati sent a dispatch to Wilson, signed by sixty-seven deputies, saying, "Your message, with its ideal beauty and political contents, brings us back to the dawn of civilization when the United States, inspired by Washington, gave the oppressed peoples of Europe and of the two Americas the fruitful example of their redemption. Your message is not addressed to the United States alone, but to all humanity, and awakens the noblest instincts among free nations. Your message is a hymn of freedom."

In France, the Stars and Stripes were flown over homes, shops, and government buildings throughout the country; President Wilson's picture was placed on government billboards. French president Poincaré wrote to Wilson, "At the moment when, under the generous inspiration of yourself, the great American Republic, faithful to its ideals and its traditions, is coming forward to defend with force of arms the cause of justice and liberty, the people of France are filled with the deepest feelings of brotherly appreciation."[12]

British prime minister Lloyd George, in a message to the American people, said that the British public, "wish me, in its behalf, to recognize the chivalry and courage which calls the people of the United States to dedicate the whole of their resources and service to the greatest cause that ever engaged human endeavor."[13]

The British House of Commons passed the resolution: "This House desires to express to the Government and people of the United States of America their profound appreciation of the action of their Government in joining the Allied Powers, and thus defending the high cause of freedom and rights of humanity against the gravest menace by which they have ever been faced."[14] Herbert Asquith, a member of Parliament and former prime minister, said "I doubt whether even now the world realizes the full significance of the step America has taken." He called America's entry into the war "one of the most disinterested acts in history."

On "America Day" in London, April 20, the American flag flew as prominently as the Union Jack and was even raised over Parliament, the first time a flag of another nation had ever flown there. Huge crowds lined the streets as a procession carried the king and queen to St. Paul's Cathedral, where they participated in "A solemn service to Almighty God on the occasion of the entry of the United States into the great war of freedom."

The chancellor of the exchequer declared that "The New World has been brought in, or has stepped in, to restore the balance of the Old. . . . I venture to express the hope and belief that a change is coming; that the long night of sorrow and anguish which has desolated the world is coming to a close."

———◆———

Recruiting and equipping an army would take some time, though. The United States military lacked both the manpower and experience of its European counterparts. Outside of the modest campaign against insurgents in the Philippines and minor expeditions to Mexico, its most recent significant combat experience—during the Spanish-American War—had occurred nearly a generation earlier. America was not prepared for war. Some advocates of isolationism, indeed, had taken military weakness to be all the protection the United States needed, since by it America would pose no threat to other nations and would thus provoke no hostility.

Preparation for war did not only entail strictly military mobilization. Besides outfitting the millions of soldiers needed to revitalize beleaguered Allied forces, America would also be called on to contribute a vast supply of provisions, to feed nations whose agricultural production had been devastated. Even if the fighting ended immediately, it would be years before

European food production returned to prewar levels. The "supreme need" of the Allies, President Wilson told farmers, was "an abundance of foodstuffs," without which "the whole great enterprise upon which we have embarked would flounder."[15] Farmers donated unused land and labor to the cause. Boy Scouts and other civic groups cultivated community "war gardens." Henry Ford and other factory owners gave workers time off to assist with the harvest. Corporations waited for planting or harvest time to close factories for repairs. High schools released students to assist on family farms. Housewives joined the United States Food Administration, pledging to reduce unnecessary household waste.

Across the country, Americans donated their time and money, to public and private organizations alike, for the war effort. One out of every three people contributed to the Red Cross, a vital relief organization on the battlefields of Europe: $283,500,000 was raised. Americans bought War Stamps— $966,270,000 worth in 1918. "Liberty Loan" war bonds were sold. A poster depicted an American soldier in combat and entreated: "Ask his mother how many Bonds you should buy." Another declared: "My boy, I backed you." The bonds were oversubscribed. More than $15 billion worth of notes were purchased, raising more capital in a shorter time than ever before in human history. [16]

On September 3, President Wilson delivered an address to incoming recruits. This was not a war of conquest, he told them, but a defense of fundamental American values. "The eyes of the world will be upon you, because you are in some special sense the soldiers of freedom. Let it be your pride, therefore, to show all men everywhere not only what good soldiers you are, but what good men you are. . . . Let us set ourselves a standard so high that it will be a glory to live up to it, and then let us live up to it and add a new laurel to the crown of America."

Recruit training, arduous under any circumstances, was intensified by the constraints of the situation, and performed by a cohort of young men who only weeks before had been students, office clerks, farmboys. As the demand grew for more rapid mobilization, by war's end some recruits found themselves on the battlefields of France just two weeks after being inducted into the Army.

A million Frenchmen gathered in the streets of Paris on the Fourth of July, 1917, to welcome the first contingent of arriving soldiers. *"Vive les Americains!"* they shouted. The troops marched in formation from Napoleon's tomb to Picpus Cemetery, burial site of Lafayette, showered the whole way with flowers and cheers. At the cemetery, one lieutenant proclaimed, "Lafayette, we are here!"

Wreaths were laid at Lafayette's tomb. Maj. Gen. John Pershing, commander of the American Expeditionary Force, declared in a speech, "I hope that here on the soil of France and in the school of French heroes, our American soldiers may be able to battle and to vanquish for the liberty of the world." Back home, the *New York Times* wrote that "an old debt is being paid."

Both the Allies and the Germans knew that it would take many months before the "doughboys" could arrive in sufficient numbers to make a difference on the battlefield.

There was no possible preparation for the brutality of modern warfare, the horror of poison gas, or life in the trenches. Yet hundreds of thousands of American boys, suddenly separated from homes, friends, and family to fight "over there," faced the challenge with genuine enthusiasm and earnest conviction in the justice of their cause. Pvt. Lloyd Staley expressed the feeling of innumerable doughboys in a letter from the battlefields of France to his sweetheart, Mary, back home in Kansas. "Maybe if America had let her task slide it would not have affected me or you materially, but we would not have held up the ideals that our country was founded on. . . . If I should fall, there certainly could not be anything nobler in my short life to fall for. So there you are, and I think that most everyone in our Army has some of the same sort of idea."[17]

From the outset, for President Wilson and the Americans, U.S. involvement in the war "over there" must be about more than merely another in an endless series of European power conflicts. On January 8, 1918, Wilson delivered his historic Fourteen Points speech to a joint session of Congress, outlining a vision for a more peaceful and just postwar world. He called for the end of that age-old instrument of international diplomacy, secret treaties: instead, "open covenants of peace openly arrived at." He called for freedom of the seas, open trade, arms reductions, decolonization, and the creation of an "association of nations . . . for the purpose of affording mutual guarantees of political independence and territorial integrity to great and small nations alike." In this noble quest, Wilson said, the Americans were not acting only in their own narrow interests, but for all mankind. "All the peoples of the world are in effect partners in this interest, and for our part we see very clearly that unless justice be done to others, it will not be done to us."[18]

Wilson's speech was lauded worldwide as marking the dawn of a new age of international relations. Across the globe, the president was praised as a prophet of a new era of global peace. "You do not know and cannot appreciate the anxieties I have experienced as a result of many millions of people having their hopes raised by what I have said," he confided to a friend.[19]

The points were well received everywhere except among their primary targets, the belligerents in Europe, where the Central Powers scornfully rejected the points as utopian, and the Allies, conscious of their dependence on American assistance, publicly acclaimed Wilson's vision and secretly continued making their own very different plans for the postwar world. Meanwhile, they pressed Wilson to accelerate deployment of the American force. "There can be little doubt that victory or defeat for the Allies depends upon the arrival of the American infantry," Lloyd George told the president.[20]

———•———

By any measure, the Americans seemed to have joined up with the losing side. German submarines had stymied Allied shipping, and German machine guns and artillery had paralyzed—and demoralized—Allied troops. There had not been a successful Allied offensive of any significance in the preceding three years. In the spring of 1917, half of the French army had mutinied, its soldiers refusing to go on the offensive. The French commander in chief, Gen. Robert Nivelle, was replaced by Gen. Henri Philippe Pétain, who immediately announced that the French army would cease offensive operations until the U.S. troops arrived—"to avoid losses and await American reinforcements." On a tour of French divisions, General Petain told them "we must wait for the Americans."[21]

As American forces were gradually placed on the battlefront, demoralized French troops sometimes called out to them *"La guerre est fini,"* "the war is over." "I am very glad that America has entered the war," Pétain remarked to Pershing. "I hope it is not too late."[22]

With about 120 submarines in their fleet by 1917, the Germans had inflicted a crippling blow to Allied shipping and were slowly fulfilling their plan to incapacitate Britain's ability to make war. In a letter to his brother in Canada, British writer F. S. Oliver described a London whose wheeled traffic was one-third its prewar level, "where nearly all the necessities of life, except air and water, have to be bought in the most sparing quantities . . . ' where coal, coke, matches, and everything of that nature have to be husbanded as if they were heaps of gold. . . . I expect we shall be pretty hungry by November."[23]

German U-boat successes, moreover, were growing. During the early stages of the war, the submarines had been sinking around 120,000 tons of Allied shipping a month. In February 1917 they sank over half a million tons; in March, three-quarters of a million tons; and in April, nearly 900,000 tons. One-fourth of the ships leaving Britain never reached their destination.[24] American military planners were taken aback at learning of the extent of the German U-boat successes. When, in April, Adm. William Sims, commander-designate of U.S. naval forces in Europe, met with the British Admiralty and was presented with the numbers, he remarked in dismay, "But this means we are losing the war." To which his British counterpart responded, "That's right—and there's nothing we can do about it."[25]

In June, Admiral Jellicoe, first sea lord of the British Admiralty, told the War Cabinet, "There is no good discussing plans for next spring—we cannot go on."[26]

Meanwhile, German infantrymen prepared for a new round of offensives, assured by their leaders that victory was near. German military strategists, in fact, felt a growing urgency to win a decisive campaign, as Quartermaster General Erich von Ludendorff said, "before America can throw strong forces into the scale."

By October 1917 the first American troops were being stationed in trenches on the Western Front. A French veteran said of the arriving Americans, "As human beings and raw material, they're the very best. . . . But they need a deal of training. The hardest thing to teach them is not to be too brave. They must first learn to hide. That's the first essential in this war."[27] To break the will of the doughboys before they could reinvigorate the Allies' fighting spirit, Ludendorff ordered his artillery commanders to give U.S. soldiers "special treatment"—in relentless barrages of gas and artillery.

The Germans launched a major offensive in hopes of deciding the war before large numbers of Americans could alter the balance. By early June 1918, German troops were within fifty-six miles of Paris. In a speech at New York City, the British high commissioner to the United States read an urgent message from the prime minister: "We are at the crisis of the war, attacked by an immense superiority of German troops," it said. "Our army has been forced to retire . . . before the pressure of a steady succession of fresh German reserves . . . It is impossible to exaggerate the importance of getting American reinforcements across the Atlantic in the shortest possible space of time."[28]

The leaders of England, France, and Italy sent a joint communiqué to President Wilson, appealing for the rapid deployment of American forces. "There is danger that the war will be lost unless the speedy arrival of additional American troops serves to restore weakened Allied reserves. . . . Thus only can defeat be avoided."[29]

But the Americans *were* coming. First in a steady trickle, then a torrent, they arrived. Wave after wave of doughboys arrived in France ready to fight, tens of thousands each week, the "inexhaustible flood of gleaming youth in its first maturity of health and vigor," as one observer called them. And what they brought with them, in the first place, was hope. A fresh breeze of possibility began to fill the air. Just when all had seemed lost, wrote French staff officer Pierrefeu, "swarms of Americans began to appear on the roads. At Coulummiers and Mieux they passed in interminable columns, closely packed in lorries, with their feet in the air in extraordinary attitudes, some perched on the tilt, almost all bare headed and bare chested, singing American airs at the top of their voices amid the enthusiasm of the inhabitants. The spectacle of these magnificent youths from overseas, these beardless children of twenty, radiating strength and health in their equipment, produced a great effect. . . . We all had the impression that we were about to see a wonderful operation of transfusion of blood. Life was coming in floods to reanimate the dying body of France."[30]

English writer Vera Brittain, who served as a nurse in France, wrote in her 1933 autobiographical work *Testament of Youth*: "[The Americans] looked larger than ordinary men; their tall, straight figures were in vivid contrast to the under-sized armies of pale recruits to which we had grown accustomed. . . . They seemed, as it were, Tommies in heaven. . . . Then I heard an excited exclamation from a group of Sisters behind me. 'Look! Look! Here are the Americans!' I pressed forward with the others to watch the United States physically enter the war, so god-like, so magnificent. . . . The coming of relief made me realize at once how intolerable had been the tension, and with the knowledge that we were not, after all, defeated, I found myself beginning to cry."

——————

It was an apprentice military. Eighty-seven percent of the soldiers in the U.S. Army were in their first year of service. Fewer than 5 percen had four or more years of service.[31] Yet, with the large number of U.S. troops now pouring into France, the German High Command understood that unless the Americans were quickly discredited as a fighting force, they would continue to revitalize the war-weary Allies. Every battle now held vast significance and, as was becoming increasingly evident, the Germans had underestimated the fighting spirit of the sons of democracy: the Americans could fight. In May, U.S. forces captured the heavily fortified town of Cantigny, in the Somme region, and then repelled a series of violent counterattacks over the following few days.

An aide to General Pershing, after meeting with the French military leadership, reported that "they were very enthusiastic over the American troops. It is in some instances touching to hear their expressions of praise and gratitude over the rapid arrival of the Americans. . . . I enclose copy of Colonel Paille's report of June 5. . . . I think I am justified in reporting him as wildly enthusiastic."[32]

Approaching the dense forest of Belleau Wood, a German stronghold, the doughboys encountered retreating French soldiers moving in the opposite direction. When the French advised the Americans that they, too, should retreat, Capt. Lloyd Williams made a reply that would live in history: "Retreat, Hell! We just got here!"

From June 6 to 20, the Marines lost eight thousand casualties, dead and wounded, in the Battle of Belleau Wood. Enemy machine gun emplacements, concealed in the dense forest, swept every inch of the terrain, and five assaults were violently repelled before the ground could be captured and held. In the costliest battle in the history of the U.S. Marine Corps to that time, the Americans had defeated the vaunted German military, denying the enemy access to railroad supply lines and effectively halting the German march on Paris, which had appeared so inexorable that the local government was preparing to evacuate.

Democracy could produce warriors, after all, when it had to. "The spirit of the [American] troops is high," declared a communication from the German front. The German units had been ordered to inflict as many casualties as possible upon the young recruits, to crush their notoriously high morale. It hadn't worked. "The various attacks of the marines were carried out smartly and ruthlessly. The moral effect of our fire did not materially check the advance of the infantry. The nerves of the Americans are still unshaken."[33] The veteran German troops were bewildered and dispirited by their defeat at the hands of the Americans. And they knew that many, many more were on the way.

General Ludendorff launched a desperate offensive against Allied forces along the Marne River. U.S. troops suffered twelve thousand casualties in the battle, fighting so ferociously that French troops began calling the Americans *"les terribles"* for their battlefield ferocity. "Had I not seen it with my own eyes," reported the French liaison officer, "I would never have believed that green troops would advance under such fire."[34] "The feature of the battle upon which the eyes of all the world are fixed, and those of the enemy with particular intentness, is the conduct of the American troops," proclaimed the London *Telegraph*.

By early August the Germans had been driven back to the positions they had held prior to the launch of the spring offensives. They had lost 168,000 men in the campaign, a million since March. From now on, it would be all defense. A despondent General Ludendorff went to talk with the chief of the German general staff, Paul von Hindenburg. "What should Germany do?" he asked in despair. "Do? Do!" shouted Hindenburg. "Make peace, you idiot!"

In the Battle of St. Mihiel, in mid-September, 300,000 U.S. troops assaulted and defeated a heavily fortified German force entrenched about ten miles southeast of Verdun, on ground the Germans had held since the earliest stages of the war. The American troops, few of whom had any battlefield experience, captured over 15,000 German prisoners and 450 cannon, themselves suffering 8,000 casualties. It was the first major Allied offensive of the year against a trench system, and it was an unqualified victory.

"The enemy has made many mistakes in this great war," Prime Minister Lloyd George wrote to General Pershing, "and none greater than when he underrated the valor, determination, and intrepid spirit of the brave soldiers of the United States of America. Now that he has tasted the mettle of the American Armies, the enemy knows what is in store for him."

Ludendorff was alarmed at the growing sense of "looming defeat" spreading through the German ranks, which he ascribed to "the sheer number of Americans arriving daily at the front."[35]

The Allies launched the Meuse-Argonne offensive on September 26, with 600,000 French and American troops, in an attempt to drive the Germans out of the region north and west of Verdun. All involved, on both sides, knew that the territory and the battle was vital to Germany's prospects. An Allied victory here might mean ending the war early, but there would be a heavy price to pay for it. Noting the exhaustion of the French forces, Allied Supreme Commander Ferdinand Foch assigned the main attacking duties to the Americans, with the French at their flanks. By the end of the offensive, more than a million U.S. soldiers would be at the front or on their way there.

Moving through a hailstorm of machine gun and artillery fire, the American advance was slow going. They pressed forward against stiff German resistance, "one damn machine gun after another,"[36] and inexorably rolled up the German line. More than 26,000 Americans lost their lives in the Meuse-Argonne offensive, and another 100,000 were wounded.

Yet it was the enemy's will that was breaking. On October 2 a representative of the German Supreme Command told members of the Reichstag that "we can no longer win the war," and that efforts must be initiated to secure peace. The fact was that Germany had simply run out of young men to put into battle, and Allied losses were being replenished by a vast reservoir of spirited American troops. The next day Paul von Hindenburg issued a letter to the Reichstag calling for an immediate "peace offer to our enemies." Due to the "impossibility of making good our very heavy losses . . . of the last few days," the chief of staff explained, "there no longer exists any prospect . . . of forcing peace upon our enemies."[37]

Now, Kaiser Wilhelm saw the wisdom of Wilson's Fourteen Points, and in early October he informed the president that the Germans would agree to an immediate "restoration of peace" based on his idealistic vision. In a series of communications, President Wilson informed the Kaiser that the Allies would draw up peace terms that would "make a renewal of hostilities on the part of Germany impossible," and called for a reform of Germany's authoritarian government. Negotiations proceeded alongside the fighting, and in early November the Allies launched their last great push of the war, overwhelming the heavily fortified Freya Stellung defensive line. On Sunday, November 10, German negotiators accepted Allied conditions for an armistice.

The prelude to the Paris Peace conference went far better for President Wilson than the conference itself. During visits to England, France, and Italy he was paraded like a conquering Roman general. Upon his arrival in France at the port city of Brest, the mayor greeted him: "Mr. President, upon this Breton soil our hearts are unanimous in saluting you as the messenger of justice and peace. Tomorrow it will be our entire nation which will acclaim you, and our whole people will thrill with enthusiasm over the eminent statesman who is the champion of their aspirations toward justice and liberty."[38]

Wounded soldiers and old women rushed up to the president to express their love and appreciation or kiss his hand. The king and queen of England feted him as a hero of the nation. King George welcomed him by saying, "It was love of liberty, respect for law, good faith and the sacred rights of humanity that brought you to the Old World to help in saving it from the dangers that were threatening it around, and that arraigned those citizen-soldiers of yours, whose gallantry we have admired . . . we thank the American people for their noble response to the call of civilization and humanity."[39] In the French capital, 2 million Parisians lined the president's route, cheering *"Vive Wilson! Vive L'Amerique!"* Italians hailed him as "the god of peace." Crowds gathered along his rail route to cheer as his train rolled by.

"Humanity leapt to accept and glorify Wilson," noted the British writer H. G. Wells. "It seized on him as its symbol. He was transfigured in the eyes of men. He ceased to be a statesman; he became a Messiah."[40] Though in the tumult of the postwar crisis his vision would not be adopted, the seeds of a future order would be planted—a global order in which the autonomy of nation-states would be increasingly respected, the use of force increasingly devalued, liberal democratic ideals widely recognized, and international power determined by peaceful economic competition rather than military conquest. These things would take time—another war and another generation—but the vision was being laid forth. It was fundamentally the American vision of how a free and democratic world could be. There was nothing new in the vision Wilson espoused. He was drawing upon ideas that had been perennial in American political discourse. Wilson was "the Henry Ford of international liberalism," as Michael Mandelbaum has called him, "taking what had already been invented and offering it to the world."[41]

In his own day (and to this one) many observers dismissed Wilson as an idealist, out of his depth among more sophisticated "realists." He was indisputably self-righteous, intransigent, and politically gawky. It was the ideas, not their exponent, that were magnetic. Yet the democratic vision he espoused would become, by the end of the century, the dominant blueprint for world order. Future generations may regard Woodrow Wilson the idealist as the most pragmatic politician of his age. "Sometimes people call me an idealist," said Wilson. "Well, that is the way I know I am an American. America is the only idealistic nation in the world."

————◆————

The conference, which opened on January 12, 1919, was attended by leaders of thirty-two Allied and associated nations, but dominated by four: Britain, France, Italy, and the United States. The Central Powers nations were not invited. At the first plenary session, President Wilson addressed the delegates, saying that the objective of the conference must be to do more than simply resolve the immediate issues relating to postwar settlements: it must also establish an international environment that would secure the future peace of the world. Neither goal, he insisted, could be attained without the establishment of an association of nations committed to the preservation of international harmony. Wilson, the optimist, had planned on the conference lasting a few weeks. Instead, it wore on for half a year.

While the Americans spoke of reconciliation and cooperation, every other delegation was transfixed upon retribution and reparations. In the end there were separate treaties for each of the Central Powers, but the primary focus of the conference was Germany, and its primary product was the Treaty of Versailles. In it, Germany admitted total guilt for causing and continuing the war, was stripped of 14 percent of its territory and 13 percent of its economic resources, and was saddled with a crippling $33 billion war reparations debt.

Amidst the inflamed postwar passions, though, President Wilson did succeed in his primary object: the establishment of a League of Nations, forerunner to the United Nations. More than any other individual, Woodrow Wilson was responsible for the creation of the most important international institution to emerge in the twentieth century.

On returning home, Wilson immediately submitted the Treaty of Versailles to the Senate and campaigned passionately for its ratification. In September, against his doctor's orders, an already exhausted president embarked upon a physically grueling cross-country trip to win public support for the treaty, often giving several speeches a day. In a speech at Pueblo, Colorado, on the twenty-sixth, Wilson declared, "There is only one power to put behind the liberation of mankind, and that is the power of mankind. It is the power of the united moral forces of the world, and in the covenant of the League of Nations the moral forces of the world are mobilized."

It was to be his last major public address. Following the speech, the president suffered a debilitating stroke. Neither he nor the treaty's prospects were ever the same. Partially paralyzed and cognitively impaired, Wilson was unable to effectively make the case, and on November 19, the Senate rejected the treaty by a vote of 39 to 55 against. The United States never did join the League of Nations. America had emerged from its isolation, for a short season, to save liberty in Europe. When that was accomplished, it withdrew back into its continental detachment.

The struggle had not been in vain. The vision of an association of nations to secure international order would become one of the seminal ideas of the age. From the darkness of the most destructive war the world had ever seen, President Wilson was able to elicit faith in a brighter future of comity among nations. Without American participation, the League of Nations was doomed to failure, but the principle upon which it rested, the idea that basic morality and law rather than might and force could form the foundation of international order, was now widely accepted. In awarding Woodrow Wilson the 1919 Nobel Prize for Peace, the president of the Norwegian Parliament said, "The President of the United States has succeeded in bringing a design for a fundamental law of humanity into present-day international politics. The basic concept on which it is founded will never die, but will steadily grow in strength, keeping the name of President Wilson fresh in the minds of future generations." By century's end, Woodrow Wilson's optimistic vision for international cooperation, dismissed by many as quixotic and impractical, would seem more like prophecy.

Woodrow Wilson's greatness, though, was only the personified reflection of the spirit of the nation he led. American involvement in the world war was an act of national self-sacrifice for a moral principle—as opposed to territorial conquest or the spoils of war—on a scale such as mankind had never seen before. In his request to Congress for a declaration of war, Wilson had summed up the position that would characterize America's efforts, not only in defeating the European dictatorships of the First World War, but in the struggle, throughout the century, to preserve human freedom. "The world must be made safe for democracy," he said. "Its peace must be planted upon the tested foundations of political liberty. We have no selfish ends to serve. We desire no conquest, no dominion. We seek no indemnities for ourselves, no material compensation for the sacrifices we shall freely make."

We seek nothing for ourselves, America had said; and against all probability, it proved to be true. At Versailles, Wilson's words were verified: in the postwar settlement, the United States sought no dominion, no indemnity, no material compensation. The nation that had turned the tide of war, the sole power to emerge from the conflict militarily and industrially vigorous, countervailed only by nations desolated and war-weary from years of fighting—the United States—sought nothing for itself. The British statesman who called America's entry into the war "one of the most disinterested acts in history" turned out to be speaking the literal truth.

In their participation in the Great War, Americans had been genuinely motivated by something greater than territorial gain or spoils. As President Wilson said in his last public address, "Mothers who lost their sons in France have come to me and, taking my hand, have shed tears upon it not only, but they had added, 'God bless you Mr. President!' I ordered their sons overseas. I consented to their sons being put in the most difficult parts of the battle line, where death was certain, as in the impenetrable difficulties of the forest of Argonne. Why should they weep upon my hand and call down the blessings of God upon me? Because they believe that their boys died for something that vastly transcends any of the immediate and palpable objects of war. They believe, and they rightly believe, that their sons saved the liberty of the world."[42]

Triumph over Fascism

WHEN THE FIRST World War ended, Americans dismantled their military as rapidly as they had built it up. Within six months after the armistice, 2.6 million enlisted men and 128,000 officers had been discharged.[1] In 1920 the U.S. military had only 30,000 more soldiers than the defeated Germans, who were limited to 100,000 men by the Versailles Treaty. Before long, America would be called on, once again, to save democratic civilization. It did not aspire to the role, and sought to avoid it when it came, but no other nation could do it.

Adolf Hitler rose to power in Germany on a wave of popular discontent and social chaos. As economists had warned, the burdensome German war debt had crippled the economy and destroyed the currency. In 1922 it took 12,000 marks to buy a dollar.[2] A year later the exchange rate was a million marks to one. When German officials pleaded for a moratorium on payments, the Allied Reparations Commission rejected the request. Hitler's rallies were attended by thousands of middle-class Germans, cheering enthusiastically for his message of national renewal, rejection of reparations, and revenge against traitorous minorities. The *Voelkischer Beobachter* newspaper described him as "the most popular and most hated man in Munich."[3]

Following a failed coup attempt in November 1923, Hitler's court trial was transformed into a national forum for the dissemination of his conspiracy theories and unltranationalist sentiments. Speaking before a courtroom crowded with journalists from throughout Germany and the world, Hitler said defiantly, "There is no such thing as high treason against the traitors of 1918."[4] Protected by a court sympathetic to his nationalist views, Hitler received only a five-year sentence, the minimum possible for a treason charge.

In addition, the judge recommended early parole. At Landsberg prison he was treated like a celebrity, receiving gifts from well-wishers, entertaining visitors in his comfortable quarters, and reading voraciously. He called the experience "a free education at the state's expense." He also had time to write his memoirs.

He did not actually write *Mein Kampf (My Struggle)* himself. Hitler, the high school dropout, was a poor writer, but he loved to hear himself speak, so he dictated the ideas to a ghostwriter, Rudolf Hess, a university student who had also participated in the "beer hall putsch." It was more an extended rant than a book: in *Four Years of Struggle Against Lies, Stupidity, and Cowardice* (as the title was to have been before the publisher intervened), Hitler spewed his disjointed racial and conspiratorial theories, and his vision for a resurgent Germany.

After serving less than a year of his sentence, Hitler was released in December 1924 and immediately set about revitalizing the National Socialist (Nazi) movement. In the election of 1930, the future dictator showed himself to be one of the most talented *democratic* politicians in history. Mass rallies were held, campaign posters put up, newspapers distributed by the millions. Hitler was only allowed to be seen in the most favorable circumstances, at masterfully staged rallies and manufactured photo-op events. Films were made of his speeches and disseminated throughout the country. The depression, he charged, was caused by the corrupt liberal politicians, the unjust international business system, the banks and—behind everything else—the Jews. The Nazi campaign slogan was "Everything Must Change."

The Nazis received 6.4 million votes, garnering them 107 seats in the parliament and making them the second-largest party in the nation. In early 1932 he lost in his challenge to the venerated (but at age eighty-four enfeebled) Hindenburg for the presidency, but forced a second round of voting and garnered 36.1 percent of the vote.[5] In elections held in July that year, the Nazis won nearly 14 million votes (37.6 percent of the votes cast), making them the largest political party in the nation and giving them 230 of 680 seats in the Reichstag.

With the Nazis now in control, the Reichstag passed a vote of "no confidence," and the government was dissolved; on the thirtieth of January, 1933, President Hindenburg appointed Adolf Hitler chancellor. Less than a month later the Reichstag burned down, and when communists were blamed, President Hindenburg agreed that Hitler should have dictatorial authority. The next day Chancellor Hitler issued a decree announcing that "curbs on personal liberty, on the right of free expression of opinion, including freedom of the press, of associations, and of assembly, surveillance over letters, telegrams and telephone communications, searches of homes and confiscations of as well as restrictions on property, are hereby permissible. . . ."[6] Trade unions and other non-Nazi organizations were banned. Opposition parties were prohibited, and unauthorized political meetings were violently broken up. Opposition newspapers were shut down. Camps were established to concentrate socialists, communists, homosexuals, the disabled, and other threats to the nation. By 1934 some 150,000 Germans were being held in such camps.

In June, Hitler used his personal bodyguard, the *Schutzstaffel* ("Defense Unit"), or SS, headed by Heinrich Himmler, to carry out a sweeping purge of suspected political opponents. The warrants read, "By order of the Fuhrer and Reich Chancellor, _____ is condemned to death by shooting for high treason."[7]

The overthrow of democracy in Germany had not provoked popular outrage. Most Germans were willing to be done with the turbulence of democracy and party politics, and once the Nazis controlled the mechanisms of state power, the silencing of opponents proceeded remarkably smoothly and largely unopposed. "It is no victory," wrote Oswald Spengler of the Nazification of Germany, "for the enemies were lacking."[8]

By the time President Hindenburg died in August 1934, the Fuhrer and the Nazis had firm control of the German state. With the support of the nation's military leaders, whom he promised renunciation of the Versailles restrictions, Hitler abolished the office of the presidency and assumed the title of "Fuhrer and Reich Chancellor." Henceforth, German soldiers would swear an oath of loyalty to Hitler himself. In a public referendum, 85 percent of German voters approved the step.

The following year, in the Nuremberg "race laws," German Jews were stripped of citizenship and declared instead to be "subjects"; they were barred from working as teachers, doctors, or lawyers or in the public sector. The Law for the Protection of German Blood and German Honor outlawed intermarriage or sexual union between Jews and Aryans, and prohibited Jews from having Aryan women under age thirty-five work in their homes. Among the world's democracies, the response was muted. Among the German people, the new laws were greeted with passive resignation by some, approval by most.[9]

More important for most Germans, the economy was rebounding. By 1936–37 the GDP was nearly double its 1932 levels, unemployment had fallen dramatically, production had grown by a third, and wages had risen 7 percent. Foreign observers of all political stripes looked admiringly upon what was being called the "German economic miracle."[10] Now secure in power, Hitler began to make diplomatic overtures to Italian dictator Benito Mussolini, whom he both personally admired (sincerely calling Mussolini "the leading statesman in the world") and regarded as a potential political ally. Goering, Himmler, and other high-ranking Nazis made a series of visits to Rome, promising economic and military cooperation. By November 1936, Il Duce was speaking of a "Rome-Berlin Axis."[11]

Already, Adolf Hitler was preparing for war, and he grew more emboldened with each new treaty violation that went unanswered. When German troops occupied demilitarized areas in the Rhineland that March, the international response consisted of diplomatic grumbling, but no action. Hitler's military buildup, in expectation of a full-scale European war, continued. On March 12, 1938, Germany declared an *Anschluss* (union) with Austria. As German soldiers poured across the border, the international community protested bitterly—but did nothing.

Immediately Hitler turned his attention to Czechoslovakia, a new nation carved from former Austria-Hungary by the Versailles accord. The country had three and a half million ethnic Germans out of a population of 14 million, most living in the Sudetenland region bordering Germany. These Germans, Hitler said, were being oppressed. At a conference in Munich on September 29, 1938, in return for Hitler's promise not to make any further territorial demands, English prime minister Neville Chamberlain and French premier Edouard Daladier (as well as Mussolini, who was crucial in helping the two sides reach agreement) consented to the German annexation of the Sudentenland. Returning to England, Chamberlain announced triumphantly that the Munich agreement would assure "peace in our time." The agreement, moreover, was popular in both France and Britain, both nations still living with the memory of the First World War and anxious to avoid another. Their leaders returned home as heroes. The London *Times* wrote that "no conqueror returning from a victory on the battlefield has come adorned with nobler laurels."[12]

Mussolini said to his foreign minister, "There will be no war. But this is the end of English prestige." He was half right. Convinced that Chamberlain was desperate to avoid war, and that he would abide nearly any abuse to do so, on March 15, 1939, Hitler ordered the invasion of all Czechoslovakia. Three weeks later, Italy invaded Albania.

On May 22, Germany signed the "Pact of Steel" with Mussolini. In it, each nation pledged to support the other in the event of war. Three months later Hitler and Stalin signed the most improbable treaty of the age, a nonaggression pact between fascist Germany and the communist Soviet Union. On the morning of September 1, 1939, just one week after the pact was signed, German troops crossed over the Polish border. More than 1.5 million *Wehrmacht* troops quickly overwhelmed the Polish troops, who retreated under the tidal wave of tanks, artillery, and aircraft. On the third of September, England and France unenthusiastically declared war on Germany, with none of the public jubilation that had accompanied the outbreak of the First World War. Too many people still remembered. This was a war of resignation, not passion. Two days later President Roosevelt announced American neutrality. On the seventeenth the Soviets invaded Poland from the east, claiming their share.

———◆———

During the six months following the invasion of Poland (a period known as the "phony war"), other than German U-boat attacks on British shipping in the Atlantic, there was little open conflict. It was the calm before the storm, as both sides prepared for the cataclysm they knew lay ahead. Then, on April 9, 1940, Germany launched Operation *Weserubung*, invading Denmark and Norway. The Danes did not resist. German troops sailed into Copenhagen harbor as the Danish navy looked on. A single German battalion captured the city. The country was occupied by lunchtime. The Danish government issued a strongly worded protest, and then fled.

Hitler unleashed Operation *Sichelschnitt* ("Sickle Stroke") on May 10 against the Netherlands, Luxembourg, Belgium, and France. Luxembourg surrendered immediately. Holland also collapsed. The French Seventh Army was sent to bolster the Dutch: it arrived in Holland on the twelfth and was in retreat on the thirteenth. The conquest of Holland took five days. Belgium surrendered on the twenty-eighth. On the day that Germany launched *Sichelschnitt*, Neville Chamberlain resigned as British prime minister, and Winston Churchill was asked to form a new government. "I have nothing to offer but blood, toil, tears and sweat," Churchill said in his first speech before Parliament.

The French Maginot Line, a series of fortified trenchworks along the border with Germany, may indeed have been impregnable, as its planners promised, but German military strategists simply went around it, cutting through Belgium. The First World War had been a war of stasis: this was a campaign of rapid movement. German troops sliced into France through Belgium in mobile units of tanks, motorcycles, and trucks, supported from the air, outflanking defenses, and emerging far beyond where the front was supposed to be. The shock of the rapid advance threw civilians and soldiers into terror. Some French units simply dissolved in the face of the onslaught, troops abandoning their weapons and melting into the flood of refugees fleeing southward.

British troops were deployed to assist in the defense of France, but it was not enough. The battle to stop the Germans at the Somme began on June 5, and was over by the tenth. Within days German armored divisions were deep inside France. Gen. Maxime Weygand, commander of the French armies, asked the government's War Council to negotiate an immediate surrender. In discussion with French leaders, Churchill called on France to fight to defend Paris, but Marshal Pétain said that there was no point in turning Paris into a "city of ruins" by resisting the Germans.[13]

The slogan adopted by French intellectuals the previous year— "Servitude rather than war!"—had turned out to be self-fulfilling prophecy. Even the Germans, already contemptuous of the French military, were astonished at the speed with which resistance disintegrated. "It was inexplicable," wrote German war correspondent Karl von Stackelberg. "How was it possible that, after this first major battle on French territory, after this single victory on the Meuse, this gigantic consequence should follow? How was it possible that these French soldiers with their officers, so completely downcast, so completely demoralized, would allow themselves to go more or less voluntarily into imprisonment?"[14]

——◆——

After the invasion, Churchill wrote to Roosevelt: "The aged Marshal Petain, who was none too good in April and July, 1918, is, I fear, ready to lend his name and prestige to a treaty of peace for France."[15] The armistice was signed on June 22, 1940, in the same railroad car in which Germany had submitted to the humiliating settlement of 1918, after its defeat in the First world War. Under the terms of the agreement, northern France, its most productive region, was to be occupied; 2 million French soldiers were to be kept as prisoners, and, adding salt to the wound, "occupation costs" were to be paid to Germany. Following the signing ceremony, Hitler had the railroad car destroyed. The next day he paraded triumphantly through Paris.

The French National Assembly voted overwhelmingly to give Marshal Pétain, a hero of the last war and now an old man, dictatorial powers. The vote was freely made. "The [deputies] knew that a change of regime was in process of coming about and that the new regime would be a dictatorship," wrote Robert Aron after the war. "The 10th July saw a free vote taken. . . . Moreover, the allegation that the vote of the members of the Assembly was not a free one is contradicted by the fact that eighty senators and deputies voted against the Government measure."[16] The new French government took its name from the site of the relocated capital, a spa town in central France called Vichy. It severed diplomatic relations with Britain.

For France's rulers the new system was not to be the imposed construct of a military victor, but an authentic reflection of French culture; a uniquely French fascism. "The new order," Pétain told the nation, "must not be a servile imitation of foreign experiments; certain of these experiments are sensible and fine, but every nation must develop a regime adapted to its climate and its genius. The new order is a French necessity."[17] Most of Pétain's countrymen acceded to that view. Mussolini wrote to Hitler in August, 1940, "I feel sure that you cannot have failed to note the extraordinary psychological phenomenon, so typical of the indomitable pride of the French, that *France does not consider herself conquered*."[18] Both French and German records indicate little public dissent during the first year of Vichy rule.[19]

Anti-Semitism was not a uniquely German invention. It was pervasive throughout Europe, and in France the Vichy regime—with the active participation or passive acceptance of most Frenchmen—not only complied with German anti-Jewish policies, but initiated its own.[20] Months *before* the first German mandates for the treatment of French Jews had been issued, the new French government had repealed a law that had prohibited popular media attacks on Jews.[21] In October, the *Statut des Juifs* ("Statute of the Jews") was passed, banning Jews from civil service posts, the officer corps, and from positions in which they might influence public opinion—which included everything from teaching to the arts to the news media. A quota system was devised to limit the number of Jews working in the professions.[22]

Within a year dozens of *camps de concentration* had sprung up in France, holding some 50,000 Jews as well as gypsies and other suspected subversives. When the mass arrests of Jews in Paris and elsewhere began in early 1942, they stirred little public opposition. Germany's removal of French Jews to the east corresponded with the desire of many Frenchmen, as one prefect put it, for "a solution that will permit a reduction in the number of Jews living in France."[23]

Hitler dangled before the French the lure of a genuine partnership which he never intended, as a means of driving a wedge between the French and the Anglo-Americans. In that he was stunningly successful, partly because he could take advantage of French national pride and its corollary Anglophobia, which already existed. "In a triumphant Anglo-Saxon world," Vichy foreign minister Jean Francois Darlan said in a national radio address, "France would only be a dominion of the second importance."[24] French leaders entreated Hitler for a more dynamic alliance and a more prominent role for France in the establishment of the new Europe following the war.

In a meeting in Germany in May 1941, Darlan assured Hitler that France would be a valuable ally in the fascist conquest of Europe. "I make a formal promise to direct French policy toward an integration with the New European Order," he said. Upon returning to Vichy, Darlan told the Council of Ministers that "if we collaborate with Germany . . . that is to say work for her in our factories, if we give her certain facilities, we can save the French nation, reduce our territorial losses to a minimum, both Metropolitan and Colonial, and play an honorable part, if not an important one, in the Europe of the future."[25]

The French contribution to the German war effort was more considerable. In time, 40 percent of France's industrial output went to supply Germany, including over two-thirds of its aeronautical, shipbuilding, and automotive production. In addition, vital raw materials such as aluminum, cotton, coal, and foodstuffs helped sustain the German war machine. As early as 1942 a German economist would report that "German orders in France are the dominant factor in the French economy."[26]

When Vichy Premier Pierre Laval met with Hitler, he was enthralled by the idea that France might play an important role in the new Europe. "My interview with Chancellor Hitler was a surprise to me, a delightful surprise," he wrote of the encounter. "We felt the same way and ended by talking a new language: European." Laval assured Hitler, "As a Frenchman, I can only say that I desire with all my heart a British defeat."[27]

Against the fascist leviathan that now dominated Europe and much of North Africa, Britain stoutly refused to submit. Even the president of the Swiss confederation had said, in June 1940, that his people must learn to "adjust" to the new circumstances of Europe. The English people refused to adjust. Following Germany's lightning defeat of France, Winston Churchill spoke to the British people: "The Battle of France is over," he said. "The Battle of Britain is about to begin."

The main target of "the blitz" was not military, or industrial, but the will of the British people. Prime Minister Churchill was certain that, if Britain could hold out, American assistance, and then outright involvement, would be forthcoming and could turn the tide against Hitler. First, the Americans had to be shown that victory against the Nazis was achievable. When the war began, 82 percent of Americans had expected a British victory. After the fall of Norway, 55 percent did. After the collapse of France, only 32 percent did.[28] Joseph Kennedy, the American ambassador in London, doubted that England could hold out against Germany. "Sooner or later the Americans will come," Churchill said, "but on the condition that we here don't flinch."

Meanwhile, he doggedly solicited American support. It was in the United States' own vital interests to prevent democratic Britain from falling to Germany, he insisted. In this, he found a receptive audience with Franklin Roosevelt. "If we go down you may have a United States of Europe under the Nazi command far more numerous, far stronger, far better armed than the New World," Churchill told the American president.

The fascist juggernaut seemed unstoppable. Hungary joined the Axis in November. In March 1941, Bulgaria joined; and in April, Germany invaded Greece and Yugoslavia, easily overcoming British and native forces to secure victory within the month. In North Africa, General Rommel's "Afrika Korps" was pushing back British forces.

On June 22, 1941, Hitler launched the invasion of the Soviet Union, Operation Barbarossa, with nearly 3 million troops and a vast mechanized army.[29] It seemed like a good idea at the time. Even the American ambassador in Moscow informed Washington that the Soviet regime probably would not survive a German assault. British and American military intelligence estimates concluded that it would take only one to three months for Germany to succeed in an invasion of the USSR.[30]

Despite warnings from U.S. and British intelligence, Soviet forces were caught totally unprepared by the attack. Stalin himself was in a state of bewilderment, and initially ordered Soviet artillery not to fire upon the advancing German troops.[31] In the Baltic states the German forces were met with indifference, and even approval, by peoples who were trading a known despotism for a prospective one. Six hundred thousand Soviet prisoners— including over 70,000 deserters—were captured in the first three weeks of fighting.[32] In the end, it was Russia's most loyal historic ally, winter, which stalled the advance.

Hitler issued a directive on December 7 curtailing offensive operations for the winter and ordering every German soldier, on penalty of death, to put up "fanatical resistance" to hold his positions during the winter. Meanwhile, his Japanese allies were drawing the United States into the conflict on the other side of the globe. In one of the greatest miscalculations of his lifetime, the Fuhrer counted on this occupying the Americans while he completed his conquest of Europe.

———•———

At the end of the First World War the United States was indisputably the world's most powerful nation. It was not long, though, a force for global peace and stability. By 1920, America had withdrawn back into the relative placidity of its own continental isolation. The U.S. Army of the 1930s was scarcely larger than it had been prior to the Great War. It ranked nineteenth in the world, behind, for example, that of the Dutch, whose defense against Hitler had been crushed in a matter of days. A German intelligence analysis of American military potential in June 1940 concluded, accurately, that the United States would not be ready to enter the war in a meaningful way until 1941 at the earliest. The U.S. spent just over 1 percent of its GDP on defense in 1939, compared to Britain's 8 percent, Germany's 16 percent, and Japan's 25 percent.

Even while Americans deplored the violations of human rights becoming evident in Europe and grew apprehensive at the rise of aggressive dictatorships, they were reluctant to become actively involved in opposing those regimes. President Roosevelt took it upon himself to convince the public that, in an increasingly interconnected world, it was not any longer possible for the United States to simply cut itself off from the rising tide of despotism which now threatened to consume much of humanity. Like President Wilson before him, Franklin Delano Roosevelt, scion of an elite New York family, was merely expressing the will of the people in declaring American neutrality; and like Wilson, he would work to alter that will. As early as 1937, Roosevelt was comparing the spread of dictatorial government to a "physical disease" that must be quarantined and controlled before it became a worldwide plague.

Americans may have regarded themselves as isolated, removed from the horrors unfolding across the oceans, but the Europeans—including Hitler and Churchill—knew better. As both the paramount economic power and a leading exponent of democratic government and individual liberty, the United States would necessarily play a central role in the global drama, whether by its intervention or by its inaction. As the Hungarian-born historian John Lukacs wrote, "During the First World War the decisive importance of American intervention had dawned gradually on the peoples of the continent. During the Second World War the decisive importance of American intervention was taken for granted from the beginning."[33] Hitler believed that if Britain could be subdued before the United States got into the war, even America's mighty industrial capacity would be inadequate to dislodge fascism in Europe. The Americans, already reluctant to become involved in international conflicts, would resign themselves to the fait accompli. Delay was crucial. Every month that American mobilization for war could be forestalled, European fascism would be better able to consolidate its position. The agreement with Japan was designed to occupy U.S. forces in the Pacific. The German government secretly funneled money to isolationist organizations in the United States.[34]

When Hitler invaded Poland in September 1939, President Roosevelt issued a proclamation of American neutrality, in accordance with the requirements of Congress's Neutrality Acts. At the same time, he was already working to change them. In a nationwide radio "fireside chat" on September 3, the president told the American people that "when peace has been broken anywhere, the peace of all countries everywhere is in danger."[35] Three weeks later he called Congress into special session, asking it to amend the Neutrality Acts and permit nations at war to purchase American arms and supplies, as long as they paid cash for them and transported them—"cash and carry."

Isolationists in the Congress scoffed at the idea that nations unable to repay even the interest on their loans from the last war should be able to pay cash for the vast armaments needed for the next one.[36] Senator Borah, a leading isolationist from Idaho, warned that "cash and carry" would be the camel's nose under the tent. In London, Ambassador Joseph Kennedy, an Irish-American and himself an opponent of aid to Britain, believed the same thing. "They all contend that all they want is a revision of the Neutrality Act to give them an opportunity to buy in America, but I do not believe them for a minute" he wrote in a cable to Roosevelt. "If Germany does not break and throw Hitler out after the passage of the Neutrality Act, [the British] will spend every hour figuring out how to get us in."[37]

Bitterly opposed by isolationists, the Neutrality Act of 1939 was passed in the Senate on October 27 by a vote of 63–30 and approved a few days later in the House. It was not exactly an omen of American interventionism: in addition to requiring all arms sales to be cash-and-carry, it prohibited loans to belligerent nations, forbade travel on ships of belligerent nations as well as the arming of American commercial vessels, and prohibited American ships from entering British waters. Under the circumstances, though, it was the best that the president could hope for. He signed it into law on November 4.

Americans were ambivalent. Roosevelt worried that the public, rather than considering the "possible results in Europe and the Far East" should the fascist powers prevail, was instead "patting itself on the back every morning and thanking God for the Atlantic Ocean and the Pacific Ocean."[38] Most Americans opposed any actions that might draw the United States into war. In a poll taken in November for *Fortune* magazine, only 36.9 percent supported the "cash-and-carry" policy. A poll the following month found that 82 percent opposed making loans to either Britain or France.[39] This marked the crest of isolationist sentiment during the prewar period.

Henceforth, the public mind would turn toward more and more active opposition to fascism in Europe.

The Neutrality Act of 1939 was not neutral at all. Cash-and-carry was a manifest effort to assist the British, which alone had the dollars needed to make large-scale arms purchases and the control of the seas necessary to transport them. English newspapers praised the act as "A Smashing Blow to Germany." Neville Chamberlain called it "a profound encouragement to us in the struggle upon which we are engaged."[40]

There was another problem, though. Britain did not have the financial resources to sustain its prodigious armaments requirements indefinitely. One way or other, cash-and-carry was only a beginning. Isolationists feared that it would lead to greater American assistance for the British war effort. Roosevelt hoped that it would.

In 1940, Americans listened to Edward R. Murrow's nightly radio reports that "London is burning," and public admiration—and support—for the tenacious Britons grew. President Roosevelt reminded the country that should liberty in Europe be snuffed out, democracy in America could not survive "as a lone island in a world dominated by the philosophy of force." He also took more direct actions, replacing isolationist Secretary of War Harry Woodring, in June, with Henry Stimson, a Republican former secretary of war (under Taft) and secretary of state (under Hoover) who had advocated more aggressive American assistance for Britain. Frank Knox, another Republican and internationalist, was made secretary of the navy.

There were growing concerns, meanwhile, over America's military unpreparedness. At the beginning of 1940 a penurious Congress had balked at the president's request for $2 billion in defense spending; by September it had readily agreed to a succession of requests totaling more than $10 billion. The new willingness to spend reflected an awareness dawning upon many Americans of the terrible choices that lay ahead. "The old isolationism is dead," British ambassador Lord Lothian reported to his government. "Nobody is against a vast armaments program. But everybody knows that it cannot be ready for years. Some say give the Allies everything you can so as to keep them fighting. Others say 'Cut your losses and desert your European friends, and man your own frontiers.'"[41] In August, Congress passed the Selective Service and Training Act, the first peacetime military draft in American history. On October 16, in a message to the first draftees, President Roosevelt declared that the country faced a challenge "as compelling as any that ever confronted our people, and I would add that each of us must willingly do his bit if we are to hold fast our heritage of freedom and our American way of life—our national existence itself."[42]

The first tentative steps of mobilization had been taken, but they were only a beginning. Gen. George C. Marshall, the army's chief of staff, warned Congress that, despite the billions now being appropriated, the army would not be prepared to fight a war until, at the earliest, December 1941.[43]

Although the U.S. Army was in poor shape, the navy was one of the largest in the world (though not the most modern), with over 100 destroyers left over from the last war, 68 of which had been recently reconditioned.[44] In May 1940, Churchill informed Roosevelt that the German U-boat campaign against British shipping was taking a devastating toll: Britain desperately needed warships to escort its supply convoys, but could not produce them fast enough and could not afford to purchase them. The prime minister raised the possibility of a "loan of forty or fifty of your older destroyers." If it could not defend its commercial shipping, it would not be able to hold out against Germany.

Roosevelt could not comply. The move would violate the Neutrality Acts, and Congress had included in its recent defense appropriation a provision forbidding the president to transfer armaments to other nations until the chief of naval operations had deemed the matériel "not essential to the defense of the United States." Roosevelt told Navy Secretary Knox, "I fear Congress is in no mood at the present moment to allow any form of sale."[45]

Churchill persisted. In a June letter, he reminded Roosevelt of the gravity of the situation (a "matter of life and death," as he later put it) and warned of the strategic consequences for the United States if Britain were to be defeated and Germany gain control of her navy—and the Atlantic. "Although the present Government and I would never fail to send the Fleet across the Atlantic if resistance was beaten down here, a point may be reached in the struggle where the present Ministers no longer have control of affairs. . . . A pro-German Government would certainly be called into being to make peace, and might present to a shattered or starving nation an almost irresistible case for entire submission to the Nazi will."[46] Churchill also instructed Lord Lothian to press the administration on the issue, to remind it that "if we go down, Hitler has a very good chance of conquering the world."[47]

Not that there was any doubt about which side most Americans favored. In a national poll taken after the invasion of France, less than 2 percent of respondents said that they hoped for a German victory over Britain. Eighty percent favored increased U.S. assistance to England.[48] Yet, as the Battle of Britain raged in the summer and fall of 1940, support for a declaration of war against the Axis never rose above 6 percent.[49] Americans overwhelmingly wanted democratic Britain to win the war: they just didn't want to be in the war themselves. Roosevelt keenly felt the urgency of the crisis. "If Britain is to survive, we must act," he told an aide.[50]

On September 3, 1940, only a year after the war had begun, Roosevelt issued a message to the Congress informing it that the United States had acquired the right to lease several naval and air bases along the eastern seaboard, from Newfoundland to Guiana, "in exchange for fifty of our over-age destroyers."[51]

The principle effect of the complex arrangement was to draw the United States and Britain closer together, a fact that infuriated isolationists and delighted those—on both sides of the Atlantic—who hoped for a more active American role. Churchill said in a speech to Parliament, "Undoubtedly this process means that these two great organizations of the English-speaking democracies, the British Empire and the United States, will have to be somewhat mixed up together in some of their affairs for mutual and general advantage. For my own part, looking out upon the future, I do not view the process with any misgivings. I could not stop it if I wished; no one can stop it. Like the Mississippi, it just keeps rolling along. Let it roll. Let it roll on—full flood, inexorable, irresistible, to broader lands and better days."[52]

The deal was important as much for symbolic reasons as for its military impact. America was now neutral in word only. In actual fact, it had now already entered the war as a nonbelligerent ally of democratic Great Britain. "A new chapter of world history was written last week," declared the *New York Times*. "The destroyers steaming toward Halifax were not only symbols of an ever-closer Anglo-American *rapproachement*, but in the opinion of some observers, sealed what in effect was an unofficial alliance between the English-speaking nations. . . . "

It may have been an indication of shifting public opinion when in July the Republican Party defied its isolationist wing and nominated Wendell Willkie over Howard Taft and Thomas Dewey (who in the spring had campaigned on the pledge of "100 percent isolationism").[53] Willkie, a Wall Street lawyer, was an avowed internationalist and agreed with Roosevelt that the United States must aid Britain. It was, in fact, not an issue of much controversy in the general election. "An overwhelming number" of Americans, said Willkie, "believe that we should give all possible aid, short of war, of course, to the Allies."[54]

A further manifestation of public opinion came on November 5 when Franklin Roosevelt, whose views on assistance to Britain and resistance to European fascism were well known, was elected to an unprecedented third term by a popular vote of 27.2 million to 22.3 million, with an electoral margin of 449 to 82. Although most Americans still wanted to stay out of the war, if possible, polls showed that a strong majority favored support for Britain. Prime Minister Churchill called the election results "a message from across the ocean of great encouragement and good cheer."[55]

———◆———

"Cash-and-carry" had always been only a temporary fix. England could not afford to sustain the huge foreign-exchange imbalance required to carry on its war effort. Lord Lothian declared that if the war persisted for two more years, Britain would expend all its gold and negotiable securities as well as much of its foreign assets. In the first week of December, while recuperating from the stresses of the election campaign aboard the navy cruiser USS *Tuscaloosa*, President Roosevelt received an urgent letter from Churchill describing his country's dire situation. "The moment approaches when we shall no longer be able to pay cash for shipping and other supplies," the prime minister wrote.[56]

Churchill had not specified what particular actions should be taken, but simply presented the need. "The rest we leave with confidence to you and to your people," he said. Franklin Roosevelt wanted to support the British in their struggle and believed that the future of democracy—and America's own national security—depended on it, but there was the difficulty of the Neutrality Act's mandate of "cash-and-carry." After several days of contemplating the dilemma, he struck upon the answer: America would not sell the armaments to Britain, it would *loan* them.

Roosevelt explained his proposal at a press conference on December 17. "Suppose my neighbor's home catches on fire, and I have a length of garden hose four or five hundred feet away," he said. "If he can take my garden hose and connect it up with his hydrant, I may help him put out the fire. Now, what do I do? I don't say to him before that operation, 'Neighbor, my garden hose cost me fifteen dollars; you have to pay me fifteen dollars for it.' No! What is the transaction that goes on? I don't want fifteen dollars—I want my garden hose after the fire is over."

Twelve days later, in a national radio "fireside chat," the president went further, giving one of the great speeches of his life. "Never before since Jamestown and Plymouth Rock has our American civilization been in such danger as now," he said. The Germans had expanded throughout Europe, and Japan was reaching across Asia.

> In a military sense Great Britain and the British Empire are today the spearhead of resistance to world conquest. They are putting up a fight which will live forever in the story of human gallantry. . . . American industrial genius, unmatched throughout the world in the solution of production problems, as been called upon to bring its resources and its talents into action.
>
> Manufacturers of watches, farm implements, linotypes, cash registers, automobiles, sewing machines, lawn mowers and locomotives are now making fuses, bomb packing crates, telescope mounts. Shells, pistols, and tanks. But all our present efforts are not enough. We must have more ships, more guns, more planes. . . . We must be the great arsenal of democracy. . . .

In an address to a joint session of Congress on January 6, 1941, Roosevelt presented a vision of a postwar world order founded upon respect for human rights and the protection of "four essential freedoms": Freedom of speech, freedom to worship, freedom from want, and freedom from fear. Such a world was incompatible with the "new Order of tyranny which the dictators seek to create with the crash of the bomb," Roosevelt told the nation. "Let us say to the democracies: We Americans are vitally concerned in your defense of freedom. We are putting forth our energies, our resources and our organizing powers to give you the strength to regain and maintain a free world. We shall send you, in ever-increasing numbers, ships, planes, tanks, guns. That is our purpose, and our pledge."[57]

As Congress debated the lend-lease proposal, Americans, Britons, and Europeans from Germany to Greece awaited the decision. H. Duncan Hall, an attaché at the British embassy in Washington, later wrote, "For the first time in history the United Kingdom waited anxiously on the passage of an American law, knowing that its destiny might hang on the outcome."[58]

The Lend-Lease Act passed the Senate by a vote of 60–31 on March 8. It was overwhelmingly approved by the House of Representatives three days later. Roosevelt had made the case with the public as well: by the time Congress voted, 61 percent of Americans supported the bill and only 23 percent opposed it.[59] A majority of Americans now favored aid to Britain even if it meant being drawn into a war with Hitler.

The bill granted the president and secretary of war broad powers "to manufacture in arsenals, factories, and shipyards under their jurisdiction, or otherwise procure . . . any defense article for the government of any country whose defense the President deems vital to the defense of the United States," and "to sell, transfer title to, exchange, lease, lend, or otherwise dispose of, to any such government any defense article . . . " On the same afternoon that the House passed the bill, President Roosevelt signed it into law. By evening he had sent the British government a list of weapons that would be available. And by the following morning he sent to Congress an appropriation request, under the new law, for $7 billion.[60]

It was the "fifteen-dollar garden hose" that saved the world. The future prime minister of Britain, Harold Macmillan, wrote that "the provision of American aid in the shape of Lend-Lease saved us from something like disaster."[61] By the end of the war the United States would provide some $50 billion in Lend-Lease aid to dozens of nations. Britain received over half. The supplies of Lend-Lease, of course, were neither loaned nor leased: the program was aid, pure and simple. Only a few billion of the total amount would ever be repaid. Churchill later called it "the most unsordid act in the history of any nation."

Soon, the United States was doing more than merely providing supplies. U.S. destroyers were presently escorting convoys of merchant ships part of the way to Britain; and though prohibited from firing upon German ships, gave their positions to the British fleet, so that its ships could. In addition, British naval vessels were now being refueled and repaired in U.S. ports.

President Roosevelt and Prime Minister Churchill met from August 9–12, 1941, in Placentia Bay, off the coast of Newfoundland, to discuss the challenges facing their two nations and global democracy. Fascism was ascendant in Europe. German success in Russia seemed certain. Britain was holding on, but could not do so indefinitely. Both leaders agreed that the United States must enter the war soon.

On August 14 the two leaders issued the Atlantic Charter, spelling out the shared principles of Great Britain and the United States that would guide the foreign policies of their nations, and upon which, they declared, the two leading democracies "base their hopes for a better future of the world." The two countries sought no aggrandizement from the war and no territorial changes, not in "accord with the freely expressed wishes of the peoples concerned." Following the destruction of the Nazi threat, they "hope to see established a peace which will afford to all nations the means of dwelling safely within their own boundaries."

When the U.S. destroyer *Greer* was attacked by a U-boat on September 4, 125 miles southwest of Iceland, Roosevelt took the opportunity to respond aggressively. In a national radio address, he called German U-boats "the rattlesnakes of the Atlantic . . . one determined step toward creating a permanent world system based on force, terror and murder."[62] The president announced that American naval vessels would henceforth "shoot on sight" German warships rather than wait to be attacked by them. From that time on, the United States was involved in a Battle of the Atlantic with Germany. In a Gallup poll taken shortly after the speech, nearly two-thirds of those surveyed approved of the president's response. "So far as the Atlantic is concerned," said Admiral Stark, "we are all but, if not actually in [the war]."[63]

American involvement in the Battle of the Atlantic would, in time, reverse German successes there, secure the shipping lanes, and shape the outcome of the war. As Rommel later wrote, "the greatest production of tanks, guns and vehicles would have availed America nothing if she could not have carried them across the seas. But this 'Battle of the Atlantic' . . . was soon lost by us with frightful casualties among our U-boats . . . and we were now doomed to inevitable defeat at any place which was accessible to the Anglo-American fleets."[64]

———◆———

It is not correct to say that the United States did not become involved in the war until it was attacked. It was attacked precisely because it was already involved; because it had remained defiantly resistant to the rising tyrannies. By the time of the raid on Pearl Harbor, there was little doubt as to which side America was supporting, and that its support would continue to expand. It had only been a matter of time. (By the time of Pearl Harbor, fifteen thousand Americans had already gone to Britain to join in the war effort, as volunteers. Two hundred and forty-four American pilots—selected out of thousands of enlistees—had flown for the RAF in defense of England. Seventy-seven had been killed. With the U.S. entry into the war, the aviators of the "Eagle Squadron" would be brought into the U.S. Army Air Force).

Prime Minister Churchill had been right. Americans did come to understand what was at stake, and when they did, public opinion shifted overwhelmingly in support of the fight for freedom, first passively, through the supply of needed materials, and then more and more actively. After the collapse of France, Churchill had vowed that Britain would persevere, would "go on to the end . . . until, in God's good time, the New World, with all its power and might, steps forth to the rescue and liberation of the Old."[65] Now, Churchill's faith, and Britain's, would be vindicated.

In the United States, the isolationists were silenced overnight. Four days after the attack on Pearl Harbor, the principle mouthpiece for the isolationists, the America First Committee, quietly disbanded. In later years its high-profile members (which included Potter Stewart, a future Supreme Court justice, and Gerald Ford, a future president) would avoid publicly discussing their participation in it. Ultimately it had not been the democratic leader Franklin Roosevelt, but the dictators of Japan and Germany who had quieted the isolationists.

Politics makes strange bedfellows, as had been shown earlier in the war with the union of Hitler and Stalin. The Fuhrer personally held his Japanese allies in disdain. In *Mein Kampf* he described the Japanese as an inferior race that, without "Aryan influence," would "fall back into the sleep out of which it was startled seven decades ago by the Aryan wave of culture."[66]

Once engaged in the war, the American people threw their whole spirit into it. Like many before and since, Japanese and German strategists had discounted the strength of U.S. national will: Americans, they believed, were soft; they would recoil from the hardships of war and not persist for long. "Hitler always argued that [the Americans] were not a tough people, not a closely knit nation in the European sense," wrote the Fuhrer's confidant Albert Speer. "If put to the test, they would be poor fighters."[67] It was a familiar mistake. "Silly people—and there were many, not only in enemy countries—might discount the force of the United States," Churchill wrote after the war. "Some said they were soft, others that they would never be united. They would fool around at a distance. They would never come to grips. They would never stand blood-letting. Their democracy and system of recurrent elections would paralyze the war effort. . . . Now we should see the weakness of this numerous but remote, wealthy and talkative people." But Churchill, a student of American history, knew better. He was reminded of a remark made by Edward Gray thirty years earlier: that the United States is "a gigantic boiler. Once the fire is lighted under it there is no limit to the power it can generate."[68]

Americans had not wanted war, but once it was upon them they pursued victory with a unity and tenacity which surpassed that of any fascist state. As the statesman George Kennan later wrote in his classic work *American Diplomacy*: "A democracy is peaceloving. It does not like to go to war. It is slow to rise to provocation. When it has once been provoked to the point where it must grasp the sword, it does not easily forgive its adversary for having produced this situation. . . . Democracy fights in anger—it fights for the very reason that it was forced to go to war."

Hitler had thought that a conflict with Japan in the Pacific would keep the United States too occupied to engage him in Europe, giving Germany time to sew things up there. He took comfort from a U.S. military estimate, leaked to the press, that America would not be prepared to fight a two-front war for a year and a half. By then, he believed, the war would be over.[69] The object of collaboration with Japan, the Fuhrer had stated in a March 15 memo to the German Foreign Office, must be "to induce Japan as soon as possible to take active measures in the far East." By so doing, he believed, "the center of gravity of the interests of the United States will be diverted to the Pacific. . . . " That, combined with a timely victory over England, would prevent Americans from entering the fighting in Europe. "The common aim of the conduct of war is to be stressed as forcing England to her knees quickly and thereby keeping the United States out of the war."[70] Following the attack on Pearl Harbor, German foreign minister von Ribbentrop expressed elation at Japan's entry into the war. It was "the most important event since the beginning of the war," he said. "This was a heavy blow for America and even worse for England."[71]

The miscalculation proved fatal. The attack on Pearl harbor, which happened sooner than Hitler had expected, brought the United States into the European conflict earlier, and more aggressively, than he could have imagined. President Roosevelt adopted a "Europe first" strategy: resist the Japanese in the Pacific, but give military priority to the defeat of fascism in Europe, which he regarded as the greater threat. By January 26, 1942, less than two months after the attack on Pearl Harbor, American soldiers began arriving in England.

Prime Minister Churchill, who understood the Americans far better than Hitler did, knew what U.S. involvement meant. He wrote of his emotions upon hearing that America had entered the war: "So we had won after all! Yes, after Dunkirk; after the fall of France . . . after the threat of the invasion . . . after seventeen months of lonely fighting and nineteen months of my responsibility in dire stress, we had won the war. England would live. . . . Our history would not come to an end. . . . Hitler's fate was sealed. Mussolini's fate was sealed. As for the Japanese, they would be ground to powder. . . . Many disasters, immeasurable cost and tribulation lay ahead, but there was no doubt about the end. . . . Being saturated and satiated with emotion and sensation, I went to bed and slept the sleep of the saved and the thankful."[72]

Opponents of the draft, so vocal before December 7, were nowhere to be found on December 8. An overwhelming majority of Americans now favored total mobilization for war and said that they were willing to put up with rationing and other hardships to defeat the fascist aggressors.[73] Military recruiters were inundated with more volunteers than they could process. As a result of the 1940 draft, by December 1941, there were already 1.8 million personnel in the U.S. armed forces. Within four years there would be over 12 million. These included, for the first time, a large number of female enlistees: around 100,000 in the Women's Army Auxiliary Corps (WACS), in addition to the Navy's WAVES, the Coast Guard's SPARS, and female Marines.[74] Millions of young men eagerly waited to turn eighteen, old enough to enlist. Many didn't wait. Thousands lied about their age and joined up early, some as young as fifteen. White stars began to appear in the windows of homes, signifying a family member in uniform. Soon gold stars began to appear, indicating that one had lost his life.

Eighty-five million Americans bought war bonds. An astonishing $157 billion was raised, providing much of the $389 billion spent by the government between June 1, 1940, and June 30, 1946. Movie stars traveled the country urging Americans to buy bonds.[75] Dorothy Lamour alone was responsible for the sale of $350 million worth. Carole Lombard died in a plane crash on a war bond tour.

About 40 percent of citizens were engaged in some type of active volunteer work in civic organizations for the war effort, and most of the rest were contributing indirectly. Ten million volunteers joined thousands of local defense councils, collecting scrap, promoting frugality, providing child care for mothers newly employed in the wartime industries. Forty thousand civilian pilots joined the Civil Air Patrol, flying lookout for U-boats or transporting vital materials or documents.[76] The Women's Ambulance and Defense Corps attracted 25,000 volunteers. The corps' slogan was "The Hell We Can't."

Communities held drives to collect rubber goods, paper, metal, and other scarce commodities needed for the war effort.[77] West Coast blood donors gave more blood than hospitals could store. Dockworkers offered to work on Sundays for free. Hundreds of millions of phonograph records, needed for their shellac, were donated. Millions of American families grew "victory gardens" to offset potential food shortages and enable the United States to help feed its allies. The goal of 18 million gardens was quickly surpassed, producing, by 1943, over 8 million tons of produce. Not all gardens were in rural areas. Residents of large cities individually grew smaller plots, but collectively cultivated an area the size of Rhode Island.[78]

American productive capacity would prove crucial to turning the tide of the conflict. When the war began, the United States had a population of 132 million. Britain, by comparison, had 48 million; Germany had 76 million; Italy had 44 million; France had 42 million; and Japan had 77 million.[79] Population numbers alone may not have been decisive, but American workers were already more productive than those of any other nation, and the gap only widened during the war. Hourly productive output rose a remarkable 25 percent in four years. Farm productivity grew by one-third. By the end of the war, American workers were twice as productive as Germans and five times more productive than Japanese workers.[80]

Once engaged, the nation's immense industrial potential and technological ingenuity were turned to the production of the implements of war.

Factories that once made consumer goods were converted to produce armaments and other supplies. Textile workers now made military uniforms. Automobile assembly lines were retrofitted to build tanks and airplanes.[81]

One challenge after another was tackled and overcome by American innovation. When the war began, U.S. industry produced no synthetic rubber, had limited reserves of natural rubber, and depended heavily on imports, which were cut off when Japan took control of most rubber-producing areas of the world. By 1944 the United States had manufactured 800,000 tons of synthetic rubber.[82] The mass production of penicillin was perfected, and other medical breakthroughs were made in response to wartime demands. Despite a 17 percent decline in the farming population between 1941 and 1945, agriculture production reached record levels. While the Germans plundered occupied territories to meet their own needs, America's "Food for Freedom" program helped feed dozens of nations around the world.

American aircraft and ship construction grew tenfold during the war. In 1941 it had taken U.S. shipyards nearly a year, start to finish, for the construction of each ten-thousand-ton Liberty ship. By the end of the war it was taking around two weeks.[83] Ultimately a new ship was being built every day, a new airplane every five minutes. By 1944 the United States was manufacturing over 96,000 aircraft annually, compared to 40,600 for Germany and 28,000 for Japan.[84]

"Without American production the [Allies] could never have won the war," Stalin said afterward.[85] American provisions of food were vital to feeding the Russian army, and American trucks were crucial to its mobility. Of the Soviet army's 665,000 motor vehicles at the end of the war, two-thirds were supplied by the United States. Soviet premier Nikita Krushchev later remarked, "Just imagine how we would have advanced from Stalingrad to Berlin without [American transport]."[86]

———◆———

Now under attack from German U-boats in the Atlantic, U.S. shipping losses steadily mounted. Adm. Karl Doenitz, commander of the German submarine fleet, had calculated that about 700,000 tons of shipping sunk each month would sap, and ultimately defeat, Britain. By June 1941 that figure was surpassed.[87] U.S. rear admiral Samuel Morison later called the U-boat campaign "the greatest threat to Allied victory over the Axis."[88]

There were other threats as well. While losses in the Atlantic were staggering in the spring of 1942, things elsewhere were going just as badly. In the Middle East, Rommel's Afrika Korps was closing in on the Suez Canal. In Russia, *Wehrmacht* forces had pushed to the edge of Moscow. In Asia, the Japanese had won a succession of stunning victories over American, British, and native troops to capture much of East Asia. In March, Gen. Douglas MacArthur had been compelled to flee the Philippines: he promised to return, but 75,000 American and Filipino soldiers were taken prisoner by the Japanese, and then forced on the murderous Bataan Death March.

Throughout it all, the Americans' most characteristic trait, optimism, never wavered. In a poll taken in the spring of 1942, at the depth of U.S. fortunes in the war, only 4 percent of Americans held the view that "the Axis has a pretty good chance to win the war."

Stalin had pressed the Americans to open up a "second front" that year, forcing the Germans to divert troops and relieving pressure on the Red Army. The Soviet leader had lobbied President Roosevelt for an immediate invasion of Western Europe, but FDR agreed with Churchill that the Allies were not yet prepared for such an undertaking. They settled upon an invasion of North Africa instead. During the preceding two years British and Axis forces had waged a fierce desert war, back and forth across a six-hundred-mile swath of North Africa in Egypt, Libya, Morocco, Algeria, and Tunisia. Things had initially gone well for the British, fighting primarily against Italian forces, but the tide turned with the arrival in February 1941 of Gen. Erwin Rommel (already famous for his victories over the French) and his Panzer divisions. By May the Axis powers had recovered all territory lost the previous year.

Operation Torch, the Allied invasion of North Africa, was to be commanded by Gen. Dwight David Eisenhower, a West Point graduate who had remained in relative obscurity during most of his military career. Ike spent the First World War training recruits, seeing neither action nor promotion. He later developed a reputation as a competent staff officer and served as chief of staff to a succession of a half dozen different generals, but desk work, however capably done, was not a prescription for rapid advancement. He held the rank of major for sixteen years. As late as 1941 he was still a lieutenant colonel.

In 1941, Eisenhower was promoted to brigadier general and put on the War Plans Division by army chief of staff George Marshall. The Kansan's plain speaking and tireless work ethic impressed Marshall, who in March 1942 put him in charge of the Operations Division, and in June made Eisenhower commander of U.S. forces in Europe. On November 5, 1942, Ike arrived in Gibraltar, where the forward headquarters for Torch was established in a network of damp, narrow tunnels and cramped rooms cut deep into the mountain, secure from German bombers. The invasion force of 110,000 was a novice army. The ships' companies on the flotilla from the United States were composed largely of naval reservists. For half of the "sailors" aboard the escort carrier USS *Sangamon*, this was their first time at sea. Of the aviators aboard the USS *Santee*, only five were experienced. There were the expected snafus of an inexperienced military. Some infantrymen who had trained in machine gunnery were given M-1 rifles; others were given bazookas without having any knowledge of their use.[89]

Hitler had permitted Vichy France to keep its colonies if it fought to defend them against the Allies. French troops had done so when the Allies took Syria in 1941, and again in Madagascar in 1942.[90] Now the Vichy regime had over 100,000 soldiers stationed in the French North African nations of Algeria, Morocco, and Tunisia. Would they, too, fight? At midnight on November 8, 1942, just before the invasion commenced, President Franklin Roosevelt affirmed a "deep friendship for the people of France" in a radio address—translated into French—to the residents of North Africa. "My friends, who suffer night and day under the crushing Nazi yoke, I speak to you as one who in 1918 was in France with your army and navy. . . . " The president urged the French colonials to support the unfolding operation. "We arrive among you with the sole object of crushing your enemies. . . . Do not, I pray you, oppose this great design. Lend us your help wherever you can, my friends, and we shall see again that glorious day when liberty and peace once more reign over the world. *Vive la France, eternelle.*" In the dank, cramped shelter within the Rock of Gibraltar, General Eisenhower and his staff anxiously waited to learn what the answer would be.

The reply was not long in coming. The Allied ships had all flown large American flags, and loudspeakers boomed in French: "We are your friends. Do not fire." French destroyers and artillery batteries overlooking the harbor opened up with a machine gun and artillery barrage. On deck and below, the terrifying crackle of machine gun fire cut through the bewildered Americans, packed into the ships' holds or waiting on deck to offload. Soon the larger French guns had found their range, sending several ships to the bottom. Hundreds of men never made it off their boats. Of those that did, some were killed in the water by French sailors firing with rifles and machine guns. Survivors were paraded through the streets of the city before French and Arabic onlookers—many of whom spat and threw stones—two miles to the military prison.[91] As the men were being marched to prison, an enthusiastic French soldier fired one last shot, killing Cpl. Alvin Ronning, a Minnesota farm boy.[92]

The invading forces underwent the mishaps of a green army in its first major encounter. Some landing craft sank from being overloaded. Many landed well away from their designated positions. A few drifted into range of a French artillery battery and were sunk. But by midday, 30,000 Allied troops had fought their way ashore, surrounded Algiers, and taken its airfields. Later that afternoon Admiral Darlan, who was by coincidence visiting a polio-stricken son in Algiers at the time, negotiated a surrender of the city and its 7,000 French troops.

Had the French initially cooperated, the plan called for the capture of Tunisian airfields at Bizerte and Tunis by Allied paratroopers on November 11.[93] The defense put up by the French forces did not thwart the invasion, but it imposed a crucial delay. Field Marshal Albert Kesselring, commander in chief of all Axis forces in the Mediterranean, organized a massive air transport of elite German paratrooper regiments, scrub Italian draftees, anyone who could be quickly rounded up and thrown into the mix. By November 25 there were already 15,000 German and 9,000 Italian troops, and 100 aircraft, in Tunisia under the command of Gen. Jurgen von Arnim, in place to oppose the Allied advance. Furthermore, Rommel's tank army was racing westward, toward Tunisia, with another 70,000 German and Italian troops. Because of the delay caused by the French resistance, the Allies had lost the race for Tunisia. Now they would have to win the battle for it.

The crucial Tunisian port cities of Bizerte and Tunis are roughly four hundred air miles from Algiers, though almost twice that distance over-land, across rugged terrain and through narrow mountain passes. It was slow going for the advancing army. From the nearby airfields in Tunisia now under their control, *Luftwaffe* pilots were able to locate and harry Allied troops, stalling the advance. By the end of December the drive into Tunisia, fiercely resisted by Arnim's growing force, had advanced to within twenty-five miles of Bizerte and Tunis but became bogged down, literally, by torrential winter rains. One war correspondent described tanks sinking up to their turrets in the mud.[94] Entrenched German units were easily able to defend the muddy mountain passes. Supplies had to be transported by mule the final two miles to the front. Casualties—250 daily—had to be evacuated the same way. The men slept in holes dug in the mud, protect-ing themselves from the bitter cold with carpets, blankets, anything they could find.

Churchill and Roosevelt met near Casablanca, Morocco, in mid-January 1943 to discuss developments in the war. Stalin had been invited but declined to attend, staying in Russia to oversee the winter defensive campaign. The Casablanca Conference marked the first time that an American president had ever flown on an airplane while in office, and Roosevelt's aides worried that the seventeen-thousand-mile round trip would take a toll on the sixty-year-old president's health. The trip—and the summit itself—was grueling. FDR and his entourage left Miami on January 11 and did not arrive in Casa-blanca until late on the fourteenth. The central issue of the summit was the opening of a "second front" against Hitler in the west, to relieve pressure on the Red Army fighting in the east. Also, Roosevelt secured an agreement to demand the "unconditional surrender" of the Axis powers, effectively fore-closing the possibility of a negotiated settlement and ultimately sealing the fate of European fascism.

General Eisenhower spent one day at the conference, speaking with Churchill, Roosevelt, and the assembled American and British chiefs of staff. He assured them of victory in Tunisia and, when pressed for a date, took a stab in the dark: May 15. With the anticipation of success in the North Africa campaign, Chief of Staff George C. Marshall favored a 1943 invasion of France, a position shared by Stalin. Churchill, who believed that the Allies were not yet prepared to launch such a massive assault, advocated attack-ing the "soft underbelly of the Axis" in southern Europe. After eight days of discussion, during which the president and the prime minister often worked past midnight, the two leaders had agreed upon an agenda: following suc-cess in North Africa, the Allies would turn to Sicily. Meanwhile, there would begin a large-scale buildup of forces in Britain, in preparation for a cross-Channel invasion of France the following May.

Against the stiff resistance of German forces making their last stand, American and British troops advanced slowly but steadily across North Africa, capturing a succession of hill strongholds in hard—often hand-to-hand—fighting. On May 7, Tunis and Bizerte fell to Allied forces. Residents took to the streets, throwing flowers at the Allied forces marching through the town and shouting *"Vive la France!"* and *"Vive l'Amerique!"*[95]

"Our losses there are enormous," Goebbels wrote in his diary. He called the defeat "a second Stalingrad."[96] At North Africa the tide of war had turned, decisively, in favor of the Allies. Italy had been disabused of its illusions of empire, and its national morale was reeling. Between Germany's losses in North Africa and those at Stalingrad, Hitler's Reich would never launch a successful major offensive again. Hereafter, fascism in Europe would be on the retreat.

As for North Africa, it was a start. It marked the first important, active American involvement in the struggle against European fascism and the first major Allied victory. The United States possessed a different military in May 1943 than it had the previous November. The U.S. Army, Bradley said, had learned "to crawl, to walk, then run." The Allies had lost over 70,000 casualties in the campaign to liberate North Africa. The American cemetery at Carthage, in Tunisia, holds twenty-seven acres of headstones.[97]

———◆———

As agreed at the Casablanca Conference, within two months after the expulsion of Axis forces from North Africa, Allied troops invaded Sicily. An island the size of Vermont, Sicily was to be, for the Allies—as it had been to armies for millennia—a stepping-stone between North Africa and Europe.[98] In the south, the island lies only ninety miles from Cape Bon in Tunisia; in the north, only two miles separate it from the mainland, across the Strait of Messina. Violent battles—in rugged mountain terrain favorable to the defense—at Gela, Comiso, Scoglitti, Vittoria, San Fratello, and elsewhere tested the fighting abilities and spirit of the Allied soldiers. In every instance they prevailed, often at the cost of heavy casualties.

In Rome on July 25, Mussolini, now regarded by many Italians as a puppet for Hitler, was ousted from power. He was replaced by Marshal Pietro Badoglio, put under house arrest, and moved to an isolated villa in the mountains. The new premier declared that Italy would continue as an ally to Germany and a participant in the war against the democracies, and he immediately commenced negotiations to the contrary. Hitler himself had been uncertain whether the Italians would offer any resistance to an invading Allied force. "The Italians never lose a war," he grumbled. "No matter what happens, they always end up on the winning side."[99]

Once Mussolini fell, all remaining Italian resistance collapsed. German forces continued to fight the advancing armies in order to buy time for an evacuation to Italy across the Strait of Messina. United States and British armies entered Messina on August 17. The German army had, only hours earlier, completed its withdrawal of over 100,000 troops and 10,000 vehicles.

When the Allied invasion of the mainland was launched, in early September, the surrender of the Badoglio government had already been proclaimed, and soldiers complained that they had endured months of arduous training for nothing. An unopposed landing would bring no glory.

There would be glory enough. The Americans were not met by acquiescent Italians, but by hostile German troops. The Germans had anticipated a landing at Salerno, and there were artillery emplacements all along the heights overlooking the beach from the front and both sides, and mortar and machine gun positions closer to the shoreline. The Americans were forced to fight their way ashore under blistering fire, but managed to slowly establish a foothold.

The next major objective was Rome, just a hundred miles away. They would be some of the hardest, and costliest, miles of that or any war. The terrain of steep hills (the rugged Apennines rising to over eight thousand feet), deep valleys, and ubiquitous rivers was inherently hostile to offense, accommodating to defense. In addition, the German forces had had plenty of time to plant land mines, destroy bridges, conceal machine gun nests, and position artillery placements. The soldiers sent to Italy were among the most dedicated and experienced troops of the Reich, and now they were embedded in the scraggy mountainsides. Winter rains soon began, dissolving the dirt roads, turning streams into torrents, washing out bridges. Snowstorms followed. More than anywhere else during the Second World War, historians have compared the fighting in Italy to the futility and soul-numbing stasis of the First World War. Soldiers lived, fought, and died up to their knees in mud, chilled to the bone in the freezing rain and snow, with entire units lost for a few hundred yards of ground.

Attacking mountain strongholds required making assaults up steep slopes, scaling cliffs, and advancing through dense minefields against unrelenting machine gun fire, amidst freezing rain, wind, and dense fog. The heights were commanded by heavy German artillery and, everywhere, machine gun nests. The fog sometimes lifted long enough for units to find themselves face-to-face with the enemy and forced into violent and bloody hand-to-hand warfare. The toll was staggering. One division lost eight hundred casualties in four days of nonstop fighting, for a few hundred yards of ground. This was no "soft underbelly."

From November 28 to December 1, 1943, Roosevelt, Churchill, and Stalin, the "Big Three," met for the first time together at Teheran to discuss the conduct of the war and the postwar world. The campaign in Italy was already having an effect on the fighting in Russia. Hitler had been forced to move thirteen divisions to the peninsula, among them two crack SS divisions from the

Eastern Front.[100] To Stalin's delight it was agreed that the invasion of France, code-named Operation Overlord, would be launched in May the following year. General Eisenhower was chosen to command it.

Already planning for a postwar world, President Roosevelt called for the establishment of an international organization along the lines of the defunct League of Nations, which would have a role—albeit still only vaguely defined—in promoting global peace. He also continued to insist that American soldiers could not be stationed indefinitely in Europe following the war to help oversee reconstruction there. American public opinion, notwithstanding its support for the struggle against fascism, remained fundamentally isolationist and would not support such a policy.

The joint declaration issued at the conclusion of the Teheran Conference reflected Roosevelt's opposition to colonialism and his determination to help promote a global community of democratic societies following the war. "We recognize fully the supreme responsibility resting upon us and all the United Nations to make a peace which will command the goodwill of the overwhelming mass of the peoples of the world and banish the scourge and terror of war for many generations. . . . We shall seek the cooperation and active participation of all nations, large and small, whose people in heart and mind are dedicated, as are our own peoples, to the elimination of tyranny and slavery, oppression and intolerance. We will welcome them, as they may choose to come, into a world family of Democratic Nations."

The conquest of Italy slogged on, meanwhile. For another half a year an army of citizen soldiers suffered all manner of physical and psychological hardships, endured unendurable conditions, witnessed their friends die around them, and came close to dying themselves. And still they persisted, and not only persisted but prevailed against a skilled and entrenched enemy. On June 4, 1944, Rome was liberated. The streets were lined with cheering Italians as Allied forces marched through the city. Soldiers were showered with flowers and given gifts of bread and wine. President Roosevelt announced the fall of Rome in a radio fireside chat. "One up and two to go," he said.[101]

The war in Italy would drag on for another year, but the attention of Allied planners was already elsewhere, as the attention of the world would shortly be. The invasion of Western Europe was two days away.

———————

Normandy would be one of the great and seminal battles, one of those pivotal moments in history that impact everything which follows. Should the Allies be defeated in the attempted invasion, more than time, equipment, and lives would be lost. The blow to Allied morale would be devastating. It would be years before another comparable attempt could be made. Hitler planned to send fifty more divisions to Russia after it was over, perhaps enough to settle the issue there. Already there was widespread sentiment in the United States that America should first defeat Japan before focusing on Germany. Further delay here might lead to a shift of priorities to the Pacific. Some leaders feared that a negotiated settlement might ultimately follow. Europe could remain indefinitely mired in its slough of authoritarian and antidemocratic rule.

Everyone knew an invasion attempt was coming. Gen. Alfred Jodl, Hitler's chief of operations, believed it would be "the decisive struggle for the outcome of the war and our future."[102] Everyone knew, furthermore, that it was likely to come in late spring—weather precluded an earlier attempt. All up and down the Atlantic Wall, defensive preparations were intensified. Rommel was put in charge of the coastal defenses and built up a formidable bulwark of concrete and steel fortifications: bunkers capable of surviving anything less than a direct hit, countless machine gun pillboxes dominating the beaches from every angle, massive concrete artillery batteries, millions of land mines, rows of barbed wire, and other impediments designed to impede a seaborne landing.

The fifty-eight German divisions deployed to meet the invasion force included some of the most highly trained and battle-hardened soldiers in the *Wehrmacht*. They would be opposed by an Allied army composed mostly of men who were seeing combat for the first time in their lives.

The buildup of forces in Britain was without precedent. Nearly 3 million Allied soldiers were involved in the enterprise. Over 1.7 million American GIs were stationed in England in preparation for the invasion. They wrote "in event of death" letters to their loved ones. "Now that I am actually here I see that the chances of my returning to all of you are quite slim," Lt. Jack Lundberg wrote to his parents and siblings back in Woods Cross, Utah. "I want you to know how much I love each of you. . . . I am sorry to add to your grief—but at all times realize that my thoughts are of you constantly and that I feel that in some small way I am helping to bring this wasteful war to a conclusion. We of the United States have something to fight for—never more fully have I realized that."[103] Like thousands of others, Jack would be killed in Normandy, leaving a young wife behind.

By 6:00 a.m. on the morning of June 6, Hitler's High Command was notified of the invading force. The Allies would be landing at Normandy, not farther north, at Pas de Calais, as expected. But no one dared to wake the Fuhrer to inform him. He would not hear of the invasion until noon. By sunrise the waters off Normandy were already dark with blood and crowded with corpses and war debris. GIs pushed past the floating bodies of dead comrades to get to the shore. The most ferocious resistance was met by the GIs coming ashore at Omaha Beach. Recognizing it as a potential landing site, Rommel had fortified it most intensely. An elaborate trench system connected machine gun nests, mortars, and artillery bunkers. Land mines were ubiquitous, offshore and on, as were concertina wire and landing obstacles jutting out of the sand. The bluff rising sharply over the open stretch of beach offered a dominating panorama of the ground below for

German mortar and machine gun positions, which now strafed every inch of the beach. Wave after wave of GIs fought the pounding surf and fierce German resistance, struggling at first simply to make it ashore alive. Many did not. By midmorning the German High Command received word that the Allied force was stranded on the beach and that the invasion attempt had been repulsed.

Gradually individuals, and then small groups of men, and then units began inching forward, toward the German emplacements. Army Rangers scaled the 117-foot cliff face of the Pointe du Hoc, engaging the defending force there and repelling it. By the end of that "longest day," the Allied forces had taken all of their beachhead objectives. One hundred and seventy thousand soldiers had made it ashore against violent resistance. There were already 11,000 casualties.

Retrospection often makes an achievement seem inevitable, but it was far from so at the time. As late as the evening before the invasion, British field marshal Sir Alan Brooke was apprehensive. "I am very uneasy about the whole operation. At the best it will fall so very short of the expectation of the bulk of the people. At the worst it may well be the most ghastly disaster of the whole war."[104]

After ordering the go-ahead for the invasion, General Eisenhower drafted a message which he intended to transmit in the case of failure. "Our landings in the Cherbourg-Havre area have failed to gain a satisfactory foothold and I have withdrawn the troops. My decision to attack at this time and place was based upon the best information available. The troops, the air, and the Navy did all that bravery and devotion to duty could do. If any blame or fault attaches to the attempt it is mine alone."[105]

Above Omaha Beach there is a vast cemetery, 172 acres, row after endless row of white marble crucifix or Star of David headstones, the resting place of over 9,000 Americans who had crossed the ocean to fight in defense of liberty. On the limestone memorial colonnade is inscribed these words:

> THIS EMBATTLED SHORE, PORTAL OF FREEDOM
> Is Forever Hallowed by the Ideals
> The Valor and the Sacrifices
> Of Our Fellow Countrymen

The push through the French *bocage* countryside of hedgerows and earthen embankments was slow, and costly in human lives. Six weeks after the invasion, the Allies had lost 100,000 casualties. On August 1, Gen. George Patton was put in command of the new Third Army that had been building up in Normandy, composed of the vast stream of reinforcements that had been daily arriving there. His orders were to break out of Normandy and across Brittany. Within a week Patton's Third Army had pushed out of the Cotentin

Peninsula and was racing through Brittany, covering forty miles in a day. It was the Americans' turn for blitzkrieg. "The Allies are waging war regardless of expense," complained a Panzer corps commander. Hitler began executing his generals. Field Marshal Gunther von Kluge, who had replaced von Runstedt as "commander in chief west," was ordered back to Germany, his fate certain, but poisoned himself before arriving there, cheating Hitler of the pleasure of killing him. Rommel, Germany's most popular general, was provided cyanide and permitted to commit suicide; his death was publicly blamed on wounds received in the war.

By mid-September 1944 the Allies were within sixty miles of the Ruhr, Germany's industrial heartland. They had liberated all of Belgium and Luxembourg, and part of Holland. In Italy, they were advancing on the Po Valley.

In the East, meanwhile, the Red Army was pushing toward Germany. Stalin launched the summer offensive he had promised as a follow-up to Normandy, and by September the Soviets had captured Romania, Bulgaria, and parts of Hungary and Poland.

As the Red Army reached the Vistula River, on August 1, the Polish Home Army staged an uprising against their occupiers in the capital city of Warsaw. Fighting only with small arms and Molotov cocktails, the force of thirty-seven thousand had expected to engage the Germans for ten days, by which time the advancing Soviets would be in the city. Thousands of civilians took up the fight. But the Red Army paused at the Vistula, holding back and allowing the Polish insurgents—potential opponents of a Soviet occupation—to be annihilated. President Roosevelt proposed a massive airlift of supplies to the freedom fighters, but the transport planes would have to proceed to nearby Soviet airfields to refuel. Stalin refused. It was a portent of things to come. The Kremlin's refusal, U.S. ambassador Averell Harriman wrote to Washington, "is based on ruthless political considerations—not on denial that the resistance exists nor on operational difficulties."[106]

The Germans retaliated savagely against the Warsaw Poles. The resistance force was exterminated and a quarter million civilians massacred. By early October the city had been razed. In January 1945, Soviet troops "liberated" Warsaw. They would remain there as occupiers for half a century.

As one of the harshest winters in memory descended upon Europe, the freezing weather took a devastating toll upon the Allied ranks. At night the men hunkered down in gravelike foxholes and did not move until morning light, hoping not to succumb to hypothermia in the darkness. Epic battles were waged, often at huge loss of life, their names today scarcely known. In the Battle of Hurtgen Forest (September 1944–February 1945), tens of thousands of GIs fought in the bleak woods south of Aachen, near the German-Belgian frontier, in a ruinous assault on a heavily fortified network of German bunkers. In the Battle of Metz (September–December 1944), Third Army forces captured the fortress city after a prolonged siege and intense building-to-building combat. In liberating the Lorraine region, the Third Army suffered fifty thousand casualties. The German army lost over three times that number.[107] It was at a terrible cost, but the Allies were winning the war of attrition.

Still, Hitler madly held out hope. He believed that a decisive defeat of the Allies might win an armistice in the west, allowing him to turn Germany's full might to the destruction of the Soviet threat in the east. In September he announced to his astonished High Command, "I have made a momentous decision. I shall go over to the offensive." At 5:25 a.m. in the frozen predawn of December 16, the sky over the Ardennes forest lit up and the ground shook from the thunder of heavy German artillery. A thick fog cut visibility to a few hundred feet. Following the preparatory bombardment, three German armies, North, Center, and South, attacked and overwhelmed the four American divisions caught entirely by surprise, strewn sparsely along the sixty-mile Ardennes front. A few of the inexperienced, noncombatant soldiers fled in panic. But most—many not trained for combat—stayed and fought, slowing the German advance during those crucial early hours and days. Soldiers armed with nothing more than a carbine or machine gun harried the German columns from the forest. Cooks and engineers blew up bridges and created the roadblocks that one German commander called "the most essential reason for the slowing up of the attack."[108] By the second day the Ardennes offensive was already behind schedule. At Trois-Ponts, a company of engineers who had been trained to operate sawmills waited surreptitiously for a German armored column to advance onto the bridge over the Salm River, and then blew it up.

The town of Bastogne, in the heart of the Ardennes, held the strategically vital crossroads through the region. Hitler's plan depended on the town's capture. On December 18 the 101st Airborne Division raced over a hundred miles by truck to get to the town before the Germans, whose advance was decisively slowed by small groups of Americans fighting on their own. When the 101st arrived at Bastogne late that night and began to establish defensive positions, the German army was only a few miles away.

After being repelled in several attempts to capture the town, on the twenty-first the German commander there attempted to get the outnumbered and outgunned Americans at Bastogne to surrender. A message was sent by emissary to the U.S. commanding officer, Gen. Anthony McAuliffe, threatening extermination of the entire American force unless they abandoned their positions.

McAuliffe wrote his one-word reply on the note and sent it back: "Nuts."

The Bastogne defenders were still holding off the German thrust when the first reinforcements from Patton's forces broke through on Christmas day. Bastogne would not fall.

After two weeks of heavy fighting, the Germans were driven back to the original battle line. The field commander requested permission to withdraw his troops from the bulge, which was now threatening to become an encirclement, but Hitler refused, giving his customary order to resist to the last man, thereby ending any possibility that the German army might survive the battle in a condition capable of making an adequate defense of the homeland. Not only had the Germans been repulsed in the largest land battle of the European war, they had suffered losses (81,000 casualties, 300–400 tanks) that they could not afford. The Americans also incurred heavy losses (77,000 casualties, 733 tanks), but these would be quickly replaced.[109]

When Winston Churchill, Franklin Roosevelt, and Joseph Stalin met at Yalta, in the Soviet Crimea, on February 4–11, 1945, the negotiations were less about the conduct of the war than about the disposition of Europe—and the world—following the war. President Roosevelt pressed for and got agreement on the inaugural meeting of the United Nations, to convene on April 25, 1945, at San Francisco. He and Churchill acquiesced to Stalin's demand that the Soviet republics of Ukraine and Belarus be admitted as full voting members of the UN, and agreement was also reached on veto power for the five permanent members of the Security Council. Also, Stalin agreed that the USSR would enter the war against Japan once Germany had been defeated, in exchange for receiving the Kurile Islands, Sakhalin, and domination in Manchuria.

On several occasions Roosevelt reiterated the American opposition to colonialism and pressed for recognition of the right of all people to self-determination. In this he was opposed by both Stalin and Churchill. The issue would have to wait. Also, America had no interest in war reparations, but Stalin succeeded in eliciting assurances of German indemnities to Russia, in the form of capital equipment, production, and the ambiguous "use of German labor."[110]

The leaders agreed to the partition of Germany following the war, including a zone for France. Stalin expressed astonishment that France "demands full rights with the Americans, British and Russians, who've carried the burden of the fighting."[111] Roosevelt was able to get a grin out of the Soviet dictator by revealing that, at Casablanca, de Gaulle had compared himself to Joan of Arc. The French would be given a zone of occupation, Roosevelt said, "but only out of kindness." Stalin replied, "That would be the only reason for giving them a zone."[112]

The most contentious issue at the conference, and the agreement with the most pernicious consequences, had to do with Soviet domination of Eastern Europe. This was necessary, Stalin insisted, as a buffer for Russia against further aggression from the West. Liberty for the freedom fighters in Poland and elsewhere was subordinated to the immediate imperatives of realpolitik. Shortly, the peoples of Poland, Hungary, Yugoslavia, Romania, Czechoslovakia, Bulgaria, and the Baltics were all to fall under Soviet mastery.

Roosevelt was visibly exhausted during the conference, and when he made his report to the Congress he was forced to do so sitting down. He would be accused of "selling out" Eastern Europe. That overstates it. The facts were already on the ground.

Franklin Roosevelt died on April 12, 1945. Having been elected on his New Deal domestic agenda, he had proven to be one of the ablest war presidents in American history. When the American people balked at entry into war, he spelled out what was at stake and used his immense communication skills to prepare the public mind for the great national sacrifices that would be required to prevail. More important, he did not bring America into the conflict until the nation was ready to make those sacrifices. In the meantime, he provided vital support which enabled Britain, and then Russia, to resist Germany until the United States did enter the struggle. In war, he fostered and sustained the largest and most complex coalition of allied nations in history; and, even as the fighting raged, he undertook meticulous planning to establish, in the aftermath of war, a more stable and peaceful world order.

Upon receiving news of Roosevelt's death, Hitler and his advisers were exuberant, hoping that, under new leadership, the Americans would switch sides. The fascist dictator had misapprehended the American mind at every step.

The advancing Allied armies encountered some of the most gruesome spectacles ever witnessed in human history. As they liberated the Reich's concentration camps, war-hardened soldiers were unprepared for the horrors they witnessed there. Grown men broke down into tears. Like many others, General Patton, the veteran of two world wars and countless battles, became sick and vomited.[113] One of the American liberators of the Buchenwald concentration camp described "stacks and stacks and rows and rows of human bodies stacked like cordwood. . . . Inside [the crematorium] you could see the bones and ash. Some of the bodies and bones were partially burned. It was the most horrible thing that a person could ever imagine."[114]

Of the 8 million Jews who had been living in the lands conquered by European fascism, 6 million were dead, some 40 percent of all Jews living in the world. "A thousand years will pass," said a Nazi official as he was being led to his execution after the war, "but still the guilt of Germany will not be wiped out."[115]

Could more have been done to prevent the Holocaust? Reports of the mass executions of Jews were reaching American and British officials at least by 1942. Critics have condemned Allied leaders for failing to act more aggressively to prevent the genocide, but those leaders did not know then what we know now. The journalist William Shirer, as knowledgeable as anyone on developments in Germany, and who had also heard the stories, later said, "I couldn't believe it . . . I did not get the story, really, until the war-crimes trials at Nuremberg. The Holocaust was recognized as the Holocaust only after victory opened up the death camps."[116]

Even today the Holocaust defies comprehension. History held no precedent for it in 1943–44. It was scarcely possible to imagine that human beings could sink to such a level: surely a plan to coldly and systematically eradicate an entire people could only be one of the rumors of war. A British Foreign Office analysis concluded that the rumors of mass exterminations were "a rather wild story." The American envoy in Berlin reported, "There is what is apparently a wild rumor inspired by Jewish fears. . . ."[117] Most Jews who heard the rumors were skeptical of them. Even those arriving at the camps could not believe them. "This is the greatest strength of the whole crime, its unbelievability," said Lilli Kopecky, a survivor of Auschwitz. "When we came to Auschwitz, we smelt the sweet smell. They said to us: 'There the people are gassed, three kilometers over there.' We didn't believe it."[118]

Nevertheless, Allied leaders had became aware of an unprecedented scale of extermination under way. On March 24, 1944, President Roosevelt read a statement to reporters in the Oval Office: "In one of the blackest crimes of all history—begun by the Nazis in the day of peace and multiplied by them a hundred times in time of war—the wholesale, systematic murder of the Jews of Europe goes on unabated every hour." He warned of dire consequences for all those "who participate in these acts of savagery . . . "[119]

But what could have been done to end the slaughter? The terrors were unfolding well within German-occupied territory. America was already waging a total war against Germany. The recommendation to bomb railroad tracks leading to the camps was clearly ineffectual: such damage was invariably repaired within a day, and would have required diverting men and resources away from the war effort on bombing runs spanning all Europe. No lives would have been saved by such an effort, and the war may have been prolonged. Assistant Secretary of War John McCloy, to whom such proposals were referred, believed that bombing rail lines would be of "doubtful efficacy" and "could be executed only by the diversion of considerable air support essential to the success of our forces now engaged in decisive operations" in the war.[120]

More feasible was the suggestion, made by some American Jewish leaders, that the concentration camps themselves should be targeted. However, this certainly would have inflicted untold deaths and injuries upon the inmates, for no clear benefit: even if some facilities had been destroyed, that alone would not have deterred the Nazis from carrying out their plan. McCloy later recalled that when he took the proposal for bombing Auschwitz to the president, Roosevelt grew "irate," insisting that bombing the camp "wouldn't have done any good." "Why, the idea!" Roosevelt said. "They'll say we bombed these people, and they'll only move it down the road a little way. . . . We'll be accused of participating in this horrible business."[121]

The head of the World Jewish Congress's Rescue Department opposed the bombing plan, as did nearly all members of the Rescue Committee of the Jewish Agency in Jerusalem.[122] The fundamental problem would not be addressed by it: the Jews of Europe would remain within the power of the fascist state and would continue to be slaughtered by it, until that state was destroyed. The only sure way to rescue European Jewry, and to save all other Jews in the world from a similar danger, was to defeat European fascism with troops on the ground.

Others have made compelling arguments for bombing the camps. Elie Wiesel, himself a survivor of Auschwitz, wishes that the Allies had bombed even if it meant the deaths of inmates. "We were no longer afraid of death—at any rate, not of that death."[123]

The debate over whether the Allies should have bombed the rail lines, or the camps, will never be finally resolved. What is not subject to dispute is that it was the involvement of the United States that prevented one of the most diabolical programs in human history from reaching its fulfillment; that, as historian Arthur Schlesinger has written, Franklin Roosevelt, "more than any other person, deserves the credit for mobilizing the forces that destroyed Nazi barbarism."[124] As one concentration camp survivor said of the last days of the war, "We heard the Americans were coming even here, and we were so happy we cried."[125]

One major political consequence of the Holocaust was to convince Jews that they must create their own sovereign nation to protect them. The death camps also turned American public opinion in favor of the Zionist movement, and the establishment of the state of Israel. In this, too, United States support was to prove vital.

———•———

As American troops dispersed across Western Europe, they were not so much feared by the local civilian populations as they were regarded as a source of rations, chocolate, protection, and liberation. It is rare in history when the local inhabitants run *toward* an invading army. "Whenever our convoy would stop," recalled Pvt. Richard Courtney, "kids would appear from all over and grin and turn their eyes up pleadingly, 'Hey Joe! Gumie? Schokolade? Cigarette for Papa? Gut American!'" The GIs, far from their own families, missing their own brothers and sisters, were soft touches. "The folks back home would have been so proud if they had seen their sons and how well they responded to the children of Europe," Courtney wrote.[126]

A tide of humanity, waves of refugees from throughout eastern Germany and the newly "liberated" nations of Eastern Europe, flowed westward to flee the approaching Russians, who engaged in a systematic policy of looting, rape, and the massacre of civilians. At the Elbe, the boundary of the American zone, infantryman Roscoe Blunt observed one of the great dramas of the century unfold, as the river became clogged with boats, rafts, and swimmers trying to get to the western side. The Americans were adhering to Roosevelt's Yalta agreement with the Russians, and some soldiers attempted to keep the crowds back, even firing warning shots into the air, but to no avail. The Russians were more fearsome. "We crawled back to the ditch and watched the constantly growing swarm of humanity crowding the shoreline. Many women [were] fearful of their lives and the treatment they would receive at the lust of the advancing Russian troops. . . . To one of them I called out *'Wo gehen sie?'* ("Where are you going?") *'Amerika,'* she answered without a moment's hesitation. *'Vereinige Staaten.'*" United States.[127]

Fascism was everywhere in collapse. In Italy, Mussolini was shot on April 28 by nationalist partisans while attempting to escape to Switzerland. On April 30, as his nation died around him, Adolf Hitler committed suicide. On the morning of Monday, May 7, at the Supreme Allied Headquarters in Reims, Gen. Alfred Jodl signed the unconditional surrender of all German forces.

"Human rights break state rights," Hitler had written.[128] SS security chief Reinhard Heydrich envisioned a time when there would be "total and permanent police supervision of everyone."[129] That vision was thwarted. More than 405,000 American servicemen died during the war, and another 671,000 were seriously wounded. They were only a portion of the total killed, but they were decisive to the outcome. The men who fought and died on the shores of Normandy, and in North Africa, and in the dark woods of Belgium, and the icy slopes of Italy, and the killing fields of Germany and across Europe, and in the skies and on the sea, did not fight to conquer territories or establish new markets for American commerce. They fought for freedom, and human history would be much different if they had not.

For many, of course, the struggle was not over in May 1945. America was still at war, half a world away, against another polity that aspired to subjugate innocent peoples.

When the Japanese attacked Pearl Harbor, the island nation had already been at war, unremittingly, for over a decade, and its leaders believed that if their expansion was to continue, it meant a collision course with the world's leading democracy. No other nation in history, East or West, had accomplished the transition to modernity in so short a time. The greatest Japanese "economic miracle" came not following the Second World War, but preceding the First. What had been regarded as a quaint, backward society in the 1850s was, by the late nineteenth century, ready to join the Western nations as an imperial power. In fact, it was not colonialism that the Japanese objected to; they merely wished to be among the colonizers rather than the colonized.

As soon as Japan was militarily able, in 1876 it coerced Korea, the "Hermit Kingdom," to accept an unequal trade agreement. In 1894, Japan declared war on China, which it quickly defeated, and seized territory in Korea and Manchuria as well as received trading concessions in China accorded the Western powers. In 1904 it went to war against Russia. Portentously, it made a surprise attack on the Russian fleet at Port Arthur, Emperor Meiji declaring war only two days later. Defeat of Russia sent shock waves throughout the established order. For the first time, an Asian nation had defeated a European power.

Russia agreed to recognize Japan's sphere of influence in Manchuria, which became an increasingly important source of raw materials for Japan. Korea was made a Japanese protectorate, and then annexed. In Manchuria, a garrison of some ten thousand soldiers, the Kwantung Army, was stationed to protect Japan's growing commercial interests there.[130] Amidst the national zeal, the tenuous separation between military and civilian authority set forth in the Meiji constitution, but lacking any historical tradition, withered. The creation of a Japanese empire, designated by the government *Dai Nihon Teikoku*,"the Great Empire of Japan," with its cornerstone in Manchuria, captured the imagination and enjoyed the support of the citizenry.

In 1937, Japan invaded China, capturing the major seaboard cities in some of the most savage campaigns against civilian populations in a century replete with such campaigns. Now, Japanese strategists believed, only America stood in in the way of Japan's total mastery over Asia. In fact, Japanese strategists had known it for years. As early as 1925, Shumei Okawa, a member of the Army General Staff, had written a popular strategic manual asserting that before Japan could achieve its divine destiny of Asian dominance, it must engage in an epic battle with the United States and defeat it. "Before a new world appears there must be a deadly fight between the power of the West and the East. This theory is realized in the American challenge to Japan. The strongest country in Asia is Japan and the strongest country that represents Europe is America. . . . These two countries are destined to fight. Only God knows when it will be."[131] In 1927, Gi-ichi Tanaka, the Japanese prime minister, had presciently warned, "If we want to control China in the future, we must first crush the United States."

In July 1941, Emperor Hirohito met with his closest military and political advisers to discuss the options. Prime Minister Konoye was present, as were War Minister Hideki Tojo, several ranking military officers, and Admiral Nomura, Japan's ambassador to the United States. Konoye told the emperor that the military had decided for a "strike south" against the Dutch East Indies and Philippines.[132] Hirohito agreed. Everyone present acknowledged that such a course would result in war with the United States. With the emperor's approval, the military accelerated its preparations. The *zaibatsu* increased armaments production. A bomb shelter was built beneath the emperor's palace. American code breakers, meanwhile, had intercepted communications indicating plans for a Japanese offensive in the Pacific.

As imperial forces moved into place for the occupation of Indochina, on July 26, President Roosevelt declared an embargo of all trade—including oil—with Japan. Within days Britain and the Netherlands, Japan's other key oil suppliers, followed suit. An energy crisis loomed. "Oil is the weak point of our Empire's national strength and fighting power," a military report concluded. "We are now gradually consuming oil that has been stockpiled. We will be self-sufficient for two years at most. Meanwhile the naval and air forces of the United States will improve remarkably as time goes by."[133] If Japan was going to act, it would have to act soon. Military planners assured Japanese leaders that "the end of British resistance [against Nazi Germany] is only a question of time," and "the United States' preparedness will not be completed before 1944."[134]

A meeting was held on September 6 at the Imperial Palace to finalize war plans. It was agreed that acquiescence to American demands for withdrawal from China would mean national humiliation. There were more than material interests at stake: there was national honor. "It is impossible for Japan to withdraw troops from China without losing face," Hirohito said. "If Ambassador Nomura does not succeed in reaching an accord with America by October tenth, Japan will move toward war with the United States and Britain."[135]

Isoroku Yamamoto, drafted to be the main architect of the battle plan against America, had been a vocal opponent of entering into war with the United States, predicting that it would bring calamity. Yamamoto, a highly intelligent man who had studied English at Harvard (where he also developed an affinity for poker), warned his military colleagues that Americans were not, as the prevailing view held, "weak willed and spoiled by luxuries." In addition, "Anyone who has seen the auto factories in Detroit or the oil fields in Texas, knows that Japan lacks the national power for a naval race with America."[136] Yamamoto cautioned that "it is a mistake to regard the Americans as luxury loving and weak. I can tell you that they are full of spirit, fight and justice. Japan cannot vanquish the United States. Therefore, we should not fight the United States."[137]

Nevertheless, Admiral Yamamoto dutifully set out to devise a plan that would give Japan the greatest chance for success in the coming conflict. For Yamamoto, though, "success" did not mean victory over the United States after a prolonged war, but the avoidance of such a war altogether. He knew that if America threw its resolve and vast resources into the conflict with Japan, it would mean cataclysm for his people. The only hope was to make quick territorial gains in the Pacific and inflict so much damage on the U.S. fleet that Americans would regard Japan's gains in distant Asia as a fait accompli, not worth a costly and destructive struggle. The plan for the conquest of the Pacific called for a simultaneous invasion of Burma, Malaya, the Philippines, and the East Indies. The conquered territories would provide the Japanese with the resources they would require for a defensive struggle against the United States, which would eventually tire of the conflict.

As preparations for war proceeded, smokescreen negotiations with the Americans also proceeded—Japanese diplomats continued the talks, but with no intention of achieving an agreement. On December 5, Secretary of State Cordell Hull told Roosevelt, "With every hour that passes, I become more convinced that [the Japanese] are not playing in the open. . . . I'm convinced that they don't intend to make any honorable agreement with us about anything, or to come to any understanding." Japan maintained the pretense of earnest negotiations up to the end. Ambassador Nomura was in Hull's office on the morning of December 7, even as the bombs were dropping on Pearl Harbor.

Eight U.S. battleships were sunk or badly damaged in the attack, along with three destroyers, three light cruisers, and 187 aircraft. Two thousand four hundred and three military personnel and civilians were killed, and another 1,178 wounded. In one day Japan had become the dominant force in the Pacific. According to Admiral Yamamoto's plan, it would have six months of unopposed conquest before the Americans would be able to fight back. Many Japanese leaders believed that perhaps the effete Americans would not choose to fight back at all.

For the Americans, although the raid was an unmitigated defeat, it could have been much worse: all three of the Pacific Fleet's aircraft carriers— *Enterprise, Lexington,* and *Saratoga*—were fortuitously at sea at the time. Things were bad enough in any event. Half of the U.S. Pacific Fleet was destroyed. The following day, President Roosevelt addressed Congress. "Yesterday, December 7, 1941—a date which will live in infamy—the United States was suddenly and deliberately attacked by the naval and air forces of the Empire of Japan. . . . "

The militarists who had counted on American democracy's indolence miscalculated badly. Within a day, recruiting stations were overrun. Recruit training centers became overcrowded, and many aspiring citizen soldiers had to be told by recruiters to come back in a few months. Some members of Congress stayed long enough to cast their last vote—for war—and then volunteered for military service.

In Tokyo, a blare of trumpets signaled the reading of the emperor's war proclamation. Japanese citizens celebrated in the streets, though a few informed Japanese did not share in the national euphoria. When Kiheiji Onozuka, former president of the prestigious Tokyo University, was told that Japan had sunk the U.S. fleet at Pearl Harbor, he whispered sadly to a friend, "This means that Japan is sunk, too."[138] Admiral Yamamoto, architect of the stunning victory, was also reticent. When asked why he was not celebrating the triumph, he is reported to have answered, "I fear all that we have done is to awaken a sleeping giant and fill him with a terrible resolve."

With America immobilized, Japan could now turn to its long-envisioned conquest of Asia. In fact, the Pacific War had begun a half hour before the attack on Pearl Harbor, when Japanese forces commenced an invasion of Malaya. Singapore had been an important naval base for the British since early in the century. Heavily fortified, it was considered impregnable. And it might have been had the attack come from seaward, to the south, where the fortifications were, but the Japanese landed to the north, on the Malay Peninsula.

In the Philippines, Gen. Douglas MacArthur received warning of a possible assault but had made little preparation against one, and when it came on December 8, the American air force of about 250 planes was destroyed on the ground. There were 35,000 U.S. soldiers stationed on the archipelago, in addition to another 100,000 native troops. On December 10, Japanese forces came ashore on the main island of Luzon, and with absolute air superiority rapidly pressed toward Manila. Within two weeks they had landed over 50,000 men and were pushing the American and Filipino force into the mountainous Bataan Peninsula. General MacArthur declared Manila an open city and moved his HQ to Corregidor, a tiny fortress island in Manila Bay. The U.S. and Filipino forces in Bataan fought on.

In the Battle of the Java Sea, in late February 1942, the Japanese dispelled any illusion that their success was due solely to the advantage of surprise. The two sides seemed evenly matched, but superior Japanese firepower and torpedoes proved decisive. In a series of engagements, two Allied cruisers and three destroyers were sunk and most of the other ships badly damaged. The Japanese suffered serious damage to just one destroyer.

General MacArthur was ordered to abandon Corregidor on February 22. He was instructed to flee to Australia, where he would set up a new command. "I shall return," he promised. On April 9, 1942, Gen. Edward King, commander of the remnant on Bataan, surrendered to the Japanese. Japan's Greater East Asian Co-Prosperity Sphere was taking shape. By mid-1942, in all of South and East Asia, only India had not been "liberated" by Japan, though what constituted liberation remained to be seen.

A 1942 Japanese government report entitled "An Investigation of Global Policy with the Yamato Race as Nucleus" indicated that it was, from the outset, part of Japan's agenda to subjugate other Asian peoples to the purposes of the *shido minzoku*. Each race, each nation, would fulfill the functions determined by its unique attributes. Each people's "proper place" was to be determined by the Japanese, whose function—and grave responsibility—it was to govern.[139] It was the "white man's burden" rendered into Japanese. The report said that, because of their unique moral attributes, the Japanese had been able to distill the highest qualities of orientalism and combine these with "the merits of Western civilization." Now they had an obligation to elevate their Asian neighbors by bringing them under the sway of this superior culture.[140] Most Japanese embraced the belief in their own racial superiority and accepted the responsibility of Japan to govern. As the popular monthly magazine *Bungei Shunju* put it, the qualities of brightness, strength, and uprightness made the Yamato people "the most superior race in the world," and the natural leaders of Asia and mankind.[141]

The subjugation of East Asia, accomplished in less than six months, confirmed the Japanese people's belief in their own primacy. As for the country's military rulers, the campaign had gone more smoothly than they had dared to hope. There had been less resistance than expected, and casualties had been lighter than anticipated. Warship losses were just one-tenth of projected levels.[142] Prime Minister Tojo asked the Navy High Command when the United States would be in a condition to launch a counterattack: not until the end of 1943, he was assured.

———◆———

Adm. Chester William Nimitz, an Annapolis graduate who had risen to be chief of the navy's Bureau of Navigation, was given the formidable task of rebuilding the Pacific Fleet and dislodging an enemy that was now securely entrenched in its newly acquired territories, with a wide defensive perimeter extending well beyond its core possessions. A division of labor emerged between MacArthur, whose forces would push northward from Australia back toward the Philippines, and Nimitz's Pacific Fleet, which would fight its way across the Pacific, one island at a time, in an "island-hopping" campaign toward the Japanese mainland. Nimitz's prejudice, shared by most U.S. military leaders, about the supposed backwardness of the enemy, was conclusively dispelled at the Battle of the Coral Sea, off of Australia, on May 7–8, 1942. In the first naval engagement in which neither sides' ships ever saw the other's, and waged entirely by aircraft launched by vessels out of sight of the battle, it was the Americans who were forced to withdraw after suffering the loss of an aircraft carrier, severe damage to another, and the loss of most of its 122 planes.

Even after the bitterly contested Battle of the Coral Sea, the Imperial Navy remained the dominant force in the Pacific and retained strategic initiative. Now Admiral Yamamoto wanted to deal a death blow to the American fleet. He devised a complex plan to lure Nimitz's Pacific Fleet out of Pearl Harbor and into a decisive naval duel by staging an attack on Midway, which was by this time America's westernmost outpost in the Pacific. If the airfield at Midway could be taken and the fleet broken, Hawaii would be vulnerable. Then, he believed, the Americans would be forced to pursue peace on terms favorable to Japan.

Through intercepts by the increasingly effective Magic code-breaking unit, the Americans had foreknowledge of the plan. By the time the immense 145-ship Japanese armada (which included four large fleet carriers), approached Midway Island, Nimitz had already dispatched two task forces to meet it. These included three carriers and an escort of seven heavy cruisers. The four Japanese carriers had a total of 325 aircraft. Nimitz had three carriers and 233 planes.

Launched in the predawn darkness of June 4, 1942, the Battle of Midway at first looked to be a total victory for the Japanese fleet. The military installation on the island was devastated, and not a single plane from the American task force survived the first wave of attacks against the Japanese fleet, which met them with a maelstrom of antiaircraft spray and Zero fighters, which were more agile than the American planes. U.S. air-dropped torpedoes failed to detonate. In all, of the forty-one planes sent against the Japanese fleet, only six survived. Yamamoto's flotilla was unscathed. The invincible Imperial Navy had achieved another glorious triumph, and Japan seemed on the verge of winning not only a great battle, but the war.

The Japanese sailors' celebrations were premature. From out of the blue there appeared thirty-seven dive bombers, from the *Enterprise*. Flying without fighter protection for an hour and a half, the pilots had gone to the very limit of their fuel supply, desperately searching for the Japanese ships, a moving target in a vast ocean expanse. Now the planes raced down from fifteen thousand feet, on top of the Japanese fighters that had descended almost to sea level to oppose the earlier attacks. "Consequently it may be said, that the American dive bombers' success was made possible by the early martyrdom of their torpedo planes," Japanese military officials later reported.[143] Bombers from the *Yorktown* shortly followed.

What followed has been called "five minutes that changed the world." The American pilots were almost unopposed by enemy aircraft, though anti-aircraft fire was intense. Between 10:25 and 10:30 a.m. the tide of the battle— and the war—turned. By 11:00 a.m. the message was relayed to Admiral Yamamoto on the bridge of the battleship *Yamato*, far in the rear: of Japan's eight aircraft carriers, the foundation of its naval might, three were on their way to the bottom of the ocean. By evening another had been badly hit, and it sank the next morning. Just as important, many of Japan's most highly trained and experienced pilots had been lost, along with over three hundred aircraft. Yamamoto withdrew his depleted force westward. In one day the balance of power in the Pacific Ocean had been transformed. It would never again be in Japan's Furthermore, American industrial production would soon become decisive. Better torpedoes and better aircraft were on the way. More aircraft carriers, many more. Between 1942 and 1944 the Japanese would add six new fleet carriers to their navy; the United States added fourteen.

It was one thing to dominate the seas, but Japan still held the land, territory that it would fight to its utter destruction to hold on to. In November 1942, following months of brutal land, sea, and air battles, Japanese troops were expelled from Guadalcanal, an island on the southern tip of the Solomon Islands, east of New Guinea.

The tide was turning. Eisenhower had landed in North Africa and was in the process of pushing the Germans off that continent. The Russians were turning back the Germans at Stalingrad. "It would seem that a turning point in this war has been reached," Roosevelt said in a November 17 speech. That month the Imperial Navy requested the use of some desperately needed ships from the German fleet. The Germans, who were having troubles of their own, refused.

Henceforth, in no year of the war was Japan able to produce more tonnage of ships than the Americans were able to sink. The United States had been in the war for just a year, but the American genius for production and distribution was at this early point already evident. In the United States a new line of powerful, faster aircraft carriers, the *Essex* Class, was coming into production. There were plans for the construction of five hundred aircraft carriers, if necessary. The P-38 and F-4U Corsair would prove more than a match for the celebrated Zero. From the North Atlantic to the South Pacific, from battleships to boots, the American productive leviathan was operating at full steam. A Marine on Guadalcanal summed it up: "We had Spam for Thanksgiving. But for Christmas, we had a turkey dinner."[144]

On April 18, 1943, while on a morale-building tour of his command, Admiral Yamamoto's plane was intercepted and shot down by American fighters. Just when Japan desperately needed new answers, it had lost the best strategic mind in the Imperial military.

———•———

The first objective of Admiral Nimitz's island-hopping campaign was to be Tarawa, in the Gilbert Islands, some 2,400 miles west of Hawaii. It was an atoll, a submerged ring of volcanic islets, their tips often poking just a few feet above sea level. Though it was tiny, from Tarawa Japanese planes could strike at the advancing U.S. fleet. It had to be captured. For three hours on the morning of November 20, 1943, American naval vessels off the atoll sustained one of the most intense bombardments in history, three thousand tons of fire—ten tons per acre. The men—including their officers—expected to walk ashore unopposed. In fact, none of the enemy's main battlements had been destroyed. There was a brief pause between the end of the shelling and the landing, but it was enough: the Japanese dug out of their excellent defenses and were waiting for the Marines as they came ashore. Of the first wave of men to assault Tarawa, only 30 percent even made it to shore. Of the second wave, fewer. Of the third, almost none.[145]

By the end of the first day, 5,000 Marines had managed to fight their way onto a 100-yard stretch of coral beach, advancing a mere 20 feet inland. Of those 5,000 men, 1,500 were dead or dying. The lagoon was red with blood. After three days of fighting, 6,000 dead and dying men lay rotting there, crowded into a space of less than one square mile. Most of the survivors had not slept, and many had not eaten, in three days. Tarawa was declared to be "secure," though it would be several more days before all of the isolated snipers had been rooted out. Of the 4,700-man Japanese garrison on the island, only 17 soldiers (some who had been too badly wounded to commit suicide) were captured alive. The Americans lost 3,500 casualties in what may have been the most concentrated destruction of the war. Among Marines, the little scrap of sand and coral would forever be remembered as "Bloody Tarawa." Radio Tokyo reported that the emperor's forces were in the process of winning another glorious victory.

The American task force relentlessly fought its way across the Pacific in its costly "island-hopping" campaign against a fanatical enemy resolved to fight to the death. Saipan. Tinian. In July, Guam fell: in Japan, the fall of the

Marianas Islands was a psychological blow to the population. The nation was now losing territory it had held *before* it embarked upon its mad spree of aggression. Government propaganda could no longer conceal the scope of the catastrophe. "About that time they began telling the people the truth about the war," observed Admiral Wenneker, a German naval attaché in Tokyo. "They began preparing them for whatever must happen."[146] General Tojo resigned as prime minister in late July. He was replaced by Gen. Kuniaki Koiso, the notorious "Tiger of Korea," who had complained that Tojo was not fierce enough in his execution of the war.

———

During their astonishing sweep across Asia in 1941, in some places the Japanese had been initially welcomed. Indonesians hated their Dutch colonizers and had embraced the Japanese as liberators, cheering enthusiastically as Japanese troops paraded through the streets of their cities. The French were similarly despised by the Vietnamese in French Indochina. Many Asians looked forward to emancipation from European dominion, and opposition to Western imperialism was exploited by Japanese propagandists. Leaflets distributed in China had enjoined the population that "to liberate Asia from the white man's prison is the natural duty of every Asiatic! All of you Asiatics who have groaned under the yoke of the white man, unite!" In Malaya and Singapore, leaflets assured residents that the Japanese were fighting to liberate native inhabitants from "many years of tyranny under white rule."[147] Hopes were soon dashed. The peoples of Asia had not been delivered from foreign domination, but had exchanged one subjugation for another, more brutal one. Their lands were needed by Japan for raw materials. Their men were needed for labor.

Throughout Asia, in every instance the Japanese occupation regime was more vicious than the one it replaced. The fundamental object of Japanese domination, as a prewar government report stated, was to establish "an inseparable economic relationship between the Yamato race, the leader of the East Asia Cooperative Body, and other member peoples, whereby our country will hold the key to the very existence of all the races of East Asia."[148] Japan's military leaders planned for the administration of newly conquered areas in East Asia to be "a source of raw materials and a market for our manufactured products. Measures will be taken to prevent the development of industry in this area. Wages will be kept as low as possible."[149]

More than 100,000 Chinese laborers died in Japanese coal mines in Manchuria.[150] Over 40,000 Chinese were sent to the Japanese mainland as slave laborers, forced to do hazardous work in dehumanizing conditions. At least one-third of these were dead by the end of the war. Construction of the Burma-Siam railroad, from October 1942 to November 1943, involved the use of about 300,000 slave laborers from throughout Asia, of whom at least one-fifth died under the oppressive conditions.[151]

From 1939–45, 670,000 Koreans were transported to Japan for forced labor in mines and heavy industry. Of these, over 60,000 died from abuse or neglect.[152] In addition, 200,000 Korean men were conscripted into forced service for the Imperial Army.

Co-prosperity it was not. The emperor's new colonies, already often wretchedly poor, were bled dry to supply Japan's growing resource needs. In the Philippines, sugar production was abandoned in favor of cotton, which was in greater demand in Japan. Imports were cut off. Mass starvation ensued. In Indochina much of the rice production was discontinued in favor of jute, which was needed for military use. A famine resulted, causing the death of some 200,000 Vietnamese. Much of the food crops that were grown were sent abroad for use by the Japanese. Starvation and disease were the inevitable consequence of the occupation government's policies, and sometimes seemed to be an object of the policies. People wasting away from malnourishment could offer little organized resistance. By 1945 the population of Hong Kong had declined from 1.6 million to 750,000.[153] In all, over 6 million Chinese lost their lives under Japan's rule of terror.

Native inhabitants of New Guinea, the Marianas, and other Pacific islands were routinely executed without trial for suspected resistance. When a revolt erupted in North Borneo, the Japanese used it as an pretext for waging a campaign to eradicate a native race of dark-skinned people, the Suluks, who inhabit islands off the western coast of Borneo.[154] Occupation of the Philippines—a Christian nation friendly to the United States and ardently opposed to Japanese rule—was also especially brutal.

Nearly a quarter million Asian women, mostly Koreans, were enlisted in forced prostitution, as "comfort women" for the Imperial Army.

One of the great horrors of the war unfolded at a "medical research" facility run by the Imperial Army outside the city of Harbin, in Manchukuo. At that camp, innocuously called Unit 371 and disguised as a water purification center, thousands of prisoners were subjected to monstrous biological experimentation that spanned more than a decade. The "research" was actually nothing more than an excuse for plumbing the depths of human depravity. In the name of scientific inquiry victims were hung from their feet, to measure how long it would take different body types to suffocate. People were injected with horse urine. Air was injected into veins. Subjects were forced to consume large quantities of heroin. Victims were infected with every conceivable bacteria, gassed with every imaginable gas. In the gas chambers, three of the walls were glass, so that the dying victims could be closely observed and photographed. Bomb canisters of gas gangrene were exploded within feet of test subjects, to measure the effectiveness of the weapon in cold conditions. "Seven days later they died in great torment," a technician noted.[155]

The facility produced anthrax, cholera, typhus, and other biological agents, which were field-tested on Chinese populations. When the war ended, preparations were under way for a campaign of biological warfare against the western United States.

The American advance across the Pacific was met with increasingly ferocious resistance as it neared the Japanese mainland. In September 1944, at "Bloody Peleliu," a tiny island of the Palau Group just six miles long and two miles wide, U.S. Marines suffered 40 percent losses in rooting out Imperial troops deeply ensconced in a network of fortified caves, bunkers, and tunnels. In the naval Battle of Leyte Gulf (which was in fact several distinct naval engagements over three days) in October, Japan lost its four carriers, three battleships, six heavy and four light cruisers, and nine destroyers—most of its remaining navy. In an act of desperation during the battle, fanatical Japanese pilots—unable to contest the Americans in the air—began crashing their aircraft in suicide attacks upon the U.S. ships. The era of the *kamikaze* ("divine wind") pilot had arrived.

U.S. troops went ashore on Luzon, in the Philippines, in early January 1945 and began fighting their way southward toward Manila, again encountering fierce opposition. About a quarter million Japanese troops remained on the island, ordered to fight to the death. Unable to halt the American advance, in February the Japanese unleashed a vengeful massacre of the Filipinos. All major Catholic institutions, including venerable old Cathedrals, convents, hospitals, and the oldest Catholic university in Asia, were destroyed. Seventy percent of Manila's factories were destroyed, along with 80 percent of its residential areas and the entire business district. Civilian casualties in the Manila Massacre exceeded a hundred thousand.[156]

Another battle was raging in the western Pacific. On February 19, a Marine invasion force had landed on Iwo Jima, eight square miles of barren volcanic rock and ash just 650 miles southeast of Tokyo. The island's terrain of jagged ridges and fifteen hundred caves was custom-suited to the defense. The Japanese considered the island their "unsinkable aircraft carrier" and had intensively fortified it with concrete-reinforced tunnels and bunkers bristling with armaments.[157] An extinct volcano, Mount Suribachi, rose five hundred feet above sea level on its southern tip. Garrisoned on Iwo Jima were 22,000 of the Imperial Army's best troops, who were consigned to death for the emperor and determined to take as many Americans as they could.

Casualty rates exceeded 40 percent. The battle for tiny Iwo Jima was on its way to becoming the bloodiest in which Americans had participated since Gettysburg.[158] Iwo Jima was finally declared to be secure on March 26, though mopping up exercises continued for weeks. Of the 60,000 Marines who went ashore, one-third were casualties by the end of the battle—17,000 wounded, 5,900 killed. They had captured the most densely fortified piece of ground in the world, with some divisions suffering casualty rates exceeding 75 percent.

Even before the last Japanese troops were dislodged from their entrenched positions, the runways at Iwo Jima's airfields had been extended to accommodate B-29s. The Pacific War was in its final phase, the assault on the Japanese homeland. Strategic bombing now incinerated large sections of Japanese cities, killing tens of thousands. Still, Japan's militarists persisted in their hopes of victory.

The logical springboard for an invasion of the Japanese home islands was Okinawa, largest of the Ryukyu chain, only 350 miles south of the island of Kyushu, and 1,000 miles from Tokyo. The Japanese expected an assault there and had prepared a formidable defense. For the destruction of the approaching American fleet, the High Command placed its hopes upon the *kamikaze*.

The American invasion fleet included 1,200 ships and half a million men, with a combat force of nearly 200,000. The landing, launched on Easter Sunday, April 1, 1945, was uncontested, but the Americans quickly came up against the enemy's fortified defensive line. Every inch of ground was covered by traversing lines of fire, in rugged, mountainous terrain perfectly suited for defense. So masterful were the enemy's emplacements that soldiers were often unable to locate the source of the fire pouring down on them. The protracted, close-up, and grisly combat on the ground took a toll upon minds as well as bodies. There were over 15,000 cases of "battle fatigue" on Okinawa, a euphemistic name for a crippling neurological disease that reduced brave men to immobility, eyes staring blankly, often sobbing uncontrollably or shrieking madly. Yet slowly, inexorably, the Japanese force was pushed back and whittled down, the final defensive barrier being breached on June 17. The Japanese commander of the Okinawa defense sent his deepest regrets to the emperor for failing to stave off the Americans, and then committed suicide.

Okinawa had been the bloodiest campaign of the Pacific War. More than 100,000 Japanese soldiers had chosen to fight to the death rather than surrender; of the 7,000 who did surrender, many had been reluctant native Okinawan conscripts. Thousands of civilians committed suicide rather than face the horrors that they believed would befall them at American hands. There were 50,000 American casualties in the battle for Okinawa; 12,000 were killed, including 5,000 sailors.

The resistance became more fanatical, and the fighting more ferocious, as the Americans drew nearer to Japan. Okinawa was the bloodiest campaign of the war, but it was only a stepping-stone, a prelude to a battle that would be infinitely costlier: the conquest of the mainland. Planning for Operation Olympic, the invasion of Japan, was already in the advanced stages. It was to involve 767,000 troops. The Joint Chiefs put casualty estimates at over a quarter million men. Based on the experience at Okinawa, MacArthur believed that the figure would be closer to 1 million.

Blinded by ideological zeal, the Imperial Army had not been deterred by the succession of devastating defeats. It prepared for a "decisive battle" that would force the Americans to negotiate a settlement. After all, Japan still controlled Korea, and much of China. Perhaps it could hold onto its prewar possessions. Following the loss of Okinawa, the government issued a communiqué: "We shall throw everything conceivable, material and spiritual into the battle and annihilate the enemy landing force by fierce and bold offensive attacks."[159]

Japanese media gave scant coverage to the unconditional surrender of Japan's ally, Nazi Germany, on May 8. Instead, the prime minister declared that Japan would fight to the end rather than surrender. Many younger officers insisted that, for honor's sake, it would be better for the country to fight to the last man than agree to any terms that would allow a foreign occupation and desecration of Japan's sacred soil. Both the military, and the general populace, were getting geared up for a cataclysmic struggle. Civilians were trained in fighting techniques with bamboo spears and small arms.

In the predawn of August 6, a B-29 took off from the airfield on Tinian Island, heading for the port city of Hiroshima, carrying a uranium bomb. The atomic blast at Hiroshima killed around 70,000 people instantly, and a similar number over the following months from injuries associated with the bomb. Three days later another atomic explosion, of a plutonium device, was detonated over Nagasaki, killing another 35,000. The bombs were horrifying in their power and their effect. And they ended the war.

Monday-morning warriors have in retrospect said that, with the submarine blockade and strategic bombing, Japan would have shortly been forced to do the rational thing, and surrender. Nonsense. If the Japanese had been acting rationally, they wouldn't have attacked America in the first place.

The Japanese were not the victims in World War II. They were the aggressors. Had Japan possessed a hundred atomic bombs, it would have used every single one of them, and obliterated all America and Asia, if necessary, to preserve its divine Empire of the Sun. Millions of Japanese had been prepared to fight to the death against an invasion. Many more would have committed suicide. Their lives, too, were saved by the bombs.

One suspects that Truman's intrepid critics, who have decried the cruelty of using the atomic bombs on the grounds that perhaps "only" one hundred thousand *more* American casualties would have been lost in an invasion of Japan, would themselves not have risked being among that number. They are heroic, like many intellectuals, with other peoples' lives.

Hundreds of thousands of young American men, most of whom had already faced the prospect of death, and witnessed much of it, in savage battles across both Europe and Asia, were readying themselves for the bloodiest battle of all, the assault on Japan. Countless of them would surely die there. "We were going from the Oki slaughter to a much worse one," said a Marine.[160] For them, the dropping of the atomic bombs was not a philosophical abstraction to be polemicized by those comfortably removed from the hazards of the arena. It was a horrible weapon in a horrible war in which they faced death, and in which many of their comrades had died. Hiroshima "lifted a great blanket of impending doom," recalled army sergeant Donald Dencker.[161]

One man heard the news while recovering from battle wounds in a military hospital. "My whole body shouted, 'Thank God for the A-bomb!' Because otherwise I'd have been sent out to more combat as soon as I was patched up—and killed sooner or later. Those were the odds. I was overjoyed."[162] Paul Fussell, then an infantry platoon leader, described his emotions and those of his fellow soldiers upon hearing of the atomic blasts: "For all the fake manliness of our facades, we cried with relief and joy. We were going to live. We were going to grow up to adulthood after all."[163]

Infantryman Jack Thompson was wounded in the fighting on Iwo Jima, and after hospitalization returned to his outfit to prepare for the next battle. "For the first time, we knew in advance what island we were headed for," he recalled. "It would be Japan, the sacred island of the cherry trees, and as veterans knew, the island of coming death. The bombing of Hiroshima and Nagasaki may be somewhat controversial now, but believe me, it wasn't in August '45. To me it meant I would be going home whole and not in a box."[164]

Members of the peace faction in the Japanese government called the atomic bomb "a gift from heaven," certain to hasten the end of the war. The militarists were not swayed. "We have but one choice," said War Minister Anami: "We must fight on." After all this, many in the military leadership still dreamed of a final battle to turn the tide. Militants in the War Council still refused to surrender. For the first time during the entire war, the emperor made a policy decision. Surrender. The militarists staged a coup, and when it failed, killed themselves.

In a taped message broadcast on August 15, Hirohito spoke to the nation. It was the first time the people had ever heard the voice of their sovereign, the Son of Heaven. "The war situation has developed not necessarily to Japan's advantage," he told them. "We must endure the unendurable," and surrender.

The United States' allies called for a punitive settlement with Japan, but for the American leadership, the time for hostility was past. As General MacArthur declared upon accepting Japan's unconditional surrender aboard the battleship *Missouri*, in Tokyo Bay, on September 2, 1945, "It is my earnest hope—indeed the hope of all mankind—that from this solemn occasion a better world shall emerge out of the blood and carnage of the past, a world founded upon faith and understanding, a world dedicated to the dignity of man and the fulfillment of his most cherished wish for freedom, tolerance and justice." A member of the Japanese delegation later said that the deck of the *Missouri* had been "transformed into an altar of peace."

More than 405,000 American servicemen lost their lives in the defense of liberty during the Second World War, with another million severely wounded, but the war was over and the peace had begun. How would the victor, the predominant power in the world, act toward the vanquished? Japanese writer Toshikazu Kase observed of the ceremony on the *Missouri*: "Here is a victor announcing the verdict to the prostrate enemy. He can exact a pound of flesh if he so chooses. He can impose a humiliating penalty if he so desires. And yet he pleads for freedom, tolerance, and justice."[165]

More broadly, the war forced Americans to reconsider their nation's role in the world. It was no longer morally acceptable, and perhaps no longer possible, for the United States to close itself off, to detach itself from developments in the larger global arena. As journalist Walter Lippman had written in 1941, the United States, as the world's leading democracy, could no longer evade its responsibility in the vacuum of isolationism. "What Rome was to the ancient world, what Great Britain has been to the modern world, America is to be to the world of tomorrow. We might wish it otherwise. I do. But our personal preferences count for little in the great movements of history. . . . "[166] Freedom-loving peoples around the world now, more than ever, looked to America as a standard-bearer of individual liberties and democratic government. If Japan's warlords had been right about the American spirit, and the United States had lacked the will to resist Japanese aggression, there would have followed generations of upheaval and atrocity across Asia. Instead there has ensued a period of unprecedented improvement in the quality of life, growing political and economic cooperation, rising living standards and life expectancy, and a flowering of individual liberty and democratic governance.

Wendell Willkie, the Wall Street lawyer and industrialist Republican who ran against Roosevelt in 1940, became an activist for an internationalist foreign policy after a 1942 tour of the world revealed to him the extent to which peoples across the globe share basic aspirations in common. In his 1943 best-selling book *One World*, Willkie wrote that, although he had traveled 31,000 miles, "the net impression of my trip was not one of distance from other peoples, but of closeness to them. If I ever had any doubts that the world has become small and completely interdependent, this trip would have dispelled them altogether.[167]

Wherever Willkie traveled, from Europe and Russia to the Middle East and Asia, he found people who yearned for the economic and political freedom that Americans took for granted, and waited expectantly for the United States to use its great power to foster liberty in the world. "When I say that this world demands the full participation of a self-confident America, I am only passing on an individual invitation which the peoples of the East have given us. . . . Other peoples, not yet fighting, are waiting no less eagerly for us to accept the most challenging opportunity of all history—the chance to create a new society in which men and women the world around can live and grow invigorated by independence and freedom."[168]

That positive participation would require, for better and worse, the United States to maintain a substantial military capability—something Americans were not accustomed to. Before the outbreak of the Second World War, the United States armed forces had numbered only 160,000 troops, poorly equipped and trained, barely ranking in the top twenty armies in the world. Joint Chiefs chairman George C. Marshall concluded his 1945 report to the War Department: "We have tried since the birth of our nation to promote our love of peace by a display of weakness. This course has failed us utterly." The imperative of maintaining a standing military in defense of liberty, without becoming militaristic, was a delicate feat in 1945, and would remain one. Nevertheless it was an imperative. If only aggressive and authoritarian nations armed themselves, then freedom would remain forever vulnerable.

For the establishment of a world in which freedom could flourish, it was not sufficient that the United States merely stand aside and let it happen. Without active American participation, such a world would not happen.

3

A New and Changed World

FROM EUROPE TO Asia, the postwar world lay in ruins, and the international system was in disarray. The United States, which a few years earlier had fielded an army the size of Norway's, emerged from the war a leviathan whose military bestrode the earth, supported by an industrial might that far surpassed all of its nearest rivals combined. Per capita income in the U.S. was twice the level of the next richest group of nations (which included Switzerland, Canada, New Zealand, and Great Britain). Americans, just 6 percent of the world's population, manufactured half of all industrial output and had 42 percent of all income.[1] Innumerable American lives had been lost in the war, and vast treasure spent. The nations of Europe and Asia lay desolated and vulnerable: the triumphant Americans could have easily followed the pattern of millennia of victors in wars, and pursued a course of plunder and national self-aggrandizement across the globe. They chose another path.

The United States could have imposed any reparation, inflicted any retaliation, upon its defeated adversaries. The German people awaited that fate. Indeed, it had been what they had imposed upon those they had vanquished. But Americans sought none of these things. They wanted nothing for themselves. They only sought to foster a more peaceful and stable and prosperous world, to help restore democracy and individual liberties where they had once existed, and to cultivate them where they had not existed before. "It is much easier to make war than peace," Clemenceau said during the Paris Peace Conference following the First World War. America won great wars during the twentieth century, but the most distinctive feature of its foreign policy was not the ability to vanquish in war, but the capacity to triumph in peace. In a radio address on December 9, 1941, following the attack on Pear Harbor, President Roosevelt said that the United States was embarking upon war "not for conquest, not for vengeance, but for a world in which this nation and all that it represents, will be safe for our children." He promised that "we are going to win the war and we are going to win the peace that follows."

Short of stature, with thick glasses that some said made him look owlish, Harry Truman had been unable to attend college due to family financial difficulties. He lacked both the physical bearing and the natural social grace of his aristocratic predecessor. What he possessed was Middle American common sense, straightforwardness, moderation, and a genuine concern for justice. He was the American everyman. Harry Truman, the happenstance president, proved to be an excellent one.

There were, of course, divisions within the administration on how to deal with Germany following the war. There had been generations of bitter experience with German belligerence, and it was unanimously agreed that a German impulse to aggression must be subdued. But how? General Eisenhower had favored a punishing "hard peace" with Germany following the war, as did Henry Morgenthau, treasury secretary under both Roosevelt and Truman. The Morgenthau Plan proposed stripping Germany of her industrial centers in the Ruhr and Saar and making it into a primarily agrarian economy, largely isolated from intercourse with the rest of Europe, with a population living at subsistence levels, but little more.

The French also advocated a rigidly punitive approach. They believed that the German people were innately aggressive, and the only protection against them was to declaw Germany by deindustrializing it. France was unhappy at having been excluded from Potsdam and other negotiations over postwar reconstruction, and the new government frantically pressed its case for harsh reparations, including special economic privileges for France in the Ruhr and Saar, and a permanent French occupation of the Rhineland,[2] though its increasing reliance upon public pronouncements rather than diplomacy attested to its shrinking international relevance. (It was only on the insistence of the Americans, in opposition to the Russians, that France was given a role at all—and an occupation zone—in postwar Germany).

Truman's secretary of war Henry Stimson favored punishment for German aggression, but not its reduction to a nation of rural peasantry. "The question is not whether we want the Germans to suffer for their sins," he said. "The only question is whether over the years a group of seventy million educated, efficient and imaginative people can be kept within bounds on such a low level of subsistence as the Treasury proposals contemplate. . . . It would be just such a crime as the Germans themselves hoped to perpetrate upon their victims—it would be a crime against civilization itself."[3]

Ultimately the United States was not interested in keeping Germans in a condition of open-ended destitution. "Americans," said Gen. Lucius Clay, the man Truman appointed as military commander of the American Zone in occupied Germany, "are not a vindictive people."[4] From the day the war ended, individual American citizens and charitable institutions began shipping food and other aid to the devastated Germans. Thousands of tons of used clothing were donated by concerned families. American physicians traveled to Germany to help restore its medical system, which had languished under the Nazis. Relief agencies organized fund-raising campaigns for the German people and donated vast amounts of food and medical supplies. At Truman's behest, former president Herbert Hoover launched an aggressive aid drive, touring the country to encourage citizens to contribute to their former adversaries.

The central objective of the postwar occupation of Germany was to prepare the nation, as the directive from the Joint Chiefs put it, "for an eventual reconstruction of German political life on a democratic basis."[5] Civil and political liberties were guaranteed in a new, democratic constitution, and a free German press and broadcast industry was fostered with American aid, even when it was critical of some U.S. occupation policies. By 1949 there were fifty-nine independent German newspapers in the American zone.[6] Agriculture experts were sent from the United States to help increase German farm productivity.

The American forces in Germany were astonishingly well-behaved for an occupying force, treating—in accord with their orders—the local population with respect. They were well-received by the German population. A 1950 survey published in the *Frankfurter Rundschau* found that, among Germans in the American zone, 31 percent found the Americans to be the most sympathetic among the occupying powers, 7 percent the British, 4 percent the French. Sixteen percent had no opinion, and 42 percent said, not surprisingly, that they preferred no occupier at all. In the British zone, 30 percent favored the Americans, 9.8 favored percent the British, .6 percent the French, and .4 percent the Russians. In the French zone, 22.6 percent preferred the Americans, 14.6 percent the French, 2.6 percent the British, and .1 percent the Russians.[7] Sixty percent of Germans said that the conduct of American troops was good, an astonishing figure in a postwar environment; in Berlin, it rose to 80 percent.

Indeed, most West Germans—cognizant of American isolationism—were afraid that the Americans would pull out early while the feared Russians were still in place, leaving them vulnerable. The memory of the Russian rampage across east Europe and Germany was still fresh, and there was growing awareness of the miserable fate of the nations in Eastern Europe that had fallen under Soviet control. On a trip to Germany in September 1946, Secretary of State James Byrnes spoke to an audience of German citizens at the Stuttgart Opera House—and by live radio broadcast, translated into German, which was heard by millions of citizens across the nation. He pledged that the Americans would remain so long as Russian troops were stationed across the border in East Germany. "We will not shirk our duty.

We are not withdrawing," he said.[8] "We [Americans] have learned that, whether we like it or not, we live in one world, from which we cannot isolate ourselves. . . . The American people who fought for freedom have no desire to enslave the German people. The freedom Americans believe in and fought for is the freedom which must be shared with all willing to respect the freedom of others."[9] Americans wanted the German people, and indeed all the world, to share in the blessing of liberty. "The American people want to help the German people to win their way back to an honorable place among the free and peace-loving nations of the world," said Byrnes.[10]

The speech was met with "enormous enthusiasm," General Clay later recalled. "It was unbelievable to me. Here was an American Secretary of State out there signing autographs for the Germans, little over one year after the end of the war."[11]

Nevertheless, Germany faced an existential crisis. The economy was in ruins, unemployment was dangerously high, productivity was low, and falling. Agricultural output was dropping, and famine loomed. Americans, who had already provided billions of dollars in aid to help rebuild Europe, responded to the crisis by sending tens of millions of tons of grain, fertilizer, and agricultural equipment. Such contributions were valuable, but they would not be sufficient.

It was not only Germany that was in turmoil. Two years after the war ended, all Europe remained prostrate. The postwar economies remained stagnant. Poverty and hunger were rampant. Populations were demoralized and dispirited. The Communists were making inroads among the economically and socially disaffected. In a general election held in October 1945, the Communist Party of France polled 5 million votes, more than any other party. In June 1946, 19 percent of Italian voters cast their ballots for communist candidates; another 21 percent supported the closely aligned Socialists, for a total of 40 percent.[12] In countries in Eastern Europe where the Communists had taken power, they demonstrated an unwillingness to give it up again. Personal and political freedoms were systematically suppressed. Their governments retained power by terror and fear. All opposition was prohibited.

On a tour of the United States in March 1946, former prime minister Winston Churchill warned in a speech at Westminster College, in Fulton, Missouri, that "an iron curtain has descended across the continent." He urged Americans to accept the leadership of the free world, to which they had not aspired but which was now upon them. "The United States stands at this time at the pinnacle of world power," Churchill said. "It is a solemn moment for American democracy. For with primacy in power is also joined an awe-inspiring accountability to the future."

Truman made Gen. George C. Marshall secretary of state in January 1947. The lifelong professional soldier who had overseen America's military triumph as chief of staff, the man described by Churchill as "the true organizer of victory," would later be described by German chancellor Willy Brandt as the "organizer of the peace."[13] Marshall was the right man for the job, an able administrator, universally respected for his integrity and judgment.

Marshall's task was formidable. Europe seemed close to collapse. Agricultural production across the Continent was stagnant. Caloric intake had fallen to just three-fourths of prewar levels, and malnourishment was widespread. In France, the bread ration in 1947 was a mere 200 grams daily, as low as at any time during the war.[14] The maintenance of industrial equipment had been given reduced priority through years of conflict, and much of the plant and equipment that had not been destroyed was now obsolete. Shortages of basic commodities such as coal and steel exacerbated problems in other industries. German industrial production was less than one-third of prewar levels; Austria, Italy, and Greece had not reached two-thirds of prewar production, and productivity in every European nation lagged far below prewar levels.[15] "We do not see why you have to read the *New York Times* to know that the Germans are starving," General Clay wrote in a cable to Washington.[16] "The crisis is now." Churchill called Europe "a rubble heap, a charnel house, a breeding ground of pestilence and hate."

In a hugely portentous report in February, the British government informed the United States that it no longer had the capacity to support the beleaguered government in Greece, which was under attack by Communist insurgents. The United Kingdom could no longer afford its global role. Like it or not, America was the world's leading democracy. Americans had not aspired to the role and were not entirely prepared for it. Yet it was upon them. As Robert Hutchins, president of the University of Chicago (and a former isolationist supporter of the America First Committee) said, "This country has been thrust against its will into a position of world leadership."[17]

No single action or event produced the shift. It had been under way, gradually, perhaps inevitably, for decades. Generations. Yet here it was. The question now was only, how would the country respond to the new global situation? The United States did not retreat back into isolationism, as it had done at the end of the First World War. Half a century of almost unremitting international conflict had made many Americans aware of the growing interconnection between nations, and with increasing acknowledgment of the United States' status as the leading democratic power came increased acceptance of responsibility in the global arena. The self-conception of Americans as keepers of the democratic flame, long a largely inward-focused vision, would now be turned outward. The previous half century of human history had been a chamber of horrors, of tyranny and bloodshed upon a scale never before seen. Perhaps with constructive American involvement a better world could be shaped, a world more prosperous, free, democratic, and safe.

On March 12, 1947, President Truman requested $400 million from Congress in economic aid for Greece and Turkey, to resist Communist subversion of their governments. "The free peoples of the world look to us for support in maintaining their freedoms," he said. "I believe it must be the policy of the United States to support free peoples who are resisting attempted subjugation by armed minorities or by outside pressure." A new vision of America's role in the world had been given expression for all mankind to hear: the United States was committed to the vitality of global democracy. Congress appropriated the full $400 million that the president requested.

All the information he was receiving convinced George Marshall that the situation was critical. He feared that the patient was dying "while the doctors deliberate." In a landmark address at Harvard University on June 5, 1947, Marshall outlined a program of sweeping economic assistance to all the nations of Europe. He said that the United States would "do whatever it is able to assist in the return of normal economic health in the world"; for, so long as Europe was racked by economic turmoil, there could be "no assured stability, no assured peace." The program, Marshall said, would be directed "against hunger, poverty, desperation and chaos." America had already given over $5 billion in postwar aid to Europe, to help relieve immediate and short-term crises such as hunger. Henceforth, assistance should be targeted at fundamental challenges of economic recovery, "a cure rather than a palliative."

The effect of the proposed program upon the Europeans was like a jolt of adrenaline to the demoralized Continent. Upon hearing of Marshall's address, British foreign secretary Ernest Bevin exclaimed, "This is manna from heaven!" The Soviet Union, fearing foreign influence, forbade its satellite states from taking part in the recovery plan. Sixteen nations participated: Austria, Belgium, Denmark, France, Greece, Iceland, Ireland, Italy, Luxembourg, the Netherlands, Norway, Portugal, Sweden, Switzerland, Turkey, and the United Kingdom. A Committee of European Economic Security, consisting of high-level representatives from all the participating nations, was established to formulate a plan for recovery.

Among other things, the nations pledged themselves to modernize production, achieve monetary stability, and "to cooperate with one another and with like-minded countries in all possible steps to reduce the tariffs and other barriers to the expansion of trade both between themselves and with the rest of the world."[18] At first the Germans were excluded from the plan. Far from supporting German industrial recovery, the French were adamant that Germany be transformed into a primarily agrarian society—"pastoralized"—and they refused even to discuss German reintegration.

Georges Bidault, the French foreign minister, told Clayton that France "does not desire to reduce Germany to misery . . . but it must not take precedence. It is therefore necessary that the dismantling of [German] factories be pursued at an accelerated rate; that France receive a much more substantial share of reparations in equipment and capital goods. Finally, the problem of raising the level of German industry must be reserved for the time being."[19] It soon became apparent to the other nations, though, that there could be no integrated Europe that excluded Germany; and the United States, furthermore, insisted that Germany be included in any blueprint for recovery. Ultimately the French accepted this (or, at least, went along with it) rather than risk being excluded from the program themselves.

In the fall and winter of 1947–48, congressional hearings were convened to study the possibility of a dramatic expansion of economic assistance to Europe. Some congressmen traveled there, including behind the "Iron Curtain," to see conditions firsthand. Both the testimony before the committees and the personal visits had the same effect, of strengthening support in Congress for the view that economic deterioration in Europe threatened democratic institutions there. Former isolationists reversed their positions. "I became a convert on this trip, and I want to statthe that for the record," said Rep. Lawrence Smith (R-Wisconsin). Rep. Pete Jarman (D-Alabama), who traveled to several Eastern European nations, said "I am impressed that it is necessary actually to experience that feeling of pressure, that feeling of strangulation that one has behind the iron curtain, in order to appreciate the situation that exists there, and the absolute necessity of doing whatever is necessary to prevent its spread."[20]

"So long as hunger, poverty, desperation, and resulting chaos threaten the great concentration of people in Western Europe," Secretary Marshall said in testimony to Congress, "there will steadily develop social unease and political confusion on every side. Left to their own resources there will be, I believe, no escape from economic distress so intense, political confusion so widespread, and hopes of the future so shattered that the historic base of western civilization . . . will take a new form. . . . There is no doubt in my mind that history hangs in the balance."[21]

There were misgivings among the public, many of whom were eager to return to an insular foreign policy now that the war was over, and any immediate danger passed. Americans were in the unaccustomed position of leadership among democratic nations. "Whether we like it or not," said Jarman, "this great country of ours . . . has grown . . . into a position of leadership and power in the world which places on the shoulder of our country a responsibility which heretofore had not rested there. . . ."[22] Congressman Everett Dirksen of Illinois insisted that, when given the information about what was at stake in Europe, most Americans would support the Marshall Plan. "I am not afraid of the reaction in this country," he said. "I am confident that in proportion as we do our jobs as representatives to bring them the story, that they will go along with [the aid program]."

Although, as a practical matter, any legislation must be advocated on the basis of national self-interest, for most Americans who listened to the public discussion over the plan, it signified assistance to friends in need, plain and simple. "The Marshall Plan is potentially a turning point in world history," declared an editorial in *Life*, a leading magazine of the day. "It may be difficult for some Europeans to realize how unmixed, how altruistic even, is this American aim [of the economic revival of Europe]. To most of us, European revival through unity is not merely a means of 'containing Russia'; it is an overwhelmingly sensible idea for its own sake. We may haggle over details, special privileges and guarantees. But the *quid pro quo* we really want is simply this: that Europe will be rebuilt into a going concern."[23]

A few months earlier, nobody had even heard of the Marshall Plan. Now, a strong majority of Americans supported it. In a poll taken in early December, only 17 percent opposed the plan.[24] And Americans supported it, furthermore, on largely humanitarian grounds. Fifty-six percent believed that the plan was best considered an act of charity; only 8 percent believed it would "curb communism."[25] "It would be a far happier circumstance if we could close our eyes to reality, comfortably retire within our bastions, and dream of an isolated and prosperous peace," said Sen. Arthur Vandenberg, a leading advocate of the plan. "But that which was once our luxury would now become our folly. . . . This legislation seeks peace and stability for free men in a free world. . . . [This plan] can be the turning point in history for a hundred years to come. If it fails, we will have done our final best. If it succeeds, our children and our children's children will call us blessed."[26]

The European Recovery Program was passed by Congress on April 2, 1948. It declared that "the restoration or maintenance in European countries of principles of individual liberty, free institutions and genuine independence rests largely upon the establishment of sound economic conditions, stable international economic relationships. . . . The accomplishment of these objectives calls for a plan of European recovery, open to all such nations which cooperate in such plan. . . . " The vote in the House of Representatives was 329 to 74; in the Senate, it was 69 to 17. President Truman signed it into law the next day. "Few presidents have had the opportunity to sign legislation of such importance," he said.

Stalin regarded the assistance program, rightly, as an obstacle to Communist aspirations in the West, and as soon as the program was proposed, Communist parties in Western Europe began propagandizing against it, calling it an instrument of American economic imperialism. For the vast majority of Europeans the propaganda campaign had no effect; the plan was regarded as a program of aid from a friend in a time of need, and the assistance was gratefully received. In France and Italy, where the Communists dominated the labor unions, American motives behind the economic assistance were widely suspect. In a September 1947 survey conducted in France, only 18 percent of the French public said that the Marshall Plan was motivated by America's sincere wish to aid European recovery; 17 percent believed it reflected the United States' desire to interfere in European affairs; 47 percent believed that the Americans did it to avoid an economic crisis of their own; 18 percent had no opinion.[27] Yet, though they said they doubted the Americans' intentions, the French scrapped for every dollar of the aid that they could get for themselves.

———•———

Hopelessness had thrown Europe into convulsions following the First World War, and it had been in real danger of doing so again. What the Marshall Plan offered, above all, was that most elusive and essential of all economic resources: faith in the future. Ernest Bevin called the program "a lifeline to a sinking man. It seemed to bring hope where there was none."[28]

By 1950 the economic effects of the new investment in plant and materials were being widely and dramatically felt. At midyear, two years into the program, industrial production among the recipient nations was 28 percent higher than it had been in 1947, and 18 percent above what it was prior to the war.[29] Output in Germany had more than doubled, from 41 percent of the prewar level to 90 percent. Production in Sweden and Denmark had risen 69 percent; in Norway, 47 percent; in Britain, 49 percent.[30]

Agricultural and industrial production rose spectacularly. In 1947, Western European shipbuilding had been stagnant at 75 percent of prewar levels; cement production was 73 percent; steel at 81 percent; yarn for textile production at 81 percent; coal at 83 percent; motor vehicle production at 77 percent. By the end of the American assistance program in 1952, cement production had risen to 157 percent of prewar levels; steel was at 133 percent; yarn 96 percent; coal 96 percent; motor vehicles 181 percent. In 1952, aggregate industrial production in Western Europe was 35 percent above prewar levels.[31] Between 1948 and 1952, meat production among recipient nations rose from 71 percent to 102 percent of prewar levels; bread production increased from 62 to 104 percent of prewar levels; sugar rose from 78 to 153 percent; coarse grains rose from 82 to 114 percent of prewar production.[32] By 1952, European agricultural output had not only recovered from the postwar levels, but was 15 percent above what it had been in 1938.[33]

The days of food shortages were over. Unemployment was down sharply. It was a different world from 1947. As Paul Hoffman, chief administrator of the program, noted, "Europeans were eating, they had jobs, they were working and working hard."[34] Economist Imanuel Wexler wrote in 1960 that "if one is permitted to project beyond 1952 and to measure the economic distance traveled by Western Europe in less than ten years after the aid program had ended, then one can, indeed, hail the Marshall Plan as one of the great economic success stories of modern time."[35] Western Europe was on the path to economic recovery, and would remain a cornerstone of global democracy.

———◆———

The transformation was most dramatic in Germany. From 1945–55, U.S. government aid to America's former adversary exceeded $3.6 billion, a huge sum. That figure did not include the independent contributions of American individuals and charitable institutions, or the nonmonetary aid provided, in the form of donated food and clothing, technology transfers, and other assistance. The stimulus of the American contribution was matched in West Germany by an industrious population and a highly skilled and disciplined workforce. The resulting economic growth was staggering. Only two and a half million tons of steel had been produced in Germany in 1946; by 1949 it had risen to 9 million tons, and by 1953 to 14.5 million tons. In 1953, German automobile production was twice what it had been prior to the war.[36] The transformation of West Germany was made all the more striking by the growing disparity with its East German neighbor, whose population stifled under oppressive state control. The material fruits of liberty were readily apparent, as living standards in Eastern and Western Europe grew more divergent. By the mid-1950s, a worker in the ineffectual state-run enterprises of East Germany had to work three times as long as his West German counterpart to maintain the same standard of living.

Economists were already beginning to speak of a German "economic miracle." "We found ourselves isolated from the world economy and had a largely useless currency," Germany's chancellor Adenauer later wrote. "Gratefully we remember the aid we received in those difficult times from those countries which only shortly before had been our enemies. Among them the United States took a leading position. Without this help, it is very likely that we would not have been able to prevent total chaos. Then came the Marshall Plan. It gave us the chance to close many gaps which the war had left in our productive plant and to get the productive process underway again."[37]

Liberal democracy took root and flourished. When in mid-1948 the Soviets attempted to seize total control of Berlin (which lay entirely in the Russian-controlled eastern zone) by blocking Allied truck and rail access through its sector, the United States and Britain undertook a massive effort to supply the city by air. The over 2 million brave citizens of West Berlin, many of whom had fled the Russian-controlled sector in the first place, stoutly refused to yield to the intimidation, enduring cold and hunger and spiraling unemployment rather than accept Soviet profferings of aid—or yield to intimidation—at the cost of their liberty. "I have only one life to lose," said one resident, a survivor of Nazi concentration camps, "and this life belongs to freedom."[38]

The Soviet government insisted that "Berlin lies in the center of the Soviet zone and is part of that zone." In Washington, Secretary of State Marshall proclaimed America's unconditional support for the Berliners: "We are in Berlin as a result of agreements . . . and we intend to stay. . . . Maximum use of air transport will be made."[39] The Soviet blockade of Berlin dragged on for nearly a year, from June 24, 1948, to May 12, 1949. A giant American transport plane laden with supplies landed in West Berlin an average of every three minutes. Two million tons of food, fuel, and other supplies were delivered, at a cost of some $350 million. Forty-five American and British airmen lost their lives in making the airlift.[40]

In September, the foreign ministers of the three Western occupying powers issued a statement announcing that their nations would regard "any attack against the Federal Republic of Berlin from any quarter as an attack upon themselves." They proclaimed that "the three Governments pay tribute to the continued steadfastness of the people of Berlin in the valiant struggle of the city to preserve its freedom. They will continue to oppose aggression in any form against the people of the city, and are taking steps to strengthen allied forces there."[41]

In West Germany the transformation continued. On May 8, 1949, a democratically elected parliamentary council approved a new Basic Law—constitution—which was ratified by over two-thirds of the German states by May 23. The Federal Republic of Germany was born. The new constitution established a bicameral legislature and a chancellor elected by the Parliament. Its first nineteen articles involved civil rights. It asserted that "Human dignity shall be inviolable. To respect and protect it shall be the duty of all state authority," and it guaranteed equality under the law, freedom of religion and conscience, freedom of expression and assembly, declared the home to be inviolable and secured from unauthorized police search, and also protected property rights.

Gen. Lucius Clay wrote to Chancellor Adenauer that the new document "combines German democratic tradition with the concepts of representative government and a rule of law which the world has come to recognize as requisite to the life of a free people." For the Germans who had been under occupation by the United States, Britain, and France, the adventure of liberal democracy had begun; for those under Soviet control, it was still generations away. The transformation of German society must be considered one of the great achievements of the twentieth century. An authoritarian and recurrently belligerent nation was to become one of the buttresses of global democracy. "The success of this occupation can only be judged fifty years from now," Eisenhower had told his staff in 1945. "If the Germans at that time have a stable, prosperous democracy, then we shall have succeeded."[42]

The American effort to restore European democracy following the Second World War succeeded on an epic historical scale. Free Europe flourished, and enjoyed a greater duration of tranquility than ever before in its history. The path of European economic cooperation that was a central feature of America's reconstruction effort (and a requisite for nations wishing to receive U.S. aid), set Europe on a course of greater integration: by 1952, trade between European nations was already 70 percent higher than it was before the war. The most important development in modern European history, the European Union, had its roots in the Marshall Plan.

The gift of $13.3 billion in Marshall Plan aid over four years was, to that time, the greatest peacetime transfer of wealth between nations in history. In 1949 the United States gave 2.4 percent of its gross national product in Marshall Plan donations. Chancellor Adenauer said in 1951 that never before in history had a conqueror done so much for the nation it had conquered.[43]

Some criticized the Marshall Plan, oddly, on the grounds that it was, after all, in America's national self-interest to promote the recovery of Europe; that the plan was "self-serving." But throughout history, victors in war had considered it to be in their interest to subjugate, despoil, and exploit. It is all the more remarkable that there should be a nation which considered it to be in its national interest for other nations to be prosperous, and democratic, and free. Democratic pragmatism is little distinguishable from idealism. As Senator Vandenberg put it, "We have no enemies unless aggressors nominate themselves as such. Our common cause is human rights, fundamental liberties, and a free world of free men."[44]

———◆———

In Europe, the challenge had been to revitalize latent democratic values, and to sow the seeds of democracy where it had never taken root before. It is easy to forget nowadays, when democracy is so widely accepted as the sole legitimate governmental form, that as recently as 1945 it was alien to nearly all the world. In Asia, there had never been a functioning democracy: no state in the region guaranteed to its people basic civil or political liberties, or ever had. Also, there was a view held in much of the West, even after the horrors of Germany's war were known, that Asian peoples were inherently more vicious, and perhaps unfit for democracy.

As with Germany, there were differing conceptions in the United States about how best to render Japan peaceful. Many saw the solution in eradicating its industrial capacity and making of it an agrarian nation. The military analyst George Fielding Eliot, writing in the *New York Herald Tribune*, advocated the "destruction of Japanese industry so that not one brick of any Japanese factory shall be left upon another, so that there shall not be in Japan one electric motor or one steam or gasoline engine, not a chemical laboratory, nor so much as a book which tells how these things are made."[45] To eradicate the perils of Imperial Rule, Harvard anthropologist Ernest Hooton called for the government to "exile, imprison, and sterilize all members of the Japanese Royal family and all of their blood relations."[46]

As for the Japanese themselves, who had waged a campaign of butchery across Asia, they anticipated—as their leaders had warned them—a slaughter of retaliation from the triumphant Americans. They were expecting to experience some of what they had been inflicting for so long. After the emperor announced the surrender, Premier Suzuki had warned the nation that "a bloody and tearful life will begin for the people, beginning today."[47]

The United States' dealings with postwar Japan, though, were aimed at reform, not revenge. The Basic Initial Post-Surrender Directive, which spelled out America's intentions with respect to the nation that had inflicted so much suffering upon the world, described the object of occupation as "to foster conditions which will give the greatest possible assurance that Japan will not again become a menace to the peace and security of the world and will permit her eventual admission as a responsible and peaceful member of the family of nations."[48] The plan had three main features: 1) disarmament and demilitarization; 2) democratization of political, economic, and social institutions; and 3) economic development (added as a priority after the occupation was under way). American leaders believed that a democratic Japan, with a free and open society, would serve as a role model for other nations in Asia.

The Japanese had expected a carnage of retribution. Instead, the young American GIs who descended on the country (600,000 at first, but rapidly declining to around 200,000), comported themselves astonishingly well, befriending the local population, sharing their rations, playing with children. When Americans and Japanese first came into real contact with each others' cultures, it was a pleasant discovery for both sides. The manifest goodwill and good conduct of the occupying Americans belied all the fears that the Japanese population—indoctrinated by a generation of military rule—had held, and helped facilitate mutual cordiality. Although the Occupation came as a humiliating blow to a proud people, most Japanese took warmly to the new relationship. Many felt that their old leaders and old traditions had failed the nation, and enthusiastically embraced the democratic reforms introduced by the Americans. The old vision lay in ruins, in the rubble of Japanese cities and in the devastated societies and lost lives that lay in the empire's wake across the Pacific. It had all been to no avail. And now, for the first time ever, the sacred home islands were being occupied. The Japanese people needed a new national vision. Democracy and liberty were to become part of that vision.

There were, of course, unpleasant incidents, as there would be among any population of hundreds of thousands of young men. There were isolated assaults by—usually drunken—former Imperial soldiers against GIs; and by drunken GIs, usually against former soldiers. Rapes were reported, and perpetrators punished. But on the whole, relations between members of the two disparate cultures were better than either side had expected, so that historian Kazuo Kawai could write in 1960 that "on balance, no occupation of an enemy country in all history had turned out to be such a happy surprise as this one for both the conqueror and the conquered."[49]

The desire to use defeat as an impetus for change was widespread among the Japanese. They had lost some 1.8 million soldiers, and nearly as many civilians, in a futile and now discredited effort, and endured years of suffering, but if the national nightmare could become the basis for a societal transformation, perhaps all the suffering would not have been in vain. Just as the Japanese people had gone to war as a group, they seemed to embrace the new era of democracy and peace in a similar fashion. There was an overwhelming desire to start anew, to create a new Japan. Novelist Jiro Osaragi, writing in the *Asahi Shinbun* newspaper a few days before the arrival of the first American forces, expressed the feelings of many of his countrymen: on the night of the emperor's surrender broadcast, he had been unable to sleep, thinking of the many friends and acquaintances who had been killed during the fruitless episode of militarism. "What can we do to ease your souls?" he wondered. For Osaragi, as for many Japanese, the answer was apparent: a new Japanese society must be called into being, "shaking off old filth." Perhaps, after a new and better Japan had emerged from the wreckage of the old, the dead would be able to "smile and rest in peace."[50]

Gen. Douglas MacArthur, appointed by Truman to head up the Occupation's military government, was Japan's interim shogun. As Supreme Allied Commander for the Allied Powers (SCAP), he wielded near-absolute power. His orders upon receiving the command: "You will exercise your authority as you deem proper to carry out your mission." From its General Headquarters (GHQ) based in the staid Dailchi Insurance Building, just across from the Imperial Palace, General MacArthur's "SCAP" (as the entire occupation apparatus came to be called) established policies that helped reconfigure a great nation. These policies were then disseminated and implemented (often with greater alacrity and cooperativeness than one would expect to find between, say, the Pentagon and the State Department) by an efficient and accommodating Japanese bureaucracy. The link between SCAP and the Japanese administrative structure was provided by the newly established Central Liaison Office, composed largely of Japanese diplomatic professionals of the former Foreign Ministry, most of whom were fluent in English. In this way directives could be implemented throughout Japanese society, down to the local level, with minimal requirement for enforcement by American personnel. In Japan, even an occupation is efficient.

Americans had no appetite for empire. Most wanted a quick occupation. So did MacArthur. The general, who had had experience in the Philippines before the war, envisioned a short occupation, to avoid creating a "colonial" mentality corrupting to both sides: of combined dependence and resentment on the part of the Japanese, and imperialistic hubris among the Americans.[51] While some American and foreign commentators called for an occupation that would last for several decades, MacArthur believed that a measure of the success of the American intercession in Japan would be how *quickly* it ended. As early as 1947 he began calling for a treaty to normalize relations between the two nations.

———•———

In August 1945, Japan was in ruins, literally and figuratively. Its people had been physically and spiritually exhausted by a war that had dragged on since 1931. Before the emperor's announcement of surrender, millions had accepted the prospect of death in a suicidal defense of the homeland, like the death throes of a vast cult. Over 5 percent of the population had been killed in the war. Most urban areas had been desolated. Cities were wastelands of rubble, dotted by occasional chimneys or vaults protruding from the ruins. Urban populations had been uprooted: one-third were homeless. Of Tokyo's prewar population of 7 million, only around a million remained. The nation lay prostrate and vulnerable. Where the Japanese had expected a reign of destruction, one of the first actions of the Americans was to ensure, in the war-ravaged country where millions were near starvation, that everyone had enough to eat. As MacArthur's aide Gen. William Marquat put it, "The Japanese are prisoners of war, and we don't let our prisoners starve, do we?"[52] Where the Japanese people had feared a rampage of vengeance, what they got instead were shiploads of food, blankets, and medical supplies. Right from the beginning the Americans' good intentions were clear. Even when some food donations collided with local cultural traditions (many Japanese found that when they steamed wheat, as they did with rice, it made them sick), it quickly became apparent that American policies in their country were not aimed at humiliating Japan, or even extracting punitive reparations, but were a well-intentioned effort to establish a more free and just society there. This goodwill of the Americans was, above all, vital in securing popular support. "In the first place, the Occupation policies were in general benevolent, constructive, and sound," wrote Kawai. "The overall character of the occupation was eminently good, and the Japanese could not help being impressed by it."[53] The Americans were to become known as "the honorable conquerors."

The idealism of the Americans in postwar Japan was palpable, from MacArthur on down to the lowliest private. Most deeply believed that they were part of something historic, helping to reshape Japan into a more open and free society. In retrospection, from the distance of half a century and a Japanese resurgence, this may appear as cultural arrogance (and there certainly was some), but in the wake of a cataclysmic war against a fanatical aggressor, it signified—to the Japanese themselves—an almost incomprehensible benevolence. U.S. agricultural advisers spent their own money to purchase fertilizer for Japanese farmers. Young GIs bought food for families whom they referred to as "my Japanese family." By June 1946, 77 percent of the daily food ration in Tokyo came from donated U.S. Army rations.[54] During the first two and a half years following the war, private American donors sent 3.5 million tons of food supplies to the Japanese.[55] A massive public health campaign was launched, which included inoculating virtually every man, woman, and child in the country against infectious diseases.[56]

Even the destruction of the old regime was done in accord with the rule of law. The trials of accused Japanese war criminals offered greater protections for the rights of the accused than had ever been offered before in their country. Japanese and other Asian observers were bewildered at the process. Russian observers were stupefied. In Moscow, the *New Times* reported that "Another peculiar feature of the trial is that the defense includes a score or more of American lawyers. They are no less zealous than their Japanese colleagues in whitewashing the criminals whose hands are stained with the blood of thousands of American citizens."[57]

Sweeping reforms were enacted within the first few months. The secret police was disbanded, censorship was abolished, and Shintoism was detached from the state. A statement issued by Emperor Hirohito disavowed the divinity of the emperor and rejected the idea that the Japanese are superior to other races. Some of the most sweeping land reforms in history were enacted, permitting 5.7 million farm families to own their own land for the first time. Under SCAP supervision, the government purchased 4.5 million acres, one-third of all cultivated land in the country, and resold it at low prices to the farmers who actually worked the fields, and who were given thirty-year loans at 3.2 percent interest.[58] Communists in Japan opposed the land reform because they were given no role in it. In the United States, some business leaders opposed the reforms for being too radical and subverting property rights. But rural misery, one of the driving forces behind Japanese militarism, was greatly alleviated as a result of the changes. Social and economic disparities in Japan were diminished. Japanese farmers would still toil incredibly hard on small plots of ground, but now they would do it on their own land. Writing a decade after the land reforms, British sociologist R. P. Dore concluded that the changes had resulted in "a considerable increase in the sum of human happiness in Japanese villages."[59]

An independent labor union was actively encouraged, and within a year membership had risen from 125,000 to 4.5 million.[60] Academic freedom was guaranteed. Coeducation was established, and compulsory education was extended from six years to nine.

On April 10, 1946, less than a year after war's end, the first postwar national election was held. SCAP wanted the Japanese public to begin practicing democracy as quickly as possible. SCAP speakers spread out across the country to encourage voter participation, and on election day SCAP observers monitored the voting and oversaw the counting of ballots.[61] Fears of political apathy in the fledgling democracy proved unfounded when 72 percent of all registered voters took part in the election.[62] The cadre of professional politicians who made up the Diet in the prewar years was largely supplanted. There were fewer lawyers and representatives of big business in the new legislature, which included 32 educators, 22 authors, 13 physicians, and 49 farmers.[63]

Within a year after their defeat in war, the national vision of the Japanese had been fundamentally transformed. Masaki Kobayashi, a soldier who had been kept on Okinawa following the war, returned to the homeland a year later to find a bewildering transformation. "Japan had become extremely democratic. Everyone was moving in that direction. Everyone was racing off in the direction of a democratic kind of humanism. . . ."[64] The word most commonly used to describe a future of individual rights and democracy was *akarui*—"bright." On the first anniversary of the occupation, the *Jiji Shinpo* declared that "Practically every Japanese holds it a supreme fortune to find General MacArthur as the Supreme Commander for the Allied Occupation forces in Japan. . . . No wonder that a booklet containing General MacArthur's biography has proved the postwar best-seller here, selling to the extent of 800,000 copies."[65]

———

Perhaps the most effective missionaries for the democratic spirit were, paradoxically, the GIs of the occupation—America's citizen-soldiers, with the emphasis now back on *citizen*. "Their exuberant good spirits came as welcome release to the Japanese, who had long been repressed by the humorless authoritarianism of their militarists," wrote Kazuo Kawai. "The enthusiasm with which Japanese children waved and shouted at passing GI's had little to do with gifts of chewing gum and candy, which generally were quite unexpected. . . . The elders also, laughing at the good-natured antics of the GI's, were charmed into letting down their suspicions against American influence. The Americans acted as the Japanese would have liked to act, but could not because of their social inhibitions, and thus the Americans became the envied models of a desired conduct."[66]

They generally treated the local population with respect, albeit across a cultural chasm, and far better than the Japanese knew their own troops had treated conquered populations. "The American GI has done more for friendship between the Americans and the Japanese than all the ambassadors ever sent here," said Takashi Komatsu, president of the America-Japan Society.[67] An elderly Japanese man from Okayama city wrote to MacArthur that "the leaders deceived the people by telling them that Americans are terrible. American soldiers are kind. Contrary to the rumors, they did nothing wrong. Because Japan was doing evil, they lied to us that Americans would go wild, but instead they are kinder than the Japanese."[68]

"The Japanese people have been enlightened by the well-mannered occupation forces," wrote another. "I doubt the Japanese people would have been as fortunate at the hands of another people instead of your country."[69]

———

The Potsdam Declaration, which required that "the Japanese Government shall remove all obstacles to the revival and strengthening of democratic tendencies among the Japanese people," was interpreted by conservative Japanese politicians as requiring modest revisions of the existing Meiji constitution, and more thorough enforcement of existing provisions, rather than a fresh start.[70] MacArthur had other ideas. He requested Japanese officials to draw up a draft for a new constitution. They proceeded gingerly, anxious to avoid group discord, and made little progress toward real reform. One proposal, for example, called for changing the existing constitution's description of the emperor's role from "sacred and inviolable" to "supreme and inviolable." When a proposed draft leaked out, Japanese citizens who supported thoroughgoing democratic reforms were dismayed. A *Mainichi Shinbun* newspaper editorial expressed disappointment "that it is so conservative and does nothing more than preserve the status quo."[71]

Finally, MacArthur ordered lawyers on his own staff to formulate a "draft" constitution. The Diet made thirty or so revisions to the draft, most minor, some surprising. It inserted a requirement that all Cabinet members be "civilians." It eliminated all peerage outside of the imperial family, and guaranteed that "all people shall have the right to maintain the minimum standards of wholesome and cultured living."[72] In February 1946, when the new charter for a democratic society was presented to Emperor Hirohito, he announced that "Upon these principles will truly rest the welfare of our people and the rebuilding of Japan."[73] Public support for the constitution was assured. Indeed, Hirohito was actively cooperative throughout the transition to democracy, vindicating those who had argued for keeping the millennia-old imperial office. Retaining the emperor rather than abolishing the office and trying Hirohito on war crimes charges had the paradoxical effect of facilitating the transition to democratic government.

The Japanese constitution existed in English before it existed in Japanese. In a telling incident, a citizen was asked if he had read the new constitution. "No," he replied, "has it been translated?" The Meiji constitution of 1889, an apparently democratic document, had embedded ultimate political sovereignty in the emperor (and gave disproportionate power to those who could entice, threaten, or cajole their way into the emperor's inner circle). Under the new constitution, the emperor was described as a national "symbol," with no real political power whatever, "deriving his position from the will of the people in whom resides sovereign power." Individual rights were no longer derived from the concession of the emperor, but were inalienable. Religious freedom was guaranteed. The right to vote was given to all men and women twenty years old or older. Equal rights were guaranteed to women, for the first time in an Asian society.

A national legislature or Diet—"the highest organ of state power"—was to consist of a House of Representatives, elected to four-year terms but subject to new elections if the House was dissolved before that time; and a House of Councillors, elected to six-year terms. As in the British parliamentary system, the prime minister would be chosen by the Diet, from among its members, serving at its discretion. He and his Cabinet would be subject to it. A vote of "no confidence" could remove the prime minister or, at his discretion, dissolve the House and bring about a new election. An independent judiciary with a Supreme Court was also established.

The new constitution was adopted by a vote of the Diet on August 24, 1946, and went into effect on May 3 the following year. It marked the ascendancy of individual rights, which was a breakthrough not only for Japan, but for all Asia. Chapter III of the constitution reads, in part:

> Article 13. All of the people shall be respected as individuals. Their right to life, liberty, and the pursuit of happiness shall, to the extent that it does not interfere with the public welfare, be the supreme consideration in legislation and in other governmental affairs.
>
> Article 14. All of the people are equal under the law and there shall be no discrimination in political, economic, or social relations because of race, creed, sex, social status, or family origin.
>
> Article 15. The people have the inalienable right to choose their public officials and dismiss them. . . . Universal adult suffrage is guaranteed with regard to the election of public officials. In all elections, secrecy of the ballot shall not be violated.
>
> Article 21. Freedom of assembly and association, as well as speech, press, and all other forms of expression are guaranteed.

But constitutionalism was not simply a matter of restoring power to the people. The people had never had real power. For a vital, functioning democracy to flourish in Japan, it would be necessary not only to alter the external formulations of governance, but the internal expectations of the people. How do you convey democratic values to a people who have had little experience of them? Town meetings were held across the country to discuss the importance of active citizen involvement in the political process, a concept unfamiliar to most Japanese. Citizens were told that they should expect to have a voice—and real power—in the new Japan. A pamphlet was produced illustrating concepts of civil rights, gender equality, and individual autonomy, and included the text of the constitution itself. Twenty million copies were distributed, one for every household in the nation. Never before in the history of Asia had the common man—let alone woman—had a say in the running of the central government. Now they were being told that they were not only permitted to participate, but had a civic obligation to do so. Tokujiro Kanamori, the new government's enthusiastic minister for constitutional affairs, penned a children's book entitled *The Story of the Constitution for Boys and Girls*, espousing the new ideals of peace, popular sovereignty, and human rights.[74] The postwar constitution marked the dawn of a new era for individual liberties. It marked a new Japan, and ultimately, a new Asia.

———◆———

The third vital element in the American agenda for rebuilding Japan was economic vitality. Japan could not flourish as a free and democratic state, or serve as a model for the nations of Asia, unless she had a thriving economy.

Rebuilding her would be no simple task. Postwar Japan was possibly in even more desperate straits than Germany. Most of its larger cities had been destroyed by the B-29 fire bombings. Only Kyoto had been spared, because of its cultural and religious significance. Two-thirds of Tokyo had been destroyed; 80 percent of Osaka. A reporter visiting Yokohama described it as "being closer to a name than a town." Blackouts were common. Energy was scarce. It had been easier to maintain coal production under conditions of forced labor: after the war, when workers were free to leave their jobs in what may have been the most derelict and dangerous mines in the world, nearly half did, preferring the uncertainty of the bleak postwar economy to the certain hazards of the Japanese coal mines.

Industrial production stood at 10 percent of prewar levels. Factories that had not been destroyed were obsolete. SCAP reports concluded that one-third of the nation's total wealth had been destroyed in the war, and up to half of its potential income. In rural areas, living standards had fallen by one-third; in urban areas, by two-thirds.[75] Furthermore, the single most important prewar export that placed little dependence upon imports, silk textiles, were being replaced by cheaper, more durable synthetic products.[76]

The food situation was even more pressing. Japan had been reduced from an empire at its zenith encompassing 774,000 square miles to a few islands of less than one-fifth that size.[77] The country had depended on food imports from across the Pacific to sustain a growing citizenry; the home islands were incapable of feeding the population under the best of conditions, and these were the worst. Most Japanese were malnourished, and many (10 million, according to a government estimate) were near starvation. Urban residents traveled to the countryside to scavenge for subsistence. Family heirlooms were traded away to farmers for rice, sweet potatoes, or other provisions. The people began to speak of an "onion existence," the peeling away of successive layers of their material possessions in exchange for food and necessities on the black market.[78] Even before the war ended, as much as half of all economic crime in the country had related to food, and police warned of "vegetable thieves."[79]

By war's end, the government's grain collections had fallen to one-third of what was required to meet the nation's needs. Overseas sources of foodstuffs and raw materials had been cut off. Domestic agriculture was nowhere near adequate to feed a population which in 1945 approached 80 million people. Even the modest official ration—amounting to 1,050 calories per person—was unavailable. Newspapers printed charts of edible weeds for housewives to forage.[80]

It was upon this hopeless situation that the Americans arrived. To meet the immediate crisis, SCAP scrounged its own food supplies to provide some 800,000 tons of foodstuffs, which it gave to the new government for distribution. Back in the United States, charitable institutions held aid drives and sent tons of urgently needed supplies. A humanitarian crisis was averted.

GHQ in Tokyo made an emergency aid request from Congress for $270 million for emergency assistance in 1946–47. That would provide 2 million tons of staples (equivalent to Japan's average for the prewar years 1936–40), other food products, fertilizer, and medical supplies. Congress provided the entire amount. The following year MacArthur requested $330 million for food aid—and got it. The next year he asked for, and received, $497 million;[81] over $4.0 billion in 2001 dollars.

The shipments from America, said a local yearbook, were "like a merciful rain during a drought." A local newspaper recorded that they "kindled a light of hope in the hearts of depressed residents."[82] By mid-1948, food consumption among nonfarm Japanese had tripled from the levels that existed at the end of the war, surpassing 2,000 calories daily. Over nine-tenths of the staples were from the massive U.S. food donations. Food stocks, at virtually zero when the war ended, were at 3 million tons by 1949. "By that time the Japanese could not eat the food as fast as the United States was shipping it in."[83]

As in Europe, social and economic malaise had followed the devastation of the war in Japan. And (as in Europe) with the promise of American assistance in recovery, despair was gradually replaced by a renewed faith in the future by a people culturally inclined to take the long view. "The national traits of energy, diligence, and ambition—temporarily paralyzed by the shock of defeat—readily revived when hope was rekindled by American aid," wrote Kawai. What the Japanese had lost was less important, in the long run, that what they had retained: group cohesion, self-sacrifice, a long-term view, a work ethic. In due course the bombed-out cities were spruced up, cleared of rubble, and began to come back to life. "Never have I seen debris from bombing so quickly and cleanly cleared away," observed a *New York Times* reporter.[84] By contrast, years after the war Manila still lay in ruins. When General MacArthur visited there in July 1946, he was dismayed to find, as one aide put it, that "the Filipinos seemed primarily interested in what they could extract from the Americans, whereas the Japanese were simply trying to get things going again."[85]

The American policy for Japan, like Germany's, was not economic revenge, but reform; not pastoralization, but revitalization. Under the direction of Detroit Bank president Joseph Dodge, who was brought to Tokyo as MacArthur's finance adviser, postwar inflation was tamed, and Japan became fully integrated into the global economy. (Among Japanese to this day, Dodge is second only to MacArthur as the most admired of the Occupation figures). Over $2 billion in financial assistance was given to Japan during the Occupation, for procuring raw materials, rebuilding industry, and getting the nation's economy back on its feet.

The acumen for industrial productivity that would catapult Japan to a position of leadership in global commerce was already becoming discernible. Military optics makers started producing cameras (including Canon and Nikon). A manufacturer of fighter plane pistons began making irrigation pumps.

A maker of tank parts became a leader in bulldozers and heavy machinery (Komatsu).[86] A company that in an earlier age—the year before—had been producing machine guns retrofitted its factory to manufacture sewing machines. Swordsmiths made kitchen cutlery. Fighter plane designers turned to making motor scooters. To satisfy the crude American penchant for chewing gum, by mid-1946 there were several hundred Japanese companies producing the stuff.[87]

One vital but little-recognized contribution to Japan's economic resurgence was SCAP's Economic and Scientific Section, Scientific and Technical Division, which provided invaluable support in the revitalization of Japan's nonmilitary scientific community. The United States provided funds, experts, technical assistance, and moral support. As a noted University of Illinois chemist told Japanese scientists at a nationwide conference on scientific renewal, "The scientists of the United States and the world have their eyes focused on Japan. You can expect friendly sympathy and cooperation from the scientists of America. . . . "[88] A steady stream of American scientists and engineers made their way to Japan to provide scientific training. Programs were established to send Japanese scientists to American universities and research institutions for training and research. (When Hideki Yukawa became the first Japanese ever to win the Nobel Prize, winning the 1949 award for physics, he was a visiting professor at Columbia University.)[89] Grants were provided to buy equipment for Japanese industrial research and development. Direct technology transfers were made, and patented American manufacturing processes were made available to Japanese firms. Quality control standards were promoted, which proved invaluable to Japan in its ascent as an industrial power.[90]

In addition, United States spending for the Korean War, which had begun toward the end of the Occupation, also had a dramatic effect. Stimulated by U.S. spending on defense contracts, Japanese industrial output grew 28 percent in the second half of 1950. By 1951, American procurements from Japanese firms were already nearly $1 billion, equal to three-fourths of all other Japanese foreign trade.[91] Spending by servicemen on leave from the war was also economically important. Most important in the long run, the United States gave Japanese industries access to the vast American markets. As an island nation poor in natural resources, Japan's dependence upon imported resources necessitated an export-based recovery, and the primary focus of that recovery was the United States, which permitted access to its markets while allowing Japan to protect its own incipient industries from American competition. Five years after the end of the war, Japan was running a foreign trade surplus. Prosperity was on the way. The future was *akarui*. Already, by the end of the Occupation, wrote Kawai, "impressive new buildings were transforming the landscape, shops were overflowing with goods of every kind, streets were jammed with new cars, and smartly dressed people were working and playing in an almost carnival atmosphere of buoyancy and vitality."[92]

As early as 1955, *Business Week* would write that Japanese manufacturers were turning from making inexpensive toys to higher-end consumer goods: cameras, microscopes, cashmere sweaters. "Most retailers report that the high quality of these new Japanese products is overcoming whatever sales resistance there might have been in the past to Japanese imports."[93] A sign of Japan's growing success came in 1956 when Southern states began calling for protection against competition from Japanese textile imports.

The stimulus of United States foreign aid and investment in Japan, Korean War spending, and an open American marketplace combined with the fiscal austerity and discipline of the Japanese to launch the nation on one of the most dramatic economic expansions in human history. Just a decade after the devastation of 1945, the *New York Times* declared that "From the utter economic prostration at the end of the war, Japan has risen to become the leader of the world in fishing, second in shipbuilding (first in number of ships built for export), third in cotton textile production, and sixth in steel output. And every month sees new postwar records in production."[94] The Japanese themselves spoke of the "Jimmu Boom," by which was meant the greatest economic boom since Emperor Jimmu had founded the nation in 660 BC.[95] In September 1962, *The Economist* published a series of influential articles describing a "Japanese economic miracle." In the course of less than two decades since the end of the war, Japan had become one of the most capable practitioners of capitalism in the world. Its economic progress was virtually unprecedented, said the magazine. The Japanese had achieved "one of the most exciting and extraordinary sudden forward leaps in the entire economic history of the world."[96]

So-called "economic miracles" in both Germany and Japan helped make those nations among the most prosperous and stable democracies in the world. They were not the result of miracles, though. The recovery that followed the war was a product of the discipline and creativity of the people— and of the determined friendship and support of the United States, the power that set those nations upon their new path and altered the course of their destiny, and history. As Professor Takashi Takasaka of Kyoto University, living a generation after the Occupation, expressed in a television interview, no nation wants to be occupied, but the American intervention in Japan was vital to breaking the culture's powerful traditional framework, thus enabling the dramatic transformation that followed.[97]

The American preference for rebuilding former adversaries rather than punishing them was satirized in the 1959 British film *The Mouse That Roared*, in which the tiny Duchy of Grand Fenwick set about to solve its economic woes by declaring war on America, in order to be defeated, and then "rehabilitated." Explained the prime minister, Count Rupert (played by Peter Sellers), "There isn't a more profitable undertaking for any country than to declare war on the United States, and to be defeated. No sooner is the aggressor defeated, than the Americans pour in food, machinery, clothing, technical aid, and lots and lots of money for the relief of its former enemies.

In other words, gentlemen, in effect, we declare war on Monday, are defeated on Tuesday, and by Friday we will be rehabilitated beyond our wildest dreams."

Had Americans pursued the usual course of victors in war, seeking revenge and plunder rather than reform and renewal, the history of Europe, Asia, and the world would have also taken a very different course. Instead of exploiting vulnerable nations, Americans had the idealistic notion that their society would be better off in a world where other peoples were also free and prosperous; and the naive belief that democracy could take root and flourish in countries where it did not exist. Both views were borne out.

Socially, politically, and economically, the relationship with the United States was an overwhelming boon to the Japanese people. Few objective analysts on either side of the Pacific could dispute Walt Sheldon's observation that "Japan, as a nation, gained more from losing the 'Pacific War' than she could have gained by winning it. . . . "[98] Japanese businessman Yagi Chosaburo wrote to SCAP to say that the Japanese people could "find no words to express our gratitude" for America's benevolence in the reconstruction. "This is only possible because of the extraordinary generosity that is your national character. It is embarrassing to say so, but I wonder what attitude Japan would have shown if the outcome of the war had been reversed."[99]

Yasukichi Yamaura, a resident of Nagasaki, wrote in a letter to SCAP that "At a time when we were liberated from a war that was like a terrible nightmare, and when the light of peace had begun to shine, like a messenger from God you offered us your hand in love and sympathy. For the unexpected treatment we received, we offer you our gratitude and pledge everlasting friendship to the American people. . . . "[100] "It is due entirely to your providential . . . occupation policies which saved [Japan] from eternal ruin," wrote S. Momikura.[101] "I believe that the Japanese race will appreciate your kindness forever," wrote another.[102]

As embodiment of the American presence in Japan, MacArthur was inundated with thousands of gifts from ordinary citizens, "to express gratitude for your Excellency's generous politics," as one note said. There were fresh fruits and vegetables from farmers concerned for his health; an elegantly handcrafted walking stick; paintings; wood carvings; fish; a Japanese fan inscribed with the entire constitution in delicate calligraphy; a suit of black-threaded armor from a metallurgist. A grateful embroiderer isolated himself in a shrine for three years to produce a magnificent kimono containing seventy million stitches. Members of the Ainu tribe in Hokkaido, long an outcast and persecuted minority in Japan, sent MacArthur the hide of a deer, "as a token of our grateful appreciation for what he has done to secure land for our people and to give to Japan a democratic society, based on law and order."[103] He received letters calling him a "living savior" for Japan and expressing gratitude for his "exalted and godlike benevolence." A fisherman thanked America for helping the Japanese to accomplish "what we could not have attained even in many years of struggle."[104]

When President Truman replaced MacArthur as supreme commander, Allied Powers, in April 1951, the Japanese public were as crestfallen as if they had lost their own emperor. But the Occupation was winding down in any case and would soon be over. For the Japanese, the American occupation would always be associated with one man, and that association was overwhelmingly positive. The *Asahi Shinbun* declared that "Japan's recovery must be attributed solely to his guidance. We feel as if we had lost a kind and loving father. . . ." Another leading newspaper, the *Mainichi Shinbun*, wrote that "he gave us . . . a new way of life, the freedom and dignity of the individual. . . ."[105] A bronze statue of MacArthur was erected in Yokohama, with the words: GENERAL DOUGLAS MACARTHUR—LIBERATOR OF JAPAN. Among villagers, rumors persisted that MacArthur himself was actually part Japanese, related to the emperor, perhaps even a descendant of the gods.

But MacArthur was all-American, his weaknesses and his strengths, and the efforts of Japan's Solon to set Japanese freedom upon a firm footing reflected a transmission of basic American values that transcended one individual's personal characteristics. A conservative and somewhat authoritarian figure, MacArthur had helped establish the foundations of a thriving liberal democracy. Douglas MacArthur in Japan was not an individual, but a symbol, a personification of a set of social and political ideals. "We will follow the way you clearly showed us during the past five years," Kuzuko Horiki wrote to MacArthur, "and work for the eternal peace of the world."[106]

The nation that a few years earlier was the scourge of Asia had been transformed into the bulwark of democracy and individual liberty there. Japan would be a stable, peace-loving nation in a turbulent world, and a loyal ally for democracy in a troubled region. At the end of the century, economic power in Japan was as widely distributed as in any nation on earth; and voter participation was typically 20 to 30 percent higher than in the United States. The occupation officially ended on April 28, 1952, but the two nations had already ceased to be conqueror and conquered; they were now allies for the common cause of peace and liberty in Asia. When the Americans left, Japan's constitution remained intact. The social and political liberties that had been introduced during the Occupation were secure: they had ceased to be American impositions—they were embraced by Japanese citizens as their own natural rights.

It is easy to forget nowadays, when democracy is so prevalent, how rare it was just fifty years ago. This may be especially true for Americans, who have enjoyed the fruits of liberty for generations. For most peoples across the globe, these are new blessings. A 1985 public opinion poll taken in both Japan and the United States asked citizens of both countries what they thought was the greatest consequence of the American occupation of Japan. The Americans believed that the greatest accomplishment of the occupation was Japan's economic revitalization. The Japanese thought that it was the legacy of freedom and democracy.[107] The Americans, in their occupation of Japan, did more to expand the liberty of the average Japanese citizen than any Japanese regime in history had ever done. America had given Japan, like Germany, the opportunity to start anew, and its people took that opportunity. A generation after their cataclysmic defeats in the Second World War, the Japanese and the Germans—who had terrorized Europe and Asia for half a century—were among the most prosperous societies in the world and among the leading bulwarks of democracy. In both cases, critics had argued that democracy could never flourish among those people. In both cases, some had called for postwar vengeance rather than social and political reform and renewal. Yet both nations embraced their liberty, and both nations enjoyed greater prosperity and well-being under democracy than they had or ever would have under their authoritarian systems. Both would be shining examples of the power of freedom in a world that was still choosing its course. If not for America's courage in defeating those nations in war, and its visionary policies following the war, human history would have taken a very different course.

In a book of cartoons commemorating the first year of the American occupation of Japan, author Etsuro Kato depicted the widespread view of the futility and folly of the war. One cartoon depicted a weary Japanese couple, armed with spear and firefighting bucket, listening in shock to the emperor's radio address on August 15, announcing surrender. The story did not end there, though. What could have been the beginning of an era of retaliation and suffering for the Japanese people instead took a different direction. In another cartoon, entitled "A Gift from Heaven," a group of Japanese was depicted reaching skyward as familiar American aid canisters parachuted down. But these canisters did not contain food or medicine. They were labeled DEMOCRATIC REVOLUTION. The caption read: "The downpour of bombs and incendiaries abruptly ceased. Then, from the very same sky, the gift of peace began to descend. Democratic revolution! Bloodless revolution! Well, we Japanese, who lost the war, who were exhausted by war, how did we receive this gift?"[108]

4

Establishing a Community of Nations

AMERICA EMERGED FROM the Second World War not only victorious, but paramount. It was a superpower the likes of which the world had never seen before. "The United States has become a Great Power . . . different in quality and texture from any Great Power hitherto known to the Old World, with the exception of Athens during the short half-century of her political greatness," wrote the distinguished British scholar of international relations, Sir Alfred Zimmern.[1] America's rise to a position of unquestioned preeminence permitted the fulfillment of a vision for global relations that had been espoused earlier, but remain unfulfilled. Where President Wilson had been rebuffed at the Paris Peace Conference a generation earlier, Roosevelt and those who followed him would succeed in creating a more open and stable international system. What followed was one of the epochal periods of transition in human history.

In calling for the establishment of a League of Nations, Woodrow Wilson had advocated nothing less than the creation of a new world order, one where relations between nations were organized not by the clandestine machinations of ruling elites, but by "open covenants of peace, openly arrived at." Aspirations for the development of a genuine community of nations, never fully extinguished even in the wake of the failure of the United States to join the League, and the subsequent inadequacy of that organization, were revived amidst the sacrifices demanded by the Second World War. "From the moment when Hitler's invasion of Poland revealed the bankruptcy of all existing methods to preserve the peace," Secretary of State Cordell Hull later recalled, "it became evident to all of us in the State Department that we must begin almost immediately to plan the creation of a new system."[2]

President Roosevelt instructed State Department planners to draft plans for an international organization modeled after the League of Nations, plans that were formulated in consultation with Congress. In September 1942, Congress passed a resolution calling for the creation of an international organization "with the power adequate to establish and maintain a just and lasting peace among the nations of the world. . . . "[3] The following month Secretary Hull publicly outlined a proposal for "an international organization under the title of 'The United Nations,'" which would work to "maintain international peace and security, develop friendly relations among nations . . . establish international cooperation, and afford a centre for harmonizing the actions of nations in the achievement of these common ends." This became a centerpiece for America's postwar planning.

At Yalta, in February 1945, an ailing President Roosevelt pressed Stalin and Churchill on the issue of the establishment of a community of nations. Indeed, the last address the president ever wrote, remaining undelivered because of his death on April 12, related to the topic that had become his central preoccupation: establishing the foundation for a community of nations that would allow a more enduring world peace. "The work, my friends, is peace; more than an end of this war—an end to the beginning of all wars. . . . Today, as we go forward toward the greatest contribution that any generation of human beings can make in this world—the contribution of lasting peace—I ask you to keep up your faith. . . . "[4] When Franklin Roosevelt died just days before the opening of the San Francisco conference, there were fears that American support for an international peace organization would be derailed for a second time. But the United States was a different nation in 1945 than it had been in 1920; and the world was different, too. Technology had brought nations closer together than they had ever been before. On his first day in office, Harry Truman announced that the United Nations conference would go forward, and the delegation chosen by Roosevelt would attend.

In contrast to the League of Nations at the end of the First World War, there was no doubt about public support. Two decades of destructive international conflict and reluctant involvement in a second global conflict had convinced most Americans of the moral and material hazards of isolationism. Leading politicians from both parties actively supported the proposals. Such diverse national organizations as the American Federation of Labor, the Catholic Association for International Peace, the American Legion, and the Federation of Women's Clubs—cognizant of the fate of the Versailles Treaty—worked together to rally public support for the proposals.[5] It was not a hard sell: a Gallup poll taken the previous June had showed that 74 percent of Americans favored the establishment of an international organization for the preservation of world peace.[6]

On June 26, 1945, representatives from fifty nations (representing 80 percent of mankind), signed the Charter of the United Nations in San Francisco, pledging to "save succeeding generations from the scourge of war" and "establish conditions under which justice and respect for the obligations arising from treaties can be maintained," and "to promote social progress and better standards of life in larger freedom." By century's end there would be 189 members of the United Nations, representing nearly all of mankind.

Funding for the site for the UN headquarters in New York was donated by American philanthropists, and during the early years the United States paid nearly all of the budget of the organization. It also paid three-fourths of the UN's postwar Relief and Rehabilitation Administration, which by 1946 was providing support for more than a million refugees.

When the brutal struggle of the Second World War finally ended, Americans sought no vengeance, no territory, no spoils. When the moment of truth arrived, and ideals were matched by power, Americans adhered to the ideals that they had long espoused in foreign affairs. Instead of exploiting the many nations that were weak and vulnerable, the United States used its new position of predominance to help establish a global system in which the weak and vulnerable were more secure from the predations of the stronger.

———————

One of the features of the prewar world order, broadly despised by Americans and doomed by the shifting power balance from 1920 to 1945, was the system of colonialism through which European powers had maintained domination over most of the less developed world. By it, a measure of a nation's greatness had become the scope of its empire. At the end of the Second World War, over a third of mankind, more than 700 million people, lived under colonial rule.[7]

A generation earlier, Woodrow Wilson had insisted in his Fourteen Points upon the right of "self-determination" for all peoples. Every nation, he said, must be liberated from foreign subjugation, free to pursue its own destiny. At the Paris Peace Conference following the First World War, in accord with Wilson's vision of self-determination the borders of Eastern Europe were redrawn with consideration for the political aspirations of national peoples. The nation-state of Poland was created, from part of West Prussia. Estonia, Latvia, and Lithuania were established as independent states, as were Czechoslovakia and Yugoslavia.

But the basic structure of the old system remained intact, and on this Wilson was unable to successfully oppose the Europeans' combined vested interest in colonialism. Germany was stripped of its overseas empire, but its colonies were divided up among the other imperial powers, as "mandates" under the new League of Nations. Even the mandate system itself was a concession to American anti-imperialism. European leaders, as one observer noted, "merely tolerated it in order to silence the anti-colonial rhetoric of the American President Woodrow Wilson."[8]

This was better than nothing, though only a little. At least the mandate system formalized, for the first time, the idea that the colonial territories were not the properties of the European powers, to do with as they liked. The League's mandate to Great Britain and Belgium in taking over Germany's former colonies in East Africa directed that "the Mandatory shall be responsible for the peace, order and good government of the territory, and shall undertake to promote to the utmost the material and moral well-being and social progress of its inhabitants."[9] The mandates were ostensibly a system of allotting stewardship to developed nations, to assist former colonies in preparation for self-rule; in fact, they were spoils by another name. The Great Powers—and some lesser ones—meanwhile clung tenaciously to their own far-flung dominions.A U.S. senator spoke for most Americans in denouncing colonialism as "earth hunger."

British prime minister David Lloyd George tried to convince Wilson to accept an American mandate, thinking it would neutralize the Americans' anti-imperial fervor. "The British would like us to accept [a mandate] so that they might more freely take what they desire," Colonel House remarked to Wilson.[10] The president would not consider it.

America never had an empire, though "in a fit of absent-mindedness" (as was said, less aptly, of the British Empire) it acquired several territories in the Spanish-American War of 1898, a conflict precipitated by American support for the independence movement in Cuba. The new territories included Guam, Puerto Rico, Cuba, and the Philippines (acquired for $20 million). Most Americans objected to these acquisitions as being a deviation from American political ideals. The United States was itself, after all, a former colony that had acquired its independence only after bitter struggle. Though most of the Cuban elite lobbied for annexation by the United States, within two years the country had a new constitution and was holding democratic elections as an independent nation, in one of the smoothest transitions to independence of any former Spanish colony.

Industrialist Andrew Carnegie offered to pay the government $20 million to give the Philippines its independence. Others, though, became caught up in the missionary zeal of spreading Western civilization to the Filipinos. The strongest faction advocating colonization of the Philippines was not industrialists, but Christian fundamentalists. "I went down on my knees and prayed to Almighty God for light and guidance more than one night," President McKinley told an audience of protestant ministers. "And one night it came to me this way . . . 1) That we could not give them back to Spain—that would be cowardly and dishonorable; 2) that we could not turn them over to France and Germany—our commercial rivals in the Orient—that would be bad business *and* discreditable; 3) that we could not leave them to themselves—they were unfit for government, and they would soon have anarchy and misrule over there worse than Spain's was; and 4) that there was nothing left for us to do but to take them all, and to educate the Filipinos, and uplift and civilize and Christianize them, and by God's grace do the very best we could by them. . . . "[11]

Even with that admixture of paternalism and cultural chauvinism, what America could do for the Filipino people, it turned out, was a great deal more than Spain had done for several centuries, and more than any other colonial power in Asia was doing for a subject people. William Howard Taft, a federal judge from Ohio, was chosen to be governor of the new territory. "We hold the Philippines for the benefit of the Filipinos," he said, "and we are not entitled to pass a single act or approve a single measure that has not that as its chief purpose."[12] The Americans earnestly worked to prepare the Philippines for democratic self-government, improved health, education, and public services, promoted local business, and extended life expectancy on the archipelago beyond what it had ever been before. A Japanese teacher assigned to the Imperial Army force occupying the country during the war noted that, unlike the relationships of other East Asian peoples with occupying powers, the Filipinos "had been satisfied with American democracy and the civilization which huge American capital had introduced."[13]

Nearly as soon as the Americans took over, they began the process of systematically turning over governmental power to the Filipino people; by 1935 the Philippines had become the first self-governing state among all the colonies of East Asia, with an elected, indigenous president.[14] So congenial were relations between the two nations, and so lucrative the American aid, that the Philippines' first president, Manuel Quezon, persistently lobbied for *increased* U.S. involvement in his country. "Damn the Americans!" he once exclaimed. "Why don't they tyrannize us more?"[15]

When, in 1934, Congress passed an act to pull the United States out of the Philippines after ten years (an interim needed, it was thought, to prepare the nation for democratic self-government), it marked, for most Americans, a welcome rejection of imperial ambition, regarded as antithetical to the values of a democratic republic. "If this is accomplished without complications during the next ten years," wrote the historian Samuel Bemis, "it will bring to an end the great aberration of 1898."[16] (When the Second World War ended, the United States promptly fulfilled its promise to grant full independence to the Philippines.)

———◆———

From Woodrow Wilson to Franklin Roosevelt, the United States helped create a climate of opinion worldwide that eroded the legitimacy of colonial subjugation and encouraged nationalist movements for independence. As Raymond Betts, a leading historian of imperialism, has written, "The United States enjoyed a long-established anti-colonial tradition. Not only did she have the well-used historical example of her own revolt against the British colonial system, but she also evolved a diplomatic style which depended on democratic idealism. . . . Although the United States had her fervor of overseas imperialism at the end of the nineteenth century, this soon subsided;

in its stead again grew a suspicion of old-fashioned power politics and the European colonialism characteristic of them."[17]

Like his predecessors, President Roosevelt disdained imperialism. He scoffed that "the British would take land anywhere in the world, even if it were only a rock or a sandbar."[18] And Roosevelt recognized in America's growing power the opportunity to chip away at the old system. It was a hope shared by most of his countrymen. Americans held a "general mistrust" of British imperialism, writes English historian A. N. Porter. "It was felt to obstruct free trade, prevent self-determination and reinforce the worst features of Britain's class-ridden society."[19] In October 1942 the editors of *Life* magazine wrote in "An Open Letter . . . to the People of England" that although Americans had been divided over participation in war aims, there was unanimity on one matter: "One thing we are sure we are not fighting for is to hold the British Empire together. . . . If your strategists are planning a war to hold the British Empire together they will sooner or later find themselves strategizing alone."[20]

On the other side, the war had not only highlighted the inability of Britain (and, indeed all of the colonial powers) to hold its empire together, but had indebted it, economically and politically, to the United States. The war also energized anticolonial sentiment in the United States. Many regarded it as an opportunity to foster historic change in the world. "The western nations must now do what hitherto they lacked the will and imagination to do: they must identify their cause with the freedom and security of the peoples of the East . . . " wrote Walter Lippmann.[21] As Japan's nascent empire spread across Asia, the Senate Foreign Relations Committee called for Britain to give greater autonomy to India. When the White House pressed the British on the matter, Prime Minister Churchill said that a declaration was being considered that would assure India of dominion status, and the right to secede from the British Empire after the war.

"I can't believe that we can fight a war against fascist slavery, and at the same time not work to free people all over the world from a backward colonial policy," Roosevelt said to Churchill.[22] Roosevelt's Four Freedoms were to be applicable, as he had reiterated, "everywhere in the world." At the Newfoundland Summit in August 1941, Churchill felt compelled to go along with the president's insistence that the Atlantic Charter include a commitment to "the right of all people to choose the form of government under which they live." That pledge, in Article 3 of the Charter, writes British historian Denis Judd, "undoubtedly signified the determination of the United States to act as the midwife and guarantor of colonial liberties and to drag a supplicant Britain along in the process."[23]

Though even at the time Churchill had no intention of yielding the empire altogether, the more pressing matter at hand was securing American support in the war. To do so, he made the concession to American anti-imperialist sentiment. Later, in one of the low points of a great political life, he would say that the Charter had been "primarily intended to apply to Europe."[24]

When Churchill attempted to waffle on the issue, Roosevelt expressed the matter plainly: "The Atlantic Charter applies not only to the parts of the world that border the Atlantic, but to the whole world."[25] Undersecretary of State Sumner Welles put it even more succinctly: "The age of imperialism is ended."

In November 1942 the State Department issued a "Declaration on National Independence for Colonies," calling on colonial powers to establish firm timetables for granting independence to their colonies: "that the *independence* of those nations which now possess *independence* shall be maintained; that the *independence* of those nations which have been forcibly deprived of *independence* shall be restored; that opportunity to achieve *independence* for those peoples who aspire to *independence* shall be preserved, respected, and made more effective. . . . "[26] Britain—ironically the only colonial power that was itself independent at the time—responded defensively. "It's far worse than I had supposed," wrote Richard Law, parliamentary undersecretary at the Foreign Office. "The whole tenor of it is to look forward to the end of the British Empire and the substitution for it of a multiplicity of national sovereignties."[27] "Hands off the British Empire is our maxim," Churchill would later say.

British diplomats, conscious of growing dependence on American support but unwilling to surrender the empire, tried to sidestep the issue altogether. This was not always possible. When the State Department asked for input on a joint Allied statement on colonial independence, Lord Hailey wrote in a confidential memo that any attempt to alter the intention of the Atlantic Charter provision on self-government must be handled with extreme caution. "To imply that there is a distinction between self-government and independence suggests a refinement which will be viewed with a great deal of suspicion in the USA. . . . Americans feel we are already repenting of having committed ourselves to it; and . . . it would be asking too much of them to expect that they will forgo the opportunity of making us 'toe the line' in regard to Article 3."[28]

President Roosevelt proposed an international trusteeship to assist all former colonies in the transition toward stable independence. These colonies "ought for our own safety to be taken away from the weak nations," among which he expressly included France.[29] Roosevelt was particularly adamant on the dismantling of the French empire. He held little regard for the French (whom he considered spineless) or for their efforts at empire (which he called "hopeless"). He condemned French colonial policy as negligent of the welfare of native populations: "After one hundred years of French rule," he said, "the inhabitants [of Indochina] were worse off than they had been before."[30] French Indochina yielded to Japanese power as submissively as France itself had yielded to the Germans. "Why was it a cinch for the Japanese to conquer that land?" Roosevelt once asked his son Elliott. "The native Indo-Chinese have been so flagrantly downtrodden that they thought to themselves: Anything must be better than to live under French colonial rule."[31] At the Cairo and Teheran conferences, Roosevelt suggested placing Indochina under the administration of an international authority in order to prevent the return of the French there.

As the end of the war drew nearer, Franklin Roosevelt grew more insistent in his anti-imperialism. At the Yalta Conference in February 1945, he recurred repeatedly on the right of peoples around the world to achieve national self-determination, though in this he was alone: Churchill had the empire to think of; Stalin, the newly acquired lands of Eastern Europe. The nations rescued from Nazi occupation, the president said, seemed to think that the three Great Powers had been obligated to liberate them. "Now they are scolding the great powers for failing to take into account the rights of the small powers."[32] The British prime minister meanwhile considered it as one of his fundamental duties to preserve Britain's colonial system. Three years earlier he had said, "I have not become the King's first Minister in order to preside over the liquidation of the British Empire." He still meant it. "I believe you are trying to do away with the British Empire," he told Roosevelt.[33]

The president did not deny it. He opposed all colonialism, as inimical both to individual human rights and to the prospects for enduring international peace. "The colonial system means war," he had once remarked. And the world was changing, he earnestly hoped and believed. America was now presented with the opportunity to engorge itself on the spoils of war. By forgoing that opportunity, it would help to show a new way. Roosevelt told Churchill, "You have four hundred years of acquisitive instinct in your blood and you just don't understand how a country might not want to acquire land somewhere if they can get it. A new period has opened in the world's history and you will have to adjust yourself to it."[34]

The British, French, and Dutch were all driven easily from their Asian colonies by the Japanese, and all made plans for their reoccupation following the war. But the old order would never return. The war had simultaneously weakened the European nations and increased the resolve of national groups opposing them. The Japanese not only swept away the colonial powers, but did so rather easily. The illusion of European invincibility had been shattered. "The war," as a Belgian colonial officer remarked, "had assuredly not raised the prestige of Europeans."[35]

The Europeans failed to comprehend the tectonic shift that was already under way. At a conference on French colonial policy held in 1944 at Brazzaville, capital of French Equatorial Africa, attended by administrators for French sub-Saharan colonies, the delegates announced that "the objectives of the civilizing effort accomplished by France in the colonies lead to the rejection of any idea of autonomy, of any possible evolution outside of the French bloc of empire; the eventual constitution of self-government in the colonies, no matter how far off, is rejected."[36] The scope of France's national self-delusion about its place in the world was summed up in General DeGaulle's radio address from London on June 18, 1940, following the perfunctory French resistance to the German invasion. "France is not alone!" said DeGaulle. "She is not alone! She has a vast empire behind her."[37] DeGaulle, who set up a government-in-exile in French North Africa after it was liberated by the Americans and British, like his countrymen regarded the empire as essential for preserving what remained of France's greatness. The French, who had since at least 1870 been preoccupied by their declining international power and prestige, saw in their overseas empire a last vestige of greatness. "I know that you are preparing to aid France materially, and that aid will be invaluable to her," DeGaulle said to Roosevelt at the end of the war. "But it is in the political realm that she must recover her vigor, her self-reliance and, consequently, her role. How can she do this if . . . she loses her African and Asian territories—in short, if the settlement of the war definitely imposes upon her the psychology of the vanquished?"

After the war, the Dutch launched a violent campaign to restore rule over the resource-rich colony of the Dutch East Indies. The effort, wrote one observer, "based on the conviction that they were still much loved by their colonial subjects, has been called one of the major pieces of self-deception in the annals of empire . . . equaled only by the French campaign to recover Indochina."[38] The UN Security Council passed a series of resolutions condemning the bloody "police action" in Indonesia, but the Dutch were unmoved. Only when the United States government threatened to cut off Marshall Plan aid to the Dutch unless they granted independence for Indonesia did they abandon their effort to reimpose colonial rule there. Indonesia became an independent state in 1949. The American action had much broader ramifications. "No move by the Americans could have been more dramatic to the British," wrote an observer. "It became apparent that the United States was prepared to cut off economic aid to a European ally in order to promote colonial independence."[39]

The British were already having their own doubts about empire. As one historian of colonialism has noted, "The course of American anticolonialism in the 1940s helped to undermine the confidence and shatter the traditional perspectives of British colonial rulers. It also armed British liberal reformers with compelling arguments that reform was vital in order to preserve the American alliance."[40] The British, who took a justifiable pride in their colonial relationships, and under pressure from their American allies and from within the colonies themselves, generally withdrew from their colonies while they could still do so on cordial terms, rather than wait to be pushed out by violence. Britain aimed to transform its empire into a commonwealth, which alone among European colonial powers it largely managed to do. British India became independent in 1947. Following intense sectarian violence between Hindus and Muslims, the Muslim-majority region became the nation of Pakistan. Britain meanwhile moved toward preparing other colonies for independence.

As for France, its colonies even in their heyday had not been a source of much material benefit. The British journal *Nineteenth Century* commented in 1884 that "A study of history . . . is more than enough to confirm an impartial observer in the generally accepted idea that France cannot colonize."[41] Yet to the French people, their colonial domain, such as it was, was the validation of a national aspiration to international importance. France had been eclipsed in Europe by its neighbors. Its claim as a great power rested on its international holdings. Its empire was all it had left, a residue of glory days.

It was France's idea of itself that was at stake, and which delayed withdrawal from an unprofitable empire and made the process violent and bloody. Early in the twentieth century the president of the Third Republic had boasted that the territories of the French empire were twenty-three times larger than the metropolitan homeland. It did not matter to the French that these were arid deserts and malarial backwaters. An empire is an empire. As the popular writer Joseph Chailley-Bert declared in 1899, French colonialism "has become a national thought . . . and it will succeed because . . . in guaranteeing the future greatness of France, it also contributes to stability and peace in the world."[42]

Peter Leroy-Beaulieu, a prominent advocate for imperialism, put the matter in plainer terms: "Colonization is for France a matter of life or death." He believed that without its overseas territories, France would decline in international consequence to the level of a Greece or Romania.[43] "France cannot be France without greatness," DeGaulle wrote in his memoirs, and France could not be great without empire.

The French embarked upon catastrophic wars in Vietnam and North Africa in order to hold onto their colonies, and to international significance. It was ousted from Indochina by the Viet Minh in 1954 after a brutal and demoralizing conflict there. The Sudan, Morocco, and Tunisia won their independence in 1956. In Algeria, the French army slid into a ruthless and repressive campaign against growing resistance, resorting to assassination and torture. Half a million conscripted French troops were involved in the fight to hold onto the North African desert nation, and as many as half a million Arab lives were lost in the campaign.[44] After years of intense fighting, on July 1, 1962, Algeria finally won its independence from France.

The pace of decolonization accelerated. From 1960 to 1964 nearly all of sub-Saharan Africa achieved independence—from Belgium, France, and Britain—and America continued to push for decolonization. "The United States regularly lent its weight to independence for Africans," writes historian D. A. Low, "though it also opposed the emergence of a new threat to liberty, communism."[45] The Cold War was now dominating international events. Even as the Soviet Union sought to use the issue of colonialism to erode the appeal of the Western nations and drive a wedge between them, the United States continued to support liberation for subjected peoples.

On September 25, 1961, President John F. Kennedy addressed the United Nations General Assembly, asserting that "My country intends to be a participant and not merely an observer in the peaceful, expeditious movement of nations from the status of colonies to the partnership of equals." But a new sort of subjugation was being imposed upon peoples—those living under Communist tyrannies. "Let us debate colonialism in full, and apply the principle of free choice and the practice of free plebiscites in every corner of the globe," Kennedy declared.[46]

In the 1961 UN Security Council debate on Portugal's continued involvement in Angola, the United States reiterated its opposition to colonialism, voting for a resolution urging self-determination for the people of Angola. In doing so, it voted against its ally Portugal. Adlai Stevenson, the American representative, said that "the United States would be remiss in its duties as a friend of Portugal if it failed to express honestly its conviction that step-by-step planning within Portugese territories and its acceleration is now imperative for the successful political, social and economic advancement of all inhabitants under Portugese Administration. . . . "[47] The resolution failed, however, due to the abstention of Chile, China, Ecuador, France, Turkey, and Britain. Portugal, one of the first European nations to embrace imperialism, was among the last to give it up: Angola was not to win its independence until 1975.

The pullout of the British from Hong Kong on June 30, 1997, marked the end of the era of colonialism. More than any other nation, America helped bring about that end. "It was the United States which most prominently opposed European colonialism," wrote the British historian of imperialism John Springhall.[48]

The hall of the UN's General Assembly was constructed to hold seventy delegations. At century's end, its membership stood at 189 nations, two-thirds of which had not even existed as independent states in 1945. Wilson's vision of national self-determination for oppressed peoples was being realized. It was being realized because instead of using its power to gain territory for itself during its period of dominance (as ascendant powers had done for millennia), America helped foster liberation for subjected peoples around the globe. It was being realized because Americans had held to the conviction that the American struggle for liberty was, as Thomas Paine had said, "the cause of all mankind."

———————

For democracy to flourish in the postwar world, and peace to endure, it was necessary that order be restored to a global economic system that had already begun to break down long before the war broke out. Hard lessons had been learned from the failure to reduce economic nationalism in the period following the First World War; there had ensued a spiral of economic tit-for-tat, discord and distrust.

The third of President Wilson's Fourteen Points had called for "the removal so far as possible, of all economic barriers and the establishment of an equality of trade conditions among nations consenting to the peace and associating themselves for its maintenance." Had it been realized, history may have taken a different course. Instead, the strident economic nationalism that spread across the globe in the 1930s not only restricted interaction between nations, but also eroded living standards in every developed nation, helping to nurture fascist and other antidemocratic movements.

Nations aggressively depreciated their currencies, in order to make their own exports cheaper to international buyers. Freed during the First World War from the stability provided by—and the fiscal restraint imposed by—the gold standard, currencies fluctuated wildly and inflation soared. By the end of the war wholesale prices had risen 200 percent in the United States, 300 percent in Britain, 430 percent in France.[49] But the Paris Peace Conference, preoccupied with the political problems of the postwar settlement, neglected to address critical economic issues.

Tariffs, import quotas, and outright trade restrictions proliferated. In the year before the outbreak of the First World War, the volume of international merchandise trade stood at 11.9 percent of GDP among industrialized nations. The surge of protectionism caused international commerce to plummet. By the late 1930s, nearly half of all world trade had been restricted by tariffs alone,[50] and industrialized nations applied quotas to restrict imports, both to protect domestic producers and as retaliation against the restrictions placed on their own products.

The worldwide Great Depression intensified the economic belligerence, as national leaders severed international commercial relationships in a misguided effort to protect their own domestic economies. The surge of protectionism only deepened the crisis: from 1929 to 1932, the value of world trade fell over 60 percent.[51] The spiral of economic retaliation was sand in the gears of the global economy: the levels of trade reached in 1913 were not to be reached again until the 1970s.[52]

Currency depreciation, defensive tariffs, restrictive import quotas, and other protectionist measures could in theory have the desired effect of improving a nation's trade balance and bolstering its employment—if a single nation were to impose those measures against other nations and they did not retaliate. Its own products would become relatively more attractive to foreign buyers, and its own markets would be protected from foreign producers. But in practice it never worked that way. The protectionist action of one nation invariably provokes a reaction from others, who are as anxious to protect their own producers from foreign competitors. The competitive devaluation of one currency spurs others to respond. Tariffs and quotas induce tariffs and quotas. Before you know it, "protective" barriers have stifled the exchange of goods and services. Nobody is protected. The worker is unable to sell his products abroad. The consumer is unable to purchase what he wants at the best price. Commerce stifles. Economies stagnate. Unemployment soars. The beggar-thy-neighbor economic policies of the 1930s ultimately flared into more overt hostilities. It might be said that war, in modern times, had been a continuation of economics by other means.

President Roosevelt and his economic advisers believed that international peace and prosperity could be sustained following the war only if the political *and* economic tensions that had existed between nations before the war were reduced. The development of an institution to promote international political cooperation—a new League of Nations—would not be sufficient; there must be provision made for promoting economic cooperation as well. Nations are, historically, much less likely to go to war if they are bound together by a web of mutually beneficial commercial relationships. A century earlier the English philosopher John Stuart Mill had recognized in international commerce a basis for increasing the interconnections between states and peoples, advancing international understanding, and rendering military conflict less pervasive. "And it may be said without exaggeration that the great extent and rapid increase of international trade, in being the principal guarantee of the peace of the world, is the great permanent security for the uninterrupted progress of the ideas, the institutions, and the character of the human race."[53] The events of the 1930s and '40s had borne him out. Increased economic interaction between nations would be essential for the development of a more stable and peaceful global system. The old barriers to the exchange of goods and ideas had to begin to come down.

The British, traditional advocates of relatively free trade, were rightly concerned that fully open global trade would be incompatible with empire. Increasingly though, the American administration possessed the economic clout to advance its position on free trade. In Article VII of the Lend-Lease Agreement, the two nations declared their support for "agreed action by the United States of America and the United Kingdom, open to participation by all other countries of like mind, directed to the expansion, by appropriate international and domestic measures, of production, employment, and the exchange and consumption of goods . . . to the elimination of all forms of discriminatory treatment in international commerce, and to the reduction of tariffs and other trade barriers."[54]

As Hitler was declaring the creation of a "new economic order," at their meeting in Newfoundland in August 1941, Roosevelt and Churchill pledged in the Atlantic Charter to promote free trade between nations, with open access on equal terms for all, "to bring about the fullest collaboration between all nations in the economic field. . . . "[55] The two most important Allied nations had committed themselves to promoting a postwar economic system based on free trade. During the course of the war, U.S. and British economists had studied proposals for the development of a more stable global economic system.

At a press conference in the White House on May 24, 1944, Roosevelt read the contents of a letter he had sent out to leaders of the Allied nations, inviting them to send delegates to an international conference on postwar economic cooperation: "The publication of the joint statement of the monetary experts, recommending the establishment of the international monetary fund, has been received with great gratification here as marking an important step toward postwar international economic cooperation. Undoubtedly, your people have been equally pleased by this evidence of the common desire to cooperate in meeting the economic problems of the postwar world. Therefore, I am proposing to call a conference of these nations, for the purpose of formulating definite proposals for the international monetary fund, and possibly a bank for reconstruction and development."[56]

The international conference was held at Bretton Woods, a resort in the hills of New Hampshire, in July 1944. It brought together over 700 representatives from 44 nations to hammer out an agreement on international economic cooperation. Treasury Secretary Morgenthau told the delegates that the conference would have a historic purpose: "creation of a dynamic world community in which the peoples of every nation will be able to realize their potentialities for peace." President Roosevelt wrote in a greeting to the delegates: "Commerce is the lifeblood of a free society. We must see to it that the arteries which carry that blood stream are not clogged again."[57]

To prevent the monetary disarray that had fostered international tensions and economic chaos in the period leading up to the Second World War, a system of stable exchange rates was established among participating nations. In addition, an International Monetary Fund was created to help stabilize the international currency system. It would provide loans to participating nations that were running temporary trade deficits, so that they would not feel compelled to resort to protectionist practices or competitive currency devaluations. Funds would also be available to nations making fundamental currency adjustments.

An International Bank for Reconstruction and Development, more commonly known as the World Bank, was established with the goal of helping to finance postwar reconstruction and, later, of reducing poverty in developing nations by loaning funds for projects that promised to raise living standards. These would include things like transportation, communications, electric power—infrastructure projects essential for economic development. The United States was to provide much of the funding for both the IMF and the World Bank.

Roosevelt was delighted with the final product of the conference. He called the Bretton Woods Agreement "the cornerstone for international cooperation." Some members of the American delegation, meanwhile, anxiously recalled the fate of the Versailles Treaty a generation earlier. The Federal Reserve's E. A. Goldenweiser told associates that most other nations had only gone along with the plan for global cooperation because of American leadership, and without that leadership the plan would collapse. He hoped that "our Congress will find it impossible to turn these agreements down because . . . the world cannot be prosperous now without American leadership."[58]

Many Americans did view the agreement with suspicion. The United States was doing just fine on its own. Why should it get caught up in international agreements to help stabilize the currencies of other nations? How much would it cost? Chicago congressman Charles Dewey warned in a radio address that passage of the Bretton Woods accord would force "mothers and wives . . . to increase your family budgets a little more to help provide the cash through extra taxes or buy a few more government bonds."[59] American generosity would make foreign nations unwilling to address their own wasteful and inefficient policies, warned isolationist senator Robert Taft. "Every nation must solve its own problems."

Wall Street bankers feared the increased governmental role in the economy. Chase National Bank chairman Winthrop Aldrich warned that "currency manipulation will not solve the basic economic problems of a war-ridden world."[60] But the bankers' credibility had itself suffered greatly in the Depression, and they lacked the prestige to have much impact on public opinion. President Roosevelt campaigned aggressively for Senate approval of the agreement. "We have learned that just as the United States cannot afford to be isolationist in its political philosophy, neither can it stand the malignant effects of economic isolationism."[61] The institutions established at Bretton Woods, he said, were essential for mankind to produce a "more united and cooperating world."

This was not 1920. Americans had paid the price for isolationism, and most were not willing to return to it. Opinion polls showed strong public support for the Bretton Woods Agreement. When Congress took up the issue, the House Banking and Currency Committee reportedly received only 42 letters opposing the agreement, 25,000 in favor.[62] There was no mistaking which way the political winds were blowing. Isolationism was dead, at least for the time being. "America has come a long way since Woodrow Wilson," said Pennsylvania senator Francis Myers. "Let us not be penny pinchers for peace."

"We have tried self-sufficiency and it has failed," said Senator Fulbright. "Let us try cooperation and participation."

Sen. Sheridan Downey said, "I do not imagine or claim that one citizen out of a hundred in our world community possesses accurate or detailed knowledge of the provisions of the Bretton Woods proposal. But to millions it has come, nevertheless, to represent a symbol of [America's] sincerity, our determination to make good our promises and pledges of a better postwar world. A destruction or injury to that symbol would be a brutal blow to the morale and hope of the world."[63]

On July 19, the Senate ratified the Bretton Woods Accord by a lopsided vote of 61 to 16. The vote signified a new internationalism; it told the world that the United States would remain actively involved in promoting peace and prosperity, even after the war ended. There would not be a return to 1920.

Though they are now taken for granted, and are often criticized—sometimes justly—for overstepping, the development of the Bretton Woods institutions was a watershed achievement. For the first time in history, truly global institutions had been established to foster international economic cooperation and development.

———————

In conjunction with the Bretton Woods structures, in 1947 the General Agreement on Trades and Tariffs (GATT) was established among twenty-three participating nations as a mechanism for lowering the barriers to trade that had fettered the global economy in the prewar period and still remained largely in place at war's end. The agreement's basic purpose was to promote "freer and fairer trade" around the world, by reducing the obstacles to the free exchange of goods and services. To avoid the system of special bilateral trade preferences that threatened to balkanize the world economy, GATT operated on the principle of "mutual reciprocity," so that concessions made by one nation to another in trade negotiations would be available to all other countries that enjoyed normal trade relations with it; so that, for example, all nations that enjoy normal trade status with the United States would face the same tariff rates on a particular commodity—when tariffs on an import are reduced for one nation, they are reduced for all.

Thus, "rounds" of trade negotiations could be conducted on an inclusive, multilateral basis rather than on an exclusionary, bilateral one. The first round of trade talks involved 123 sets of negotiations covering 50,000 items. More than 40,000 tariff concessions were made, involving over $10 billion in international trade.

It was a starting point. Successive rounds of negotiations further lowered barriers to trade, and in the eighth and final round of GATT negotiations (the Uruguay Round, completed in 1994), participating nations pledged to lower tariffs by a further 40 percent and gradually eliminate long-standing textile quotas. It also established the World Trade Organization, a permanent international organization (whereas the GATT only had contracting parties, the WTO would have members) established to further reduce trade barriers through multilateral negotiations, and provide trade dispute settlement for member states, to ensure that each side is abiding by the agreed-upon rules.[64] The United States Congress voted to join the WTO on December 1, 1994, and it came into existence in January 1995. By 2000 the WTO had over 140 member nations, working together to foster intercourse between nations.

The aim of the IMF, the World Bank, GATT, the WTO, and the new economic order they signified was the promotion of international economic cooperation. They worked. Between 1945 and 2000, average tariffs imposed by the world's industrialized economies fell from more than 40 percent to under 6 percent.[65] From the close of the Second World War to the end of the century, the volume of world trade expanded more than fourteenfold, to

7 trillion dollars. World economic production associated with international trade rose from 8 percent to 26 percent. According to World Bank estimates, the reduction of trade barriers from the Uruguay Round resulted in an increase of purchasing power for the world's consumers of between $100 billion and $200 billion each year.[66]

The United States used its vast influence to help establish institutions that held America to the same rules as all other nations that chose to participate. It is no accident that some of the most vocal opposition to the trade agreements came from American labor unions and other organized interests, who feared that the agreements would cost millions of American jobs as they created jobs for workers abroad. In fact, free trade *has* helped developing nations create jobs and raise living standards higher than ever before. In 1960, manufacturing workers in nonindustrialized nations received just over 10 percent of the wages of American workers; by 2000 this had risen to 30 percent, and developing nations were supplying nearly 40 percent of all U.S. imports.[67] But it has not been at the expense of American workers. Wages for U.S. workers grew most rapidly—over 2.5 percent annually—during the period from the fifties to the seventies, when trade growth was most dramatic.[68]

"There is a curious notion that the protection of national interest and the development of international cooperation are conflicting philosophies," Treasury Secretary Morgenthau said in his address at the conclusion of the Bretton Woods Conference. "We have found on the contrary that the only genuine safeguard for our national interest is in international cooperation. . . . This has been the great lesson taught by the war, and is, I think, the great lesson of contemporary life—that the people of the earth are inseparably linked to one another by a deep, underlying community of purpose. This community of purpose is no less real and vital in peace than in war, and cooperation is no less essential to its fulfillment." The epochal transformation of the global system toward an increasingly open structure has been breathtaking. Its consequences are no less so. There has followed expanding intercourse between nations, growing interconnectedness, and rising standards of living such as the world has never seen before. The expansion of international commerce has helped make producers more innovative and efficient, workers more productive, consumers more prosperous, governments more bountiful than ever before. After half a century of American leadership in eradicating the barriers to global free trade, there was at the dawn of the twenty-first century a level of peaceful interaction between nations unprecedented in human history.

———————•———————

Freedom is meaningless and democracy is impossible where people are starving. If all the nations of the world were really to enjoy the blessings of liberty that America espoused, they must be lifted out of the chronic poverty and insecurity that plagued their societies. In 1948, Harry Truman was elected in his own right, campaigning on the necessity for America to remain actively involved in world affairs. The first inaugural address of Woodrow Wilson—a president remembered primarily for his place in international diplomacy—had not even touched upon foreign policy. It was to be the focus of Truman's inaugural address, delivered on January 20, 1949. The world had changed since Wilson's age; so had America. In his inaugural, President Truman proposed a "program for peace and freedom" in the world, which would entail four points of action. "First, we will continue to give unfaltering support for the United Nations and related agencies. . . . Second, we will continue our programs for world economic recovery. . . . Third, we will strengthen freedom-loving nations against the dangers of aggression. . . . Fourth, we must embark on a bold new program for making the benefits of our scientific advances and industrial progress available for the improvement and growth of underdeveloped areas."[69]

When Truman spoke those words, half of the world's population was malnourished. Most were illiterate. Three-fourths lived in unrelenting danger of sudden death or prolonged agony from preventable diseases. Life expectancy in developing nations was only forty-one years, little improved—like living standards—from the Stone Age. "More than half of the people of the world are living in conditions approaching misery," Truman said. But for the first time in its history, mankind possessed the "knowledge and skill to relieve the suffering" of peoples in distant lands. America must take the lead. "The United States is preeminent among nations in the development of industrial and scientific techniques. . . . I believe that we should make available to peace-loving peoples the benefits of our store of technical knowledge in order to help them realize their aspirations for a better life. . . . Only by helping the least fortunate of its members to help themselves can the human family achieve the decent, satisfying life that is the right of all people."[70]

It came to be popularly called the Point Four Program, as it was the fourth of Truman's proposals for fostering peace and freedom in the world. It immediately received broad public support. Here was that stubborn American idealism at work again. "In a world where man can harness the elements and tame the microbe there is a moral burden to use this new knowledge in easing the burdens that still weigh upon the majority of mankind," wrote Richard Fagley, chairman of the Council for Social Action.[71]

On June 5, 1950, Congress passed the Act for International Development, which declared that "The people of the United States and other nations have a common interest in the freedom and in the economic and social progress of all peoples." It was an unprecedented and courageous declaration. The United States has sometimes been compared to ancient Rome in the scope of its preeminence. Well, the Roman Senate never made such a remarkable statement as that one, or had the power to give it credence. "It is declared to be the policy of the United States to aid the efforts of the peoples of economically underdeveloped areas to develop their resources and improve their working and living conditions," the new law said, "by encouraging the exchange of technical knowledge and skills and the flow of investment capital. . . . " The Technical Cooperation Administration was established to implement the program.

History is replete with instances of nations using their technical superiority to subjugate foreign peoples. But here was a nation using its technological advantage to elevate and liberate others. Indeed, it would *give away* technologies and enormous resources in order to reduce suffering in remote lands, to promote health and prosperity among absolute foreigners. That's idealism. The United States, as Truman had put it in his address, would strive "to create the conditions that will lead eventually to personal freedom and happiness for all mankind." He would later say that "America cannot remain healthy and happy in the same world where millions of human beings are starving."[72] The scope of it was without parallel in human history. Historian Arnold Toynbee said that the national undertaking to improve the living conditions of the poorest of mankind "will be remembered as the signal achievement of this age."

A commission was created to look into what sorts of humanitarian aid would have the greatest benefit in raising living standards in developing nations. The International Development Advisory Board, chaired by Nelson Rockefeller, concluded that most of humanity were daily confronted with two terrors that had tormented mankind since the dawn of history: hunger and disease. "In many regions malnutrition is chronic with intermittent periods of actual starvation on a wholesale level. In many regions one half of all children born do not live to the sixth year of life and the average lifespan is less than one half that in developed areas." Yet, despite the formidable challenges, there was much that could be done. "There is no country in these areas in which food production could not be raised appreciably through simple improvements in agricultural methods and equipment or the wider use of fertilizers. There is no country in these areas where new tools of medical science could not bring under control most of the debilitating illnesses sapping the productive energies of these peoples."[73]

So America embarked upon an ambitious and unprecedented program to alleviate human suffering around the world. The State Department was flooded with requests for assistance—from thirty-five governments within the first six months. Engineers, agronomists, doctors, nurses, and vocational experts were sent abroad to provide desperately needed technical knowledge and equipment. Within six months after Congress approved the program there were 350 American technical advisers working on over 100 humanitarian projects in 27 countries. They were training local farmers in methods to increase crop yields; digging wells; distributing fertilizer and pesticides; instructing in the use of modern plows and threshers; giving inoculations; teaching health and sanitation techniques. In addition, hundreds of trainees from 34 countries had been brought to the United States to study the latest techniques in botany, agronomy, and public health.

Americans traveled abroad, and some gave their lives, in the struggle against poverty and ignorance.

Billions of people around the world—billions—would live better lives, and longer ones, because of the American aid. From India to the Andes, from Africa to Asia, Americans dug wells, purified water, built schools, established hospitals, fostered village industries, taught principles of agriculture and distributed equipment, eradicated disease outbreaks, and on and on. By the late 1960s, India had received nearly $8 billion in humanitarian aid from the United States; Pakistan, $3.67 billion; the United Arab Republic, $769 million; Peru, $460 million; and on across the Middle East, Latin America, Africa, and Asia.[74] American assistance had benefited the citizens of 99 nations and five territories, so that a chairman of the House Foreign Operations Subcommittee on Appropriations could declare, in 1969, without too much exaggeration, that "Of the three-and-a-half billion people of the world, all but 36 million have received aid from the United States."[75]

Assisted by American technical advisers and American technology, a Green Revolution unfolded in developing nations, raising harvest yields by double and triple. At century's end, infant mortality in the developing world was only one-third of what it had been when President Truman announced the Point Four program. Average life expectancy in developing nations had been raised by twenty-three years. Global literacy had nearly doubled, to over 70 percent.

By century's end the United States would give over $200 billion in humanitarian assistance to poorer nations. "This effort," wrote the British historian Paul Johnson, "in absolute or relative terms and from whatever viewpoint it is regarded, was wholly without precedent in human history, and is likely to remain the biggest single act of national generosity on record."[76]

———————

Some of America's critics, at home and abroad, have suggested that the United States only acted from its own self-interest in promoting a global community of nations, in pushing for an end to colonization, in fostering the reduction of barriers to trade between nations, in working to elevate living conditions among the poorest nations. Self-interest, whether of an individual or a nation, is a nebulous and subjective thing, open to innumerable interpretations. Individuals sometimes act in ways that seem to others to be manifestly opposed to their own best interest. So do nations. No people ever acted in ways that it believed to be *against* its own interests. The critical question in history is: What does a people consider to be in their interest? Another nation in America's position could just as easily have considered its interest to pursue territorial conquest after the Second World War. That would have been the usual course for a dominant power.

As it was, humanity made greater real progress during the period of American dominance than it made under any other power in history. In virtually every nation in the world, at century's end people lived better and longer than they had ever lived before. In nearly all, they lived freer.

National self-interest matters in international affairs, and will always matter. A democratic nation's foreign policy should never be conducted without reference to the welfare of its own people. The history of America's relations with other nations, though, reveals a concern for a set of ideals—democracy, individual liberty, limited government, international cooperation—that is exceptional in the history of great powers. Those ideals have sometimes been derided as *idealism* or *political moralism,* but the human prospect would not have fared nearly so well if America had been without them.

Promoting Justice in the Middle East

IN THE EARLY decades of the twentieth century, Arab attitudes toward the United States and its people were overwhelmingly positive. The Americans in the region, unlike the Europeans, had not come as conquerors or colonizers: the primary experience that most Arabs had with Americans were with missionaries, educators, and humanitarian workers, and these relationships were nearly always congenial. The United States had been the only anti-imperialist nation among the Great Powers. It was a driving force in the decolonization movement, and for the self-determination of Arab peoples. During the First World War, Woodrow Wilson had openly opposed the Anglo-French Sykes-Picot plan for the postwar division of the Ottoman Empire as spoils between the Great Powers.

America could easily have claimed a substantial share of those territorial spoils. Instead, it rejected them on principle. The twelfth of Wilson's Fourteen Points—which dealt with the breakup of the Ottoman Empire—declared that the peoples "which are now under Turkish rule should be assured an undoubted security of life and an absolutely unmolested opportunity of autonomous development." However, the positive attitudes of Arabs toward the United States were to grow increasingly hostile after the Second World War, as Americans' support for nations' self-determination was extended to the Jews in their midst.

There had been an uninterrupted Jewish presence in Palestine since the people of Judah first migrated to the barren land and made it fruitful three millennia earlier, though a succession of invaders claimed authority over the area, persecuted its inhabitants, and fostered a dispersion of the main Jewish population across the Middle East, Europe, and Africa. For sixteen hundred years before the arrival of Islamic warriors in the seventh century,

Jews had been the main population group in Palestine. Even afterward, and right up until the twentieth century, there never ceased to exist in Palestine a thriving Jewish community. Modern Zionism emerged as a political program in the nineteenth century, when proponents such as Moses Hess and Theodor Herzl, convinced of the intractability of European anti-Semitism, pushed for international acceptance of a Jewish state in Palestine, where Jews could finally live free of persecution. Fleeing subordination, repression, and pogroms, between 1900 and 1914 some forty thousand Jewish immigrants flocked to Palestine, where they began building settlements and developing the barren and inhospitable land. British and American statesmen gradually came to accept the need for the establishment of a Jewish homeland in Palestine.

In November 1917, British foreign secretary Arthur James Lord Balfour wrote to prominent Jewish businessman Lord Rothschild that "His Majesty's Government view with favour the establishment in Palestine of a national home for the Jewish people, and will use their best endeavours to facilitate the achievement of this object. . . . I should be grateful if you would bring this declaration to the knowledge of the Zionist Federation."

At the Paris Peace Conference following the First World War, Britain was granted its mandate in Palestine, based in part upon its promise, set forth in the Balfour Declaration, to promote the establishment of a Jewish national home there. The mandate partitioned the territory into two parts, creating the Arab emirate of Transjordan from 80 percent of the area, to be demarcated by the eastern bank of the Jordan River. This was declared to be off limits to Jewish settlement. The Zionists were to receive a narrow corridor of land along the Mediterranean. Though some Jews denounced the partition of what they regarded to be their traditional homeland, most accepted the arrangement as a necessary compromise with the political realities of the region. When the fifty-two members of the League of Nations approved the British plan, it was widely regarded as tacit acceptance of the Balfour Declaration. In September 1922, the United States Congress passed a resolution declaring "that the United States of America favors the establishment in Palestine of a national home for the Jewish people. . . . "

Jewish communities in Palestine flourished. So did the Arabs who lived among them: their infant mortality was cut in half, life expectancy extended, and per capita income rose beyond that in neighboring Arab lands. The new economic conditions created by the Jews had the unforeseen effect of attracting more foreign Arabs to the area as well (100,000 between 1922 and 1946),[1] a fact that was to have vast ramifications. Indeed, Arab immigrants to Palestine moved disproportionately *to* Jewish population centers—such as Haifa and Jerusalem—rather than to Arab villages. Many of those same Arabs were calling for the expulsion of all Jews from Palestine. Finally, after years of Arab unrest and attacks against British administrators, and anxious to preserve its own position as the dominant imperial power in the Middle East, in 1921 Britain acquiesced to Arab demands to restrict Jewish immigration while permitting continued unrestricted Arab immigration to the area.

Jewish immigrants purchased their land, often at several times the going rate, usually from wealthy, absentee Arab landlords living in distant cities like Damascus and Cairo. In 1930 the British government established a special commission to investigate Arab complaints about Jewish land purchases in Palestine. The Simpson Commission found that "They [Jews] paid high prices for the land, and in addition they paid to certain of the occupants of those lands a considerable amount of money which they were not legally bound to pay."[2] From 1919 to 1936, Jewish settlers paid over $360 million for land in Palestine.[3]

Most Arabs rejected any proposal for a Jewish homeland in Palestine, and vowed to spill more British and Jewish blood to defeat it. "Every Arab in Palestine will do everything in his power to crush down Zionism," a prominent Arab leader warned, "because Zionism and Arabism can never be united together."[4] Amidst continuing Arab violence, and fearing for its rule elsewhere in the Middle East, in 1939 Great Britain repudiated the Balfour Declaration. The government issued a White Paper promising an Arab state in Palestine within ten years, and a further reduction in Jewish immigration for five years, after which any Jewish immigration would require Arab approval—essentially halting it altogether. There were already half a million Jews living in Palestine.

When the scope of the Holocaust became understood, world opinion was shocked into action. Within and without the Jewish community, support for British emigration restrictions to Palestine dissipated. Six million Jews had been put to death while Zionist leaders negotiated with the British government over its stringent immigration controls, then set at only 18,000 annually. It was now evident that compromise and conciliation would not lead to the establishment of a Jewish state. Harry Truman had long held that view.

As soon as the Second World War ended, President Truman began sending emissaries to Europe to study the situation of Jewish refugees there and was horrified by the reports he received. Truman believed that to send the "displaced persons" back to their countries of origins, as many European leaders proposed, would be to return them to the very societies that had persecuted and massacred them in the first place. In August 1945 he wrote to the British government that "the main solution" to the refugee crisis was "the quick evacuation of as many as possible of the non-repatriable Jews, who wish it, to Palestine."[5] He also pressed for an increase in the number of Jewish immigrants allowed into the United States, and worked to keep the pressure on the British government. On October 4, 1946, on the eve of Yom Kippur, he called for the establishment of a Jewish state in Palestine.

Seeking to extricate itself from the quagmire, in February 1947 Britain brought the problem to the United Nations, expressing its desire to end the British mandate in Palestine. The United Nations Special Committee on

Palestine (UNSCOP) was established to investigate the crisis and recommend solutions. The UNSCOP proposal, issued in August, called for the partition of Palestine west of the Jordan into two nations, one Arab, one Jewish. The city of Jerusalem was to remain an independent international zone. Though Arabs comprised a majority in Palestine, the Jews formed the majority in areas included by the partition plan within the Jewish state. Those areas had attracted substantial populations of Arabs by the greater economic opportunities and higher standard of living that existed in the Jewish population centers.

Most Jews living in Palestine reluctantly accepted the UN plan. It was not what Zionists had hoped for, but under the circumstances they recognized that a sliver of territory was better than none at all. The Arabs unanimously rejected the plan and vowed its destruction. The British government also rejected the plan.

Zionists knew that American backing would be essential to the fulfillment of the dream of a Jewish state, and lobbied President Truman for support. "The choice for our people, Mr. President, is between statehood and extermination," Dr. Chaim Weizmann, president of the World Zionist Organization, wrote to Truman. "History and providence have placed this issue in your hands, and I am confident that you will yet decide it in the spirit of moral law."[6] Jewish-American support was vital, of course, but Christian Zionists were just as crucial. Motivated by biblical beliefs in Jewish entitlement to the Holy Land, by prophecies of the latter days, or by humanitarian reaction to the Holocaust, they raised funds for Jewish settlers, espoused the Zionist cause from pulpits across the country, and helped produce a social and political environment in which advocacy of a Jewish state was not identified as a strictly "Jewish issue."[7]

By contrast, the State Department bureaucracy uniformly opposed the creation of a Jewish state in Palestine. Defense Secretary James Forrestal warned that American support for Israel would weaken its position in the Arab world and imperil vital oil supplies. Certainly there was much at risk. The Arab population of the Middle East was pro-American. The United States had been the only Great Power without imperialist ambitions in the region and had actively supported independence for Arab states. There was a deep reservoir of goodwill toward the United States in the area, and with the growing importance of Arab oil, there would be great benefit to be had from influence there. (In 1944, U.S. oil companies controlled 42 percent of the Middle East's proven oil reserves.)[8] A ll of that would be jeopardized by American support for a Jewish state. U.S. oil interests would be imperiled, and the Soviet Union would surely gain influence in the strategically vital area. In short, it was not held to be in America's interest to back the proposed state.

For President Truman, as for the majority of Americans, support for the establishment of the state of Israel did not flow from a narrow calculus of national self-interest. It was simply the right thing to do. State Department personnel, Truman later wrote, were "almost without exception unfriendly to the idea of a Jewish state. . . . Like most of the British diplomats, some of our diplomats also thought that the Arabs, on account of their numbers, and because of the fact that they controlled such immense oil reserves, should be appeased. I am sorry to say that there were some among them who were inclined to be anti-semitic."[9] When the president announced his support for the UNSCOP plan, some State Department officials—"striped-pants conspirators," Truman called them—began working actively to oppose its passage in the United Nations, and even after its passage worked to prevent its fulfillment.[10]

The vote in the General Assembly was expected to be close. On November 25, 1947, an amended version of the UNSCOP plan had fallen one vote short of the two-thirds required for passage. Truman held nothing back in pushing for the two-thirds vote needed for adoption of the partition plan. The French, for example, concerned over possible reaction in their North African colonies and vacillating to the very end, were advised that American financial aid might be cut off in the event of a negative vote. It was galling for the French, once a Great Power themselves, to be subjected to such blatant external pressures, but at the last moment Premier Leon Blum announced that his country's UN delegation would vote for the resolution. The votes of an unknowable number of other delegations, but at least half a dozen, were likewise swayed.[11] On the twenty-ninth the General Assembly, in session at Flushing Meadow, New York, adopted the resolution by a comfortable margin: 33 in favor, 13 opposed, 10 abstentions.[12] Truman's efforts had unquestionably been responsible for turning several votes, and for adoption of the resolution. An editorial in the B'nai B'rith magazine the following month credited Truman for securing the votes needed for the plan's passage.[13]

It may be said that the "indispensable man" to the establishment of a Jewish state was an unassuming Baptist from the American Midwest. The president had acted on principle, with great political courage, but he had not acted in isolation. Two-thirds of Americans supported the UN's plan, and only 10 percent opposed it.[14] The practicalities of the American support for the new state may be disputed, but it is beyond dispute that for most Americans, the policy was a moral act, and not a political calculation.

Arab leaders vowed to reverse the UN decision by force. The Arab Higher Committee's spokesman Jamal Husseini warned the United Nations that the Arabs would soak "the soil of our beloved country with the last drop of our blood . . . " and there followed a campaign of violence and terror against the Jewish settlers.

With the British withdrawing in frustration from their mandate in Palestine, on May 14, 1948, David Ben-Gurion and the Jewish People's Council proclaimed the establishment of the independent state of Israel. At 6:00 p.m. Washington time, President Truman announced American recognition of the new state of Israel. Hearing the news of the American recognition, residents of Tel Aviv and elsewhere poured onto the streets, "shouting, cheering and toasting the United States."[15] A. J. Granoff, a prominent Jewish-American, wrote to Truman: "In short, Mr. President, if all American citizens of the Jewish faith throughout this land do not bless your name tonight in their houses of worship, then there is no gratitude in the world."

In New York, Chaim Weizmann was interrupted by an aide bearing the good news. Before the aide could speak, Weizmann calmly said, "The United States has recognized us."

"How could you know that?"

"Your face told me," Weizmann replied. Then he added, "Besides, didn't I tell you about President Truman?"

Ben-Gurion, a leader of the Zionist movement and Israel's first prime minister, would later say that Truman's crucial support for Israel had "given him an immortal place in Jewish history."[16]

———•———

In its support of national self-determination for the Jews and the Arabs of Palestine, the United States was acting in accord with the principles espoused by Woodrow Wilson, principles that, when they were announced, had been praised throughout the Arab world. America's policies would later be criticized as depriving the Arabs of Palestine (thenceforth, simply "Palestinians") of their national self-determination. It was not so. The establishment and defense of the Jewish state never precluded the creation of a Palestinian state as well. The original UN plan had envisaged precisely such an arrangement, and the United States had supported it. The Zionists, moreover, had supported it, too, agreeing to reside side by side with an Arab state in Palestine and appealing for comity. "It is our belief that a great Jewish community, a free Jewish nation, in Palestine . . . will be of great benefit to our Arab neighbors," said Zionist leader David Ben-Gurion. "We need each other. We can benefit each other."[17]

Arab leaders refused to admit the possibility of *any* Jewish state in their midst and embarked upon a generations-long campaign of violence to eradicate it. Israel was embattled from the moment of its birth. Forty million Arab neighbors pledged the destruction of the new state, which was comprised of just 600,000 Jews. The day after Israel announced its statehood, it was invaded by the armies of Egypt, Iraq, Jordan, Syria, and Lebanon. One percent of the Jewish population of Palestine was killed in that conflict.[18] The foundation was being laid for what would become Israel's reflexive approach to its relations with its neighbors: security first. The entire nation was only 275 miles long and ranged from 15 to 75 miles wide. It was surrounded by Arab states committed to its destruction. An attacking army could be across the border and upon its major population centers in minutes.

As for the Arabs of Palestine (who might easily have had their own state), they now found themselves without any territory at all to call their own. Egypt annexed Gaza. Jordan annexed the "West Bank."

Within six months Israel had held its first democratic election, the first in the history of the entire region.

———◆———

During the conflict of 1947–48 there was simultaneously an exodus of Arabs out of Israeli territory (the UN put the figure at around 650,000), and of Jews fleeing increasingly violent treatment in Arab states (estimated at around 550,000). Most of the roughly 650,000 Palestinian Arabs who left Israel did not go far: they remained within Palestine, traveling the few miles to the Arab side of the armistice line. Both sides had a refugee problem in 1948.

That is where the similarity ended. The Jewish refugees were welcomed into Israel, and given economic and other aid to help them assimilate. They continued to flood into Israel, and within the first two years the population had doubled to over a million. Arab governments, by contrast, refused to resettle most of the Arab refugees, preferring to keep them segregated in vast camps, which were maintained with the assistance of UN funding, most of it from the United States. When Israel was destroyed, the plan went, they would be returned. (Of the Arab states in the region, only Jordan agreed to help resettle some of the Palestinian refugees). It was a prescription for the longest-running "refugee problem" in the world; one that would persist for generations. By the end of the century there were over twice the number of Palestinian refugees that there had been at the start. Arab leaders quickly came to regard the Palestinian refugees themselves as a political implement with which to pummel Israel. "The refugees are the cornerstone in the struggle against Israel," government-run Radio Cairo declared. "The refugees are the armaments of the Arabs and Arab nationalism."[19]

The people of the Arab world were poor, largely illiterate, with insupportable birth rates and a life expectancy around thirty-five years, living in patriarchal, hidebound societies under repressive regimes. Arab national leaders, not one of whom had come to power through election, recognized the practical benefits of giving voice to the anti-Israeli sentiments of mass opinion to deflect discontent with conditions at home. The new state of Israel became the scapegoat for ills that had afflicted the Arab world long before its existence, and the panacea for those ills was increasingly seen to be the destruction of the Jewish state.

By the early 1950s, Egypt was actively supporting cross-border raids by Palestinian *fedayeen* ("self-sacrificers") into Israel, and was calling for a "second round" of warfare to eradicate Israel.[20] The Egyptian government began to recruit and train terrorists, who were regarded as an effective weapon to be used against the young state.

In 1955, Egyptian president Nasser inked a deal with the Russians (through the Czech government) for $250 million worth of Soviet military equipment. The timing seemed propitious: in the previous year, the British had, under pressure from Egypt, begun to withdraw from their massive military base that housed some eighty-thousand troops at the base of the Suez Canal zone. Though Britain had granted independence to India a decade earlier, it still clung to its sphere of influence in the Middle East. That influence was steadily being undermined by emerging Arab nationalism. Nasser was its leading exponent. The French were caught up in a violent struggle to hold on to Algeria. They were confronted there by an independence movement growing steadily in power, which received both moral and material support from Nasser. Neither Britain nor France were ready to yield their positions in the Middle East.

Israel, of course, had the greatest incentive of all to wish Nasser gone, or at least neutralized. Its security was directly at stake. During the preceding five years, over a thousand Israeli civilians had been killed in cross-border raids by Arab terrorists, a staggering figure considering the country's size. Nor was there any prospect of a change of policy: in early 1954 the Egyptian foreign minister declared that "the Arab people will not be embarrassed to declare: We shall not be satisfied except by the final obliteration of Israel from the map of the Middle East."[21] Newspapers and radio stations throughout the Arab world, all to some extent under government control, spewed an endless stream of virulent anti-Semitic and anti-Israel propaganda.

But General Nasser's leadership in the Arab world, attained in large part by his strident confrontation with Israel, was not feeding or clothing his people. Average per capita income in Egypt was under $100. The country's population was exploding, with a growth rate of 4 percent annually. And Egypt's greatest revenue-producing enterprise was controlled by Britain and France. On July 26, 1956, Nasser nationalized the Suez Canal, which had since its construction in the preceding century been under French and British control.

British prime minister Anthony Eden's understanding of the world, and Britain's place in it, had been formed in an earlier era. One U.S. diplomat said of the prime minister that he "had not adjusted his thoughts to the altered status of Great Britain, and he never did."[22] Britain promptly responded to Nasser's action by announcing that it would not allow Egypt to nationalize the canal. Eden dashed off a message to French premier Guy Mollet, insisting that Britain would take whatever action was necessary to reverse Nasser's move, and urged France's cooperation. The French, bogged down in Algeria, blamed Nasser for fomenting unrest there. Now, with the nationalization of the canal, Paris had the provocation it needed for striking back at the Egyptian dictator.

With no specific knowledge of their military planning, President Eisenhower nevertheless grew alarmed by the increasingly belligerent tone of the Anglo-French reaction. The prospect of an international conflict for the sake of restoring to imperial powers a vestige of the colonial era held no appeal for the Americans. British and American international lawyers had agreed that Egyptian nationalization of the canal had been legal. As a sovereign state, Egypt had the right to nationalize the Canal Company, which existed on Egyptian territory, was registered in Egypt, and subject to Egyptian law.[23] There was no legal justification for action against Egypt's nationalization of the canal. For Eisenhower, the resort to force was to be prevented if at all possible.

In France, where the Algerian conflict had already inflamed anti-Arab sentiment, the public strongly supported the war. In Britain, though a majority favored a firm response, there was greater misgiving over the prospect of military action. Opposition members of Parliament formed the Suez Emergency Committee to mobilize public opinion against war. The *Manchester Guardian* warned that the use of military force would have calamitous long-term consequences for Britain in the Middle East. *The Economist* pointed out the weakness of Britain and France's legal case and advised negotiation.[24]

Eisenhower wrote to Eden cautioning against the precipitous use of military force. Secretary of State John Dulles traveled to London, where he met in tense talks with the British and French. He made clear what the former imperial powers had already learned in the preceding years, that on matters which involved colonial disputes, American policy might diverge from that of its European allies.[25] Nasser played his hand shrewdly, keeping traffic on the canal moving, preventing violence against foreign lives or property in Egypt. Traffic on the canal flowed at about the same rate as before the crisis.

France and Britain prepared for war. On September 2, President Eisenhower wrote to Eden, "I am afraid, Anthony, that from this point onwards our views of this situation diverge. As to the use of force or the threat of force at this juncture, I continue to feel as I expressed myself . . . some weeks ago . . . new military preparation and civilian evacuation . . . seem to be solidifying support for Nasser. . . . I must tell you frankly that American public opinion flatly rejects the thought of using force."[26] Americans believed, as Vice President Nixon later put it, that British and French conduct in the Suez manifested "policies toward Asia and Africa which seemed to us to reflect the colonial tradition."[27]

Lingering French and British hopes that the United States might be drawn into the conflict once its allies became engaged were dashed. In a press conference on the eleventh, President Eisenhower was asked whether the United States would go to war to support Britain and France if they resorted to military force in the Suez. The former general answered that under his presidency the United States would only go to war if Congress voted to do so, or if the country were in imminent danger. "So far as going into any kind of military action under present conditions, of course, we are not."

The French foreign minister, Christian Pineau, made overtures to the Isreali government to draw it into the plan. A raid against military bases throughout the Sinai would surely be defensive. France would veto any Security Council resolution condemning Israel and would quadruple its monthly shipment of fighter jets if Israel went along with Anglo-French war plans. By early October a secret agreement had been reached.[28] Israel was to invade Egypt; then France and Britain would send troops into the area to separate the combatants, permitting them to seize the canal.

Eisenhower received intelligence of Israeli military mobilization on October 26 and sent an urgent message to Prime Minister Ben-Gurion, requesting that Israel take no action that would destabilize the tenuous peace in the Middle East. America's commitment to Israel's security was unwavering, but it could not sanction aggression.

Israel launched its attack against Egypt on the twenty-ninth. The following day, as planned, Britain and France issued a joint communiqué, asserting that "the outbreak of hostilities between Israel and Egypt" threatened to disrupt freedom of navigation through the canal. It requested Israel to withdraw its military forces to ten miles east of the canal, and the Egyptians to "withdraw their forces from the neighborhood of the Canal, and to accept the temporary occupation by Anglo-French forces of key positions at Port Said, Ismalia and Suez." There is no telling what the French and British were thinking, but the flimsy gauze of conspiracy covering the collusion was transparent to everyone else. The Israeli forces, who at the time were not near the canal, would actually have had to *advance* farther into Egypt in order to meet the demands of the Anglo-French cease-fire ultimatum.

The American president first received word of the ultimatum through news reports. The usually unflappable Eisenhower was infuriated. He sent an urgent message to Eden, warning that precipitous military action would escalate and prolong the violence in the region. The White House issued a statement expressing the president's hope "that the United Nations organization would be given full opportunity to settle the items in the controversy by peaceful means . . . "

On the day that the ultimatum was issued, President Eisenhower made a national radio address, discussing the brutal invasion of Hungary by the Soviet Union and the events unfolding in the Middle East. "The actions taken [by Britain, France, and Israel] can scarcely be reconciled with the principles and purposes of the United Nations to which we all subscribed," he said. "There can be no peace without law. And there can be no law if we were to invoke one code of international conduct for those who oppose us and another for our friends."[29] Eisenhower sent a message to Ben-Gurion "expressing my grave concern and renewing a previous recommendation that no forcible initiative be taken which would endanger the peace."[30]

The next day the United States called for an emergency session of the UN Security Council, where the American representative Henry Cabot Lodge introduced a resolution condemning Israel's invasion and called for member states to refrain from assisting Israel. It was promptly vetoed by Britain and France.[31]

Anthony Eden never grasped the nature of America's opposition to the aggression in Suez and harbored a sense of betrayal that endured to the end of his life. "It was not Soviet Russia, or any Arab state, but the Government of the United States which took the lead against Israel, France and Britain," he wrote in his memoirs.[32]

By now, though, the characters were all upon the stage, and the tragedy had to be played through. On October 31, British and French bombers began attacking Egyptian airfields. The conflict had been joined. In the British Parliament, when opposition members asked the prime minister whether Britain was at war in Egypt, Eden could not say. The discussion grew so fractious that the session was suspended, the first time that had happened in thirty years. In Paris, Premier Mollet was having an easier time of it. French public opinion strongly supported the action, and the National Assembly had given him a vote of confidence the previous day.

Eisenhower stood on principle. Britain and France were close allies, and the United States had a special relationship with Israel: this had not changed. Yet the same international rules of conduct must apply to all nations. On November 1 the resolution that had been vetoed in the Security Council was put before the General Assembly for a vote. The Americans derived no pleasure from denouncing the actions of their closest allies, but the United States could not refrain from doing so and still remain loyal to the principles it had long espoused in international affairs. "I doubt that any delegates ever spoke from this forum with as heavy a heart as I have brought here tonight," Secretary Dulles said as he presented the resolution. "We speak on a matter of vital importance, where the United States finds itself unable to agree with three nations with whom it has ties, deep friendship, and respect, and two of whom constitute our oldest, most trusted and reliable allies."[33] The resolution, which called for an immediate cease-fire and withdrawal of troops, passed by a vote of 65 to 5.

By the fourth, Israel had captured all the Sinai Peninsula, the Gaza Strip, and the Red Sea coast. As directed by his government, Abba Eban announced in the United Nations that Israel would abide by a cease-fire agreement, if Egypt would. The announcement caught the French and British off guard and threatened to upend their entire scheme. Anglo-French military forces were still en route to Egypt: they could scarcely justify an invasion to separate the warring sides if the two sides had already stopped fighting. The two governments pressured Israel to resume the fighting, and later in the day it withdrew its cease-fire offer.[34]

Given all the political capital that had been expended in the preceding weeks, Britain and France had to have something to show for their efforts. On the fifth, commandos from the combined force landed in Egypt, capturing Port Said by the end of the day. But the Israeli and Egyptian armies had long since stopped fighting, and UN peacekeepers were already being sent to monitor the truce. Anthony Nutting, minister of state at the British Foreign Office, resigned, saying that he was unable to defend the government's policy. Sir Edward Boyle, economic secretary to the Treasury, soon followed.

Seeking to capitalize on the fiasco, Soviet Premier Nikita Khrushchev condemned "the aggressive war being waged by Britain and France against Egypt, which has the most dangerous consequences for the cause of peace." The Soviet Union, he promised, would restore peace in the Middle East—at any price. Alluding to the Russian nuclear arsenal, he ominously warned, "We are determined to crush the aggressors and restore peace in the Middle East through the use of force."[35] President Eisenhower promptly advised the Soviets that any missile attack against Britain or France would result in a devastating American response, and the American Supreme Commander of NATO issued an even blunter warning. Soviet rhetoric was toned down.

But Eisenhower continued to pressure Britain and France to withdraw. When a run started on the British pound in the global currency markets, the United States conspicuously refrained from halting it, convincing many observers that the "special relationship" between Britain and the United States was at risk.[36] On the seventh, when the UN voted on a U.S.-sponsored resolution calling for the immediate withdrawal of French, British, and Israeli forces from Egypt, France and Britain could not even bring themselves to vote against it. They abstained. The resolution passed, 65 to 1, Israel being the sole dissenting vote.[37]

Prime Minister Eden, desperate to salvage what he could from the affair, announced that the British and French troops would remain at the canal until the two nations were assured that it would operate under international administration. The White House quietly made it clear that hundreds of millions of dollars in promised economic assistance, as well as oil supplies that were by now urgently needed, would not be provided until Britain unconditionally withdrew its forces from Egypt, which it presently did.

Israel, too, expressed reluctance to withdraw its troops. Acting American secretary of state Herbert Hoover Jr. (John Foster Dulles was now on his sickbed, dying of cancer) warned of a cutoff of all public and private American assistance if it did not withdraw, and possible expulsion from the United Nations. Ben-Gurion recalled that Abba Eban's cables from the United States "sowed fear and horror . . . " It was, he said, "a nightmarish day."[38] With the threat of American sanctions looming over it, by the end of February Israel had returned all the territory it had captured.

Inexplicably, the French blamed the failure of the ill-conceived scheme on the faintheartedness of the British. *Le Figaro* wrote that "France . . . was the only one in the Suez Affair who viewed the situation properly and conducted herself energetically."[39] Eden and Mollet also condemned the United States for abandoning them, but America had never been with them in the gambit. Their two nations' imperial days were largely finished in the Middle East, and elsewhere. They had revealed not only residual imperial ambitions, but ineptitude: it was hard to say which was more detrimental in international affairs.

The Suez Crisis helped propel Nasser to unchallenged leadership of the Arab world, and the Soviets were now firmly established in the region. British prime minister Anthony Eden resigned from office on January 10. America's relations with Britain, its closest ally, fell to their lowest point in a century, though shared history, culture, interests, and values assured that the freeze would be short-lived.

The crisis had demonstrated that the United States would not be bound to any single state in its international diplomacy, but would adhere to values that were the bedrock of its foreign policy. France and Britain were its closest allies. Nasser was certainly no friend. America had stood on principle, and voted with its adversary the Soviet Union in the General Assembly to help end the aggression, even at cost to its relations with key allies. "Seldom in history has a nation's dedication to principle been tested as severely as ours during recent weeks," Eisenhower said in a January 5 address before the Congress. "We have shown, so that none can doubt, our dedication to the principle that force shall not be used intentionally for any aggressive purpose and that the integrity and independence of nations of the Middle East should be inviolate."[40] America had proven that it was not the reflexive supporter of one side or another in the region, but was committed to justice for all peoples.

Although any imminent threat to Israel's national security had been removed, the fundamental situation remained unchanged. Its Arab neighbors continued to refuse to recognize its existence and continued to call for its annihilation. From 1957 to 1962, Israel filed over four hundred separate complaints with the United Nations over Syrian and Egyptian incursions, and other violations of the 1948 armistice, with little effect.[41] In 1962, Nasser boasted that Egypt's new Soviet-made ballistic missiles "can hit any target south of Beirut."[42] Arab political and religious leaders actively worked to foster the hatred of the Jews that was already deeply rooted in their culture. As a matter of public policy, Arab schoolchildren were indoctrinated in anti-Semitism. The Syrian minister of education remarked that "the hatred which we indoctrinate into the minds of our children from their birth is sacred."[43]

As in the Suez Crisis, American policy in the region continued to be directed toward a solution to the turmoil based on principles of equity rather than on unquestioning support for one side or the other. President John F. Kennedy, a Democrat who had been elected in 1960 with the help of over three-fourths of the Jewish vote, maintained a Mideast policy that differed little in fundamentals from that of his Republican predecessor Eisenhower, who had garnered less than a quarter of the Jewish vote. Both men worked to advance a comprehensive Middle East peace and assure Israel's security against enemies pledged to destroy it, while preserving America's national interests in the region—which included fostering, where possible, cordial relations with more moderate Arab states.

President Kennedy believed that in order for lasting peace to be achieved, the issue of the Palestinian refugees must be resolved. He appointed Joseph Johnson, the distinguished president of the Carnegie Endowment, to search for some resolution, but little headway was made on the matter before the young president's assassination in November 1963.

In May 1964 the Palestine National Conference met for the first time since the 1948 war and announced the establishment of the Palestine Liberation Organization. Funded by Arab states, it would soon encompass a force of over 10,000 guerrilla fighters, living in camps near the Israeli border, with the avowed objective of destroying the Jewish state. By 1965 there was an almost constant succession of violent cross-border attacks against Israelis by Arab terrorists, supplied and supported by Israel's Arab neighbors. Retaliatory strikes by the Israeli Defense Force (IDF) had no deterrent effect, and only angered an international opinion already antagonistic to Israel.

Arabs living in Israel, meanwhile (the 160,000 who remained there following independence had grown to 312,000 by 1966, mostly by natural increase), continued to enjoy more political rights, civil liberties, and economic opportunities than those living under any Arab regime. Between 1949 and 1966, fewer than 6,000 had emigrated.[44]

Although the United States had been committed to Israel's security since its inception, it had also worked to reduce tensions and hostilities in the region; one way it did this was to sharply restrict arms sales to Middle East states, including Israel. Truman, regarded by many as Israel's greatest friend, maintained an arms embargo against it throughout his presidency. Only as the national security dangers to Israel became apparent, and its avowed enemies were inundated with Soviet weaponry, did the United States gradually begin arms sales to Israel. When Lyndon Johnson took office in 1963, these still included only defensive weaponry.[45] It was only in 1965, as the military threat to Israel grew and the Cold War heated up, that President Johnson agreed to sell Israel 250 M-48 tanks, assault aircraft, and other potentially offensive systems.[46]

Bristling with Soviet arms and assurances, and preoccupied with his status as the leading anti-Zionist among Arab leaders, Nasser gradually revived his mission of destroying the state of Israel. On May 15, 1967, he deployed 90,000 troops into the Sinai, and ordered the UN peacekeeping force (which had been in place since the Suez Crisis, proving a buffer between Egypt and Israel) out of the country. The Egyptian defense minister said that the army was like a wild horse, chomping at the bit to be unleashed against Israel.

The Syrians were also impatient for war. The Golan Heights, in the south of the country, had been fortified with a massive complex of artillery batteries and became the source of nearly daily shelling of Israeli settlements near the border. "The Syrian Army, with its finger on the trigger, is united," declared Syrian defense minister Hafez Assad. "I, as a military man, believe that the time has come to enter into the battle of annihilation."[47]

On May 22, Nasser closed the Straits of Aqaba to Israeli shipping. In 1956, Eisenhower had pledged to keep the Straits open if Israel withdrew from the territories it occupied in the Suez Conflict. The closing of the Straits meant the gradual economic strangulation of Israel. Nasser knew that it would be forced to respond. He hoped that it would. Announcing the closure, the Egyptian leader declared that the situation in the region had been transformed since the Suez Crisis. Whereas Britain, France, and other nations had been supporters of Israel then, the growing power of the Arab states, and the Cold War (and latent anti-Semitism in some places), had transformed the situation. America stood nearly alone in support of Israel. "Israel today is not backed by Britain and France as was the case in 1956," said Nasser. "It has the United States, which supports it and supplies it with arms. . . . " The Kremlin announced that Israel was to blame for the escalating tensions and pledged support for the Arab states.

President Johnson denounced Nasser's closure of the Straits as "illegal" and warned that it "brought a new and grave dimension to the crisis in the region. To the leaders of all the nations of the Near East, I wish to say what three presidents have said before—that the United Sates is firmly committed to the support of the political independence and territorial integrity of all the nations of the area. The United States opposes aggression by anyone in the area, in any form, overt or clandestine. This has been the policy of the United States led by four presidents—President Truman, President Eisenhower, President Kennedy and myself—as well as the policy of both of our political parties."[48]

Johnson remained in constant contact with Arab, Russian, and Israeli leaders, working to keep a lid on the crisis. He submitted a peace proposal that provided for a return of United Nations peacekeepers and UN administration of Gaza until the emergency was resolved, and pullback of both Egyptian and Israeli troops from the borders where they now faced off. Leaders throughout the Arab world called for war and the destruction of Israel. There were mass demonstrations urging war. The government in Cairo promised a struggle that would bring about the destruction of Israel, "this racist base," and Damascus predicted that "the war of liberation will not end except by Israel's abolition."[49] On the thirtieth, Egypt entered into a military alliance with its former rival, Jordan. "All of the Arab armies now surround Israel," declared Jordan's King Hussein. "There is no difference between one Arab people and another, no difference between one Arab army and another."[50] On June 4 the military pact was extended to include Iraq.

Nearly half a million Arab troops, along with 3,000 tanks and 810 aircraft, were now massed along the entire length of Israel's vulnerable border, from Syria in the north to Jordan and Egypt in the south, within striking distance of Israel's population centers. It was clear that diplomacy would not succeed. Prime Minister Levi Eshkol determined that Israel must act now to save itself from destruction. On June 5, Israeli planes were launched against Egyptian air bases in the Sinai. Flying at 150 feet to avoid detection, 183 planes struck a dozen airfields. The Soviet-made Egyptian air force was destroyed. Radar installations and other targets in Jordan, Syria, and Iraq were hit. By nightfall, Israeli jets controlled the skies. Egyptian tanks commenced a chaotic retreat back across the Sinai, pursued by IDF ground forces.

Early on the fifth, Eshkol transmitted an urgent message through American diplomats to King Hussein, explaining that Israel's fight was with Nasser, not Jordan. Only when Jordanian forces began shelling the Israeli-held section of Jerusalem were Israeli troops sent against the Old City of Jerusalem and the West Bank of the Jordan river. By the seventh, Israeli soldiers captured the Old City, and the West Bank the following day.

Next Israel turned to the Golan Heights, towering three thousand feet above the Galilee, from where Syria had launched repeated missile attacks. By the tenth, IDF brigades had ruptured Syrian defenses, and the Syrian army was in retreat toward Damascus, whereupon Eshkol ordered the army to halt its advance.

A cease-fire went into effect at 6:00 p.m. on June 10. In less than six days, Israel had routed the enemy armies and captured the Sinai Peninsula, the Golan Heights, the Gaza Strip (a narrow swath of land running along the western Mediterranean, 26 miles long and four to five miles wide), and the West Bank (the territory, roughly 2,300 square miles, between the Jordan River and the nation of Jordan). Within those territories were nearly a million Palestinian Arabs: Israel had solved one security problem, but now had a new one on its hands.

In the UN Security Council, the United States, and Britain led a small group of democratic countries in linking Israeli withdrawal from the newly occupied territories to a cessation of Arab hostilities against it. The Soviet Union and France led the chorus of Third World states condemning Israel for its "unprovoked aggression" against the Arabs.

France's President De Gaulle, who himself had ambitions for leadership in the Third World, castigated Israel for starting the conflict. Nasser praised his good judgement. When De Gaulle was reminded that Israel had withdrawn from the territories it acquired in the Suez Crisis in part because of French guarantees that it would have access to the Gulf of Aqaba, he replied, "That was 1957. This is 1967."[51]

At an address in Washington on June 19, President Johnson proposed a bold five-point plan for Mideast peace while emphasizing that "the main responsibility for the peace of the region depends upon its own peoples and its own leaders." He called for the withdrawal of Israeli forces from the newly occupied territories, in conjunction with a workable peace agreement that would secure Israel against Arab assaults from those territories. "The first and the greatest principle is that every nation in the area has a fundamental right to live," Johnson said, "and to have this right respected by its neighbors."[52]

The Israeli government offered to return the Sinai to Egypt and the Golan Heights to Syria in exchange for promises of peace, but neither country would accept any agreement that, even implicitly, recognized Israel's right to exist. Meanwhile, the U.S. ambassador to the United Nations, Arthur Goldberg, was working tirelessly to quash Arab-backed resolutions placing blame for the war on Israel, and attempting to advance an American-backed framework for a sustainable peace in the region. The product of that effort, Resolution 242, "Concerning Principles for a Just and Lasting Peace in the Middle East," was passed unanimously by the Security Council on November 22. It called for "termination of all claims or states of belligerency," and for the "withdrawal of Israeli armed forces from territories occupied in the recent conflict." Resolution 242 was to become the starting point of all subsequent peacemaking efforts in the Arab-Israeli dispute for a generation. "Land for peace" was to become the catchphrase of Middle East diplomacy. Neither the Israelis nor the Arabs were entirely satisfied with the Resolution, though Israel and Jordan accepted it. Iraq and Syria, still refusing even to acknowledge the existence of Israel, rejected 242 out of hand. Nasser, having suffered a humiliating defeat, needed time to regroup. He made some obliquely conciliatory statements in public, but in private told his generals, "You don't need to pay any attention to anything I may say in public about a peaceful solution,"[53] and was soon sponsoring renewed violence against Israel. The Palestine Liberation Organization denounced the resolution, reaffirmed its refusal to recognize Israel, and embarked on a new wave of terrorism.

By the end of the year there were several hundred "incidents" monthly of Egyptian military attacks and Israeli retaliation. Within two years Nasser had repudiated the 1967 cease-fire agreement altogether and renewed open, low-level warfare against Israel. Hafez Assad, now the dictator of Syria, was also providing bases and equipment for PLO terrorists operating from his country. "We have never committed ourselves, nor shall we ever do so, to restrict terrorist activities," President Assad boasted. "Syria is the lung through which terrorist activity breathes, and it will remain that."[54] In the West Bank and Gaza, the PLO attempted to foment popular uprisings, planted land mines along roads, and launched attacks against Israelis. The PLO also expanded its operations in Lebanon. By 1972 over 5,000 Palestinian and other Arab guerrillas resided in camps around southern Lebanon, which came to be known as "Fatahland," a state within a state.

Arab terrorism now ranged far beyond Israel. In 1970, seven elderly Jews living in a retirement home in Germany had been slaughtered by Arab terrorists. In Switzerland, forty-seven passengers and crew were killed in an airline bombing. During the Olympic Games at Munich in September 1972, PLO terrorists stormed the Olympic Village and murdered eleven Israeli athletes and two Germans.

President Richard Nixon viewed the Middle East as being of pivotal importance to international stability. He, his national security adviser Henry Kissinger, and his secretary of state William Rogers placed an enduring Arab-Israeli peace near the top of their foreign policy priorities (Vietnam, of course, was the overarching concern); and on February 5, 1969, the incoming president announced that the United States would work to forestall another war in the region by launching a new peace initiative.[55] After months of high-level discussions, in October the administration put forward the "Rogers Plan," a comprehensive agreement that included points on Israeli withdrawal from occupied territories, Egyptian guarantees of Israel's use of the Straits of Tiran and the Suez Canal, "fair settlement" of the refugee problem, and mutual recognition.[56] By his second year in office, though, Nixon, like those before him, had abandoned hope of mediating a final and all-encompassing resolution to the Arab-Israeli dispute and began to focus on achieving more modest, narrow agreements between particular actors on specific issues.

By 1972, Arab leaders were again banging the drums of war. In January, Egyptian premier Aziz Sidky announced the implementation of austerity measures to put the country on a war footing in preparation for "total confrontation" with Israel. Alluding to Arab oil production, he warned the United States that its continued commitment to the existence of Israel was jeopardizing its national interests in the region.

For the first time, Arab leaders were effectively using their greatest resource—the oceans of oil beneath their desert sands—to advance their geopolitical interests. They began cutting production, reducing exports to a world that had grown dependent on their commodity, and they threatened to cut further. As oil exports declined and prices soared, the Arabs believed, the Western nations would reconsider their support for Israel. They did. The "oil weapon" proved to be one of the most effective instruments of foreign policy in history. Oil dependence helped explain why Europe was turning away from support for Israel and toward the Arab side: Britain depended on imports from the Arabs world for 63 percent of its oil; Spain, 69 percent; Italy, 79 percent; France, 77 percent; West Germany, 74 percent.[57] The Third World and the Communist bloc were already solidly with the Arabs. That left only America in unwavering support of Israel. Saudi Arabia's King Faisal issued a statement warning Washington that it would be "extremely difficult" for his nation to continue supplying America with oil, due to America's "complete support of Zionism against the Arabs."[58]

The Arab nations were well armed for a fight and by all indications were preparing for one. From 1970 to 1973 the Soviet Union had supplied hundreds of aircraft and tanks to Egypt and Syria, along with sophisticated anti-tank and antiaircraft missiles that had never before been sent out of the USSR, even to Eastern European allies.[59] "War is now inevitable" Egyptian President Anwar Sadat had told the Egyptian parliament in March 1972. By October, 200,000 troops were massed along the Egyptian side of the Suez.

On Saturday, October 6, Yom Kippur, Judaism's holiest day, Egypt and Syria launched a surprise attack against Israel. An Israeli counterattack in the Sinai on the eighth was repelled, with devastating results. One hundred of 170 IDF tanks were destroyed or abandoned. Defense Minister Moshe Dayan grew despondent and confided to advisers that not a single Israeli tank stood between the Sinai and Tel Aviv.[60] In a meeting with Prime Minister Golda Meir on Tuesday morning, Dayan urged the use of Israel's modest—a couple dozen weapons—nuclear arsenal. Meir refused, for the time being. But nothing could be taken off the table: Meir and Dayan believed, along with most Jews, that an Arab military defeat of Israel would mean another Holocaust.[61]

Henry Kissinger, who had recently replaced Rogers as secretary of state while retaining his post as national security adviser, now dominated U.S. foreign policy-making. (President Nixon was preoccupied with the growing Watergate crisis.) At 1:45 a.m. on Tuesday, the ninth, Israel's ambassador in Washington, Simcha Dinitz, called Kissinger on the phone to plead for American assistance. The IDF was running short of vital supplies and could not sustain a defense for long.

The two men met that morning in the White House, and for the first time the American government was presented with the full scope of Israel's plight. Nearly 50 aircraft had been lost in ninety-six hours, and 500 tanks. There may or may not have been talk about the possible Israeli resort to nuclear weapons in the face of imminent defeat, but in any case Kissinger was convinced. He began pushing for an airlift to resupply the beleaguered Israeli army. In a meeting with key foreign policy advisers that afternoon, Nixon announced that the United States must do everything in its power to prevent Israel from being defeated, which could precipitate a humanitarian catastrophe in Palestine. Ambassador Dinitz had presented the government with a list of urgently needed materials. All required supplies would be provided.

American supply efforts were hampered by the refusal of nearly every European ally to permit overflight of their territory. France, Britain, Italy, West Germany, and Spain, fearful of the Arabs' oil weapon, refused U.S. flyover of their territory to assist Israel. American transport planes could not refuel, land, or even fly over virtually all of Europe. Soviet transport planes, meanwhile, were arriving in Egypt and Syria with ammunition, missiles, and other supplies from bases relatively near to the conflict, in Central and Eastern Europe, and Russia. The Israeli chief of staff was informed that within forty-eight hours there would be insufficient planes and material to keep the air campaign going. They were running out of aircraft, bombs, air-to-air missiles, everything. And without airpower, the war was lost.[62]

Finally, the State Department negotiated permission from Portugal to use Lajes field, in the Azores, as a landing area. Nearly overnight the sleepy airfield, which normally averaged one or two flights daily, became the site of an airlift operation that during its operation exceeded in magnitude the

Berlin airlift. By October 17, fifty tons of American weapons, ammunition, and other desperately needed supplies were arriving in Israel every hour, dwarfing the Soviets' resupply efforts for the Arabs despite Moscow's numerous logistical advantages. Huge C-5s and C-141s unloaded vast amounts of matériel—more than a million and a half pounds of it by the end of the first day.

Saudi Arabia, the world's largest oil producer, threatened to halt all oil exports to the United States if Washington persisted in its support for Israel. Nixon replied that America would not be blackmailed into abandoning Israel. On the twentieth, Saudi Arabia announced a total cessation of all oil exports to the United States. The other Arab oil producers followed, making the oil embargo complete. Other nations were threatened with similar treatment if they supported Israel. The West German Foreign Ministry told the U.S. government that it must halt all shipments to Israel from U.S. bases on German territory, in order for Germany to maintain its "strict neutrality" in the Middle East conflict.[63] Michel Jobert, the French foreign minister, continued to defend the Arab attack, asking whether "trying to set foot on one's own territory necessarily constituted an unexpected aggression."

By the time Secretary of State Kissinger flew to Moscow on the nineteenth to negotiate terms for a cease-fire, Israel had clearly taken the upper hand, completing an encirclement of Egyptian troops on the eastern bank of the Suez. Kissinger hoped to delay the talks long enough for Israel to weaken the Egyptian army a little more, but without waiting so long that the Egyptians became routed and humiliated, in which case prospects for peace after the war would be diminished. By the twenty-first, Sadat was making urgent calls to the Soviet ambassador, imploring the Kremlin to "take all possible measures to arrange an immediate cease-fire."[64] The agreement reached by Kissinger and Soviet Premier Leonid Brezhnev became the basis of Security Council Resolution 338, which called for a cease-fire within twelve hours of its adoption, implementation of Resolution 242, and for the parties to undertake negotiations for "a just and durable peace in the Middle East."[65]

The Security Council adopted the U.S.-Soviet backed resolution by a vote of 14–0. Three days later the Security Council voted 14–0 for a resolution establishing a United Nations peacekeeping force to be positioned in the Sinai between the Egyptian and Israeli troops. Ultimately most of the funding would come from the United States.

The conflict had convinced Anwar Sadat that the United States held the key to stability in the region, and he requested Secretary Kissinger to mediate peace discussions. Kissinger agreed. On November 7 the State Department announced the resumption of diplomatic relations with Egypt, severed since the 1967 conflict, and on the ninth a peace plan was announced, negotiated by Kissinger in intense discussions with Arab and Israeli leaders, which called for strict adherence to the UN cease-fire, access to provisions for the encircled Third Army, and discussions between Egypt and Israel on return to the October 22 positions. The two nations signed the accord on November 11 and began exchanging prisoners a few days later.

Arab oil-producing nations announced another 25 percent cut in production and outlined a rating system so that pro-Arab states would not be hurt by the cuts. For Americans, the embargo meant oil shortages, long lines at gasoline pumps, and spiraling fuel prices. But the oil extortion did not induce Americans to abandon their support for Israel. A poll showed that two-thirds of Americans favored continued support for Israel, even if it meant further oil shortages and further increases in gas prices.[66] The United States stood by embattled Israel, and its own principles, even at great economic cost to itself. Ultimately oil prices quadrupled.

Elsewhere, nations were clamoring to get on the Arabs' good side. On November 14, Singapore's prime minister Lee Kuan Yew, under the threat of an oil cutoff, announced that his country would repudiate contracts to supply fuel to U.S. military forces in the Pacific. European governments ignored Egypt's surprise attack on Yom Kippur and scrambled to reiterate opposition to Israeli "aggression." Belgium, previously considered neutral, shifted to the pro-Arab position. The Dutch government reversed its policy, issuing a statement calling for withdrawal of Israel from the occupied territories, and denouncing the Israeli presence as "illegal." Italy and West Germany grew increasingly vocal in their demands for unconditional Israeli withdrawal, and soon they were added to the list of the Arabs' Most Favored Nations. With its economy reeling from the "oil shock," on November 22 the Japanese government called on Israel to withdraw from Arab territories captured in 1967, and threatened to break off relations if it failed to do so. The Japanese foreign minister met with ten ambassadors from Arab states to inform them of a shift in Japan's Mideast policy to a pro-Arab stance.[67]

On November 14, with the military crisis over, the United States ended its massive airlift to Israel. In all, nearly 600 transport plane flights had carried over 22,000 tons of equipment and supplies to Israel during the four perilous weeks, replacing losses incurred in the fighting and enabling Israel to maintain its defensive campaign. Israel had had only one real ally in the world, but it was the right one. When at the height of the emergency Prime Minister Meir visited an airfield to survey the monumental American supply effort, she fought back tears at the sight of it. "For generations to come," she said, "all will be told of the immense planes from the United States."[68]

———•———

Like presidents before him, Jimmy Carter came to office in January 1977 with high hopes of using American power and influence to help bring about a just and lasting peace to the Middle East. The Holy Land was a region in which the devout Baptist, like many Americans, took a deep personal interest.

The United States was now recognized by nearly all involved as the only actor capable of bringing the contentious sides to the bargaining table and making progress there. "Americans hold ninety-nine percent of the cards in the Middle East," Sadat said.

Within four months after taking office, Jimmy Carter had met with the individuals most crucial to peace in the Middle East and was encouraged that a significant breakthrough was within reach. Jimmy Carter's concern for the situation in the region was deep, genuine, and needed little prodding. "Looking back," he later recalled, "it is remarkable to see how constantly the work for peace in the Middle East was on my agenda, and on my mind."[69] In early 1978, Carter undertook an exhaustive trip through the region to keep the peace process moving forward. But the impasse seemed insoluble. On July 26 he received a message from President Sadat saying that negotiations between Egypt and Israel were getting nowhere, and that further discussions between the two sides could not be justified.

Some dramatic new initiative was urgently needed, lest the entire momentum toward peace be lost. On August 3, President Carter sent letters to Begin and Sadat, inviting them to meet together with him, to discuss peace between their nations. "Although recent discussions have produced minimal progress," he wrote to Begin, "broad areas of agreement do exist, providing the basis for sustained hope." Carter informed the leaders that the presidential retreat at Camp David was available as a possible site for the meeting, though "I have no strong preference" as to location. Both men accepted the invitation.

Camp David, Maryland, verdant and cool, a tranquil mountain sanctuary, is as removed as one could possibly be from the heat and ancient animosities of the Middle East. For thirteen days the attention of the world was upon it, the hopes for peace and the destiny of an entire region.

On Tuesday, September 5, 1978, the three heads of state descended with their entourages in a fleet of helicopters upon the rural retreat. Anwar Sadat offered his plan in a meeting with Carter on Wednesday morning. It was lengthy (eleven pages) and detailed formula that Carter immediately recognized to be a nonstarter. It called for total Israeli withdrawal from all occupied territories, demolition of all Israeli settlements, self-determination for Palestinians, and compensation or right of return for refugees who had left Israel. But Sadat also advised Carter in advance of a number of concessions that he would be willing to make at critical junctures in the talks, including full normalization of diplomatic and economic relations, limitations on the Palestinian right of return, and acquiescence on Israeli control over all of Jerusalem.[70]

Still, the gap between Begin and Sadat remained wide. The former enemies met together for the first time that afternoon, with Carter present, and Begin sat silently as Sadat read his long proposal. When the three leaders met again the following day, Begin went over the Egyptian proposal point by point, giving his reasons for rejecting each one. Sadat accused him of wanting land more than peace. They both got up and began walking to the door, prepared to break off negotiations, but Carter blocked their way, refusing to let them leave until they had agreed to at least let him try to work out a plan agreeable to both sides. Both remained at Camp David, but any goodwill that may have existed at the beginning of the process had been dissipated. It would be up to the Americans to generate a proposal. The two leaders were not to speak to one another until the summit was over, and a peace accord was ready to be signed.

For the next week the two old warriors clung tenaciously to their initial positions. Israel would not withdraw from its settlements and military installations in the Sinai. Egypt would not make peace unless the problems of the West Bank and Gaza were resolved. Tension and distrust pervaded the "talks" in which neither of the principal actors would talk to the other. The delegations communicated through President Carter or his advisers or, commonly, not at all.

On Friday the fifteenth, Sadat, convinced that nothing further could be accomplished by staying, packed his bags and told the Egyptian delegation to prepare to leave. President Carter went to Sadat's cabin and implored him not to go, citing consequences to Sadat's reputation among Arab nations, to relations between the United States and Egypt, and to their friendship. Sadat agreed to stay two more days.

In discussions with the Israeli delegation, the Americans had become convinced that there was room for maneuver on the Sinai problem. After intense negotiations, and with the support of Moshe Dayan (now Israel's foreign minister), Begin agreed to withdraw from airfields that Israel had built in the Sinai, if the United States would help pay for the construction of new bases in the Negev Desert. Carter agreed. That left the settlements, which Begin had taken a solemn public oath never to give up. Members of the prime minister's own delegation advocated compromise, and leaders of his own and opposition parties in Israel were pressing for some agreement. Hard-liner Ariel Sharon, now agriculture minister, told Begin in a phone call not to let settlements in the Sinai be the obstacle to a peace agreement with Egypt. Finally, Carter proposed a plan that would extricate Begin from personal responsibility for the withdrawal: the question would be put before the Knesset to decide. In that way the final obstacle to a historic agreement between the two nations was overcome.

The problem of the West Bank and Gaza proved more intractable. Carter finally managed to get Sadat to relinquish his demand for total Israeli withdrawal and settle instead for a provision calling for self-determination for Palestinians, reaffirming Resolution 242 and including an "exchange of letters" in which the United States reiterated its position that East Jerusalem was part of the West Bank. In reality the problem was simply being put off for resolution at some future time rather than allow it to become a barrier to the achievement of any agreement at all.

The Camp David Accords did not terminate the Middle East conflict. It had persisted for generations, millennia, and it would not be resolved in a few weeks of discussions. But the history of the region had come to a crossroads, and taken a new direction. An Arab state had, for the first time ever, recognized Israel's right to exist, and promised to make peace. In a land where since 1948 there had been unrelenting hostility and conflict, that in itself marked a watershed.

In a ceremony in the East Room of the White House on Sunday, September 17, Carter, Begin, and Sadat signed the Camp David Accords. "After four wars during thirty years, the Middle East, which is a cradle of civilization and the birthplace of three great religions, does not yet enjoy the blessings of peace . . . " declared the preamble. "[Egypt and Israel] are determined to reach a just, comprehensive and durable settlement of the Middle East conflict through the conclusion of peace treaties. . . . Their purpose is to achieve peace and good neighborly relations."

It was only a beginning. Other Arab states immediately renounced the Camp David Accords, denounced Sadat as a traitor, and threatened the expulsion of Egypt from the Arab League, along with economic retaliation, if it signed a peace treaty with Israel. In Israel, Begin was criticized by hardliners for giving up land in exchange for mere promises.

Camp David had been a starting point, not a destination. Carter had hoped that the destination, a peace treaty between Israel and Egypt—and the beginnings of a comprehensive peace for the region—would be achieved by year's end.

By November, though, some observers were predicting that peace might not be achieved at all. There were immense obstacles to success. The Accords had been roundly condemned in the Arab world, and Sadat was facing both foreign and domestic pressures to repudiate them. Israelis were worried that once Israel had given up Sinai, Egypt would return to belligerency. The ruler of Iran, Shah Reza Pahlavi, an American ally and one of the relative moderates in the region, faced growing unrest from Islamic fundamentalists who wished to establish a theocracy there. Shortly, he would be out. The Organization of Petroleum Exporting Countries (OPEC) continued to raise oil prices, helping to fuel inflation and slowing growth in the United States and world economies. Lebanon, once an oasis of stability and tolerance in the Middle East, was collapsing into a dark hole of sectarian violence from which it would not emerge for decades. Begin had announced plans to expand Israeli settlements in the West Bank. The peace talks had broken down.

It was increasingly apparent that without more active American involvement to move the process along, the two sides would remain deadlocked. Carter sent Secretary of State Cyrus Vance on a trip through the Middle East in December to restart the negotiations. In mid-February, he invited Israeli foreign minister Dayan and Egyptian prime minister Mustafa Khalil to Camp David for further discussions. On March 2 he met with Begin at the White House, and on the seventh embarked on a trip to Cairo and Jerusalem. After heated discussions with the two nations' leaders, and at times close to giving up in despair, on March 13 a breakthrough was made, when Begin agreed to turn over the Alma oil fields in the Sinai if the United States would guarantee its supply. UN peacekeeping forces would provide a buffer between the two sides, and the United States promised to support Israel if Egypt violated the treaty. In addition, America had promised billions of dollars in aid annually to each nation.

On March 26, 1979, Carter, Begin, and Sadat met for another signing ceremony at the White House, this one on the north lawn. It was not the all-encompassing solution to the Mideast conflict that Carter had hoped for during his early months in office, but the peace treaty was indeed an event of epic historical importance. During the grueling Camp David negotiations, in which he had worked to exhaustion as both mediator and advocate, Carter had scribbled a line to himself in the margin of a page of notes when an agreement seemed near: "First Egyptian-Jewish peace since time of Joseph." Then, he crossed out "Joseph," and penned in "Jeremiah."[71]

The success confirmed the view of both sides that America was the only nation capable of acting as an honest broker in the region, able to mediate further progress toward peace. Accompanying the treaty were letters of understanding from both Begin and Sadat, which stressed that the United States was to be fully involved in negotiations over the Palestinian issue and subsequent Egyptian-Israeli negotiations.[72]

Would peace have been made between the two nations without American participation? The fact is that, in the absence of U.S. involvement, they *weren't* moving toward peace. Indeed, without American security guarantees for Israel, there is no reason to believe that the Arabs would have ever abandoned their rejection of its very existence. With American support, the survival of Israel was assured. Sadat had come to grips with that reality, as other Arab leaders would have to do.

The Middle East was a dangerous place to be a peacemaker. On October 6, 1981, President Sadat was assassinated by Islamic extremists opposed to peace with Israel. Other developments in the region were also unpromising. During the late 1970s and early '80s, France had facilitated the acquisition of nuclear technology by Iraqi dictator Saddam Hussein, who was pledged to the elimination of the state of Israel. Hussein, who controlled one of the largest oil reserves in the world, insisted that he was building a nuclear reactor for strictly peaceful purposes, but Israeli intelligence reports indicated that he was pursuing the development of a nuclear weapon capability. On June 7, Israeli fighter jets attacked and destroyed the Iraqi reactor.

In September, President Ronald Reagan, Carter's successor, proposed a new formula for a broad Middle East peace, which called for a self-governing polity in Palestine and a freeze on new Israeli settlements in the occupied territories.[73] Israel continued to resist U.S. pressures to halt settlement construction in the occupied territories, and from 1982 to 1986 the number of

Israeli settlers there tripled. On April 18, 1983, a suicide bomber whom Islamic clerics had promised immediate entry into Paradise for killing enemies of Islam, exploded a van loaded with a ton of explosives outside the American embassy in Beirut, killing 63, including 17 Americans. The terrorist group Islamic Jihad claimed responsibility for the attack. Members of Congress began calling for the withdrawal of U.S. forces from Lebanon, but President Reagan still held out hopes for the precarious peace agreement between Lebanon and Israel, and was reluctant to abandon Lebanon to the Syrians.

Then, in the predawn of October 23, another suicide bomber drove a truck full of explosives through the security barricades outside the barracks of the U.S. Marine peacekeeping forces in Beirut. The explosion killed 241 Marines as they slept and seriously wounded another 80. Fifty-eight French peacekeepers were killed when a bomb was simultaneously detonated outside the French compound in Beirut. Again, Islamic Jihad claimed responsibility for both bombings. In early 1984, Reagan withdrew the Marines from Beirut, and the Lebanese government, now fully under Syrian control, repudiated its peace agreement with Israel.

In Palestine on December 8, 1987, after four Palestinians were killed in an auto accident with an Israeli troop carrier, demonstrations began as a spontaneous, largely unorganized reaction, but quickly became organized for specific political goals. PLO leaders, detached and ineffectual, were not the driving force. A fundamentalist group called Hamas (meaning "enthusiasm," and also an Arabic acronym for Islamic Resistance Movement) emerged in leadership, and soon set forth a list of objectives for the *intifada* (a term it first used in the crisis, meaning "a shaking off," or, roughly, "uprising"): wage holy war against the Zionists; oppose all peace efforts; bring the Arab states to true Islam, and into the conflict.[74]

Facing a crisis in the occupied territories, and with a growing number of Israelis questioning whether the occupation was serving Israel's security interests at all, Shamir wrote a six-page letter to Secretary of State George Shultz, asking for a new American initiative to bring peace to the region, and suggesting that Israel might alter its position on Palestinian "autonomy."

After two extended trips to the region in two months, and detailed discussions with all the key actors—including leaders of Jordan, Egypt, Israel, Syria, the Soviets, and individual Palestinians—in March 1988, Shultz announced a new American proposal to move the peace process forward. The Shultz Plan, as it came to be called, involved linking negotiations on the transitional arrangements for the occupied territories' with negotiations on their "final status."[75] Shultz embarked upon a flurry of diplomacy to rally support for his plan, making repeated trips to Middle Eastern capitals, with little to show for his efforts.

With the election of George Bush, Reagan's vice president, to the presidency in 1988, the basic American approach to the Arab-Israeli dispute continued to be that the United States would work to foster peace in the region, but could not impose it.[76] Anti-Westernism, and especially anti-American and anti-Israeli sentiment, was surging in the region, animated by two very different ideologies: the Islamic fundamentalism of Iran's theocratic regime, and the pan-Arabism of Saddam Hussein, dictator of Iraq, who conceived himself the leader of a resurgent and united Arab world that would stand up to the West and Israel. In Palestine the *intifada* was degenerating into anarchic violence between the Palestinians themselves. They were murdering each other for religious impiety, perceived deviation from fundamentalist Islamic morality, suspected collaboration, even association with Jews. Ultimately more Palestinians than Jews were killed by Palestinians during the *intifada*. By 1991 the *intifada* had dissipated itself in exhaustion and confusion.

Although in speaking of the "Middle East conflict" one is generally referring to that between the Arabs and the Israelis, there has during the same period been almost incessant conflicts *between* various Arab nations, which have exacted a far greater toll in human lives. One of the most brutal of these was the conflict between Iran (run by an oppressive fundamentalist Islamist theocracy) and Iraq (run by an oppressive secular dictator). A year after becoming president, Hussein launched a war against neighbor Iran, which had both oil that he wanted and a fundamentalist Shi'ah Islamic government that he feared. Its leader, the Ayatollah Khomeini, had led a populist uprising against the pro-American Shah, who had been secular and one of the relative moderates in the region. Hussein, a Sunni, feared the spread of fundamentalism to his own country, where the Shi'ah majority were violently oppressed. When Khomeini took power in Iran, he staged a bloody purge of army officers loyal to the Shah, leaving the military weakened. Hussein saw an opening, and in September 1980 invaded western Iran. After a year of fighting, recognizing that the war was going to be more difficult than anticipated, Hussein offered a truce. The Ayatollah, pledging to destroy Iraq's secular regime and replace it with a theocracy, refused. The pieces were in place for a brutal and protracted struggle.

The Iraqi dictator received support from an unlikely assemblage of benefactors: from oil-rich Arab sheikhdoms that also feared the rising tide of fundamentalism beginning to sweep across the region; from France, which Hussein had for years cultivated as a supplier of military goods; from the USSR, which had its own Islamic population and fears of fundamentalism to cope with; and, sporadically, from the United States, which had become the chief locus of hostility, the "Great Satan" for the Ayatollah's fundamentalist revolution, and whose citizens had been made targets by it.

The war raged from 1980 to 1988, with virtually no movement by either side. The two nations fought to an exhausted stalemate, with boundaries precisely where they had been at the start of the murderous conflict, which had resulted in the deaths of an estimated half million Iranians and 300,000 Iraqis. They agreed to a cease-fire in July 1988, and each side declared victory.

Hussein had established absolute control over his own society, through mass murders, torture, a highly developed cult of personality, and a Soviet-style secret police. He also possessed the largest military in the region, over a million men under arms, which needed to be kept busy. His military buildup had put the country deeply into debt, its economy was in shambles, and Hussein's own reputation within the Arab world had been tarnished. He looked around for ways to reestablish himself as the region's paramount leader.

In 1990, Hussein grew increasingly belligerent toward Iraq's tiny neighbor to the south, Kuwait, accusing it of "economic warfare" through oil overproduction, and of "stealing" Iraqi oil through production at the Rumalia oil field, which spans the Iraq-Kuwait border. On August 2 the Iraqi army invaded Kuwait and within a day had overrun the tiny kingdom. From the beginning, President Bush took the lead in reversing the aggression. Bush had come to the presidency as Soviet Communism was collapsing and the Cold War winding down. In the post–Cold War era he had envisioned a revitalized community of nations, a "new world order," in which the world's nations cooperated to stem international aggression and advance democracy and human rights. The invasion of Kuwait was a flagrant challenge to that vision. Though the Bush administration had worked to foster cordial diplomatic relations with the Iraqi leader (who was regarded as a potential counterbalance to surging fundamentalist extremism), and had in 1989 issued a National Security Directive declaring that the United States "wished to improve relations with Iraq," Bush immediately denounced the invasion, froze all Kuwaiti and Iraqi assets in the United States, imposed a trade embargo on Iraq, and threatened worse to come if it did not withdraw. "This will not stand," the president declared.

At the United Nations, by a vote of 14–0 (Yemen abstained), the Security Council adopted an American-backed resolution that condemned the invasion and demanded an immediate withdrawal of Iraqi troops. American power would have been more than sufficient to dislodge the Iraqi forces, but, in accord with his goal of international cooperation, Bush pursued the creation of an international coalition to reverse the aggression. Facing stronger international opposition than he had anticipated, Saddam Hussein attempted to alter the terms of the conflict. On the tenth he called for Muslims to launch a jihad, or holy war, against the Saudi rulers, to liberate Islam's holy cities, Mecca and Medina, from the "worldly" regime, a transparent ploy from one of the Arab world's most secular rulers. Over 50,000 Iraqi soldiers were now poised along the Saudi border. Hussein warned that if the United States attempted to dislodge his forces from Kuwait, there would ensue "the mother of all battles."

By mid-January there were some 425,000 American soldiers, and an additional 300,000 ground troops from 18 other countries, along with ships from another 13. Hussein had more tanks (4,700 to the Coalition's 3,500) and artillery on the field, but the Coalition's mostly American equipment was vastly superior, and its air and sea dominance would be overwhelming.[77]

On January 12 the U.S. Congress voted to approve the use of military force to remove the Iraqi army from Kuwait. The vote was close (52–47 in the Senate; 250–183 in the House). The issues involved were not easy ones. Both Kuwait and Saudi Arabia were repressive oligarchies. Neither were democratic, or permitted any meaningful political opposition. Neither observed fundamental individual rights of free speech, press, or religion. In accord with Islamic tradition, their women were treated as second-class citizens (or, in the vernacular of fundamentalism, put on pedestals), cloaked behind incarcerating veils, and barred from the political, social, and economic life of the society. Critics of the intervention complained that America was rallying world opinion to defend undemocratic societies and to defend oil supplies. They were right on both counts.

If in diplomacy you insist upon dealing only with admirable regimes, you will find yourself with absolutely no influence upon the events of the world a great deal of the time. Neither Saudi Arabia nor Kuwait were free or democratic, but they were far preferable to any realistic near-term alternatives.

And yes, Saudi Arabia and Kuwait were vital suppliers of oil to the West. What? National self-interest played a part in the decision? The very notion seemed to alarm some idealists. It is excellent for a nation to defend its ideals in foreign affairs, but one that will not defend its interests will soon be able to defend neither. Furthermore, with Hussein as impresario of Middle East oil, he would be even better positioned to finance his known penchant for the development of biological, chemical, and nuclear weapons. Another, more catastrophic war against Israel would have been only a matter of time. Polls showed that 75 percent of Americans supported going to war to oust Iraqi forces from Kuwait.

Only the PLO, Jordan, Libya, and Sudan supported Iraq's aggression, though antiwar demonstrators protested in major American and European cities. French president Francois Mitterand engaged in extensive negotiations with Hussein in hopes of staving off the impending conflict with Iraq. France was its most important supplier of Western technology—including over $15 billion in weaponry during the preceding decade—and stood to lose the most, along with Russia, if the Iraqi leader was toppled from power. Hussein undertook a variety of stratagems to split the Coalition—attempting to rally Arab nations against Israel and its U.S. patron, and warning Europeans of American hegemony, but with little effect.

At the eleventh hour, Mitterand proposed that the United Nations agree in advance to hold an international conference to discuss Hussein's grievances on the Palestinian problem if he agreed to withdraw, but the UN had already called for unconditional withdrawal, and the French proposal was rejected.

The Bush administration had pressed the United Nations for a specific deadline for Iraqi withdrawal from Kuwait. On January 15 that deadline passed. Two days later, in the predawn hours of the seventeenth, the air campaign portion of Operation Desert Storm began. Tomahawk cruise missiles fired from ships in the Persian Gulf struck Iraqi command-and-control targets hundreds of miles away. Apache helicopters attacked positions near the border. Stealth fighter-bombers attacked air defense systems, airfields, missile launchers, command centers, and weapons sites. So effective was their radar-evading technology that enemy antiaircraft defenses often did not respond until the bombs were exploding and the planes were on their way home.[78]

Hussein ordered the destruction of Kuwait's oil wells, creating an environmental catastrophe but having little effect on the overall course of the war. Within ten days after the air war began, Coalition aircraft had established air supremacy.

After Hussein had rejected repeated ultimatums to withdraw his troops from Kuwait, the ground war was launched on February 24. By the twenty-seventh, Coalition forces had entered Kuwait city to jubilant crowds. In the Iraqi desert, units of what was left of the elite Republican Guard were being decimated. Iraqi POWs now approached 100,000. A greater number had simply deserted. Fewer than 20,000 soldiers remained in anything resembling military formation.[79] With Coalition troops driving toward Baghdad, the Iraqi ambassador to the United Nations announced that his government would accept the Security Council's resolution calling for unconditional withdrawal from Kuwait.

The Iraqi army was routed. Saddam's infrastructure of control was in disarray. Coalition forces appeared poised to deliver a death blow to the regime. Then, in a momentous decision, Bush stopped the war. Joint Chiefs chairman Colin Powell and other military leaders had warned of huge losses in the event of street fighting in Baghdad. In addition, the UN resolutions had only called for the expulsion of Iraqi forces from Kuwait, which had now been accomplished. The French and Russians were demanding an immediate cessation of all fighting. To go on would have ruptured the Coalition and alienated the Arab states. Bush stopped. Hussein remained in power; weakened, but in control of his country. He would rebuild and reconsolidate.

In international politics, nothing succeeds like success. The overwhelming military triumph of the American-led coalition, the cooperation of most Arab states in the alliance, the disintegration of the Soviet Union, and the emergence of the United States as the sole global superpower all helped recast the region's political milieu. Seizing the opportunity, the Bush administration launched an ambitious new effort to revive the stalled Arab-Israeli peace process. Bush was committed to using the global political capital achieved by the victory to press for a broad Middle East peace. "We must do all that we can to close the gap between Israel and the Arab states and between Israelis and Palestinians," he said to Congress days after the end of the war. "The time has come to put an end to the Arab-Israeli conflict."[80]

During the first eight months following the Gulf War, Secretary of State James Baker traveled to the region eight times, meeting with key Arab and Israeli leaders, developing the framework for an international conference to address the long-standing sources of contention. In June, President Bush sent invitations to Israeli prime minister Shamir, Syria's Assad, Jordan's King Hussein, Saudi Arabia's King Fahd, and Egypt's President Mubarak, outlining his plan for an international peace conference to be held in Madrid in October. The General Conference, which was to include delegations from Israel, Syria, Lebanon, Jordan (including Palestinian representatives), Egypt, the European Community, the USSR, and the United States, would consider region-wide issues such as water usage, economic development, and the environment, but would have no authority to impose solutions. Of greater importance would be a series of bilateral talks between Israel and each of its Arab neighbors, and between Israel and the Palestinians.

The Madrid Conference was a landmark in Middle East history, not so much for any substantive agreements reached (which were few) as for the nature of the process itself. Israel was now, for the first time ever, in direct diplomatic discussions with Arab states that had not long before refused even to acknowledge its existence; and with the Palestinians (and indirectly, the PLO).

The altered international environment was manifested in other ways, too. In December 1991, after intense American diplomatic efforts, the UN General Assembly, by a vote of 111 to 25 (with 13 abstentions), finally rescinded its 1975 resolution which had denounced Zionism as "a form of racism." There was, in addition, no longer any doubt but among the most fanatical Islamists that the state of Israel was there to stay.

Bush's successor Bill Clinton continued to work for a resolution to the age-old Middle-East conflict. At the White House on July 25, 1994, Prime Minister Rabin and King Hussein of Jordan issued the "Washington Declaration," a framework for negotiations and a pledge to forge a treaty between their two nations. The Declaration proclaimed that "the state of belligerency between Israel and Jordan has been terminated" and promised the development of "good neighborly relations of cooperation between [Jordan and Israel] to ensure lasting security and to avoid the threats and the use of force between them."[81] At the signing ceremony on the White House lawn, King Hussein declared, "What we have accomplished, and what we are committed to, is the end of the state of war between Jordan and Israel." To advance the agreement, the United States forgave over $700 million in Jordanian debt.

With the help of tenacious American diplomacy, the political climate of the Middle East apparently had been transformed. Less than a generation earlier it had been political—and sometimes, literal—suicide for an Arab leader even to sit down with an Israeli leader. Now there was meaningful dialogue between Israel and most of the Arab world. The number of nations recognizing the state of Israel, now 150, was double that of a decade earlier.

And Israel had entered into a historic peace agreements with a second key neighbor. On October 26, 1994, at Wadi Araba, Jordan, Clinton looked on as a peace treaty was signed between Israel and Jordan, two nations which, not long before, had been mortal rivals.

———◆———

On the morning of September 11, 2001, the world changed when nineteen Arab terrorists hijacked four American airliners, flying two of them into the World Trade Center Towers in New York and one into the side of the Pentagon. The fourth hijacked plane crashed into a field in Pennsylvania as passengers on board valiantly struggled to wrest control of the plane from the hijackers, in order to prevent it from becoming an instrument in a similar catastrophe. Approximately 260 passengers aboard the planes were killed, 120 men and women inside the Pentagon, and almost 3,000 in the collapse of the World Trade Center Towers, including hundreds of New York City police and firefighters who had rushed to the scene to provide emergency assistance. It was by far the largest terrorist attack in history, and the largest attack on American soil since Pearl Harbor. There had been attacks before, but Americans had generally felt insulated from terrorism. No longer.

President George W. Bush, son of the former president Bush, vowed to launch a "war on terror" and rallied world opinion and the support of international leaders to its cause. The first target in that campaign was Afghanistan, home to the fundamentalist Islamic theocracy Taliban, and haven for the al-Qaida terrorist network responsible for the 9/11 attacks, and its leader, Saudi-born Osama bin Laden. The terrorism highlighted the rise of extremist religious fundamentalism throughout the region, whose hatred was not fundamentally of America, but of modernity itself. The United States, the leader of the free nations, and not coincidentally a supporter of Israel, simply made the most obvious target.

In Afghanistan, under Taliban rule women were barred from education or any work outside the home. Houses with women in them had to have their windows painted, lest anyone see the female inside and be tempted to impure thoughts. Women who did venture outside were beaten with rubber hoses by roaming squads of "Morality Police" if they had any part of their skin showing. Men were beaten for excessively shaving their beards and other offenses. Television and cinema were prohibited, as were such leisure activities as kite-flying and reading most books. Spreading non-Muslim ideas was punishable by imprisonment. Those convicted of adultery were stoned, and other suspected moral offenders were shot in mass public executions. Hindus and other non-Muslims were ordered to wear distinguishing yellow symbols. It is no wonder that to such a regime and its adherents, the free people of America seemed a threat.

Critics warned of a long and protracted war, pointing to the Soviet Union's debacle in Afghanistan. However, military operations began on

October 7, and within weeks the repressive Taliban regime had been removed from power, key al-Qaida camps were destroyed, and an interim government was paving the way for a more free and democratic society.

More long-term terror concerns involved weapons of mass destruction—chemical, biological, or nuclear—with which a single terrorist could inflict incalculable damage upon a population. Iraq's Saddam Hussein had been known to use chemical weapons on his own people, killing hundreds of thousands, and had attempted to acquire a nuclear weapons capability. For years following the Gulf War he had played a cat-and-mouse game with UN weapons inspectors, and most analysts believed that he had failed to destroy all of his weapons of mass destruction, as mandated by the UN. Citing evidence of Hussein's continuing efforts to obtain nuclear and other WMDs, in September 2002, President Bush challenged the United Nations to confront the "grave and gathering danger" presented by Iraq or stand aside and let the United States and its allies do it. In February 2003, U.S. secretary of state Colin Powell made a presentation to the Security Council using satellite pictures and other evidence purporting to show that Iraq was secretly continuing to develop weapons of mass destruction. Bush worked to construct a coalition of nations to assist and sanction the American effort to oust Hussein, though to many observers his diplomatic style smacked of unilateralism and hubris. British prime minister Tony Blair remained a steadfast ally, even as his support for the war eroded his approval ratings at home. France and Russia, reluctant partners in the first Gulf War, attempted to rally international opposition. In a nationwide television address on March 6, President Bush again warned of Iraqi weapons of mass destruction and said that the United States was prepared to go to war unilaterally if necessary to disarm Hussein. "We will not wait to see what terrorists or terrorist states could do with weapons of mass destruction."

The war commenced on March 20 with missile attacks on key military sites, and in four days U.S. Army forces were within a seventy miles of Baghdad. By early April, Hussein's brutal and repressive regime had been destroyed. Crowds celebrated in the streets, toppling giant statues and defacing murals of the man who had ruled their nation by violence and intimidation for decades. For the Americans and their coalition partners, though, the most daunting part of the undertaking had just begun.

In the wake of the stunning military victory, President Bush determined to use the hard-won political capital to press for a renewal of the stalled Mideast peace process. And so, on April 30, 2003, yet another American administration advanced yet another initiative to bring greater peace and stability to the Middle East. President Bush's "Roadmap for Mideast Peace," developed in cooperation with Russia, the European Union, and the United Nations and issued with their support, outlined a path toward a permanent status agreement on Palestine, ultimately including the establishment of a Palestinian state. The Roadmap called for the Palestinian authority to restrain groups involved in terrorism, and for Arab states to cut off all funding to those groups; for the development of a draft constitution for a democratic Palestinian state and the appointment of an interim prime minister; for the freezing of all Israeli settlement activity; for international assistance in Palestinian economic development.

At a summit of Arab leaders at Sharm el-Sheikh on June 3, Bush pledged to "work with all the parties concerned" to achieve the vision of a "Palestinian state that is free and at peace." The following day in Aqaba, Jordan, he joined in a historic meeting with Palestinian prime minister Mahmoud Abbas and Israeli prime minister Sharon, both of whom expressed support for the Roadmap. Once again, American persistence—and pressure—had helped achieve a breakthrough. The Tel Aviv newspaper *Ma'ariv* wrote that "It was not the change in Sharon, if at all, that now moves the paralyzed wheels of the peace process. . . . Bush is investing the political prestige and political fortune he acquired [in the victory over Saddam Hussein]."[82] Prime Minister Sharon was now openly calling for an end to the "occupation," and Palestinian prime minister Abas condemned the "folly" of the *intifada*. There would be many obstacles along the path to peace, but by January 2005 both Afghanistan and Iraq had held democratic elections, the first and second in the history of the Arab world. Both had been held under American aegis. After the first free election in Iraq's history, the German magazine *Der Spiegel*, which had been vehemently critical of America's policy in Iraq, asked "Could George W. Bush Be Right?" It observed that, "Reagan, when he demanded that Gorbachev remove the Berlin Wall, turned out to be right. Could history repeat itself? Europeans today—just like the Europeans of 1987—cannot imagine that the world might change. . . . But in a country of immigrants like the United States, one actually pushes for change. We Europeans always wanted to have the world from yesterday, whereas the Americans strive for the world of tomorrow."[83]

In the Middle East, a land of ancient civilizations and ancient animosities, it helps to take the long view. At the dawn of the new millennium, democracy and perpetual peace were not at hand. But just half a century earlier, when the modern state of Israel was born from a United Nations partition of Palestine, its existence was immediately denounced by its Arab neighbors, and every nation in the region pledged its destruction. As the twenty-first century began, all but the most fanatical Arab political and religious leaders had come to accept the existence of Israel. Israelis and Palestinians were negotiating on a two-state solution in Palestine, with the destination seeming at last in sight. And liberty was, though haltingly, taking root in a region that had never known it before. It would not have happened without American involvement in the Middle East, which was vital, just, and honorable.

Taming the Red Dragon

DURING THE EARLY decades of the twentieth century, American activity in China was mainly private and philanthropic, not political or commercial. In 1914 the United States accounted for just 3.1 percent of foreign investment there; by 1931 it still stood at only 6.1 percent of the total.[1] Americans spoke of a "special relationship" with the Chinese people and were the largest source of foreign assistance to them. Grade schools, universities, hospitals, YMCAs, and other public service programs were established with the aid of millions of dollars of American charitable donations and the involvement of thousands of American teachers, doctors, and missionaries.

China's imperial system was already disintegrating when Mao Zedong was born into a moderately prosperous peasant family in rural Hunan province in 1893, the oldest of three boys who survived childbirth. Just months after his birth, a more modern Japan defeated a backward and insular China in 1894 and imposed a humiliating treaty on it. In 1931, Japan created the puppet state of Manchukuo, in Manchuria, and installed the last Chinese emperor, Puyi, as figurehead chief executive.

In 1937, Japan—already in possession of Manchuria—had staged the incident at the Marco Polo Bridge and used it as a pretext for an invasion of China. An isolationist American public decried the aggression but opposed intervention to halt it. Over the following months, reports of Japanese atrocities helped stir public sympathy, and growing awareness of Japan's larger territorial ambitions convinced Roosevelt and other leaders that Chinese resistance to Japanese aggression was a matter of U.S. national security. "The peace of the world is tied up with China's ability to win or prolong its resistance to Japanese aggression," Roosevelt declared. "A Japanese victory increases greatly the chances of a general world war."[2] *Time* magazine featured the Generalissimo and Madame Chiang as "Man and Wife of the Year." In 1938, Roosevelt approved a $25 million credit to Chiang's Nationalist government, to help finance its resistance against the Japanese.

Chiang Kai-shek, like Mao, was first of all a self-promoter. He shrewdly cultivated his reputation in the United States as "China's Christian warrior," established himself in the American mind as the undisputed leader of the Chinese people, hired Washington insiders to lobby the administration for more aid, and dispatched his passionate and eloquent wife on speaking tours across the United States to rally public support. Madame Chiang moved audiences with tearful addresses on how her husband hoped to build a more democratic China. By 1941, even before Pearl Harbor, America had committed itself to providing enormous quantities of war supplies to Chiang's forces. After December 7, support for Chiang's government became a key element of Roosevelt's plan to roll back Japanese expansion in Asia.

Upon hearing of Japan's attack on Pearl Harbor, Chiang Kai-shek and other Nationalist leaders celebrated. The wife of a top KMT officer later recalled, "The Kuomintang government officials went around congratulating each other, as if a great victory had been won. . . . At last, at last America was at war with Japan. Now China's strategic importance would grow even more. American money and equipment would flow in; half a billion dollars, one billion dollars . . . and that meant U.S. dollars into the pockets of officials."[3] In all, the United States would supply more than a billion dollars in aid to Chiang's Kuomintang forces (much of it transported over the perilous Burma Road), but neither they nor the Communists played a major role in evicting the Japanese invaders. KMT leaders grew increasingly corrupt and, with their ties to the landed elite, increasingly alienated from the peasantry—which accounted for over 90 percent of the country's population.

Chiang, in fact, pursued a policy of *avoiding* a costly war with the invaders, preferring to husband his growing resources, waiting until the inevitable American defeat of the Japanese, when renewed fighting with the Communists was certain. At Yenan, meanwhile, with a combination of terror and charisma, Mao was tightening his grip over the Communists. To be saved, the Chinese nation must be of one mind, Mao insisted. That mind was to be his. When the Party Congress met in mid-1945, it adopted a new constitution declaring that "The Chinese Communist Party takes Mao Zedong's thought . . . as the guide for all its work."[4]

The truce between the Nationalists and the Communists, established after Japan's invasion in 1937 had always been an unsteady one. Half a million KMT troops had been deployed to blockade Yenan, where Mao had led the Communists on the Long March. On several occasions major fighting had broken out. Now, with Japan defeated, the last American troops were withdrawn from China in 1946. The final conflict between the KMT and the CCP loomed.

Even as popular American magazines like Henry Luce's Time-Life publications extolled the Christian fighter for freedom, intelligence reports from

China depicted Chiang's regime as brutal and repressive and corrupt. The Chinese living in Kuomintang-controlled territory were growing more discontented with the government, while support for the Communists was growing.[5] The Roosevelt administration pressured Chiang to make the social and economic reforms essential to winning grassroots support, and the Generalissimo made repeated assurances that reforms were under way.

President Truman inherited Roosevelt's vision of a China that would emerge as a great world power, free and prosperous, a force for peace and stability in Asia. Thus he pushed, as Roosevelt had, to have China included among the permanent members of the United Nations Security Council. Many of the old powers of Europe—including, ironically, Stalin's Russia—would have preferred to have China remain disunited and vulnerable, an easy prey, as it had been for over a century. Truman complained to his advisers that "we were the only big nation that wanted a united democratic China."[6]

International politics rarely involves a choice between a good and a bad alternative. Official American policy called for the nurturing of a "united, democratically progressive, and cooperative China,"[7] and in pursuit of that goal, Chiang Kai-shek and his Nationalists were regarded as the lesser of two evils.

In late 1945, President Truman appointed Gen. George Marshall to travel to China on a peace mission, in an attempt to avert a civil war and help negotiate a coalition government. It was a last-gasp effort to prevent a catastrophic conflict. For over a year Marshall engaged in an unremitting shuttle diplomacy between the Nationalists and Communists, managing for a time to effectuate a truce. Both sides ultimately opted for military confrontation, Mao because he believed that total victory was within reach; Chiang because he believed that the Americans would not let him lose. Marshall was recalled to Washington—as secretary of state—in January 1947, as full-scale civil war was erupting. He left China exhausted and depressed, convinced that Mao and his followers were not mere "agrarian reformers," as some analysts thought, but that they were "playing the Russian game," posing as reformers in order to seize dictatorial power.

But Marshall also believed that the primary blame for the lack of popular support for the KMT fell to Chiang Kai-shek and the Nationalists themselves. There were no good options for American policy-makers. "I have tortured my brain and I can't see the answer," Marshall said just before leaving.[8]

Gen. Albert Wedemeyer, who had served as commander of U.S. forces in China, was assigned to make a thorough, monthlong survey of the situation in the country and candidly report back. Wedemeyer wrote to the new secretary of state that the Nationalists were "spiritually insolvent," but the alternatives were worse.[9]

American support for Chiang did not, as some journalists and academics have insisted, drive a potentially friendly Mao into hostility against the

United States and into the Communist camp. Ideologically, Mao was already there. From his college days he had been vociferously anti-capitalist and anti-Western. Mao recognized that the American political and economic system was incompatible with his vision of world socialism. He was a committed Marxist. In a 1940 essay entitled "On New Democracy," he called for "a dictatorship of all the revolutionary classes over the counterrevolutionaries and traitors," with the Communist Party playing the "leading role" in the new dictatorship.[10] As a Communist leader candidly told a visiting American, they "looked on U.S.A. as an enemy."[11]

In November 1948 the CCP issued an article entitled "Internationalism and Nationalism," in which it asserted its long-held doctrine that "the world today has been divided into two mutually antagonistic camps, composed of the American imperialists and their accomplices—the reactionaries of all the world; on the other hand, the world anti-capitalist camp, composed of the Soviet Union and the New Democracies of Eastern Europe, and the national liberation movements in China, Southeast Asia, and Greece, plus the people's democratic forces of all countries of the world."[12]

To be sure, American officials both in and outside China were dissatisfied with the choices offered by domestic Chinese politics. In March 1949 the U.S. Chamber of Commerce in Shanghai sent a letter to the State Department criticizing "the military, civil, and economic incompetence, or worse, of the Nationalist government." That same month the consul general in Tianjin reported to Washington that the necessity of containing Communism "should not oblige us to support a hopelessly corrupt government which has lost the support of its people."[13] There were simply no good options. It is entirely conceivable that if the Nationalists—who in 1945 were vastly superior in men and equipment—had been less corrupt, more democratic, more connected to the people, the Chinese civil war might have had a different outcome. It may have been that the KMT did as much to lose the war as the Communists did to win it. But circumstances were what they were, and in that vast and ancient nation, with no experience of democracy in its history or in its canon of traditional philosophy, and with a population approaching half a billion people, there may be little that any outside power could have done to alter circumstances. The Chinese people ultimately determined the course that China took.

From the outset, Mao was a Marxist, an advocate of violence to achieve totalitarian power. "To put it bluntly," he wrote as a young revolutionary in 1927, "it is necessary to create terror for awhile in every rural area; otherwise it would be impossible to suppress the activities of the [opponents] in the countryside. . . . "[14] He never in his life deviated from this.

———◆———

In addition to the more than $1 billion in aid given to Chiang Kai-shek's Nationalist government during the Second World War, from 1945 to 1949

American assistance exceeded an additional $3 billion. Perhaps no amount would have been enough. The popular Madame Chiang made another visit to the United States, appealing for more money and even hinting that if her husband didn't receive it, he might be forced into an "accord with the Soviets." Truman didn't bite. He had lost all faith in the KMT, "grafters and crooks,"[15] but doubted that their leaders would risk losing the embezzled funds they had squirreled away in American banks. Even the internationalist Senator Vandenberg, who had favored aid to the KMT, now acknowledged that "there are limits to our resources and boundaries to our miracles." He called the situation in China "the conundrum of the ages."[16]

Could it have been done differently? In August 1949 the State Department issued a lengthy White Paper on "United States Relations with China, with Special Reference to the Period 1944–1949." The transmittal letter by the new secretary of state, Dean Acheson, told Truman that billions of dollars in U.S. economic and military assistance had not been sufficient to bolster an ineffectual Nationalist government, and there had not been anything else that Americans could have reasonably done that would have altered the outcome. "The only alternative open to the United States was full-scale intervention in behalf of a Government that had lost the confidence of its own troops and its own people," Acheson wrote. "Intervention of such a scope and magnitude would have been resented by the mass of the Chinese people, would have diametrically reversed our historic policy, and would have been condemned by the American people. . . . The unfortunate but inescapable fact is that the outcome of the Civil War in China was beyond the control of the government of the United States."[17]

Chiang Kai-shek and his defeated government fled to the island of Taiwan, some 130 miles east of the mainland across the Taiwan Strait. On October 1, 1949, Mao stood at the ancient Tiananmen Gate in Beijing, outside of the old Forbidden City of the emperors, and announced the establishment of the People's Republic of China. Then he moved into the Imperial Palace. China had a new emperor. The Soviet Union immediately announced its recognition of the new government and the cessation of diplomatic ties with the Nationalists.

On Taiwan, Chiang vowed to keep up the fight, to return to the mainland and overthrow the Communist government. Most Americans wanted no part of it. The United States, still weary from its struggle with European fascism and now faced with an aggressive Soviet totalitarianism in Europe, could not get enmeshed in a civil war in the most populated nation in the world. On January 5, 1950, President Truman released a statement expressing America's determination to stay out of the Chinese civil war.

Now, the national soul-searching and political finger-pointing began. "Who lost China?"—as if it had been diverted away from the threshold of liberal democracy. Those who had any familiarity with the situation knew better. State Department official George Kennan's Policy Planning Staff had concluded a year earlier that the fate of China had been largely out of the hands of American policy-makers. "The salvation or destruction of China lies essentially with the Chinese—not with foreigners."[18]

———◆———

In the New China, the Communist Party was to be the sole source of all cultural, economic, and political power in the country. Mao, its chairman, implemented land reform, ended most trade with foreign nations, and banned all political criticism. A vast nation was now to be remolded according to the blueprint of a single half-educated dictator. Hundreds of thousands of suspected political opponents—"counterrevolutionaries"—were executed or shipped off to slave labor camps.[19] "A revolution is not a dinner party," Mao said.

The party was to control all commerce, labor, employment. To maintain stability in urban areas (where the CCP had less experience and fewer adherents), most public employees were permitted to keep their jobs if they agreed to participate in indoctrination sessions and embrace Maoism.[20] Most did. Factories were reorganized for centralized command, and party-controlled "work units" in the "collective economic enterprises" gradually became the dominant factors in citizens' social and economic existence. Only loyal party members could hold positions of social or political responsibility. By the end of 1950 the CCP had nearly 6 million members.

To produce a classless society, it would be essential to know which class each individual had come from. "Class labeling" determined one's place in the new order. Those classified as landlords or "rich peasants" faced the certain loss of all property and imprisonment or execution. "Middle peasants" were a little safer, exposed to public condemnation, loss of property, and social status, but apt to survive in some condition. It was safest to be labeled a "poor peasant."[21]

In February 1950, Mao and Stalin, two of history's most brutal dictators, signed a comprehensive military and trade pact. For Mao, like Stalin, whatever the social or political question, violence was the solution. "Power comes from the barrel of a gun," as he had famously said. Now he was proving it. The landed class, deemed the greatest threat to the new regime, was annihilated. At least a million landowners were murdered during the initial land reform process.

Internal passports were introduced, so that citizens could not travel from one place to another without the party's permission. Mandatory mass indoctrination meetings were held, part of the comprehensive new program of "thought reform." Neighbors were grouped into local "committees" to be drilled in Maoist ideology, and to keep an eye on each other. Schoolteachers told children to report their parents if they heard them saying anything suspicious. Group pressure was the most effective means for condemning unapproved styles of hair, dress, or thought. Citizens who persisted in "counterrevolutionary" thought or speech were to be turned in to the local party.

Hundreds of thousands simply disappeared. A vast network of brutal *laogai* "reeducation through labor" prison camps were established to hold "counterrevolutionnaries" and other political offenders.[22] Within five years after the Communists took power, a foreign observer would write that "there are probably few persons throughout mainland China who have not in some way participated in [thought reform]."[23] Mao himself acknowledged that 700,000 "local bullies and evil gentry" were executed between 1950 and 1952.[24] Independent newspapers in Hong Kong estimated 20 million deaths.

Soviet dictator Joseph Stalin entered the Second World War against Japan—after the atomic bomb had been dropped on Hiroshima—not to share in the fighting, but in the spoils. Truman agreed to a joint U.S.-Soviet occupation of Korea (which Japan had occupied since the beginning of the century) similar to that in Germany, with the 38th Parallel as the dividing line. On August 9, Red Army troops poured into northern Korea from Manchuria. But as in Eastern Europe, it soon became apparent that the Soviet Union had broader ambitions for its Korean occupation zone. The Kremlin rushed 120,000 men into the territory, immediately began to establish a Communist dictatorship, and closed the border to restrict the flood of refugees fleeing southward. U.S. forces arrived about a month after the Soviets. American troops were well received in the south and generally well-comported, but in the north the behavior of Soviet soldiers (reminiscent of their counterparts in Eastern Europe) was so predatory that they eventually had to begin traveling in groups of three or more after dark, as protection against enraged locals.[25] The U.S. occupation in the south began to lay the groundwork for a free and democratic political system.

Talks between U.S. and Soviet officials over Korean reunification broke down in late 1947 over the Kremlin's refusal to permit a United Nations–backed plan for free elections throughout the Korean peninsula, to be supervised by UN observers. Stalin had already chosen a ruler, Kim Il-sung, who had served in the Red Army in the Second World War and was a committed Communist. As power in the north was coalesced under one ruling institution, the Korean Worker's Party, in South Korea there emerged over a hundred fractious parties, all vying for power in the new democratic state. Often these were based on age-old clan or regional ties, with little or no experience of democracy or elections, suspicious of one another, reluctant to compromise.

In elections held in May 1948, the nation's first ever, South Koreans elected a National Assembly. Ninety-five percent of the 8 million registered voters had turned out on election day; UN election commissioners declared that the election reflected a "valid expression of the will of the people."[26] The Assembly adopted a constitution, and the Republic of Korea was formally proclaimed in August 1948. Its first president, selected by the Assembly, was Syngman Rhee, the country's best-known exile leader, who, unlike many prominent Koreans, was not tainted with collaboration during the Japanese occupation. Following the election, with the U.S. mission in South Korea complete, the withdrawal of troops was begun.

In the North, in September, Kim Il-sung was formally declared premier of the Democratic People's Republic of Korea. A national conscription was begun. Large industrial facilities were converted to armaments production. A massive Communist indoctrination campaign was launched, and all opposition to Kim was violently suppressed.

Syngman Rhee was not a paragon of democracy. His regime was corrupt and brutally suppressed Communist—and other—opposition. His nation lacked historical or cultural experience with democracy, and the Japanese had governed the country since the turn of the century, occupying all important positions of public administration. But even in 1949, South Korea was a protodemocracy, with the institutions, the rhetoric, and the espoused values—though not yet fully taken root—of a liberal democratic society. It was on the path. No nation ever suddenly became a democracy. By mid-1949, the withdrawal of American forces from Korea had been completed. They left behind only modest quantities of small arms for the inchoate army, in order, MacArthur explained in a directive from his HQ in Tokyo, "to indicate clearly its peaceful purpose and provide no plausible basis for allegations of being a threat to North Korea."[27] As Soviet forces were withdrawn from the North, they left Kim's army with an enormous cache of weapons and munitions.

When Mao rose to power in China, world communism seemed ascendant. Kim Il-sung had his own dreams of historical greatness, and for more than two years he had pressed Moscow to support an invasion of the South. "I do not sleep at night, thinking about unification," he told the Soviet ambassador."[28] Stalin had balked, concerned about U.S. intervention and fearing a broader conflict. When he finally acceded to the plan, it was contingent upon Mao's willingness to have the Chinese play the main role in the event of an escalation. Mao notified Kim of his support for an invasion of the South and raised the possibility of sending Chinese assistance. He was certain that the United States "would not start a third world war over such a small territory."[29]

The timing of an invasion was increasingly urgent. Communist agitators in the South had diminishing appeal as the situation stabilized there, and in the early summer of 1950 the legislature was scheduled to pass a land-reform bill that would further reduce their appeal. The ROK army, with fewer than 100,000 men, had been infiltrated by South Korean Communists. It lacked the equipment, discipline, or training of Kim's army, which had over 150 of the powerful Soviet-made T-34 tanks; America had left South Korea with no tanks at all. The North had an air force of 200 fighter planes and bombers; the South had none. The North had a 3 to 1 advantage in artillery.

Its Army included as many as sixty thousand combat veterans, hardened by years of warfare in China; relatively few soldiers in the ROK army had any battle experience.[30]

On June 25, 1950, an intense artillery barrage shattered the predawn darkness at the 38th Parallel. That was not unusual. Sporadic exchanges across the no-man's-land were a common occurrence, and the initial barrage provoked little concern. But the intense fusillade was followed by a lightning thrust across the parallel of 90,000 North Korean soldiers supported by 150 massive T-34 tanks. It was a rout. A force of around 35,000 ROK troops, inexperienced, ill organized, and poorly equipped, were defending the border. They were overrun almost immediately. The South Korean army, having no aggressive ambitions, was more of a national police force, bearing mainly small arms and responsible for maintaining civil order. In the face of this onslaught, entire regiments evaporated. Within a week only half of the ROK soldiers could be accounted for.[31]

By the afternoon of the first day, North Korean fighter planes were striking the capital city of Seoul. Kim's armored divisions advanced southward with impunity. Within three days Seoul had fallen to the advancing Communists.

International relations impose difficult choices. Syngman Rhee, like Chiang Kai-shek, was an authoritarian ruler, not widely liked or trusted in Washington. But the American commitment was to the fledgling democracies in their countries, not to particular leaders. Should the United States get involved in what the Communists were calling the "internal affairs" of a country a world away, in which there was no compelling security interest? If America did not act quickly, the fledgling democracy in South Korea would soon cease to exist. Truman got word of the invasion around 9:20 p.m. while on a visit to his hometown of Independence, Missouri. He asked Secretary of State Dean Acheson to request a special session of the United Nations Security Council for the following day, and then returned to Washington.

In a sense, Korea provided a clear-cut test case for the callow United Nations as an instrument for international peacekeeping. The circumstances were undisputable. As one American diplomat later recalled, when the Security Council met to consider the aggression, "no nation dared ask for a delay on the excuse that the facts were not known."[32] Following vigorous efforts by the American ambassador, the UN Security Council adopted a resolution calling for an immediate cease-fire in Korea and withdrawal of North Korean forces. It called on member nations to "render every assistance to the United Nations in the execution of the resolution." The measure passed 9 to 0, with Yugoslavia abstaining. Two days later the Security Council adopted a U.S.-sponsored resolution calling on member nations to give South Korea the assistance "necessary to repel the armed attack." There *would* be an international response to the aggression. The Communists had underestimated the resolve of the United States and the democratic West.

The United Nations action itself was historic: it marked the first time that a global organization had denounced aggression, and then organized to act against it. As a member of the British Parliament noted in London, "We are witnessing something quite unique in the enforcement by arms of collective security by a world organization. . . . That is something that has never before occurred in the history of the world."[33] The Korean vote itself was something of a historical anomaly: the Russians had begun a boycott of the Security Council several months earlier, demanding that Mao's government be given a seat on the Council. Except for that boycott, their representative would have been able to veto the resolution. Because of Cold War politics, it was not to be replicated for over forty years, until the Persian Gulf conflict in 1991.

Any UN response would take time, though, and the government in South Korea had a matter of days, not weeks. "Mr. President, the news is bad," Secretary of State Acheson reported to Truman. The Communists were close to succeeding in their conquest of the Korean peninsula. Truman did not waver. "Dean, we've got to stop the sons of bitches no matter what." By the time the South Korean ambassador in Washington went to see President Truman on June 26 to formally request U.S. assistance, the decision had already been made. "Many years ago, when Americans were fighting for their independence, at Valley Forge, our soldiers lacked food, medicine, clothing," the president said. "In 1917, western Europe was about to fall to pieces, Europeans were in despair, but some friends went over and helped them."[34] Now, the United States would do the same for the Koreans. In South Korea, when it was announced on the radio that America was going to come to the nation's assistance, there were joyful demonstrations in the streets, and grown men wept in relief. The following morning, just two days after the invasion, Truman announced that he had ordered American air and sea forces in the region to go to South Korea's defense. Also, warships would be sent to the Strait of Taiwan, to deter the invasion of Taiwan that Beijing had planned.

It had been reasonable for Beijing and Pyongyang to expect that the United States would stay out of the Korean conflict. For most Americans, Korea was an unknown and inconsequential nation somewhere in Asia, with no conceivable strategic importance. Kim had expected that Korea would be too distant to defend, and too remote to matter, for the Americans.

But public sympathy for the embattled South Koreans, and support for President Truman's actions, was overwhelming. Reflecting national sentiment, Congress quickly voted to extend the draft (by a vote of 315–14 in the House, and 70–0 in the Senate), and then passed a Military Assistance Plan to provide military aid to the Republic of Korea. "Democracy Takes a Stand," declared the *New York Times*.[35] "Virtually all shades of opinion wholeheartedly support the President," British ambassador Sir Oliver Franks reported to London.[36] "I have worked in and out of Washington for twenty years,"

Joseph Harsch wrote in the *Christian Science Monitor*. "Never before have I felt such a sense of relief and unity pass through the city."[37]

———◆———

America was not prepared to go to war. This was nothing new, of course. America, the greatest military power in history, had displayed the least affinity for warfare of any leading nation during the twentieth century. For all its might, America was a nation of producers and merchants, not warriors. It had been caught unprepared at the beginning of both the First and Second World Wars; its armed forces had been inadequately staffed, equipped, and trained. Now, again. Following the war, Truman had wanted to reduce the 12-million-person wartime military to 2 million. The American public had wanted it to be cut even further. Responding to popular pressure, Congress voted in the spring of 1946 to restrict the military to just over a million men. A vast arsenal of equipment was mothballed.

By 1950 almost every unit in the U.S. military was undermanned, and underequipped for battle. Shrinking military appropriations were incompatible with the commitments that America had undertaken—in part because no other democracy was able—for the defense of the free world. "Perhaps the best result of the Korean affair," remarked the Canadian ambassador in Washington, "is that it has made it possible for the people of the United States to accept the load involved in making their military power equal to their world responsibilities."[38] On July 19, Truman formally requested a $10 billion emergency appropriation from Congress to begin a massive rearmament program. Within days Congress voted to appropriate $11 billion, and authorized a 3.2-million-person military.

Thousands of young American men went down to their local recruiters and enlisted. Bill Patterson of Stillwater, New York, twenty-year-old son of an industrial worker, went with a group of forty-five friends to sign up for military service. It seemed like the right thing to do. "They had a problem over there," he later recalled. "We wanted to do something about it."[39]

On the thirtieth, Truman authorized MacArthur to send U.S. ground troops to Korea. Soldiers stationed in Japan would be rushed to the Korean front, to stem the tide and buy time for a larger force to mobilize. In the meantime, as it had already done in the North, Kim Il-sung's advancing army was giving South Koreans a foretaste of what life would be like under the Communist utopia. Thousands of suspected "reactionaries," landowners, businessmen, and potential critics were arrested, imprisoned, and executed—all without trial. Mass murder was used to frighten potential opposition: between June and September alone, at least 26,000 South Korean citizens were murdered.[40] The South Koreans recognized the American arrivals as their sole hope. Handmade American flags flew from homes in the South, away from the front. Arriving U.S. troops were applauded and tearfully thanked by Koreans gathered along their route. Chong Suk was a young girl in a small village south of Seoul when the North invaded. "We did not know why our country was at war," she later recalled. "We just knew that our dads were gone and we were hungry. At night, we would seek protection in bunkers or foxholes." Suk writes that she knew nothing about the United States, "but I had heard of 'Yankees,' and how they were here to save us. One morning, a few children ran through the village yelling 'The Yankees are here!'"[41]

On July 5 and in the following days, the Americans engaged the vastly larger North Korean force, suffering heavy losses and being slowly but inexorably pushed back. Two days later the UN Security Council named General MacArthur Supreme Commander of the United Nations force in Korea. The entire U.S. Eighth Army would be sent to Korea. But it would take time. In the meantime, the battered American force in Korea, outnumbered 10-to-1, must prevent a total defeat before the war had even started.

By early August, U.S. and ROK forces had been pushed into a corner, a defensive cordon about fifty miles across and a hundred miles long around the port city of Pusan, Korea's second largest city, on the southeastern tip of the peninsula. The North Koreans, sensing victory, threw human wave after wave at the "Pusan Perimeter," under orders from Kim Il-sung to complete the invasion by mid-August. Time was of the essence. New American troops and supplies were arriving daily, but for many international observers, the outcome on the Korean peninsula was already certain. "Enough of this nonsense," declared the British newspaper *The Statesman*. "The United States should recognize a lost cause and stop pouring men into this Asian sinkhole."[42] The years of military demobilization now showed. An American field commander reported that the troops "have all the guts in the world and I can count on them in a fight. But when they started out, they couldn't shoot. They didn't know their weapons. They'd been nursed and coddled, told to drive safely, to buy War Bonds, to give to the Red Cross, when somebody ought to have been telling them how to clear a machine gun when it jams."[43]

Yet they held the line. By the second week of September it was evident to both sides that the Pusan defensive cordon would not be broken. U.S. forces (and now units from Britain and other UN allies) were still arriving in large numbers. Large tanks capable of destroying the massive Russian T-34s were arriving. In addition, U.S. aircraft had established air supremacy, battering Communist force concentrations and restricting daylight movement. The invaders had been halted.

General MacArthur launched a bold amphibious assault at Inchon, on the western coast of Korea, on September 15. U.S. forces broke through North Korean lines and pushed toward Seoul. Kim Il-sung had wanted to prevail with his own North Korean forces, but for weeks before the Inchon landing, Mao had been considering intervention in Korea. "If the U.S. imperialists win [in Korea], they may get so dizzy with success that they may threaten us," Mao told a Politburo meeting on August 4, a month before the Inchon landing.[44] Party leaders in Beijing, still consolidating their grip on

their own country, worried that a Communist defeat on the Korean peninsula might undermine their position at home. On July 17, the party launched
a massive "Hate America" propaganda campaign. By August, Mao had sent
more than three hundred thousand PLA (People's Liberation Army) troops
to the Korean border.

Mao had expected that the entry of U.S. forces into the conflict would
produce a reversal for the North, but the disintegration of Kim's "People's
Army" in the days following Inchon took everyone by surprise. Soon the
Communists were in full retreat, with U.S. forces in pursuit.

MacArthur believed that the North Korean aggressors could not simply
be allowed to retreat behind the 38th Parallel, lick their wounds, and regroup
for an inevitable future aggression. Officials in Washington agreed. "Your
military objective is the destruction of the North Korean armed forces," the
Joint Chiefs cabled him on September 27. Two days later George Marshall
(whom Truman had persuaded to come out of retirement to serve as secretary of defense) instructed MacArthur that he should feel "unhampered"
tactically and strategically by the 38th Parallel.

Eighth Army troops crossed the parallel into North Korea on October 7.
If anything, resistance grew more fierce as the battle moved north. Kim
Il-sung had issued a general order to his army: "Do not retreat one step further," and to encourage the troops he established a 'supervising army' with
the mission of summarily executing deserters. By the nineteenth, Pyongyang had fallen, and Kim Il-sung had fled north toward China. The end of the
war seemed imminent. GIs began making plans for after the war. MacArthur
promised that the boys would be "home for Christmas," and was so certain
of an imminent victory that some arriving munitions and supplies were
sent back.

By October 2, Mao had already ordered PLA generals to prepare for
deployment into Korea, "ahead of our schedule."[45] He concurred with those
who dismissed young American soldiers as rich, spoiled, soft. They lacked
the ideological fervor of Communist troops and were "afraid of dying" for
their cause.[46]

Less imperialistic and more philanthropic than the major European
powers had been, even after the Communist revolution the United States
continued to be widely admired and liked among ordinary Chinese. To rally
support for the war at home, in late October the CCP Central Committee
escalated the "Hate America" campaign that it had been waging. Party officers throughout the country received an agenda for a propaganda campaign, entitled "How to Regard the United States (Outlines for Propaganda),"
which conceded that many Chinese had been beguiled by "the outward
appearance of American democracy" and the popular misconception that
the United States was "a democratic and peace-loving" nation. Also, the
widespread belief that America was a model for modernization and could
be crucial to China's development had to be refuted. And finally, the public
had to be convinced that the perception of American power was overblown,

that it was a "paper tiger" that could be defeated by Chinese arms. To this end, people had to be reminded that the United States had a relatively small army, stretched thinly around the globe; that a war conducted halfway around the world in Korea would overburden its logistical capabilities; and that it had no really strong allies, as Germany and Japan were unarmed, and Britain, Italy, and France were no longer military powers.[47] The Chinese people must be taught that it was "wrong to either adore or be afraid of the United States."[48]

The bulk of the forward U.S. force had halted around Pyongyang, preparing for a final offensive against the North Korean People's Army, which had retreated toward the Yalu. On November 26, Gen. Peng Dehuai launched the Chinese counterattack. A flood of humanity swept down upon the frontline units, blowing whistles and bugles, hammering gongs and shouting American profanity as they came. The Chinese "human wave" tactic inundated positions across the peninsula. A Turkish brigade was obliterated after making a gallant defensive stand.

In the end there was nothing to be done against the onslaught but attempt to survive it. The Eighth Army was ordered to withdraw. On the ground, another enemy had joined the battle: winter. The weather combined with the hilly Korean topography to produce some of the most brutal conditions in the history of warfare. The longest and most deadly retreat in American military history had commenced.

In a nationwide radio address on December 15, President Truman vowed that America would "continue to uphold and if necessary, to defend with arms, the principles of the United Nations—the principles of freedom and justice."[49] Even as the Chinese sent reinforcements and supplied their army from behind the Yalu River, Truman assured concerned allies that the United States would limit the conflict to the Korean peninsula and not strike China itself.

Nations participating in the UN force were also expressing misgivings at the duration and cost of the war, and pressed Washington for a quick treaty with Pyongyang and Beijing. Truman publicly explained that the United States would continue to pursue a cease-fire, but not at the cost of abandoning the peoples of Korea, Taiwan, or Southeast Asia to Communism. And if the Communists persisted in their aggression against South Korea, he said, America would continue to stand by it, and see the conflict through to the end, with or without the participation of other nations.[50]

———◆———

With prospects for victory in sight, Mao ordered General Peng to cross the 38th Parallel and push the Americans into the sea. "The imperialists will run like sheep," Peng told his commanders. "Our problem is not Seoul. It is Pusan. Not taking it—just walking there."[51]

GIs began calling it the yo-yo war. For the second time in six months, all roads, paths, and trails southward were clogged with fleeing refugees. This exodus, though, was being conducted in midwinter conditions, on icy, frozen ground. Tens of thousands of refugees died in the mass migration. Thousands more were murdered, as both the North and South Korean armies committed atrocities against civilians who were suspected of collaborating with the enemy or were simply in the way. Communist forces captured Seoul for a second time on January 4.

Under the new command of Gen. Matthew Ridgeway, Allied forces launched a series of lightning strikes at the vast Chinese force, and as the engagements continued, confidence grew. By January the Eighth Army had absorbed the worst of the Chinese offensive, was holding firm, and had begun pressing back. Henceforth, there would be no more talk of a Korean Dunkirk, either from troops in the field or policy-makers in Washington.

On January 21, General Ridgeway issued a statement entitled "Why Are We Here?" to be read to every soldier in the Eighth Army. "What are we fighting for? We are here because of the decisions of the properly constituted authorities of our respective governments," the statement said. "The issue now joined right here in Korea is whether communism or individual freedom shall prevail; whether the flight of fear-driven people such as we have witnessed here shall be checked. . . . You will have my utmost. I shall expect yours." The effect on the men was electric. By the first week of April the Eighth Army had fought its way back to the 38th Parallel. Back to where the war had begun.

In the United States, President Truman was being criticized by some for not being aggressive enough in opposing Communism in Asia, and by others for being in Asia at all. Isolationists such as Joe Kennedy (the former ambassador to Britain) and Herbert Hoover called for a retrenchment from the United States' extensive security commitments abroad and the establishment of a "Fortress America" at home. Korea was not America's problem. When Hoover made a speech critical of America's international commitments, the Soviet newspaper *Pravda* reprinted it in its entirety. A leading Chinese newspaper ran an editorial declaring "American Ruling Class Is Confused and Split."[52] For the oligarchs in Beijing and Moscow, political disagreement bespoke chaos. For Americans, it was part of the normal functioning of the democratic process, a system where, unlike in Beijing or Moscow, there was no unified "ruling class" at all.

With UN forces back at the 38th Parallel, the president saw a chance for a negotiated peace. The Joint Chiefs cabled MacArthur in Tokyo, ordering him not to send troops across into North Korea. MacArthur responded by issuing a public statement calling for the conquest of all of Korea and condemning a negotiated peace. He also wrote to members of Congress expressing his critical views, some of which were made public. On April 11, Truman announced what he knew would be an unpopular decision. In the message relieving MacArthur of his command, the president wrote that "Full and vig-orous debate on matters of national security is a vital element in the consti-tutional system of our free democracy. It is fundamental, however, that military commanders must be governed by the policies and directives issued to them in the manner provided for by our laws and Constitution."

In most societies, for most of history, military power was preeminent. Warriors imposed their will upon society. In the sacking of MacArthur, the principle of civilian supremacy over the military was reconfirmed. MacArthur continued to make public statements critical of the president's refusal to carry the war to China itself. Critics of the president in Congress held hear-ings to inquire into MacArthur's firing, but their primary impact was to highlight the general's egoism and declining judgment. He made a speech to Congress, famously remarking that "Old soldiers never die, they just fade away." (Though the line is remembered, the speech was rambling and self-glorifying). In fact, MacArthur did not just fade away, or at least tried not to. He quietly promoted himself as a possible Republican nominee for the 1952 election, but by then the sheen was gone.

By now Mao had abandoned his hopes for a swift triumph in Korea, but he remained committed to his plan for Communist domination of the entire peninsula and was willing to expend a limitless number of lives to achieve it. "Win a quick victory if you can," he told General Peng. "If you can't, win a slow one."[53]

The Chinese launched a series of violent counterattacks in the spring to dislodge the UN force, or demoralize it, but without success, and at a cost of two hundred thousand casualties. U.S. forces and equipment were now firmly deployed in Korea, and there was no longer any doubt about American resolve.

Cease-fire talks, begun in July, continued sporadically at Panmunjon, in the neutral zone, for the next two years. So did the fighting, as ferocious and bloody as ever, but now confined to a swath of land on both sides of the 38th Parallel. In obscure places given improvised names like Old Baldy, Bloody Ridge, Heartbreak Ridge, and Pork Chop Hill, savage battles were waged, courage displayed, lives lost. But there would henceforth be no dra-matic offensive dashes or major territorial gains. Instead, artillery pounded away and opposing armies fired at each other with machine guns and mor-tars and carbines from trenchworks separated by a few thousand yards or less of barbed wire and land mines: a return to trench warfare.

A key sticking point in the talks was whether the UN would forcibly return all Chinese and North Korean POWs. Many did not want to go back. Most of those in the "volunteer" Chinese force had been impressed into service, and estimates based on interviews with the prisoners suggested that half or more of them would not return home if given a choice. Large numbers of North Korean soldiers also expressed the desire to remain in the South. For the Communist leadership, the prospect that half of their "volunteers" would refuse to return home signified a propaganda catastrophe. They insisted that all of the 130,000 POWs being held in South Korea be returned, against their will if necessary. In October 1952 the talks broke down.

Peace could undoubtedly have been reached in Korea much sooner if the United States had acceded on the forced return of POWs, but to Truman it was a moral issue, and polls showed that most Americans felt the same way.[54] "We shall not trade in the lives of men," declared Secretary of state Acheson. "We shall not forcibly deliver human beings into Communist hands."[55]

Harry Truman had held public office for three decades and had already decided not to run for reelection months before the Korean War broke out. It was the decision of a practical Midwesterner, prudently suspicious of the seduction of political life. "There is a lure in power," he wrote in his diary. "It can get into a man's blood just as gambling and lust for money have been known to do."[56] Dwight Eisenhower, who had campaigned on a pledge to end the war, was elected president in November 1952. During the campaign Eisenhower had promised "to bring the Korean War to an early and honorable end. . . . "[57] In December he made a trip to Korea, where he witnessed the heavy toll that the protracted, "forgotten war" was having. On his return, Eisenhower announced that, unless progress was made toward a peace accord, the United States would launch a major new offensive against North Korea.

The one point that Eisenhower was adamant about was the question of the forced repatriation of the tens of thousands of Chinese and North Korean POWs who wished not to return to life under Communist tyranny. For the Americans, the principle of granting political asylum was a genuine and core political value. "Perhaps in this matter we were idealistic," Eisenhower's secretary of state John Foster Dulles later wrote. "But the one thing for which Americans had been willing to fight and die was their ideals. We did not apologize for this."[58] The armistice agreement was signed on July 27, 1953.

From 1950 to 1953, 1.3 million Americans served in Korea, at a monetary cost to the United States of approximately $20 billion. In defense of democracy in that distant and foreign land, 55,000 Americans were killed and 103,000 wounded.

Half a century later, U.S. and South Korean troops still gaze warily across the Demilitarized Zone, the most heavily fortified border in the world, still on guard against aggression today. Was the Korean War not a success? It is true that at the end of it the country was still divided, as it had been before the Communist invasion. But it is also true that tens of millions of human beings have lived freer and fuller lives who otherwise would have subsisted—and would today still subsist—under one of the most soul-numbing tyrannies in history. For South Koreans, defeat of the Communist aggression has meant all the difference in the world.

Korea is sometimes called "the forgotten war" by those who served there, because during the years of static fighting a war-weary nation turned its attention elsewhere, but the war left an indelible mark upon history, the course of which it indelibly altered, much for the better, and upon the lives of millions of Koreans. At the outset of U.S. involvement, the Truman administration had announced that American intervention in Korea was "solely for the purpose of restoring the Republic of Korea to the status prior to the invasion from the North."[59] That objective had been achieved. America had gone to war to halt Communist expansion. It succeeded in doing so.

More broadly, by 1953 the prospects for Asia seemed very different than they had in 1949, when Mao had promised that the Red Dragon of Communism would sweep across the region. The United States government was giving billions of dollars in military and economic assistance to Korea, Japan, Taiwan, the Philippines, Singapore, and other bulwarks against Communism. American ships now patrolled the Strait of Taiwan, and U.S. forces were pledged to come to Taiwan's aid in the event of a Chinese attack: because of America's unwavering support, Mao had indefinitely postponed a planned invasion. The Communist world had been startled by the vigor and tenacity of America's response to the aggression in Korea. There would be Communist-backed insurgencies, to be sure, but there would be no Communist juggernaut in Asia. It is easy to forget now, but halfway into the twentieth century totalitarian Communism was poised to be the dominant political system in the world. It was not inevitable that freedom would triumph in Asia and elsewhere. It did so because courageous people made enormous sacrifices for it.

———◆———

For a time following Korea, Mao suspended plans for aggressively expanding Communism elsewhere in Asia, but in 1954 he again put to the test Washington's support for Taiwan. In August, Beijing announced its determination to "liberate" Taiwan, and a blockade was commenced of offshore islands in the Strait of Taiwan. A month later the PLA began a bombardment of the islands, the two largest being Quemoy and Matsu. The Eisenhower administration never wavered. Provisions were supplied to the Taiwanese forces on the islands, and Secretary of State Dulles reiterated that the United States stood firmly with Taiwan, even if it required the use of military force to defend Taipei's sovereignty. In January 1955, Congress enacted the Formosa Strait Resolution, authorizing the president to use force to defend the "security of Formosa, the Pescadores, and the related positions and territories in that area."

Hundreds of millions of American aid dollars had already flowed to Taipei (and more were on the way—a billion dollars by the end of the decade), but with increasingly bellicose Chinese pledges to "liberate" the island nation, on February 11, 1955, President Eisenhower signed a Mutual Defense Treaty with Taiwan, which was ratified overwhelmingly by the Senate two days later. The treaty's stated purpose was "to declare publicly and formally [the two nations'] sense of unity and their common determination to defend themselves against armed attack, so that no potential aggressor could be under the illusion that either of them stands alone in the West Pacific Area. . . . " The pact called for the U.S. and Taiwan to cooperate in economic development, to promote "by self-help and mutual aid" their defensive capabilities, and to act together to defend against aggression." If America was invaded, Taiwan would come to its defense. And vice versa. On May 1, China ended its shelling of the islands.

———◆———

Responding to Washington's criticisms that his regime suppressed free expression and other human rights, in a speech in May 1956, Mao asserted that, as a scientific truth, Marxism did not fear free speech. He quoted a traditional Chinese saying: "Let a hundred flowers bloom, let a hundred schools contend." The following March he went even further. The government should be "open wide" to opposing viewpoints, Mao said, "to let all people express their opinions freely . . . "[60]

Something approaching the kind of freedom of expression taken for granted every day in the democratic West existed in Communist China from May 1 to June 7, 1957. Pent-up criticisms, ideological disagreements, and condemnations emerged, slowly at first, then in a torrent. Almost immediately it was evident that the party—indeed, socialism itself—did not have the popular support that its leaders had imagined. Chairman Mao, isolated and detached, had expected any criticisms to be as clement as "a breeze or a mild rain."

As students, workers, and writers began to speak out against the party's corruption and monopoly of power, the deputy minister of education cautioned that unrestricted criticism could open the floodgates of revolution. "The students have many problems today and things have reached a saturation point. Once they are in the streets, the townsfolk will gather together and the situation will worsen. For the masses are also dissatisfied with the Party. . . . "[61]

China's brief experiment with freedom of speech was over. Premier Chou Enlai warned that those who criticized the government would be declared enemies of the state.[62] The Communists had had enough of the experiment with controlled freedom. There ensued a violent crackdown on those who had criticized socialism. Scientists, writers, and other intellectuals who had disparaged the chairman or the party found themselves scrubbing toilets for a living, or imprisoned, or facing execution. Millions were sent to hard labor in prison camps or collective farms for "thought reform."

Show trials were held; an indeterminable number were executed, as the Communists had been forced to violently suppress their critics. Mao's belief that the party could withstand criticism had been wrong.

In a move designed to stir up nationalist sentiment at home, on August 23, 1958, Beijing renewed talk of "liberating" Taiwan and resumed its bombardment of Quemoy and Matsu islands. President Eisenhower responded that the United States would not abandon its ally "in the face of armed aggression" and dispatched a massive naval force to the Strait. Provisions were supplied to the embattled Nationalist forces on the islands by U.S. naval ships running the blockade, and support from U.S. warplanes enabled the Nationalists to establish air superiority over the islands. Khrushchev held back support for Mao, unwilling to get involved in a situation that might escalate into conflict with the United States. He confided to aides that he had misjudged American will. Mao backed down.

Large landowners had already been eliminated in China. Now small landholders, potentially entrepreneurial and capitalistic, came to be regarded as a potential threat. They, too, had to be eliminated. In 1955, Mao decreed that the existing agricultural cooperatives, comprised of 20 to 40 families, must be further combined, into enormous collectives of 100 to 300 families. Chinese would not live on, or work on, or own their own land. All property would be owned by the state—the party. Ninety-nine percent of the peasant population was herded onto vast communal farms.[63] Private property had been abolished; now private life was to be abolished as well. In the new communal world, everything was collectivized. Each commune's party secretary supervised committees, which regulated every aspect of existence. Meals were eaten in common dining halls; Mao called these a "key battlefield of socialism." Children were raised in communal boarding schools by communal, party-approved child rearers.

China was about to take a "Great Leap Forward" into modernization and prosperity, unprecedented in human history, Mao promised. Within a few years China would surpass America as the richest country in the world. Millions believed Mao's promises. Millions more were afraid to raise objections.

The Great Leap Forward was a human catastrophe on a scale unequaled in history. The 1959 harvest was 30 million tons below the previous year, but the party cadres in the communes did not dare report their shortfalls, as this often resulted in charges of "defeatism" and imprisonment. In reporting output, party officials were expected to exhibit "public consciousness": that is, to present data that would be encouraging to the masses.[64]

When grain shipments from the communes fell far short of the tremendous yields reported, it was taken as evidence of subversion. Peasants must be concealing the grain. "There is plenty of grain," declared the first secretary of Xinyang Province, "but ninety percent of the people have ideological problems."[65] Farmers and cadres suspected of withholding grain were imprisoned, publicly beaten, tortured, or executed. The party's propaganda machine meanwhile worked frenetically to boost flagging public zeal and inspire the workers to work harder. It published posters of crops grown so densely that children could walk atop them. One poster proclaimed: "China Surpasses U.S.A. in Wheat Production."

Between 1957 and 1960, China's death rate doubled. In 1960 the population of the most populous nation in the world declined by 4.5 percent.[66] In some localities, up to half of the villagers perished. Yet long after it was apparent that the Great Leap was a disaster, the policies were stubbornly maintained. Even as peasants starved, Mao, eager to establish his system as an economic model to be emulated by other developing nations, continued to export food "surpluses" abroad to China's allies.

In the government-created famine of 1960–61, 20 million Chinese lost their lives. Measured by its death toll, Maoism had created the most catastrophic famine in human history. It was systematic famine, created and administered by government policy. It marked the first time in history that famine had reached every part of the enormous nation, including regions that normally produced great food surpluses, and should have in 1958–61.

Only Defense Minister Peng Dehuai, commander of the Korea campaign, had the courage to openly question the effects of Mao's Great Leap. Mao dismissed reports of famine as "defeatist" and accused General Peng of being a "rightist." Within a month Peng had been forced to write a self-deprecating confession and was under house arrest. A few years later, during the Cultural Revolution, he was tortured and executed.

Apologists for Mao's statism continually recur to the fact that China must feed one-fifth of the world's population. But China's population *density* is less than many nations. It is a populous country, but it is also enormous. Its population density per hectare of arable land is barely half that, for example, of South Korea, and only 40 percent of Japan's.[67] Commune-ism continued to have disastrous consequences for the Chinese long after the Great Famine had passed. China's agricultural productivity continued to languish while that of its Asian neighbors such as Japan, Taiwan, and South Korea grew by up to sixty-fold. Twenty years after the Great Leap, the World Bank reported that farmers in China were only half as productive as those in such underdeveloped nations as Indonesia, Pakistan, and Thailand. [68]

After the failure of the Great Leap Forward, Mao determined that a new revolution was needed to rejuvenate the flagging public zeal and tighten his own grip on power. He launched a "Cultural Revolution" to purify Chinese society. At its vanguard were to be groups of ideologically zealous youth, the Red Guards, fanatically devoted to the chairman, recruited from throughout the country. They would sweep away the remnants of pre-Communist traditions and institutions and usher in the era of true socialism. Millions, and then tens of millions, of students were mobilized. Mao Zedong, who had long denounced Stalin's cult of personality, was elevating himself to a state of ferocious adulation perhaps equaled by no other human in modern times. Weeping, hysterical youths, a million or more at a time, gathered in mass demonstrations, shouting "Chairman Mao is the red sun in our hearts! We will smash whoever opposes Chairman Mao!"[69]

They waved their *Little Red Book* of Mao's quotations and roamed the country, ravaging anything that denoted the "Four Olds": old thought, old culture, old customs, old habits. Vestiges of the corrupt past—including books, ancient art, and religious artifacts—were vandalized and destroyed. "There is no construction without destruction," Chairman Mao had told the youths. "Put destruction first, and in the process you have construction."[70] First tentatively and then with growing vehemence, school-age youths began censuring adults suspected of subversion. Aspiring politicians jumped onto the bandwagon of national hysteria. In mass "struggle meetings," those accused of antiparty activities or beliefs were brought before large crowds, where they were verbally and physically abused before they confessed. Frozen by fear, hoping for a reduced punishment, millions of men and women confessed to political crimes they never committed. The list of offenses and offenders grew. Anyone who had ever been abroad, especially to America, was suspect. Blue jeans, Western art, and decadent American hairstyles were banned. Doctors were prohibited from using English when writing prescriptions. People were imprisoned for owning foreign books or for having made some offhand remark, long-forgotten, criticizing Mao or the party. It was a crime for any home or vehicle not to display a picture of Chairman Mao.

"I love a great upheaval," Mao had said, but by 1968 the mayhem that he had instigated was slipping beyond his control. Factions emerged between Red Guard groups, sometimes resulting in violent clashes over interpretation of the chairman's quotations. The Red Guard had become a cult, and its units sects, fighting each other over dogma. Disillusioned with his latest social experiment, Mao decided to end it. He called out the army to suppress the Red Guards. In August the state-controlled radio announced that numerous "illegal" student and worker organizations had been disbanded.[71] Thousands were killed in public executions as the Red Army violently put down factional strife. Internationally, China suffered an irreparable loss of face. By 1969 any remnant of attraction that it had held for Third World oligarchies and Western intellectuals had largely evaporated. It could list as its confirmed allies only Albania and North Vietnam.[72]

———◆———

America's relations with the totalitarian regime in Beijing can only be understood in the context of the larger protracted struggle between the free world and international Communism, which during the 1960s and 1970s continued to be pledged to the destruction of liberal democracy by violent revolution.

The question was, how best to spur change within politically repressive societies? In 1966 the Council on Foreign Relations issued a voluminous study, chaired by former CIA chief Allen Dulles, which showed that many leading U.S. foreign policy experts favored a liberalization of the American policy toward China.[73] Testifying before the Senate Foreign Relations Committee in March 1966, Columbia University scholar A. Doak Barnett described the U.S. approach toward the PRC since its creation as "containment and isolation." He believed that the United States should move toward "containment but not isolation," a view shared by many authorities, including within the administration of President Lyndon Johnson.[74]

"Lasting peace can never come to Asia as long as the seven hundred million people of mainland China are isolated by their rulers from the outside world," Johnson said in a speech on July 12. "We persist because we believe that even the most rigid societies will one day awaken to the possibilities of a diverse world. And we continue because we believe that cooperation, not hostility, is really the way of the future."[75] But how to coax China out of its insularity, which had long preceded the Communists? Administration officials believed that by presenting Beijing with the prospect of improved relations, the United States might "preclude the possibility that the only place they can move for improving their international position is through reconciliation with the USSR."[76] That is, they would attempt to widen the gulf between China and the Soviet Union. Johnson's new policy came to be referred to as "containment without isolation."

China's millennia-old tradition of isolation was compounded by the paranoia natural to a totalitarian regime. There were innumerable obstacles to fostering closer relations. In April 1967, in response to the outbreak of epidemics across China, the U.S. State Department announced a humanitarian program to send drugs to help treat and fight the spread of meningitis, cholera, and contagious hepatitis. Beijing rejected the offer and denounced it as a "dirty trick."[77] The *People's Daily* wrote that America was attempting to "present heinous U.S. imperialism as a god of mercy to deceive the people of the world." Hundreds of thousands of Chinese died of the preventable diseases.

In 1964, China had become a nuclear power, and since then Mao had repeatedly spoken of China's ability—with its huge population—to survive and prevail in the event of a nuclear holocaust. "If worst came to worst and half of mankind died," he said in 1968, "the other half would remain while imperialism would be razed to the ground and the whole world would become socialist; in a number of years there would be 2,700 million people again and definitely more."[78]

Despite its insane rhetoric, Beijing had abundant reason to be interested in an overture with the Americans. In 1968, under its leader Alexander Dubcek, the Czechoslovak Communist Party had initiated several liberalizing reforms, including a relaxation of state censorship. In response to the "Prague Spring," the Soviet Union invaded Czechoslovakia, justifying its aggression with what would become known as the Brezhnev Doctrine, which held that the USSR had the right to interfere in the internal affairs of any socialist state that was deviating from the one true path of socialism. This was disconcerting to the leadership in Beijing, for they too were following their own brand of Communism. During the early 1960s, Chinese government propaganda had described the paramount global conflict as being "between the socialist and imperialist camps"; by 1969 that had been modified to "between the oppressed nations on the one hand and imperialism and social imperialism on the other." "Social imperialism" signified Moscow's version.[79] There was an increasing frequency of border clashes between the two nations, which had escalated into sporadic firefights. Mao began warning his people to prepare for a possible invasion by the "number one enemy," Russia's "social imperialists."[80]

Richard Nixon, elected president in November 1968, seemed an unlikely prospect for making a major breakthrough in relations with Beijing. He had, after all, risen to prominence as a vocal red-baiter, supporter of Chiang Kai-shek's Nationalists, and congressional inquirer into "Who lost China?" At least by 1967, presidential-hopeful Nixon was calling for the integration of China into the global community. "Any American policy must come urgently to grips with the reality of China," he wrote in *Foreign Affairs*. "There is no place in this small planet for a billion of its potentially most able people to live in angry isolation."

"We seek an open world," President Nixon said in his inaugural address on January 20, 1969. "Open to ideas, open to the exchange of goods and people, a world in which no people, great or small, will live in angry isolation. . . . "[81]

In a message to Congress in February 1971, Nixon reiterated what would become one of the landmarks of his administration—bringing China into the international community. "An international order cannot be secure if one of the major powers remains largely outside it and hostile toward it," the president said. "In this decade, therefore, there will be no more important challenge than that of drawing the People's Republic of China into a constructive relationship with the world community, and particularly with the rest of Asia. . . . "[82] In April, the United States lifted a decades-old travel ban to China, and Beijing responded by inviting an American table-tennis team that had been playing in a tournament in Japan to visit the country. On April 14, as Chinese officials met with the American Ping-Pong team, the White House announced the easing of a trade embargo with China, the relaxation of currency controls, and permission for U.S. ships to carry Chinese cargo between non-Chinese ports.

On July 16 the president made a nationwide television address to announce that National Security Adviser Henry Kissinger had just returned from a weeklong trip to China, and that Nixon had accepted an invitation to visit there the following year. "I have taken this action because of my profound conviction that all nations will gain from a reduction of tensions and a better relationship between the United States and the People's Republic of China," he said.[83] On February 21, 1972, Nixon arrived in Beijing for the epochal visit. During the following week he attended cultural performances, toured historic sites, and met with an ailing Chairman Mao and Premier Zhou Enlai. At the end of the trip, the two sides issued the "Shanghai Communiqué," asserting that "countries, regardless of their social systems, should conduct their relations on the principle of respect for the sovereignty and territorial integrity of all states." They pledged to advance mutual understanding and ease tensions by promoting "people-to-people contacts" and trade.[84]

On the issue of Taiwan there remained broad differences between the two governments. Beijing reiterated its position that Taiwan was a province of China that must eventually be "liberated." The American government declared that U.S. troops would only be withdrawn from Taiwan "as the tension in the area diminishes," and following a peaceful resolution of the conflict between Taipei and Beijing.[85] Washington also announced that it would support "seating the People's Republic of China" in the United Nations, but would continue to oppose the expulsion of Taiwan. U.S. opposition to China's admission had been decisive, and when the opposition ended, the admission was soon forthcoming.

The phrase "Only Nixon can go to China" would find its way into colloquial usage. Was a rapprochement with China the right thing to do? International politics is not an arena that presents us with choices between optimal alternatives. During World War II the Allies had sided with Stalin in an effort to defeat Hitler. "If Hitler invaded Hell," Churchill said of the pact with the Soviets, "I would make at least a favorable reference to the Devil in the House of Commons." In attempting to exploit differences between the two Communist powers, Nixon was responding to events as he found them. Not all repressive leftist regimes were necessarily tied together as allies, any more than all democracies were. Advocates of an opening to China believed that better relations with it would bolster the American position in dealings with Moscow. "To have two Communist powers competing for good relations with us," Henry Kissinger later wrote, "could only benefit the cause of peace."[86] Ultimately, that hope was vindicated.

———◆———

When Mao Zedong died on September 9, 1976, of Parkinson's disease at the age of eighty-three, the struggle to replace him had already simmered for years, and the need for dramatic reform in China was undeniable. Its economy was inert. As the capitalist nations of Asia surged far beyond it in agricultural and industrial output, health, life expectancy, and other measures of human welfare, no objective observer could deny the failure of the Communist model or the superiority of free markets.

There was no doubt that the Chinese government remained repressive and deprived its citizens of basic civil liberties. For President Jimmy Carter, elected in November 1976 and deeply committed to advancing a humanitarian foreign policy, the question remained how to best move the huge nation toward greater openness, respect for human rights, and peaceful cooperation within the global community: by isolation or by positive engagement? Carter, like Nixon, chose the latter.

In China, meanwhile, Deng Xiaoping (who had been labeled as "antiparty" and exiled during the Cultural Revolution) was confirmed by the party's Central Committee in 1978 as the country's "paramount leader." The Central Committee announced that the main task of the party was not to wage class struggle, but to overcome the country's economic backwardness and raise the standard of living.[87] Deng's reforms were directed toward the improvement of economic vitality and living standards, where the failure of the Communist system was in increasingly stark contrast to the West, and even to China's capitalist Asian neighbors. Deng believed that U.S. economic and technological assistance were essential for China's modernization. Carter believed that engagement would moderate the oppressive and leaden Communist system.

On December 15, 1978, Jimmy Carter made the announcement that many China watchers had for decades considered inevitable: "The United States recognizes the Government of the People's Republic of China as the sole legitimate government of China." Formal diplomatic relations were to be established with Beijing, effective January 1. Carter referred to the opportunity to renew the "long history of friendship" between the two peoples and advance world peace.[88] The formal recognition of the PRC, though a logical extension of the policy of "containment without isolation," required the termination of official diplomatic ties with Taipei. Nevertheless, the basic cultural and economic relationship would remain strong. The president said that he expected the Taiwan issue to be "settled peacefully by the Chinese themselves." Meanwhile, "cultural, commercial and other unofficial relations" would be maintained between the United States and Taiwan, and the American commitment to the defense of the Republic of China was reaffirmed.[89]

The decision to establish formal diplomatic relations with the Beijing regime was not made in a vacuum. For Carter, in addition to the prospect of improving human rights in China, there was always looming in the background the menace of Soviet Communism. It was also a concern for the Chinese. "If we really want to place curbs on the Russian bear," Deng told Carter on a visit to Washington in early 1979," the only realistic thing is for us to unite."[90]

There were reasonable arguments, moral and pragmatic, to be made on both sides of the case. Americans supported the easing of tensions with China, but favored keeping diplomatic pressure on the Beijing government to promote human rights there, and favored maintaining the security relationship with the nascent democracy in Taiwan. Nobody expected Communist

China to become suddenly democratic with the improving relations, and it did not. But the process was sparking new hopes for reform, including in China itself. The Beijing government desperately sought inclusion as a legitimate member of the international community and had adopted in early 1978 a new constitution, guaranteeing "freedom of speech, correspondence, the press, demonstrations. . . . "

Though the party's professed liberalism was a sham, its shift toward capitalism was not. "Isolation landed China in poverty, backwardness and ignorance," said Deng. "I am afraid that some of our old comrades have this fear, after a generation of socialism and Communism, that it is unacceptable to sprout some capitalism. . . . It cannot harm us. It cannot harm us."[91] The communes were dismantled and a system of contract farming put in their place. Peasants were allowed to cultivate small, personal plots of land and keep the profits from their labors. Western firms scrambled to establish business relationships in hopes of tapping into the vast "China market." In China, the profit-motive was no longer malicious. "To get rich is glorious," Deng declared. It was announced that some wasteful and inefficient state-run enterprises would be allowed to go bankrupt. Conservative critics of the reforms warned of "spiritual pollution" to socialism resulting from free markets, but the economic effects of Communism had been so ruinous, and the benefits of economic liberalization were so apparent, that Deng enjoyed broad support for his policies.

Economic freedom was one thing; politics was altogether different. Economic reforms proceeded alongside political oppression. Many things had not changed. There was still the subordination of the individual to the state. There was still the suppression of civil liberties. There was still a dictatorship, if not of the proletariat. China's rulers had retained everything from Marx except the Communism.

When, in mid-April, students gathered in Tiananmen Square to demonstrate for political reforms, they were denounced by the state as Western collaborators. The crowds continued to grow. By the eighteenth a million people a day were gathering in Tiananmen. In the square, students erected a huge styrofoam and plaster "Goddess of Democracy and Freedom." It was modeled after the American Statue of Liberty, raising its torch of liberty into the air. It became the rallying point for the demonstrators.

Martial law was proclaimed on the nineteenth. The party leadership was conscious of the propaganda catastrophe that the demonstrations represented for their regime. Images of millions of Chinese citizens demanding reform in the symbolic center of the nation were being broadcast throughout the world. Something had to give. On June 3, Chinese leaders ordered the People's Liberation Army to clear the square. A quarter million troops now surrounded the city.

Groups of workers and students organized to obstruct the advance of army units toward the city center, building barricades, letting the air out of tires, imploring the soldiers not to fire upon their fellow citizens. It is not known who first gave the order to fire on civilians, but it had to have come from the Party's Central Military Commission, and probably from its chairman, Deng Xiaoping. Most of the killing done on the morning of June 3–4 in what has come to be called the Tiananmen Square Massacre was not done in the square, but along the approaches to it. By the predawn of the fourth, PLA troops had reached the edge of the square. As a dense fog of tear gas descended on Tiananmen, government loudspeakers warned all of those still gathered there that they would be considered participants in a "counterrevolutionary action" and be treated accordingly. Tanks and troops flooded into Tiananmen, and more shots rang out in the night. The small number of students who chose to remain behind in the square were never heard from again. For the next week army reinforcements continued to arrive in the city to secure control.

The Red Cross estimated that around 2,600 were killed in Beijing on June 3–4. In the ensuing crackdown on the pro-democracy movement, between 10,000 and 30,000 citizens were arrested. Most were held without trial or convicted in show trials. Under torture and threat of death, some confessed to antistate activities. Others fled abroad.

Although in the election campaign of 1992 candidate Bill Clinton criticized Bush for his complaisance toward the Communist regime's actions, President Clinton determined—as presidents before him had—that constructive engagement was more likely to integrate China into the global community and facilitate its democratization than a policy of isolating it would.

———◆———

How shall we assess America's encounter with China since the rise to power of Mao and the Communists? Though the Beijing government had begun to embrace the system of private enterprise and free markets that the United States had fostered throughout the world in the twentieth century, politically it remained repressive and authoritarian. Reforms had been made, but there was far to go. Yet there may have been little more that the United States could have done to alter the course of internal affairs in the most populous nation in the world; and America was remarkably successful in its policy of containing Mao's expansionist impulses, preventing the Beijing regime from forcibly extending its brand of Communism to other Asian nations. That is not a small thing. From 1945 to 1978 the United States gave over $43 billion in economic assistance to promote democracy and free markets among Asian societies.[92] At the end of the century democracy and free markets were burgeoning across Asia, and people were living more freely and more prosperously than ever before in their history.

Consider the fate of one of those societies—Taiwan. A tiny island outpost just off the Chinese mainland, it stands as a flourishing reproach to Beijing's socialist ideology and exists as a free and independent nation only because of America's unwavering and persistent, persistent, persistent commitment to it.

A 1954 CIA report concluded that Chiang's Nationalist government in Taiwan was able to subsist in the face of the danger from the mainland "only because of U.S. support. . . . The future fortunes of the Chinese Nationalist Government will be determined to a very large extent by U.S. policy, and will depend increasingly upon the scale and character of U.S. aid and support."[93] Dwight Eisenhower, while wary of Communist China and supportive of Taiwan, held Chiang Kai-shek in no greater esteem than Truman had. As had been the case in China, there were no optimal choices in 1950 Taiwan. International affairs are often a delicate balancing act between disagreeable alternatives. Eisenhower's secretary of state John Foster Dulles wrote that "Chiang is bitter, arrogant, and difficult for us. . . . He has a vested interest in World War III, which alone, he feels, might restore his mainland rule."[94]

American economic assistance was linked to liberalization, including an aggressive program of land reform, for which the United States provided both technical assistance and funding through the Joint Commission on Rural Reconstruction.[95] One-fourth of all cultivated land in the country was affected by the reforms. The proportion of owner-farmers increased from 33 to 57 percent by 1953. The Taiwanese were becoming more prosperous, more educated, more politically demanding. Under continuing pressure from the United States and its own people, the KMT gradually expanded the sphere of political freedom from local and regional to national politics. "The regime's prime constraint," wrote one analyst, "was U.S. assistance."[96]

From 1951 to 1965 the United States gave Taiwan $1.5 billion in nonmilitary aid to assist in economic development.[97] It also promoted private economic investment there and gave Taiwan's manufacturers broad access to the immense American market. The shift in formal diplomatic recognition to the mainland in 1979 had little substantive effect upon U.S. relations with Taiwan, or its economic performance. Taiwan's external trade rose 31 percent that year, and foreign investment in Taiwan increased by over 50 percent, to $329 million.[98]

The men who established Taiwan's first major opposition party, the Democratic Progressive Party, counted on American pressure on behalf of the incipient democracy. "If we are persecuted, our candidates can refuse to participate in the year-end elections," said a party leader. "Such an action of protest will elicit great public sympathy, and the KMT will be the target of great international pressure, especially from the United States."[99]

Fifty years after the Seventh Fleet was dispatched to defend the people of Taiwan against certain invasion from the mainland, the nation remains, against all odds, an independent state—democratic, free, and prosperous. By the end of the twentieth century the Chinese who had fled to Taiwan had established a democratic polity with aggressive opposition parties, freedom of speech, and a free press, and had made a peaceful transfer of power, one of the tests of a free society. With unwavering American support, the people of Taiwan had established the first functioning democracy in the long history of Chinese civilization.

———•———

Or, consider the 50 million people of South Korea, liberated from Communist aggression by American action and defended for half a century by it. The 38th Parallel today marks not only a geographic border, but a cultural chasm. On the North lies one of the most closed, repressive and impoverished societies in the world; on the South lies a free and democratic people with a vibrant and prosperous culture. Like everywhere else—including the United States—democratization took time in Confucian South Korea; it proceeded in fits and starts, but with resolute American encouragement and assistance, by the 1980s it was clear that democracy was there to stay. At the dawn of the new century South Korea stood as a dynamic, thriving democracy, contrasting starkly with the squalid totalitarian regime in the North.

The mechanisms of state control are all-pervasive in North Korea. There is no "judicial system" separate from politics and party. As in other twentieth-century utopias, the secret police are everywhere, and everyone is a potential informant. Neighbor is enjoined to inform upon neighbor, brother upon brother, children upon parents. To know of a "political crime" against society and not report it is to be part of it. To travel beyond one's town requires written permission from the local party office, the director of one's work group, and the Security Police. Citizens are still protected from all potentially corrupting influences (everything foreign), and are indoctrinated from infancy on: everything they hear, see, and read must be sanctioned by the state. North Korean radios are manufactured to receive only government stations. To be caught listening to South Korean radio is an offense punishable by life imprisonment. It is also a crime for citizens to talk to foreigners. The few foreigners who *are* allowed to visit the country—now mostly relief workers—find their movement severely restricted and their every action monitored by government watchers.

More than a decade before the elder Kim's death in 1994, he began preparing the public mind for the acceptance of his son as ruler. By decree Kim Jong-il's portrait was hung next to the father's in public places, homes, billboards, and on the sides of buildings. In 1997 the younger Kim was named general secretary of the Korean Workers' Party. No election was required, as he received "unanimous approval."[100]

The public is maintained in a constant state of heightened ideological alert by ceaseless warnings of a coming Great Conflict. Children spend countless hours in military drilling exercises, preparing for the war always just around the corner with world capitalism. While every other segment of North Korean society suffers deprivation, the military flourishes, a means of assuring its continued support for Kim. Out of a population of 22 million, the Korean People's Army is one of the largest in the world, comprising an estimated 1.2 million personnel, twice the size of the armed forces of the much larger and more prosperous South. Military spending absorbs over one-fourth of the nation's meager GDP.

In North Korea mankind has witnessed the tragedy of Communism played through to its final scene, apparently unmoderated by any significant public pressures upon the regime for reform. Factories are obsolete and unproductive. The archaic transportation system has broken down, so that food which *is* produced often rots before it can be shipped. The roads are nearly devoid of traffic. The vitality of the nation, its spirit, seems to have been sapped. There are few pedestrians on city streets, and many of those are in military uniforms. When *Washington Post* correspondent Don Ober-dorfer traveled to Pyongyang, he counted a total of twenty-three vehicles (on both sides of the road) along the twelve-mile drive on the main highway from the airport into the city. It was a Monday, around noon.[101]

Upon acceding to power, Kim Jung-il announced his economic priorities for the nation: everything would be top priority. "Agriculture first. Light industry first. Foreign trade first."[102] The twentieth century has showed ideological zeal to be a poor promoter of individual work effort, much less creativity. Prosperity by decree did not deliver the goods. Factory supervisors, fearful of failing to meet party quotas, learned how to fudge numbers and appear busy, if not productive.

The country's collective farms were designed to run according to the dictates of party ideologues, not agriculture specialists, but nature does not bow to ideology. They could order what seeds were planted, but they could not command them to grow. Isolated from the outside world, North Korean bureaucrats had not even learned about important advances in seed varieties. When in 1995, Kim finally admitted to the outside world the existence of a famine and requested aid from the United Nations World Food Program, North Korea was one of only two nations (along with Cuba, another economic basket case) that still dogmatically adhered to the Communist model.

Conservative estimates put the death toll from the state-induced famine of 1994–99 at over 1 million—5 percent of the population. The Pyongyang regime never admitted to its own people that it had been forced to ask for international assistance. Instead, it drummed the message that their privation was a result of the global imperialist conspiracy against their socialist paradise. Kim initiated a series of propaganda campaigns urging the people to work harder and be more frugal. The media ran stories of Koreans who had selflessly decided to move from comfortable lives in the city to go to work in the mines, or to the farms, in order "to give happiness and satisfaction to the respected and beloved general [Kim Jong-il] with bumper crops."[103] A "Let's Eat Two Meals a Day" campaign was launched. There were public executions of Agriculture Ministry officials, before audiences of 20,000 to 30,000, but they did not spur productivity.[104]

At the dawn of the new millennium the Pyongyang regime continues to use mass meetings, indoctrination sessions, and incessant propaganda to maintain the allegiance of the public—although it is impossible to know how deep that allegiance is. Also, the Secret Police has become more active than ever in rooting out dissent. And North Koreans are constantly warned that those who defect to the South are tortured and then executed by the imperialist regime there. But fear underlies all other mechanisms of control, and underlying that fear is the nation's formidable gulag system. Around two hundred thousand political prisoners are held in six massive camps, one larger than the District of Columbia, and by all accounts the figure is rising as Kim desperately clings to power. Citizens are arrested and imprisoned without trial for a variety of offenses as diverse as the whims of party officials: having a religious faith, singing a South Korean pop song, making even mildly critical political statements, refusing an official's request for a bribe, being born into a dubious family. Around half a million people are believed have died in North Korea's prison camps in the past generation. But in fact, as escapees to the South have pointed out, the entire country is a kind of gulag.

As for the party elite themselves, their insularity and self-deception rose to bewildering levels. In May 1991, Kim Jong-il made a speech to top party officials warning that "the imperialists and reactionaries, loudly advertising the 'advantage' of private ownership, are urging socialist countries to abandon social ownership and restore private ownership. . . . The people in our country experienced through their actual lives that social ownership alone provides them with an abundant and cultured life."[105] The Dear Leader himself (who has ordered the kidnapping of foreign citizens, the assassination of critics abroad, and the bombing of a Korean Airlines flight) prohibits his subjects from learning anything of the outside world, for there are few places that would not seem appealing by contrast Now, Kim is developing a nuclear bomb–making capacity.

The isolation and repression of North Koreans contrasts glaringly with social and political life south of the 38th Parallel. An airplane arriving at Pyongyang from Beijing may be the only flight landing in the entire nation that day.[106] In the South, tens of thousands of travelers pass through dozens of airports, arriving from and departing to all points of the globe. In South Korea civil liberties are protected. A free press scrutinizes a popularly elected government. The streets of Seoul and other South Korean cities are hubs of cultural vitality, seething with the happy anarchy of freedom.

South Korea's 48 million people live infinitely better lives today because of the American commitment to their defense during the Korean War, and since that time. The South Korean economy flourished with the help of billions of dollars in American economic and defense assistance. U.S. policies helped nurture developing Korean industries by allowing them to protect their firms from competition, while American markets were opened to their products.

At century's end, North Korea's GDP was $12.6 billion, a *decline* of $2.5 billion from fifteen years earlier. South Korea's economy, with a GDP of $450 billion, was the eleventh-largest in the world. It boasted the fifth-largest foreign exchange reserves in the world. Per capita income in the South was about $10,000, more than twelve times greater than that of the North, where per capita income was less than $800. Life expectancy for South Korean men was 72.1 years, and for women 79.5 years—more than a decade longer than their counterparts in the North.

The American struggle in Korea secured the balance of power in East Asia. It halted the advance of Communism there. But most concretely, for hundreds of millions of Koreans who have lived and are yet to live, it has made all the difference in the world. They are more free, more prosperous, more alive because of the sacrifices made by millions of Americans, 55,000 of whom gave their lives. Many Koreans have not forgotten. Like many of her generation, Chong Suk, a young girl during the Korean war, feels deep gratitude toward the 'Yankees' who fought to defend her country from totalitarianism. "You changed our lives," she wrote in a thank you letter to the men who served in Korea. "We did not know who you were, where the United States was, or why you had to be there. We only knew you as our guardian angels."[107]

----•----

As the new age dawns, China is in a state of flux. Marxism has been rejected, even by the party leadership. China has embarked upon "socialism with Chinese characteristics," but nobody knows what that means, including the leadership. The party still dominates the political sphere, and much of the social and economic, and is unwilling to yield power even though its ideology has been discredited. After countless failed social experiments, inflicting millions of lost lives, the Chinese Communist Party is trying a new experiment: free market Communism. In late 2001, China joined the World Trade Organization, signaling its desire to join the globalization phenomenon under way, and even enter the ranks of market economies. To do so, it committed to a timetable of further structural economic reforms.

No Communist regime has ever reformed its way to liberal democracy. The oligarchs in Beijing will not. But because of the increasingly free and prosperous world that their people see all around them in Asia, change is inevitable. Entrance into world trade has promoted economic growth in China, but it has also spurred entrepreneurialism, increased knowledge of the outside world, eroded the party's monopoly over patronage, and fostered competing—private—sources of power. The adoption of even semi-free markets have necessitated other freedoms: party leaders have been forced, for example, to legalize the free movement of workers. And the flow of information continues to grow. That is the paradox of liberalization in the modern era: if you don't liberalize your society, the people will see that their economy is a disaster and will rebel; and if you do, the people will yearn for political liberty, and will rebel. Ultimately the Chinese will come to recognize, as others have, that the real engines of prosperity—creativity and initiative—cannot be dictated or "planned." As Polish revolutionary leader Lech Walesa put it: "In the past, you could stand behind a man who had a pick and spade and tell him to dig a hole two hundred meters long. But you can't put a man behind someone working creatively, behind a computer, and tell him 'Devise something original.' "[108]

In the early 1900s, Americans earnestly undertook to bring China into the community of free nations. The past half century has vindicated their efforts. Had they succeeded then, the billion people of China would have been infinitely better off today: they would live more freely and more prosperously. Immeasurable suffering and millions of lives would have been spared.

That project remains unfinished. The regime in Beijing persists as one of the most repressive in the world. American leaders must continue to criticize oppression and encourage pro-democracy forces in China. "The U.S. is the chief beacon of democracy and individual freedom in a world that recently has tipped toward democracy and free markets," writes human rights activist Ross Terrill. "This light on the hill influences the Chinese mind and pressures the Chinese Communist Party. We should speak up for American values, including federalism and individual rights, while stopping short of pushing solutions to China's domestic affairs."[109] Beijing needs good relations with the free world infinitely more than the free world needs Beijing.

Elsewhere in Asia, the model of liberal democracy that the United States helped establish is increasingly ascendant, and the vitality of those nations stands as an indictment of the savagery and ineptitude of Communist regimes in China and North Korea, which increasingly resemble throwbacks to some darker age of human history. For thousands of years the peoples of Asia have been governed by authoritarian regimes. The twentieth century was a time of epic threats to life and liberty there—fascism from Japan; Communism from China and Russia. But today, from South Korea and Japan to the Philippines, Singapore, Hong Kong, and Taiwan, political and economic liberties have taken root and flourished. Nations have risen from grinding economic destitution and political oppression to become dynamic, democratic societies. It was not inevitable that, at the end of the twentieth century, social and political conditions would be far better for those societies than they had ever been in history. Across Asia, across the century, millions of Americans worked and fought, sacrificed and died to make that transformation possible.

7

Crusade for Freedom

MARXISM WAS NEVER a single ideology. It was dozens of different, sometimes incompatible doctrines; rationalizations for nationalists, patriots, self-promoters, rebels, clerics, intellectuals, artists, unionists, all seeking power in their own way. Marxism was a justification for seizing and expanding control over the individual. The utopia it promised justified the brutality it entailed. For a new society to be built, the old society must be razed. For the "new man" to emerge, the old one must be annihilated. Communism—the idea of a polity based upon coerced selflessness—proved to be one of the worst ideas in history and, along with fascism, one of the twentieth century's most destructive. A materialist doctrine, it demonstrated the power that ideas, even badly mistaken ones, can have upon history.

Karl Marx had expected Communism to emerge in developed, industrialized nations. In fact, it took power only in those societies he called 'backward,' more feudal than capitalistic, authoritarian, lacking rule of law. In November 1917, Vladimir Lenin's Bolsheviks took power in Russia following the overthrow of Czar Nicholas II. Lenin, who with Marx envisioned a "withering away of the state," presided over the development of what would become the most all-pervading and intrusive political system in history. His Bolsheviks, who insisted that they were fighting to overthrow a vicious and oppressive social order, murdered more political opponents during their first four months in power than the czarist regime had in a century.[1] Within weeks after seizing power, Lenin had created the All-Extraordinary Commission for Combating Counter-Revolution and Sabotage, called *Cheka* for its Russian abbreviation. The first modern secret police was given the task of conducting the "Red Terror": to hunt out and eradicate political opponents.

The Communists did not represent the views of more than a tiny minority of Russians, but they won the frightened submission of the former state bureaucracy, and benefited by the apathy of the larger public and were thus able to buy the time needed to consolidate control over the implements of power. "If 200,000 landlords could rule Russia, why not 200,000 Communists?" Lenin asked.[2]

The achievement of utopia required a new kind of oligarchy: a tyranny more thorough and comprehensive than any before in history. It was truly *totalitarian*: every aspect of social and political and economic existence, every nook and cranny of the individual's life, was to be controlled by the state, which was to be controlled by the party.

Such rule could only be accomplished by terror. All "enemies of the people" were to be "exterminated without pity," Lenin said. Who were those enemies? Anyone opposed to the new order. "Without mercy, without sparing, we will kill our enemies in scores of hundreds," declared the party. "Let them be thousands, let them drown in their own blood." In addition, *potential* political enemies, including "the bourgeoisie, landowners, industrialists, merchants, counter-revolutionary priests. . . " were to be hunted, arrested, and imprisoned in "concentration camps."[3] Lenin commented approvingly that, in some areas, "one out of ten of those guilty of parasitism" were being "shot on the spot."[4]

Civil institutions, potential competitors for power, were abolished. Much of the land was expropriated by the state. Eventually, all would be. Functions once performed by the marketplace, ranging from shoe repair to tailoring, came under the control of the state.[5] With agriculture collectivized, a system of food rationing had to be developed.

Many peasants, needless to say, demurred to confiscation of their property and production. In 1918, soon after coming to power, Lenin declared a war of annihilation against these "class enemies." He sent an order to provincial officials commanding them to "Hang (hang without fail, so the people see) no fewer than one hundred kulaks. . . . Do it in such a way that for hundreds of [kilometers] around the people will see, tremble, know, shout: *they are strangling and strangle to death* the blood sucker kulaks." To accomplish the terror, officials were instructed to "find some *truly hard* people."[6] There were plenty of such to be found, then and for the next seventy years, to do utopia's violent work.

In the Ukraine entire Cossack towns were destroyed and their populations killed, dispersed, or sent into forced labor. In the Cossack regions of Don and Kuban, from 300,000 to 500,000 people were executed or deported in 1919–20. Religious leaders were hunted down and butchered. Purge followed upon purge as the Communists sought to "purify" society. Allies in the revolution, now potential contenders for power, were arrested and imprisoned or executed.

A year after the Communists came to power, the country was in famine. Grain harvests fell from 78 million tons in 1913 to 48 million in 1920. Over 5 million people died in the ensuing famine, and even more would have if not for aid from the American Relief Administration, which provided food for 25 million Soviet citizens.[7]

One of the few activities Communism turned out to be relatively efficient at was mass repression. A 1918 secret police directive ordered that "suspicious persons are to be incarcerated in a concentration camp. . . . "[8] By 1921 there were 122 such camps in 43 provinces, the foundation for what was to become the most elaborate political imprisonment system in history. The term used to describe the camp system, *gulag*, was an acronym for *Glavnoe Upravlenie Lagerei*, "Main Camp Administration." The slave labor provided by the camps, ranging from logging and agriculture to construction, mining, and factory production, was to become a critical factor in the Soviet economy.[9]

By the early 1920s it was apparent to all but the most credulous believers that the world revolution the movement had foretold was not coming anytime soon. Like members of a cult for whom the millennium fails to arrive when predicted, their faith was undiminished. They turned to building "socialism in one country" instead. Russia, which Marx had derided as the last place where Communism was likely to take hold, would be the springboard for the global socialist millennium.

———●———

Born and raised in the rural Georgian town of Gori, Joseph Stalin came from an impoverished and uneducated peasant family with an abusive, alcoholic father. Sent by his mother to a seminary to become a priest, he became violently antireligious. Five foot four inches tall, of slight build, face pockmarked by a childhood bout of smallpox, he was an isolated and solitary figure his whole life. "He was depressed by his aloneness and he feared it," Khrushchev wrote of his mentor.[10] Like other dictators, Stalin's insularity grew as the years went by, fueled by paranoia. Any popular personality was threatening. (This included Marshal Georgi Zhukov, Soviet hero of the Second World War, whom Stalin was to exile to Odessa following the war.) Leon Trotsky, who had played a key role, along with Lenin and Stalin in the creation of Soviet Communism, disdained Stalin as a mediocrity, but it was Stalin who brutally consolidated power after Lenin's death in 1924; Trotsky wound up getting purged from the party, then executed while living in exile in Mexico.

For Stalin, like Lenin, there could be no allowance for dissenting opinions on the path to utopia. "The existence of factions is incompatible either with the party's unity or with its iron discipline," he declared upon taking power.[11] A "cultural revolution" was launched to indoctrinate the citizenry.[12]

Forced collectivization accelerated forced collectivization. In 1924, Stalin announced that it was time to bring about the "liquidation of the kulaks as a class."[13] Over a million kulaks, prosperous peasants who were despised as successful protocapitalists and feared for their potential anti-Communist influence, were violently removed from the countryside, their property seized. Many were shipped off to the burgeoning gulag system or executed. In all, during the 1930s and 40s, some 7 million kulak households were destroyed.[14]

Zealous urban Communists with no training in agriculture were dispatched to the countryside to oversee the herding of peasants into large, "cooperative" farms. Peasants' livestock was taken by government agents for use on the collective farms, where they were often neglected: the number of Russian livestock fell by half between 1928 and 1932.[15]

Millions of ordinary peasants who were suspected of opposing the new order were shot or removed to Siberia. Others fled the countryside for the cities—12 million between 1928 and 1932. To control this unapproved population movement, in 1932 a law was introduced establishing "internal passports." By that year, 81 percent of all tilled land in the agriculture-rich Ukraine had been collectivized; 70 percent of all farm families had been relocated to collective farms.

Life on the state-controlled farms grew increasingly bleak. Mandatory mass rallies were held to instill the peasants with ideological fervor, but to no effect: productivity plummeted. Party officials overseeing collectivization, most of them inexperienced in agriculture, created larger and larger communal farms, with disastrous results. A series of state-inflicted famines ravaged the Soviet Union in the early 1930s and, as was later repeated in China's state-induced Great Famine, those in the richest agricultural areas often suffered the most, since they were the targets of the most demanding state production quotas. Party overseers—"food detachments"—were sent to ensure that the harvest was secured in government barns. Only after the state's extravagant quota had been met would the farmers themselves receive a share of the produce. "The harvest was good, but the government took everything," a survivor recalled.[16]

It was a crime for individuals to store—"hoard"—two days' worth of bread or other foodstuffs: one must trust the party for one's daily bread. By the beginning of 1933, 55,000 had received long sentences for "stealing" a few onions or ears of corn from the land they worked, to feed their starving families; thousands had been executed.[17] A party member sent to the countryside to enforce compliance by the peasantry wrote of the scene: "I saw people dying in solitude by slow degrees, dying hideously. They had been trapped and left to starve, each in his home, by a political decision made in a far-off capital around banquet tables."[18]

As millions of citizens starved to death, even at the height of the famine Stalin continued to ship grain abroad—1.8 million tons in 1932 and 1.7 million in 1933[19]—to earn foreign currency and international prestige for his economic plans. He publicly denied the existence of famine, insisting that rumors of famine had been spread by opponents of socialism.[20] There followed a series of brutal retaliations against peasants on collectives that had not delivered their state-ordered production quotas. Hundreds of thousands were rounded up, many to die in the gulag. Many of Communism's leaders, including those carrying out the violence, were genuinely devoted to the dream of building a new, utopian world, and justified the mass murders on that basis. Others were simply opportunists, sycophants, and thugs who would have as energetically joined in the butchery if its rationale had been fascism, or any other power grab. Among the party faithful there was some misgiving, mostly muted, toward the murderous policies. A handful of Communist true believers, seeing what had become of their dream, committed suicide. Some went mad. Some, a Communist official noted at the time, "instead of going mad, became professional bureaucrats for whom terror was henceforth a normal method of administration, and obedience to any order from above a high virtue." "In [1919] we executed people, but we also risked our lives in the process," Nikolai Bukharin, an early leader of the Bolshevik movement, told a friend. "In [1930–32], however, we were conducting a mass annihilation of completely defenseless men, together with their wives and children."[21]

Though believing Marxists later blamed the brutality of the era on the particular personal characteristics of Stalin, it was not the product of an individual, but a system. Alexander Yakovlev, a Politburo member who in the 1980s helped initiate democratic reforms in the Soviet Union, and headed the Russian commission on the "rehabilitation of victims of political repressions" of the past, concluded that "The truth is that in his punitive operations Stalin did not think up anything that was not there already under Lenin: executions, hostage taking, concentration camps and all the rest."[22]

Life in the cities was no less brutal. Stalin's five-year plan to dictate industrialization had resulted in a dramatic deterioration in living standards. To inspire fervor, workers could be sentenced to long prison terms for not laboring diligently enough. And under the centrally dictated economic system, rations—and waiting in long lines for them—became a way of life. Meanwhile, the state propaganda machine hammered the population with slogans like "Life has become better, life has become merrier."[23] At the same time there was emerging a privileged class of party bureaucrats, *apparatchiks*, who had special access to food and consumer goods, housing, vacation villas, even cars and drivers.[24] All advancement within society depended upon party membership.

By the 1930s it was becoming evident that the fervid hopes of the revolutionists for social and economic transformation were not about to be realized anytime soon. And most of the old scapegoats were gone. New scapegoats had to be found. Furthermore, the remnants of the Leninist regime must be destroyed and replaced by those with unquestioned loyalty to Stalin. The dictator embarked upon a new campaign of terror to consolidate power for the party and himself. The period termed the "Great Terror," which began in 1936 and lasted until 1939, marked one of the most ferocious episodes of state violence in a century rife with it.

The Politburo set quotas for arrests and executions in each region. It was announced that the "observance of legal procedures and the preliminary approval of arrests are not necessary." The quotas were overfulfilled by ambitious party officials. Bureaucratic lists were kept of the "Groups Subject to Punitive Measures," tallying the number of those who had been executed or imprisoned, and estimates of those who yet had to be. Stalin declared that torture was to be applied to "known and obstinate enemies of the people."[25] Show trials became the entertainment of the day. The secret police, now called the People's Commissariat of Internal Affairs (or NKVD, for its Russian acronym), tortured confessions out of hundreds of thousands of innocent people.

Fearing that his Army Intelligence Directorate had been penetrated by foreign spies, Stalin ordered it eliminated. To be on the safe side, all of its officers were executed. At least forty thousand Red Army officers were murdered in 1937–38 (more than during the first two years of the war with Nazi Germany).[26] The military's officer corps was decimated.

Then, Germans working in the defense industries and key industrial sectors: 68,000 were arrested, 42,000 executed.[27] Then, a purge of other suspect nationalities—including Poles, Latvians, Estonians, Romanians, Greeks, and others: 350,000 were arrested, 247,000 were killed.[28] Other groups also fell into the expanding net. The slaughter of the clergy, for example, continued and accelerated under Stalin. In 1937 alone, over 85,000 clergy were shot. The Comintern was also repeatedly purged, including of its foreign devotees, whose loyalties Stalin had grown suspicious of.[29]

In all, some 7 million Soviet citizens were arrested in 1937 and 1938. A million of those were summarily executed. Two million more died in concentration camps.[30] Perhaps as a matter of tidying up loose ends, in 1939 Nikolai Yezhov, the head of the secret police who had overseen the terror, was arrested and convicted of conspiracy, and executed.

The object of the Great Terror was not so much to root out specific, real "enemies of the people" (as the accused were called), but to instill fear into all who might *potentially* oppose the regime—that is, everyone. Mass fear was the linchpin of the strategy of state control. The logic of the totalitarian state was being fulfilled. As George Orwell so deftly portrayed in his 1949 work on totalitarianism, *1984*, the total state must not only decide what the future was to be, but the past also. Neither thoughtcrime nor the Thought Police were fictional inventions. Accused Soviet "enemies of the state" were not merely killed. They suffered a "second death," being blotted out from permissible memory; erased from the history books, even deleted from photographs. History was written, and rewritten, and rewritten again. Former heroes of socialism became villains, then disappeared from history altogether.

Above all, the terror worked. Open political discussion, such as it had been, ended altogether. Any public criticism of the party, and criticism within the party of the ruling elite, virtually ceased to exist. Scientists learned to assert truths they didn't believe. Farmers and factory workers met in indoctrination meetings to praise a party that they despised and feared. Writers extolled a system they deplored. "Stalin was gradually eliminating shame," writes Russian historian Edvard Radzinsky. "Fear is stronger than shame."[31]

Beria performed his task with masterful bureaucratic efficiency. Between 1936 and 1941, the population of the gulag doubled, to 1.9 million.[32] Conditions in the camps were brutal. Malnutrition and disease were prevalent. Mortality rates often surpassed 10 percent per year. Wave after wave of imagined political enemies were sent to toil and die in camps scattered from the Black Sea to frozen Siberia. As purge followed upon purge, victims of one wave of repression occasionally met their torturers arriving in the camps, as accused subversives, in a later wave.

From 1935 to 1940, 7 million accused political opponents were murdered by the Moscow regime.[33] Between 1932, the beginning of Stalin's collectivization push, and the outbreak of the Second World War in 1939, the overall population of the Soviet Union declined by some 10 million people.[34]

The 1939 invasion of Poland that precipitated the Second World War, it should be remembered, was launched by Hitler *and* his ally Stalin. The Soviet Union entered the war on the side of the Nazi aggressors. By mid-1940, Moscow had annexed parts of Poland and Finland, northern Romania, and the Baltic states of Estonia, Latvia, and Lithuania. Stalin remained complacent when Hitler's armies pushed the Allied forces off the Continent at Dunkirk in June 1940. Later, at postwar conferences of the Big Three, the dictator went on endlessly about the terrible sacrifices his nation had endured in the war, which was true. He did not mention that Russia only got into the war in the first place because his ally, Hitler, had turned on him and invaded his nation, an eventuality for which his misplaced trust in the German tyrant and repeated purgings of the Red Army had left his country wholly unprepared.

In the end, though, Stalin benefited from Hitler's program. The Nazi dictator's systematic annihilation of existing and potential opposition to his Reich in the conquered nations created a power vacuum throughout Eastern Europe, into which the Soviet dictator would later impose his own minions. In his defense against Hitler, Stalin managed to establish a larger empire than he had hoped to achieve in his 1939 alliance with Hitler.

Even before the Second World War ended, there were warning signs of conflict to come. At Yalta, in February 1945, Stalin agreed that Poland would be "reorganized on a broader democratic basis," but when Franklin Roosevelt said that the election there must be as pure "as Caesar's wife," Stalin replied, "They said that about her, but in fact she had her sins." The Soviet invasion of Poland had replicated the brutality with which the Communists maintained control in their own country, and presaged what was to come for the other nations of Eastern Europe. In April 1940, 22,000 Polish prisoners, military and civilian, public officials and private citizens, were transported to remote locations around the country (including over 4,000 to the Katyn Forest), forced to dig their own graves, then murdered in mass executions. The order had come directly from Stalin and the Soviet Central Committee.[35]

Though Franklin Roosevelt favored accommodation (and during the war many Americans regarded Stalin benignly, referring to him as "Uncle Joe"), among the American leadership there had never been any illusions about Stalin or his system. Regarding the improbable alliance with the Kremlin, the president had quoted an old Balkan proverb: "My children, it is permitted you in time of grave danger to walk with the devil until you have crossed the bridge."[36] In the early 1940s, Hitler was certainly the more imminent threat.

At Yalta, President Roosevelt got Stalin to agree to a Declaration on Liberated Europe, pledging the Allies to help the newly liberated nations of Eastern Europe to resolve postwar economic and political problems through democratic processes. Both leaders, though, recognized that the United States was not in a position to alter the immediate facts on the ground: Soviet troops were there; Americans weren't. Returning from Yalta, Roosevelt glumly told an aide, "I didn't say the result was good. I said it was the best I could do."[37] Stalin told his foreign minister, Vyacheslav Molotov, "Don't worry. We can deal with it in our own way later. The point is the correlation of forces."[38]

At Potsdam in July, the new president, Harry Truman, found a Kremlin leader intent upon consolidating Soviet control over Eastern Europe. It soon became clear that the free elections Stalin had promised for the occupied countries would never take place. Though the president would later be accused of "selling out" the peoples of Eastern Europe to the Soviets, the postwar annexations were already a de facto reality before the leaders ever met. To dislodge Red Army forces would have required going to war against a new enemy as soon as Hitler was defeated.

———◆———

By shortly after the end of the Second World War, the peoples of Western Europe regarded themselves as liberated; and the peoples of Eastern Europe regarded their nations as occupied. The Soviet subjugation of Eastern European nations following the war proceeded in three general stages: 1) by force and threat of force, postwar coalitions of Communist and non-Communist parties were transformed into shams, in which real power was held only by the Communists; 2) non-Communists were purged (by violence, intimidation, or imprisonment) from all government positions; and 3) finally, even native Communists suspected of disloyalty to the Kremlin were purged.[39]

Stalin killed more people than Hitler did. For the peoples of Poland, Czechoslovakia, Hungary, and other East European nations, the defeat of the Nazis did not bring liberation. Agriculture was collectivized and industry socialized. Peasants and workers who resisted the collectivization were imprisoned in the labor camps that were sprouting up across Eastern Europe. Assassinations, tortured inquisitions, forced confessions, show trials, and incessant propaganda became part of the cultural landscape. Across Eastern Europe, non-Communist political activists began to disappear, or turn up dead. Thousands of Soviet "advisers" were sent to help establish domestic surveillance agencies, which had as their model the Soviet secret police. The new East European secret police organizations had two functions: to monitor potential anti-Communist activity among the population, for the state; and to monitor the Communist officials within the state, for the Kremlin.

———◆———

The inevitability of the conflict between Communism and liberal democracy was not just one of the tenets of Marxist dogma: it was its *central* belief. Without it, the entire ideological edifice would collapse. From its beginnings as the rages of an unemployed German philosopher to its ignominious finish, Communism defined itself in terms of its opposition to capitalism. It saw itself as entailing violent and global revolution. Later efforts by some writers—themselves often critics of liberal democratic capitalism—to blame the emergence of the Cold War on *American* actions look increasingly absurd in the light of evidence that has emerged from previously closed Soviet-bloc archives. It is no longer possible to contend that militaristic expansion was not part of the Kremlin's plan, but was merely a defensive reaction to a perceived threat from the West. Indeed, while revisionist historians in the West maintain that American provocation induced the Cold War, a number of Russian and East European historians have suggested that the West bears some responsibility for not acting more aggressively to constrain the Kremlin's expansionism *earlier* than it did.

Neither Marxism's theorists nor its activists made any effort to hide its essentially aggressive nature. It certainly must expand beyond Soviet borders, to the industrialized nations. "[In November 1917] we knew that our victory will be a lasting victory only when our undertaking will conquer the whole world," Lenin had said in 1920. "Because we had launched it exclusively counting on world revolution."[40] Stalin had likewise, as early as the 1920s, described the international system as being divided into two incompatible "centers of gravity," one centered around the socialist Soviet Union, the other around the liberal democratic "Anglo-America."[41]

Even diplomatic relations were part of the battle. "Remember, we are waging a struggle with the whole capitalist world," Stalin had said to Molotov in 1929.[42] The Soviet foreign minister proudly told an interviewer, near the end of his life, "My task as minister of foreign affairs was to expand the borders of the fatherland as much as possible. And it seems that Stalin and I coped with this task quite well."[43] Though many of its leaders were indeed true believers, there was much sheer Russianism in Soviet Communism. For Stalin, the expansion of the socialist faith was inseparable, almost indistinguishable, from the expansion of Soviet power. All of his successors, including the last one, followed this line.

Communism had no fixed timetable for the achievement of its global project. When capitalism looked weak, Communism would advance. When capitalism seemed strong, it would hold its ground. But History, with a capital H, was on its side. "Our ideology stands for offensive operations when possible," said Molotov, who was aptly called "his master's voice." "And if not, we wait."[44]

At the end of the war, liberal democracy appeared to be in retreat. The Communist moment seemed to be at hand. During the immediate prewar period, attention in the West had been on the Great Depression, and serious commentators were predicting that it was capitalism which was in danger of collapse. Some of them hoped that it was. In the chaotic aftermath of war, it was by no means inevitable that the nations of Western Europe would remain democratic. The Americans, moreover, were returning to their instinctive isolation. The Soviet Union could ill afford to go to war for the lands of Eastern Europe, particularly with the new American atomic capability, but Stalin wagered that it would not have to. "We were on the offensive," Molotov later acknowledged. "To squeeze out the capitalist order. This was the cold war."[45]

The conditions for the confrontation between democracy and totalitarianism were already in place when, on February 9, 1946, Stalin made an ominous speech in Moscow, in a tone consonant with long-espoused Marxist principles, declaring that war was inevitable between capitalism and communism, and calling for a rapid Soviet military buildup. A few weeks later, in a March 5 speech at Westminster College in Fulton, Missouri, former prime minister Winston Churchill warned that "an iron curtain has descended across the continent. Behind that line lie all the capitals of the ancient states of Central and Eastern Europe. . . . The Communist parties, which were very small in all these Eastern states of Europe, have been raised to preeminence and power far beyond their numbers and are seeking everywhere to obtain totalitarian control." Churchill believed that it would be up to the world's oldest and most powerful democracy, America, to lead the struggle against the spread of totalitarianism.

In July, President Truman asked his special counsel, Clark Clifford, to make a report analyzing the U.S. relationship with the Soviet Union. Along with his assistant George Elsey, Clifford spent weeks interviewing top U.S. officials who had been involved in diplomacy with the Soviets, examining the succession of Kremlin violations of international agreements and its aggressions in Eastern Europe. The conclusion, shared unanimously among all those who had worked closely with or studied the Soviets, was inescapable: "The Soviet Union constitutes a real menace to freedom in this world; freedom in Europe; freedom in the United States." But Americans were not prepared to take on a new adversary. They were weary of war, and wary of international commitments. The president publicly made some tough remarks about the need for vigilance in the face of manifest Soviet ambitions, and proceeded with the demobilization of the military.

After the Second World War the American people, the Congress, and the administration wished only to reduce America's global commitments. Between 1945 and 1947 the size of the U.S. armed forces was slashed from 12.1 million to 1.7 million men, while the Red Army remained at over 3 million. (By 1955 the Red Army would have nearly 6 million troops under arms.) It was only in response to the emerging Soviet threat to international order that Americans reluctantly took up the cause that Winston Churchill had urged upon them.

———◆———

Stalin was secretly funding Communist parties and guerrilla movements across Western Europe. Economic distress racked the Continent, fostering social and political instability. If the unrest dragged on, there was a real possibility that Communist parties might rise to power in France, Italy, and elsewhere. It was not only the Americans who thought so: the leader of France's Communist Party, Maurice Thorez, informed Stalin that France would soon go Communist.[46]

In Greece, Communist insurgents fought a guerrilla war to overthrow the pro-Western government. Elsewhere in the Mediterranean, Stalin (seeking, like a long succession of Russian rulers, warm-water access for the Russian fleet) had sent Turkey a demand for joint control of the Dardanelles, which would permit the USSR access to the Mediterranean from the Black Sea. He menacingly deployed Red Army divisions to the Soviet border with Turkey. In February, with its postwar economy floundering, the British government quietly informed Washington that it could no longer afford to provide military and other aid to the governments of Greece and Turkey in their fight against the Communist insurgencies.

There could be no more delay. Only one nation was capable of halting the further expansion of Communism. On March 12, President Truman spoke to a joint session of Congress. "At the present moment in world history," he said, "nearly every nation must choose between alternative ways of life. . . . One way of life is based upon the will of the majority. . . . The second way of life is based upon the will of the minority forcibly imposed upon the majority. It relies upon terror and oppression, a controlled press and radio, fixed elections, and the suppression of personal freedoms. I believe it must be the policy of the United States to support free people who are resisting attempted subjugation by armed minorities or by outside pressure. I believe we must assist free people to work out their own destinies in their own way." The Truman Doctrine, as the principle came to be called, would be the foundation for America's half-century struggle to resist the spread of Soviet totalitarianism. "There is no other country to which democratic Greece can turn," Truman told the Congress.

Many Americans had yearned for a return to quiet isolationism. Truman's message, if it was heeded, would preclude that. Senator Vandenberg called it "the most fundamental thing that has been presented to Congress in my time." In May, Congress approved the president's request for $400 million in aid to Turkey and Greece, to assist those governments in resisting Communist insurgencies. In doing so, it ratified the Truman Doctrine and launched America on a new course. The basic outline of the American policy was spelled out in an article entitled "The Sources of Soviet Conduct," which appeared in *Foreign Affairs* magazine in July 1947. The author, identified only as X, was later revealed to be George Kennan, head of the State Department's Policy Planning staff. In the essay, Kennan analyzed the nature of the Kremlin's power, describing the Soviet leadership as tyrannical, but not mad: Communism was bent by a messianic ideology upon expansion and domination, but was not constrained by a schedule. Moscow's leaders sought to expand Communism globally, but they would not do so at the cost of their own survival in power. Soviet expansion, therefore, could be restricted by patient and resolute resistance to it. "Soviet pressure against the free institutions of the Western world is something that can be contained by the adroit and vigilant application of counter-force at a series of constantly-shifting geographical and political points, corresponding to the shifts and maneuvers of Soviet policy, but which cannot be charmed or talked out of existence," Kennan wrote. "The United States has it in its power to increase enormously the strains under which Soviet policy must operate, to force upon the Kremlin a far greater degree of moderation and circumspection than it has had to observe in recent years, and in this way to promote tendencies which must eventually find their outlet in either the break-up or the gradual mellowing of Soviet power."[47]

Kennan believed that this was an epic challenge worthy of America. "Surely, there was never a fairer test of national quality than this," he concluded. "In the light of these circumstances, the thoughtful observer will find no cause for complaint in the Kremlin's challenge to American society. He will rather experience a certain gratitude to a Providence which, by providing the American people with this implacable challenge, has made their entire security as a nation dependent on their . . . accepting the responsibilities of moral and political leadership that history plainly has intended for them."[48]

The Cold War did not arise because of diplomatic failures, personality clashes, or misunderstandings. Stalin—and Mao, and other tyrants—knew what some Western observers failed to grasp: that the two systems of governance were fundamentally incompatible. Though Yalta or Potsdam are frequently given as the starting point of the Cold War, it was probably inevitable long before then. Long before Truman ever signaled the Soviet threat, Kremlin leaders regarded the world as divided irretrievably into two antagonistic camps. Yet, though Soviet rulers were ideological, they were not irrational. They were aggressive, but not self-destructive. In Europe, and later elsewhere, they endeavored to extend their domain until they were confronted by U.S. force, and then paused.[49] They pushed, and kept pushing, until they were pushed back. After studying Kremlin documents that until the end of the Cold War had been classified, Russian historians Vladislav Zubok and Constantine Pleshakov concluded that, in response to Soviet aggression following the Second World War, far from being too belligerent "the West was not firm enough, it did not check Stalin's imperial expansion."[50]

Devoted Communists around the globe believed in the ultimate messianic destiny of Soviet Communism. They believed it was historically inevitable that "scientific socialism" would prevail, by violent revolution and the subjugation of populations. The Communists believed, correctly in this at least, that ultimately capitalism and Communism were incompatible. America did not invent the Communist threat, but rose to meet it. Had there been no totalitarian system to contain, there would have been no policy of containment, no Cold War.

As the Kremlin's grip tightened across Eastern Europe, it continued to foster Communist movements in Western Europe. It counted on postwar economic instability to produce conditions ripe for socialist political takeovers. Americans, for their part, believed that if other nations were prosperous, they would be more likely to be democratic and peaceful, too. On April 2, 1948, the United States Congress approved the most massive assistance program in human history to help rebuild the shattered economies of Europe. "The restoration or maintenance in European countries of principles of individual liberty, free institutions and genuine independence rests largely upon the establishment of sound economic conditions, stable economic relationships . . . " declared the Congress. The European Economic Recovery Program—the Marshall Plan—was to provide $13.3 billion in aid over four years (equivalent to over $100 billion in today's dollars). With American aid and access to American markets, Europe embarked upon a period of remarkable economic expansion and prosperity.

Opposition to the expansion of Communism was embraced by most Americans, to the extent that Truman's foreign policy, of which it was the dominant feature, never became a wedge issue in the 1948 presidential campaign.[51] In a September article in *Life* magazine, Lutheran theologian Reinhold Neibuhr expressed the widely held view that the struggle against totalitarianism was a moral as well as a political issue. "We cannot afford any more compromises. We will have to stand at every point in our far-flung lines."[52] For the next half century, the containment of Communism would be the central—and bipartisan—feature of American foreign policy.

There were already notable successes of the policy. In Iran, when confronted with American resolve, Stalin had backed down. During the Dardanelles Strait crisis in Turkey, when Truman had dispatched a fleet of warships to the area, Stalin withdrew his threats over sharing the Strait. Massive shipments of U.S. supplies had also been sent to Greece, along with armaments and military advisers, and by October 1949 the last remnants of the Communist rebel forces had been cleared from their mountain strongholds.

Because of the deeply rooted American apprehension about any governmental secrecy, and the relatively reduced requirements of an isolationist foreign policy, the United States was the last of the great powers to establish an international intelligence service.[53] Covert action seems inherently suspicious, and all the more so in a democracy, in which the government's actions are supposed to reflect the will of the people. "Gentlemen do not read each other's mail," said Henry Stimson as a newly appointed secretary of state in 1929, after learning that the government had established a codebreaking unit.[54] He shut it down.

America had been caught unprepared for both the First and Second World Wars, at enormous national cost. Pearl Harbor itself had been a failure of intelligence. Franklin Roosevelt established the Office of Strategic Services (OSS) in 1942 to collect strategic intelligence for the Joint Chiefs of Staff and conduct covert operations. It was abolished at the end of the war, and the Central Intelligence Agency was established by Congress in 1947 as the Cold War intensified, under authority of the National Security Council, its director responsible directly to the president. The CIA was tasked with collecting and analyzing foreign intelligence and performing "such other functions and duties as the NSC will from time to time direct." The Agency was prohibited from engaging in domestic operations, which were under the purview of the FBI.

"It is generally agreed that a good intelligence service is the first line of military defense today," declared the *Christian Science Monitor*. " 'Aha!' says the average American. 'Spies!' Yes spies—such as all the major nations of the world maintain in order to know what the others are up to. There is no use being coy about the subject."[55]

The Agency and its precursor were staffed by highly educated men from predominantly upper-class backgrounds, a disproportionate number of them from elite universities. They were not innocents abroad. Nor, by the nature of their mission, could they be. To be effective, they must deal with criminals, rebels, traitors, mercenaries.

The United states was starting out the Cold War intelligence contest from behind: at the end of the Second World War the West had no agents in Moscow; the Kremlin had both Russian and Western agents in Western Europe, Britain, and the United States.[56] Within months after its creation, CIA operatives (many of them former OSS men) were engaged in a shadow struggle against Soviet totalitarianism that would continue for generations. They opposed Soviet infiltration of Western European media and labor unions. They organized resistance to Communist-supported insurgency groups in Europe and Asia. They broke codes and intercepted communications between Communist regimes.[57] They were vital in exposing Soviet penetration of certain Western European political parties, countering KGB political interference in Western nations and assisting democratic parties in organization and electoral techniques, helping to curb growing Communist influence in Italy, France, and elsewhere. In the Italian election of 1948, funds were funneled through CIA operatives to democratic parties, thwarting a Communist takeover of the government.

The following few years were crucial to the protection of Western security. When the Soviet Union detonated an atomic bomb, CIA intelligence estimates assured the president, accurately, that the Kremlin was unlikely to precipitate a direct military conflict "that would automatically involve war" with a militarily stronger United States: its program for expansion would continue to be, as earlier estimates had reported, "primarily revolutionary in nature."[58] CIA agents also worked to root out American and British diplomats, scientists, and others who were working on behalf of Moscow. In the Philippines, Agency operatives played a central role in the defeat of the Communist-supported Huk insurgency.

Certainly a few of the Agency's operations would appear questionable in the rearview mirror of history. In 1953, after Iranian prime minister Mohammed Mossadeq dissolved the country's parliament, threatened to remove the traditional monarch (Shah Reza Pahlavi), nationalized British oil fields in the country, and strengthened ties with the Communist Tudeh Party, Washington agreed to a British proposal for a joint operation in support of Iranian military officers planning a coup. The coup succeeded, Mossadeq was sent into exile, and the pro-Western Shah took control of the country. Though there followed a generation of surface stability, below the surface there percolated deep currents of discontent, driven by Iranian nationalism and a resurgence of Islamic fundamentalism, and an increasingly repressive Shah. As a consequence of the Mossadeq coup and its aftermath, writes Gregory Treverton in his work *Covert Action*, the Shah and the United States became more closely identified with each other "than was good for either of them."[59]

The year after the Mossadeq coup, CIA operatives trained and supplied rebels who overthrew Jacobo Arbenz, the socialist president of the tiny Central American nation of Guatemala. Arbenz had appointed Communists to high-level positions in his government, expropriated private land, and expanded ties to the Soviet bloc. He fled into exile in Czechoslovakia.

American involvement in the coup, which would have proceeded without it, would forever be tainted by the co-incidence of the legitimate national security goal of keeping Soviet Communism out of Latin America, and the narrow economic self-interests of U.S. firms—particularly the United Fruit Company—whose land had been expropriated.

Elsewhere, the shadow struggle continued. Among Western socialists and intellectuals who perceived a "moral equivalence" between totalitarian and democratic states, covert operations would persistently be opposed, and equated to the activities of the KGB. In fact, there had been excesses and blunders, as there are in every war, and there would be more. Yet the men and women engaged in the shadow war were vital in stemming the tide of Communism at a pivotal moment in history.

On June 23, 1948, the Soviet Union imposed a total blockade of Berlin, which it now claimed as part of its German occupation zone. All ground transport routes from the West were cut off, with the explicit aim of forcing the three Western occupying powers out of Berlin. Without a supply line to the West, the citizens of West Berlin would soon be without food, fuel, and other essential provisions. The stakes could not have been greater.

There was never any question. "We are going to stay, period," Truman announced. The city of over 2 million people would have to be supplied entirely by air. By December, 4,500 tons of provisions were reaching the city daily, 8,000 tons by the following spring. A cargo plane was landing or taking off every sixty seconds. For a year, courageous American and British pilots flew coal, food, and other supplies to West Berlin, braving wind and rain and dense fog, defying Soviet predictions that provisions would not be able to get through during the inclement Berlin winter. "We flew when birds walked," said one airman. American cargo planes delivered over 2 million tons of supplies to the doughty West Berliners—at a cost of $350 million—and the lives of forty-five aviators. International relations scholar Avi Shlaim has written of the Berlin blockade that "The future of Germany, the future of Western Europe and the future of the precarious postwar international order all hung in the balance."[60]

Stalin's advisers had assured him that a population the size of West Berlin's could not be provisioned by air. They were wrong. On May 12 the Kremlin, having suffered a political defeat of incalculable consequence, lifted the blockade. Just as Stalin's conquest of Eastern Europe had provoked an initial alarm among the Western nations, his bellicose effort to subjugate West Berlin helped unite the West as no internal pressure could have done. Berlin showed that only by resolute will would Soviet totalitarianism be checked. In the airlift, America had demonstrated its will. As Alexander

Solzhenitsyn later wrote, "It's the very ideology of Communism. . . . If you can seize something, seize it; if you can attack, attack; but if there's a wall, then go back. Only firmness will make it possible to withstand the assaults of Communist totalitarianism. . . . You [Americans] in 1948, defended Berlin only by your firmness of spirit—and there was no world conflict."

Any sense of elation over the victory in Berlin was short-lived. On August 29 the Soviets successfully tested their first atomic bomb. And in Eastern Europe, the screws of subjugation continued to be tightened. In November, a Russian marshal was named Poland's minister of defense and commander in chief of its army, which was reorganized in conformity with the Soviet model.

———◆———

The internecine wars between capitalist nations, which Marxists had antici-pated as an inevitable next step in history, never materialized. Instead, there emerged one of the most unified and effective alliances ever created, spurred by Soviet aggressions in Berlin and elsewhere in Eastern Europe. In 1947 the British government had begun making proposals about a "Western demo-cratic system," as Foreign Secretary Ernest Bevin put it, "to inspire the Soviet government with enough respect for the West to remove temptation from them and so ensure a long period of peace."[61] European anti-Commu-nists were at least as anxious to secure an American commitment to Europe as Americans were to be there. Bevin worked assiduously to tie the United States by treaty to the defense of Western Europe, and both sides of the Atlantic recognized that, if the democratic nations were to remain united against the Communist threat, there was no alternative to American leader-ship. "I am entirely convinced," wrote French political theorist Raymond Aron, "that for an anti-Stalinist there is no escape from the acceptance of American leadership."[62]

After more than a year of negotiations, on April 4, 1949, the United States, Canada, and ten Western European nations signed the North Atlantic Treaty, committing to come to each other's defense if attacked. Member nations were free to determine their own level of defense spending and their military contribution to the alliance.[63] In the treaty, the signatory nations declared that "They are determined to safeguard the freedom, common heritage and civilization of their peoples, founded on the principles of democracy, individual liberty and the rule of law. . . . " If the Soviet Union attacked the United States, the overarchingly strongest nation in the history of the world, the war-ravaged nations of Western Europe would come to its assistance. And vice versa.

The NATO Treaty was ratified by the U.S. Senate on July 21 by a vote of 82 to 13. The United States had entered into its first peacetime military alliance since 1778. If there had been any lingering doubt about American isolationism, there was none now. General Eisenhower served as NATO's first Supreme

Allied Commander, from 1950–52. Within a few years after its creation, NATO nations had seventy-five divisions positioned in Western Europe, Greece, and Turkey.[64]

Increased economic and social cooperation followed the establishment of NATO, tying the democratic nations of the North Atlantic closer and closer in a web of mutual interests and values. NATO would prove to be the most important and effective alliance system in history. With American economic assistance on the one hand, and military support on the other, the nations of the Western alliance were successful in resisting Soviet pressures, and during the second half of the twentieth century there was greater peace and stability in Western Europe than there had been for millennia.

It is not difficult to grasp the appeal that Communism held, particularly in the developing world. It promised not only shared purpose toward a common struggle, but the attainment of an earthly utopia. For peoples embarking upon decolonization and development, the Marxist promise could be intoxicating. American military resistance to Communism needed to be matched by social and economic assistance to developing nations, to address conditions that made Communism alluring to demoralized populations. In his inaugural address on January 20, 1949, President Truman listed as the main points of U.S. foreign policy: support for the UN; assisting European social and economic recovery; and military assistance to "freedom-loving nations." In his fourth point, Truman proposed "a bold new program for making the benefits of our scientific advances and industrial progress available for the improvement and growth of underdeveloped areas."[65] The Point Four Program, launched to assist development in Third World nations, had an initial appropriation in 1950 of $34.5 million, which by 1953 was raised to $155.6 million. Under the program, thousands of American technical experts worked in dozens of nations, helping to build essential infrastructure and providing training in agriculture, health care, and finance.[66] Under the Point Four program and Marshall Plan, the United States gave billions of dollars in foreign economic aid.

When Stalin announced plans to aggressively support Communist insurgencies around the world, an aide asked him whether such a policy wouldn't violate the Yalta agreement. "It does," he replied. "And to hell with it! It is true that for us this entails certain inconveniences, and we will have to struggle with the Americans. But we are already reconciled to that."[67] In April 1950 the U.S. State Department's Policy Planning Staff issued a report, adopted by the National Security Council in June as NSC-68, which predicted—accurately, as it turned out—that Moscow would foster limited wars around the world as part of its globalist ambitions, and called for increased U.S. defense spending to meet this new type of challenge. "The frustration of the Kremlin design requires the free world to develop a successfully functioning political and economic system and a vigorous political offensive," the report concluded. The United States must lead the democratic nations in confronting the Soviet Union "with convincing evidence of the determination and ability of the free world" to oppose its expansionism.[68]

The policy was put to the test when Communist North Korea, backed by China and the USSR, invaded South Korea on June 22. In immediate response, the Truman administration led an effort at the United Nations to renounce the aggression, and then waged a costly but ultimately successful war to repel it. "President Truman's decision to go to the defense of Korea in June 1950 will stand out as a shining page in the history of the United States," wrote Hungarian-born historian John Lukacs in 1961. "For it was a uniquely honest reaction in the defense of freedom, without second thoughts. . . . "[69]

———◆———

In Washington, the House Un-American Activities Committee (HUAC) responded to the public's growing sense of wartime anxiety in the late 1940s by holding highly publicized hearings in a search for Communists hidden in Hollywood, academia, and the State Department. In 1950, Sen. Joseph McCarthy (R-Wisconsin) began holding hearings into alleged Communist infiltration of government, making baseless accusations in sensational media events aimed more at self-promotion than uncovering truth.

Fears among the general public of a spreading tide of Communism were not unfounded. Totalitarianism had made substantial gains in the few years since the end of the Second World War. The Soviet empire loomed over Europe. The postwar chaos that threatened to destabilize democratic values helped fuel the development of Communist movements. In France and Italy the Communist parties, supported by the Kremlin and responsive to it, had been surging.

Much of the intelligentsia in the West, most overwhelmingly that of France and Italy, actively advocated Soviet-style socialism as the preferred form of government. Sartre spoke for many of them when he declared, in 1952, that "Any anti-Communist is a dog."[70] The Communist ideology, moreover, had made world domination (including the violent overthrow of the democratic West) a central tenet of its faith. Archives opened after the fall of Soviet Communism have shown that Stalin was making designs for Communist world expansion that justified or exceeded the fears of even his most vociferous critics in the West. "You have to understand the importance of your position and that you are fulfilling a historic mission of unprecedented significance," he told a visiting Chinese delegation. "Let's add to China's population of 475 million the populations of India, Burma, Indonesia, the Philippines. . . . "[71]

Populous and sprawling Communist China loomed over Asia. Across the globe, far more people now lived under totalitarian regimes than democratic ones. In the three years after the Communist invasion of South Korea,

Americans fought to repel the aggression at places like Pusan, Inchon, Chosin, Bloody Ridge, and elsewhere. By the time an armistice was reached in July 1953, 55,000 Americans had been killed in the defense of Korea, and another 100,000 severely wounded.

In the United States, the fact was that there *were* Communist zealots in Hollywood, academia, the State Department, and elsewhere, working to undermine American democracy and advance Kremlin interests. The dream of restructuring society according to one's own utopian blueprint, the totalitarian temptation, had always had its allurements throughout history, and modernity only seemed to have nourished the hubris: the misfit philosophy professor as social engineer. As a social model that worked infinitely better on paper than in reality, Marxism found a disproportion of its adherents not in the proletariat, but in the bourgeoisie, and particularly in the academy and arts. "I believe that totalitarian ideas have taken root in the minds of intellectuals everywhere," George Orwell wrote in 1949.

The Kremlin waged an aggressive covert campaign to assist Marxist true believers in the West to subvert their democratic political systems. Among the international front organizations established to help surreptitiously spread Communist ideology were the World Federation of Trade Unions, the World Federation of Democratic Youth, the International Organization of Journalists, the International Union of Students, and the World Peace Council. Independent trade unions and left-leaning civic and political groups in the West were infiltrated.[72] Though the members of the Communist Party of the USA (CPUSA) insisted that they were independent from the Soviet Union and received no support from it, documents released following the Cold War have confirmed that the party, and a number of front organizations, maintained elaborate covert operations to carry out pro-Soviet espionage, were funded from Moscow, and took orders from it through American Communists traveling to the Soviet Union, and Soviet agents in the United States.[73]

Perhaps most harmfully of all, several top American atomic scientists passed nuclear secrets to the Kremlin, making important contributions to the development of Soviet nuclear capability. Two of those spies, Ethel and Julius Rosenberg were sentenced to death on April 5, 1951, for delivering nuclear secrets to the Soviet Union. They were executed in June 1953. Their case was a cause celebre among the American left. Celebrities petitioned on their behalf. Demonstrations were held, in the United States and Europe— some of them organized, it later turned out, at the direction of Soviet agents. For four decades the "persecution" of the Rosenbergs for their Communist beliefs was a rallying symbol for American socialists. Here was proof that the U.S. government had gone too far in opposing socialism: the harassment and finally the execution of a couple of benign Bronx Communists. The United States held show trials, just like Stalin did. The two nations were morally equivalent.

Except for the inconvenient fact of the Rosenbergs' guilt. They were not victims, except of their own zealotry. In Khrushchev's memoirs, he praised the Rosenbergs for their "help in accelerating the production of our atomic bomb,"[74] and documents released after the opening of Soviet archives confirmed that Julius had indeed run an elaborate espionage ring in the United States, sending vital U.S. nuclear secrets to Stalin. Whereupon, American socialists changed the subject.

Some exploitation of wartime fears for political gain, as McCarthy and others had done, was probably inevitable. What was not inevitable was the outcome. The "Red Scare" was predictable, comprehensible, and, given the conditions of the time, surprisingly limited. The excesses of McCarthyism, while deplorable and in glaring contrast to liberal democratic ideals, consisted of a small number of individuals being publicly shamed, humiliated, stigmatized. Some unjustly lost their reputations. Some actors, producers, teachers, diplomats suffered ruined careers, some wrongly. A total of ten Hollywood writers and directors spent up to a year in jail for refusing to testify before the HUAC. (Most of them, it later transpired, actually were Communists, at a time when the United States was in a mortal struggle with Communism.) Dozens of others were blacklisted and suffered diminished careers. There were injustices.

President Truman called HUAC "the most un-American thing in America." In August 1954 a Senate special committee was created to consider disciplinary action against McCarthy. On December 2 the Senate voted 67 to 22 in favor of a resolution censuring him. He died shortly afterward, discredited and politically washed up.

Truman had said of McCarthy that he was "the greatest asset that the Kremlin has."[75] It might have been literally true. By his deceptions, exaggerations, and denials of justice, McCarthy did far more to assist American Communism than any Communist filmmakers or writers had done. He had helped to inoculate future Soviet apologists in the West against public reaction. The Kremlin did indeed have an ambitious program of subversion and espionage directed toward the United States—described in KGB directives simply as "the Main Enemy." But henceforth, elite political opinion in the West—not only among committed Marxists, but moderate liberals—would regard with suspicion and derision subsequent claims of an "enemy within."

A total of *two* Americans were executed during the Red Scare, the Rosenbergs, both indisputably guilty of treasonous crimes against their country. While American filmmakers and writers have in later years focused on how the Red Scare resulted in the ruined careers of a handful of innocents (often filmmakers and writers), under Soviet Communism another kind of scare was going on. In Russia there were no mass demonstrations against Stalin's terrors. The people cowered in submissive political silence under the totalitarian glare of the secret police, continuing political arrests and executions, forced labor, and, behind it all, the looming gulag. In Eastern Europe and in the Soviet Union itself, the Great Terror had never really abated. The number of prisoners held in the Soviet gulag prison camps did not peak in the late 1930s but in 1953, when its population reached at least 12 million.[76]

———————◆———————

Stalin, the aging dictator, commenced his final purge in January 1953, this one against an alleged "doctors' plot" of mostly Jewish doctors who had—in collaboration with American Jews—purportedly been responsible for murdering a number of high-ranking party officials. After being tortured, one of the accused doctors supposedly confessed that he had received orders to "eliminate the leading cadres of the Soviet Union," including Stalin.[77] Soviet citizens were assured that those involved had been arrested and shot.

Joseph Stalin died on March 5, 1953, under circumstances that continue to provoke dispute. After one of his frequent late nights of binge-drinking with his Politburo, he had retired to his room and ordered his guards that he was not to be disturbed. When he did not appear the next morning, and into the afternoon, his aides grew worried, but no one dared risk entering the room without his permission. The delay may have cost him his life. When guards finally went in the next evening, they found him semiconscious on the floor. Four days later Stalin was dead, of an apparent brain hemorrhage. Whether he was killed by one or more subordinates (some point to secret police chief Lavrenti Beria as the only one with the capacity to pull it off), either out of fear for their own lives or desire for power, may never be known.

The dictator was dead: long live the dictatorship. Stalin's death spurred a struggle for power, and survival, among the Kremlin leadership. Throughout Eastern Europe his death helped kindle hopes for greater independence. In May and June, across East Germany, Czechoslovakia, Hungary, and Romania, there were anti-Soviet demonstrations and work stoppages. When East German workers staged a general strike and mass demonstrations in mid-June, the Kremlin leadership concluded that an example must be made. Fearing the spread of the movement, Moscow ordered the Soviet high commissioner in East Germany to declare martial law. East German leader Walter Ulbricht urged the Kremlin not to "spare bullets" in putting down the strikes in his country.[78] Soviet armored divisions, including at least six hundred tanks, descended on the demonstrators in Berlin, directing machine gun fire against the unarmed protesters. Impromptu military tribunals passed death sentences and then carried them out on the spot.[79] Ulbricht was kept in power, the Kremlin calling him the "bulwark of the struggle of the German people for a united, peaceloving and democratic Germany."[80] That year, over 300,000 East Germans fled to the West through East Berlin.

Back in Moscow, the machinations for power were still going on. Nikita Khrushchev formed a troika with Molotov and Georgi Malenkov, a pragmatic party technocrat. The three feared Beria, suspecting that he might use the unrest in Eastern Europe as a pretext for seizing sole power. Before he could get them, they arrested him on trumped up charges of conspiring against socialism, then secretly tried and had him executed, publicly announcing Beria's fate only months later. With Beria gone, Khrushchev now turned on Malenkov and Molotov, gradually pushing them out of power and asserting himself as the party's undisputed leader. Throughout the remainder of his life, Khrushchev always took pride in his ability to force the others out and consolidate power for himself; for being the most cunning among a group of cunning men. Power would never again be so centralized as it had been under Stalin, but it never ceased to be a totalitarian dictatorship. Four days before being elected party chief, Khrushchev issued a directive calling for increased "terror attacks" against "traitors" and other dissidents abroad."[81]

President Eisenhower, the former general, strongly opposed the resurgent isolationist strain in American politics and cited Republican candidate Robert Taft's endorsement of an insular "fortress America" as an impetus for his own decision to run for president in 1952. "Conceiving the defense of freedom, like freedom itself, to be one and indivisible, we hold all continents and peoples in equal regard and honor," he said in his inaugural address on January 20, 1953. "We reject any insinuation that one race or another, one people or another is in any sense inferior or expendable."[82]

Eisenhower deeply believed that, as the world's dominant democratic nation, the United States had an obligation both to oppose the expansion of Communism and foster the development of social and economic conditions that would diminish Communism's appeal. "Wherever popular discontent is found or group oppression or mass poverty or the hunger of children," he had written in 1948, "there communism may stage an offensive that arms cannot counter."[83] To help raise living standards in the developing nations, the administration pushed for reduced tariffs on imported goods, liberalization of international trade, and billions of dollars in direct economic assistance to poor nations.

A crucial component of Eisenhower's strategy of containment was the establishment of a series of alliances with non-Communist nations. To NATO was added the Southeast Asian Treaty Organization (SEATO) in 1954, the Central Treaty Organization (CENTO) in 1955 (involving Turkey, Iraq, Iran, and Pakistan), and numerous other multilateral and bilateral defensive agreements. Some of these were to prove more effective, some less, but all were part of the effort to unite democratic and protodemocratic nations in a web of mutual assistance that could withstand the accretion of Communist power. To this end, Eisenhower believed, America must lead, it could not domineer. Its leadership must be based on shared interests and, where possible, shared values.[84] In 1954, as flickering hopes for freedom were being snuffed out in Eastern Europe, a democratic West Germany gained admittance to NATO, an event that was in itself a historic achievement of the U.S.-led alliance. The formerly aggressive global powers Japan and West Germany had now, through determined American efforts at reconstruction, been brought fully into the community of democratic nations.

———•———

Coming to power after Stalin's death, Nikita Khrushchev had a public relations problem on his hands. Some 40 million citizens had been executed, imprisoned, or forcibly displaced under the former dictator. The population of Eastern Europe recoiled at Soviet domination. Khrushchev began to speak of "socialism with a human face," and went abroad on a series of fence-mending visits.

Khrushchev said that world Communism was now strong enough to defeat the West by "peaceful competition," and so "peaceful coexistence" was possible, though the two systems remained ultimately incompatible. In May 1955 he signed an agreement in Vienna with the other three Allied occupying powers, agreeing to withdraw Soviet troops from Austria in exchange for its promise to remain neutral in the East-West conflict. As a counterbalance to NATO, that same month the Soviet Union established a mutual defense treaty, the Warsaw Pact, with its vassal states in Europe. The treaty was largely symbolic, and it was superfluous: in fact, the Kremlin already had functional control over both the governments and the militaries of its satellite states. The Warsaw Pact merely formalized the arrangement. Indeed, for the peoples of subjugated Eastern Europe, the death of Stalin meant little. Kremlin control over the their nations was being consolidated when Stalin died in 1953. That consolidation was not interrupted.[85] Khrushchev would be even more active than Stalin in promoting insurgency in the developing world. He increased economic and military support for Marxist terrorist groups in Asia, Africa, and Latin America.

To gain greater control over the state security apparatus, the Moscow oligarchy in 1954 established the Committee for State Security (KGB), combining wide-ranging powers for both domestic and international intelligence and propaganda, surveillance of the domestic citizenry, broad police functions, and control over the gulag. The use of terror was never renounced, in principle or in practice. But the system that Lenin and Stalin had built was now a machine that would, almost, go of itself. Khrushchev could denounce the wholesale terror by which the Communists had established control, because less was required to *maintain* control over a terrorized population whose spirit, whose will to resist, had already been broken. Now confident of his own power, at the Twentieth Party Congress in Moscow on February 24–25, 1956, Khrushchev made a closed-session speech in which, for several hours, he enumerated and denounced atrocities committed during Stalin's rule.

Khrushchev was an unlikely source for the attacks on Stalin. He had risen to power doing Stalin's will, overseeing purges in Stalin's name. He had certainly made no objections *while* the terrors were being conducted. As party chief in Moscow in 1936–37, he oversaw the arrest and imprisonment or execution of thousands of members of the Moscow Soviet. Over fifty thousand persons were arrested in Moscow under Khrushchev's supervision. During his first year as party leader for the Ukraine, 1938, over 106,000 persons were arrested on political charges there.[86] In the years after he came to power as head of the Soviet Union, he would prove no less willing to use violence to suppress opposition at home and abroad.

Surely the speech had not been meant to stay secret. In any case, copies leaked out—to the Communist and capitalist worlds. At first Western Communist parties vehemently denied published reports of the address. "Don't fall for press stories of attacks on the late J. V. Stalin at the 20th Congress," the Communist Party of Australia warned its members. The CPUSA denounced reports of the speech as capitalist propaganda. When the evidence became undeniable, Western Communists sidestepped the issue and finally rationalized it away.

For Communist leaders in power elsewhere, though, the matter was more serious. Stalinist dictators in Eastern Europe and Asia were bewildered and angered by the address. The erosion of Stalin's legitimacy eroded their own. Mao condemned it as dangerous revisionism, and later, as part of a capitalist conspiracy. For Khrushchev the speech had been a calculated effort to distance himself from one of the most vicious regimes in history. The crimes of the regime were known, anyway. He hoped to limit the blame to a depraved individual rather than to a depraved system.

In Eastern Europe, citizens tested the limits of the regime's "socialism with a human face." Industrial workers in Poland, discontented with brutal working conditions under the Communists, initiated a series of work strikes which grew into a national demonstration against the party's rule itself. On June 28, "Black Thursday," the government sent two divisions of troops (including several hundred tanks) to suppress the protests. At least seventy-four workers were killed, and hundreds wounded.

When, on October 23, thousands of students and workers in Budapest, Hungary, demonstrated against the Soviet occupation, demanding more individual liberty, government radio broadcasts condemned the "fascist reactionary elements" and announced that public meetings would be prohibited until further notice. The unrest did not subside. An interim prime minister, Imre Nagy, a reformer, was appointed in hopes that he would get a lid on the crisis. Instead, on the thirtieth, Nagy bravely announced that he would abolish one-party rule and establish a coalition government. On November 1 he denounced the Soviet occupation and declared that Hungary would withdraw from the Warsaw Pact. That was the last straw. Within two days, 15 Red Army divisions, with over 4,000 tanks, were deployed around Budapest and other major Hungarian cities. On the morning of

November 4 they moved in, to "restore order" as the Kremlin explained, annihilating all who resisted.

As it launched its military offensive against the Hungarian people, the Kremlin was already planning an international propaganda offensive. The Central Committee issued a directive that agents in the World Peace Council not agree "to the publication of any document in the name of the World Peace Council in which the activities of the Soviet troops in Hungary might be viewed as interference in the internal affairs of Hungary." In addition, the Soviet ambassador to Hungary, Yuri Andropov, was ordered "to ascertain the possibilities of setting up a link between the representatives of the peace movement in Hungary and the World Peace Council, so that they could help the Peace Council to adopt the correct position on the question of events in Hungary."[87] Also, the socialist intelligentsia in the West were to be instructed on the proper spin to put on the crisis: a telegram was to be sent, "via the Soviet ambassador to Paris, to our French friends, with a request to explain to . . . leaders of the peace movement the correct interpretation of the events in Hungary."[88]

The Soviet news agency Tass reported that, in response to a request from the Hungarian government for assistance, the Soviet military had sent troops into Hungary.[89] Between five and ten thousand Hungarians were killed in the bloodbath. A quarter million fled the Soviet occupation during the following weeks, escaping to the West. Nagy was arrested, tried, and executed (though not necessarily in that order). His body was buried in an unmarked grave.

Could the United States have intervened? The Suez Crisis was a distraction, but more important, any effort to liberate Hungary, in the center of Europe, would have certainly involved a major war with the Soviet Union, a forbidding prospect in an era of nuclear arsenals. But the events in Eastern Europe had clearly shown that, though Stalin was gone and even denounced, his successors would defend, by terror if necessary, the empire that terror had built.

While the Kremlin was asserting its dominion over its vassal empire, Khrushchev continued to concentrate his own power at home. Molotov, a potential competitor, was removed from all his party posts and ended his illustrious diplomatic career as ambassador to Mongolia. Malenkov wound up managing a power station in remote Kazakhstan.

———◆———

The Kremlin had been making important inroads in the Middle East, with Egyptian leader Gamal Nasser and other dictators in the region. On January 5, 1957, President Eisenhower made a speech to a joint session of Congress requesting $200 million annually in aid to support "the independence of the freedom-loving nations of the area," and authorizing "assistance and cooperation to include the employment of the armed forces of the United States to secure and protect the territorial integrity and political independence of such nations, requesting such aid, against overt armed aggression from any nation controlled by international Communism."[90] The Eisenhower Doctrine, of securing the Middle East from Communist encroachment, was carried on by successive presidents and would prove remarkably successful in inhibiting the spread of Communism in the region.

To help promote economic growth and stability in the Third World, in February 1957 the U.S. State Department announced plans for the establishment of an international loan fund, capable of making loans on favorable terms for development projects in the underdeveloped nations of Asia, Africa, and Latin America. In August, after a heated budget battle, Congress authorized creation of the Development Loan Fund, with an initial capitalization of $500 million, and another $625 million the following year.

The Communists' Five-Year Plans made any daydream seem possible: simply write down what the state ought to achieve, then decree it. Since the state had totalitarian control, it ought to be able to plan—and dictate—productivity. Khrushchev told graduating Soviet military cadets that "Within a period of, say, five years following 1965, the level of U.S. production per capita should be equaled and overtaken. The USSR will have captured first place in the world, both in absolute volume of production and per capita production, which will ensure the world's highest standard of living."[91]

The Kremlin's hubris was spurred by the successful launch, on October 4, 1957, of the first artificial satellite, Sputnik I, into earth's orbit. Khrushchev added to the growing fears in the West of a "missile gap" by publicly stating that the Kremlin was producing missiles "like sausages."[92] He blustered that he had ordered a study of how many missiles would be required to destroy the "vital centers" of the U.S. and Western Europe,[93] and informed the British ambassador that only six atomic bombs would be needed to destroy Britain, nine for France.[94]

Dwight Eisenhower, the amiable and trusted "man from Abilene," was the right man for the time. Unflappable, soothing like a beloved grandfather, he never questioned America's fundamental rightness in the struggle with Communism, or the certainty that it would prevail. Confident in the country's capacity for technological innovation, he was unawed by Moscow's bombast. He discounted Kremlin claims of a huge ICBM force and rightly concluded that the U.S. bomber fleet would be sufficient deterrent until a new generation of American ICBMs could be brought into production against the new Soviet threat. Moves were made to strengthen scientific education, research, and development.

Developments in the Space Race confirmed Khrushchev's already intense belief that Communism was on a trajectory of world domination. "Whether you like it or not, history is on our side! We will bury you!" he had told a gathering of Western ambassadors in Moscow in 1956. The dawn of the new age was at hand. "Our era is an era of Socialist revolutions and national liberation revolutions; an era of the collapse of capitalism," Khrushchev told Moscow university students in early 1961.[95] He ebulliently declared that by supporting the "sacred" struggle of Third World revolutionary movements, the Soviet Union was bringing the capitalist world "to its knees."[96]

As the dictator's hubris grew, so did his rashness, including almost unrestrained efforts to export revolution abroad. Africa had been largely off of the map of superpower conflict, not because of regional stability (the process of decolonization by the European powers and local self-government, for which the dozens of new nations were unprepared, had produced massive turmoil there), but because of its lack of perceived strategic value. Now, Khrushchev made it clear that nothing would be off the table. When the Belgian Congo (later Zaire) received its independence from Belgium in June 1960, it was engulfed in a violent civil war, with numerous tribal and other groups fighting for power. The Congolese army itself splintered into warring factions and began to massacre Belgian settlers. Belgium sent troops to help the new prime minister, Patrice Lumumba (formerly a beer salesman) restore order. Amidst the chaos a secessionist movement declared its own independence from Congo in the mineral-rich Katanga Province. Lumumba appealed for UN intervention, and on July 14 the Security Council called for the withdrawal of Belgian troops, to be replaced by a United Nations peacekeeping force. When Secretary-General Dag Hammarskjold refused to use those troops to aid Lumumba in quelling secessionists, he appealed to both Washington and Moscow for assistance. The Kremlin responded by supplying Lumumba with air and ground transports and hundreds of Soviet military personnel.

With Eastern bloc troops pouring into the country, Congolese president Joseph Kasavubu dismissed Lumumba, who refused to step down, instead announcing his own dismissal of Kasavubu. In September, pro-Western colonel Joseph Mobutu overthrew Lumumba, who fled and was captured by Mobutu's forces and killed. The Kremlin lost a possible foothold in the Congo but gained a propaganda asset: Lumumba was rendered a martyr to the forces of Western imperialism, and a Moscow university for Third World students was named after him. Mobutu, who was to retain power for decades, had reunited the country by 1963, though violent instability persisted in the Congo as elsewhere on the continent.

———◆———

In style, background, and temperament, John F. Kennedy was a stark contrast to the staid, aging Eisenhower. Scion of a wealthy Boston family, in 1960, at age forty-three, Kennedy became the youngest man ever elected president, defeating Eisenhower's VP Richard Nixon. Yet, though there were obvious differences with his predecessor, Kennedy, like Ike, was staunchly anti-Communist. He shared the belief of both previous Cold War presidents that America's position of predominance among democratic nations imposed upon it important moral and political responsibilities. "We are the key, the archstone, the basic element in the strength of the entire free world," he declared. Kennedy believed that Eisenhower had depended too heavily upon nuclear deterrence and called for dramatic increases in conventional arms expenditures to permit a more "flexible response." "We intend to have a wider choice than humiliation or all-out nuclear war," he said in a national address in July 1961.[97] That spending on conventional arms, though, must not come at the expense of nuclear deterrence. Overall defense expenditures would have to increase, even if it meant deficit spending. "Our arms must be adequate to meet our commitments and ensure our security, without being bound by arbitrary budget ceilings," he told the Congress. "We must not shrink from additional costs where they are necessary."[98]

Upon taking office, the young president faced a sea of troubles: Marxist insurgencies in Asia, Latin America, and Africa, the emergence of a Soviet satellite just off the Florida coast, the apparent superiority of the Kremlin's missile program, and an increasingly belligerent Khrushchev. "The only thing that surprised us when we got into office," he quipped to a reporter, "was that things were just as bad as we had been saying they were."[99] America must bolster itself for a protracted struggle ahead. In his first State of the Union address on January 30, 1961, Kennedy presciently warned that "there will be further setbacks before the tide is turned."

But the president's strategy for defending democracy was not confined to using military power. Like his predecessors, he believed that prosperous nations had both an ethical obligation and a rational self-interest in promoting the social and economic welfare of less developed countries. From the outset of his presidency, he worked to expand the policies of foreign assistance that had been established under Truman and Eisenhower. "The great battleground for the defense and expansion of freedom today is the whole southern half of the globe—Asia, Latin America, Africa and the Middle East," he said. "They seek an end to injustice, tyranny and exploitation. More than an end, they seek a new beginning."[100]

During the 1960 presidential campaign, Kennedy had proposed the establishment of a government-sponsored voluntary assistance program to improve the quality of life in developing nations. "There is not enough money in all America to relieve the misery of the underdeveloped world in a giant and endless soup kitchen. But there is enough know-how and enough knowledgeable people to help those nations help themselves," he said. And he believed that America was brimming with talented young people to "serve the cause of freedom as servants of peace."

Americans enthusiastically embraced the proposal. A Gallup poll taken shortly after the election found that 71 percent supported the establishment of a Peace Corps, with only 18 percent opposed.[101] The public response was so positive that the program became one of the early policy initiatives of the new administration: the day after the inauguration (in which Kennedy exhorted Americans, "Ask not what your country can do for you, but what you can do for your country"), he tapped his brother-in-law Sargent Shriver to chair a task force "to report how the Peace Corps could be organized and then to organize it."[102] In March 1961, Kennedy signed an executive order establishing the Corps, though if it were to have longevity, it would have to be approved and funded on a long-term basis by the legislative branch. In September the Congress voted overwhelmingly to provide $30 million to fund the creation of a Peace Corps of American volunteers to serve abroad. The new agency was swamped by applicants.

Communist propagandists tried to stigmatize the Corps as an instrument of cultural imperialism, or a vehicle for CIA operatives. And nationalist sensibilities were sometimes pricked at the prospect of receiving aid, but most governments of developing nations—and more important, the people themselves—were eager to receive it. Under Shriver's leadership, by the time of Kennedy's death in 1963 there were 7,300 Peace Corps volunteers, mainly idealistic young men and women, often living in hardship in remote Third World villages, working to improve the lives of ordinary citizens in forty-four nations in Africa, Asia, and Latin America. They dug wells, taught literacy, assisted in economic development, instructed in agriculture and sanitation techniques, and delivered food aid and medical assistance.

The good that the Corps has since accomplished in promoting social welfare in developing countries, in educating Americans about the outside world, and in influencing foreign opinion toward America and its values is beyond calculation. As a Nigerian journalist wrote, "The Peace Corps is a greater service to this country than Britain was in a hundred years with all her epauletted and sword-carrying governors." A Turkish peasant said of the volunteers in his village, "These people are giving something they alone can give: they are giving of themselves. There's nothing like [the Peace Corps] in the world."[103] At century's end, about 7,000 volunteers were serving in 69 nations around the world, with a budget of $300 million. Over 150,000 Americans had served two-year terms as Peace Corps volunteers.

The Peace Corps was only one part of a much broader effort to promote democracy in the developing world. During his years in the Congress, and in his presidential campaign, Kennedy had called for a Marshall Plan–type effort for the Third World. They were not empty words. Against those who disparaged foreign aid as an international dole, Kennedy said that the United States had a historic opportunity to help lift less-developed nations into self-sustained economic growth, to give their citizens an economic and political stake in a stable, democratic world order. The greatest threat posed by Communism was not from Soviet or Chinese aggression, but internal disorder among impoverished and alienated populations. "It makes little sense for us to assail the horrors of Communism, to spend $50 billion a year to prevent its military advance—and then to begrudge spending less than one-tenth of that amount to help other nations . . . cure the social ills in which Communism has always thrived," Kennedy told the Congress.[104] In September 1961 it passed the Foreign Assistance Act, establishing the Agency for International Development (USAID) to rationalize and streamline foreign aid efforts, emphasizing long-term social and economic development. In addition, the Development Loan Fund, the Food for Peace program, and other humanitarian programs was established. In 1962, USAID assistance to developing nations amounted to over $2.6 billion.[105]

Kennedy also proposed an "Alliance for Progress" to help promote economic development and political stability in the troubled Latin America region. In requesting congressional funding for the program in 1961, he ambitiously called for spending $20 billion over ten years to promote democracy in Latin America. "We propose to complete the revolution of the Americas," Kennedy said. "To build a hemisphere where all men can hope for a suitable standard of living, and all can live out their lives in freedom and dignity. To achieve this goal political freedom must accompany material progress. . . . "[106]

The Alliance for Progress was formalized by the Charter of Punta del Este, in Uruguay, on August 17, 1961. It asserted that "free men working through the institutions of representative democracy can best satisfy man's aspirations, including those for work, home and land, health and schools. No system can guarantee true progress unless it affirms the dignity of the individual which is the foundation of our civilization."[107] In the end, the inability to achieve far-reaching land reform probably doomed the loftiest objectives of the program. It would be some time before most Latin American societies were ready for democracy. But Kennedy's ambitious goal for the program was exceeded: Latin America received over $22 billion in aid from the United States during the 1960s.[108]

———◆———

Khrushchev continued to see Communist ascendance just over the horizon. In a June 1961 address on Radio Moscow, he declared that the Soviet Union had been able to reach "second place in the world" in just forty-four years. "Now only America is left for us," he said. "It is like an already aged runner . . . he lives on yesterday's glory, but is short of wind. By now the scientists of America are studying and reporting to the government that the Soviet Union will have caught up with America in 1970."[109]

Despite the Kremlin's global propaganda effort to tout the miracle of social and economic development under Marxism, the gap between Communist and capitalist societies was growing increasingly stark. While the Soviet and East European economies stagnated under stifling government control, Western Europe was prospering. The great danger that liberal democracy posed to Communism was not invasion, but the persistent reality of a superior alternative, a better idea. Though an imposing barrier had been constructed along the nine-hundred-mile border between East and West Germany—a vast prison wall designed more to keep East Germans in than enemy forces out—the city of Berlin itself remained as a glaring ideological reproof of the Communist regime. It was impossible to restrict travel between the Eastern and Western zones of the city, and East Europeans wishing to escape Communism simply had to cross over into the city's Western zone, and from there be transported to the West. Berlin was a vast empirical reality check for Communism, a place where the musings of abstract Marxist theories jutted up against facts. The injury it did to Moscow's international propaganda efforts was as great as the manpower costs it inflicted upon East Germany.

Something had to be done. For years in East Germany, *republikflucht* ("fleeing the republic") had been a crime. But free spirits continued to escape the stagnation and oppression of the Communist regime, to the greater vibrance, prosperity, and liberty of the democratic West. From 1949 to 1961, 2.8 million East Germans (one-sixth of the population) fled to the West.[110] One-sixth of the East German population had fled Communism in the preceding dozen years, heading for the capitalist enslavement that incessant Soviet propaganda said awaited them in the West.

It was embarrassing. It was also costly: the defectors were predominantly younger, most under thirty, with technical skills. In a speech in June, while ominously denying intentions to build a wall to keep East Germans from escaping, East German leader Walter Ulbricht insisted that "the territory of West Berlin forms part of the territory of East Germany."[111] During June and July 1961 Moscow reiterated its threat to sign a treaty with East Germany that would establish Berlin as a "free city." Germans flooded westward, over 30,000 in July alone. Now, a crisis loomed. On the twenty-fifth, President Kennedy made a nationwide television and radio address, describing West Berlin as "the great testing place of Western courage and will. . . . We cannot separate its safety from our own."

By late July, Khrushchev had decided to seal the border. Shortly after announcing that Russia had developed a one-hundred-megaton nuclear bomb, and had the capacity to strike the United States with it, the Kremlin ordered Ulbricht to begin construction of a wall isolating West Berlin. Party loyalist Erich Honecker was put in charge of the task. At around midnight on August 12–13, East German workers began constructing a makeshift barbed wire barrier between East and West Berlin. Residents of the city awoke on Sunday morning to find that the city had been cut in two. The Eastern city's rail system no longer traveled to the Western sector. Houses along the border line were being demolished. Where the East-West boundary ran down the middle of streets, they were torn up and studded with concrete pylons.

Kennedy knew that he must proceed with utmost caution. Any precipitous action in Berlin might destabilize the entire international order and would certainly threaten nuclear war. The situation was immensely complex: the wall was being built at the urging of the East German government, on East German territory, under international agreements that had been in place since the end of the Second World War, and which had been at least tacitly acknowledged by the Western nations. As for the wall itself, probably nothing could be done.

To assure West Berliners of unfaltering American support, Kennedy dispatched Vice President Lyndon Johnson to visit the city, along with the popular retired general Lucius Clay. To substantiate the commitment, a symbolic contingent of fifteen hundred additional U.S. troops was sent, up the Autobahn route across East German territory, to West Berlin. When the convoy arrived and was permitted entry into the city, it signified to the citizens that the Americans would not abandon them, and would not allow West Berlin to be absorbed into the East.

In the following weeks a hideous wall of cinder blocks, cement, and barbed wire rose up, over a hundred miles long. Eventually a second wall sprang up behind the first, and between the two a no-man's-land sewn with land mines and surveyed by 285 watchtowers was manned by thousands of border guards at machine gun emplacements. To prevent West Berlin from becoming atrophied and then assimilated, Kennedy launched a program to sustain and foster the city's economic, cultural, and political ties with the West, to nurture its continued vitality as an oasis of freedom.

In the following years thousands of East Germans, desperate for liberty, risked their lives in dangerous and sometime ingenious attempts to get across the barrier to freedom. About five thousand succeeded. Several thousand were captured in the attempt and faced imprisonment. Six hundred were shot.

There was another way. In its one capitalist enterprise, the East German government granted prosperous West German citizens the right to purchase their loved ones' freedom, if they could afford the price. Even for those who could not physically escape there, though, Western liberty was to remain an ideal against which their tyrannical regime would be judged, and by which it would ultimately collapse.

The Communist illusion was over. Churchill's metaphorical "Iron Curtain" had become visible. Communist leaders in Moscow and East Berlin commenced a propaganda campaign to depict the barrier as an "antifascist protection wall," but the guardposts were all facing east. Everybody knew what it was, and what it represented. The Wall was a barrier against the inexorable flow of mankind toward freedom. It was a monument that tyranny was compelled to build to the striving of the human spirit to be free.

A few weeks after the Berlin Wall crisis, Khrushchev broke the three-year-old U.S.-Soviet nuclear test moratorium by ordering a series of hydrogen bomb detonations. The Kremlin acknowledged that it had resumed atomic testing, and that it had detonated a fifty-megaton hydrogen bomb in the atmosphere. The bomb (equivalent to 50 million tons of TNT), was the largest explosive device ever detonated, ten times more powerful than all the explosives used during the entire Second World War, 3,000 times more powerful than the Hiroshima bomb. Khrushchev was elated. "Let this device hang over the heads of the capitalists like a sword of Damocles," he said.

The United States had advocated the moratorium, and Kennedy administration officials had been working to negotiate a permanent test ban, but the resumption of Soviet atomic testing forced a renewal of testing by the Americans In September, Kennedy reluctantly ordered the resumption of U.S. testing. "What choice did we have?" he asked UN ambassador Adlai Stevenson. "We couldn't possibly sit back and do nothing at all."[112]

As technology increased the destructiveness of bombs, it also reduced the warning time for a nuclear strike to just a few minutes. The Colorado Springs–based North American Air Defense Command (NORAD), established in 1958, monitored radar and satellite information from across the northern hemisphere and alerted the Strategic Air Command in Omaha, Nebraska, of potential incoming missiles. From missile silos on the ground and a fleet of atomic bomb-equipped B-52 bombers that maintained a constant presence in the skies, and in submarines plying the oceans, U.S. forces maintained a constant nuclear vigilance; a credible threat of retaliation in the event of a Soviet nuclear strike.

A nearby island in the Caribbean, meanwhile, was emerging as an improbable flash point in U.S.-Soviet relations. On January 1, 1959, Fidel Castro's rebel forces had overthrown the pro-Western government of Fulgencia Batista, a corrupt and brutal dictator of the island nation of Cuba, just ninety miles off the Florida coast. Across Latin America, age-old oligarchies still held sway over burgeoning populations seething with resentments. The elite resisted land reform and opposed social and political modernization. By 1943 there were revolutionary Marxist parties in every South American nation.

Long before Castro came to power, the United States had worked to promote democracy and stability in the region, giving direct aid and pressing for land reform. In 1959 the Eisenhower administration established the Inter-American Development Bank, one of the first institutions for regional development, to help promote social and economic progress in South America, with an initial capitalization of a billion dollars. Seventeen Latin American nations and the United States participated in the agreement to establish the IDB. In return for the American assistance, Latin American governments pledged to make much-needed land and social reforms.

When Kennedy announced the creation of the Alliance for Progress in March 1961, in a speech to a group of Latin American ambassadors at the White House he called the program "a vast cooperative effort unparalleled in magnitude and nobility of purpose to satisfy the base needs of the

American people for homes, work and land, health and schools." It entailed an initial ten-year U.S. contribution of $20 billion. Much of the American aid to the region was siphoned off by self-interested elites and wound up in the Western bank accounts of political leaders rather than in needed development projects. There were other deep-rooted problems. During the 1950s the region's economy had grown at a respectable 4.3 percent rate, but its population increased at a staggering, unsustainable 3 percent annually, the fastest growth rate anywhere in the world.[113] Nevertheless, with the help of often-begrudged but undeniable American political and economic assistance, most Latin American nations made halting but significant progress toward liberal democracy. At century's end only one regime in the Americas still rejected democracy outright.

Shortly after taking power, in April 1959, Castro, a former law student, made a triumphant visit to the United States, stirring leftist audiences with his socialist vision for Cuba. When Anastas Mikoyan, deputy chairman of the Soviet Council of Ministers, visited Cuba in February 1960 at Castro's invitation, he was elated by what he found there. "Yes, he is a genuine revolutionary. Completely like us," Mikoyan reported to Moscow. "I felt as though I had returned to my youth."[114]

The revolution against Batista had indeed been a popular one, supported by broad segments of Cuban society, and Castro was able to rise to power by promising to restore the democratic constitution of 1940. The pretense did not last long. Castro ordered the summary execution of hundreds of Batista supporters, established autocratic control over a one-party state, and banned all opposition. In April 1961 he officially declared what everybody already knew: that under his government Cuba was to be a "socialist" nation. By that time Soviet agents had already assisted Castro in the establishment of a Cuban KGB, the *Direccion General de Inteligencia*, which recruited informants and conducted a pervading surveillance on the population. Following the Chinese model, neighborhood "Committees for the Defense of the Revolution," directed by party loyalists, were created to promote political indoctrination and to monitor suspicious political activities. Special courts were established and show trials held to convict and sentence suspected political opponents. Castro's closest comrade, Ernesto "Che" Guevara, a devotee of Stalinism, was made minister of industry, and initiated the forced collectivization of the economy. He influenced Castro's comprehensive program of indoctrination of Cuban youth and oversaw the development of its Stalinist "corrective work camps."[115] "In Cuba a new type of man is being created," explained Guevara in 1960.

Mass media and communications were rigidly controlled. Marxist indoctrination was made the cornerstone of public education, and thousands of prospective teachers were sent to Russia and Eastern bloc nations for instruction in socialist indoctrination. The Catholic Church was persecuted as a counterrevolutionary influence, with many priests and nuns hounded into exile.[116]

Moscow had supplied Castro's rebellion, now it would supply his dictatorship, drawing tighter and tighter—as dependency grew over the following years—the purse strings of control, with a view to harassing the Americans in their backyard, and Cuba as a launching pad for Communism elsewhere in the Americas. Within two years after the takeover in Cuba, Venezuelan president Romulo Betancourt was complaining about terrorists in his country who "receive arms and money from Communist Russia, through the branch office they have set up in Havana."[117] By 1960, Castro was openly promising to export Communist revolution to all of South America.

The term "Bay of Pigs" is seldom found apart from the modifier "fiasco." This is not without reason. From the beginning, Kennedy knew that the operation was a long shot. The Joint Chiefs of Staff had concluded that the mission had "little chance of success," though the CIA (which trained and supplied the Cuban rebels involved) was more confident. The president's actions against the Cuban regime were hardly from out of the blue. Castro was establishing an outpost of the Kremlin just miles offshore and promising to export Communism elsewhere in the Americas. During the 1960 election campaign, candidate Kennedy had recommended supporting "non-Batista democratic anti-Castro forces."[118]

There was a case to be made for intervention in Cuba. There was no case for a half-intervention. But planning had already begun during the Eisenhower administration, and Kennedy gave his approval for the operation to go forward. On April 17, 1961, about 1,300 anti-Castro Cuban exiles landed at the Bay of Pigs, aiming to overthrow the Communist government. Within seventy-two hours the badly mismatched force had been defeated; 114 men were killed in the failed invasion, and 1,189 were captured by Castro's troops.

"How could I have been so stupid, to let them go ahead?" Kennedy asked aloud. The following year, the survivors were ransomed by Castro for $53 million in food and other provisions. The doomed invasion effort elevated the Cuban dictator's prestige within the Communist world, the Third World generally, and even the American intelligentsia. Kennedy's concerns about the use of Cuba as a forward base for the projection of Communism into the Americas were well founded. By 1962 there were over forty thousand Russian troops on the tiny island.

On October 14 an American U-2 spy plane photographed what were confirmed to be ballistic missile launcher sites in Cuba. The Kremlin had begun to install the first of about three dozen medium- and intermediate-range nuclear missile launchers ninety miles off the American coast, capable of striking most American cities. If they remained, American foreign policy, including its centerpiece, anti-Communism, would henceforth be conducted in the shadow of nuclear terror.

Khrushchev believed that Kennedy was "very young, too intellectual, not strong enough to handle . . . crisis situations."[119] It was Kennedy who remained calm and deliberative throughout the crisis. Though there was immense pressure for an immediate response, Kennedy did not act precipitously. On the morning of Tuesday, October 16, he met with a group of senior National Security Council advisers; in that, and subsequent meetings, a range of options were considered: a strike on the three missile bases; a broader strike against military targets in Cuba; an invasion; a blockade. On the eighteenth, President Kennedy met at the White House in a previously scheduled meeting with Soviet foreign minister Andrei Gromyko, but did not reveal that he had knowledge of the missile installations. Gromyko smilingly lied to the president, maintaining that the USSR would never place offensive weapons in Cuba. In a nationwide television address on the twenty-second, Kennedy informed the American people of the crisis and announced the imposition of a "quarantine" on all shipping to Cuba. Commercial ships would be permitted to pass through the naval blockade, while ships carrying military cargo would be intercepted. U.S. naval commanders were ordered "disable, don't sink" ships that refused to halt, and in the following days, several ships were searched. Others turned back to the Soviet Union rather than reveal their cargoes.

At the United Nations Security Council, when Soviet ambassador Valerian Zorin denied the existence of missiles in Cuba, U.S. ambassador Adlai Stevenson, armed with satellite photos, pressed for a response: "Do you, Ambassador Zorin, deny that the USSR has placed and is placing missile sites in Cuba? Yes or no?"

Zorin: "I am not in an American courtroom, sir, and therefore I do not wish to answer a question that is put to me in the fashion in which a prosecutor puts the question. . . . "

Stevenson: "You are in the courtroom of world opinion right now, and you can answer yes or no. You have denied that they exist, and I want to know whether I understood you correctly."

Zorin: "Continue with your statement. You will have your answer in due course."

Stevenson: "I am prepared to wait for my answer until hell freezes over, if that's your decision. I am also prepared to present the evidence to this room."[120]

On the twenty-sixth, the White House received what appeared to be a conciliatory and face-saving message from Khrushchev: the Kremlin would remove the missiles if the United States pledged not to invade Cuba. The following day another, more strident and seemingly contradictory message was received: the Soviet Union would dismantle the Cuban missiles if the United States removed its Jupiter missiles from Turkey. Kennedy decided to acknowledge the conciliatory offer and ignore the more provocative one. The obsolete Jupiters in Turkey were a fortuitous bargaining chip: they had already been scheduled for removal months earlier. Kennedy made a private pledge to Khrushchev to do so.

Fidel Castro, who had urged Khrushchev to launch a missile strike against the United States, flew into a rage when he learned that the Soviet missiles were being withdrawn from Cuba. Khrushchev was a "Son of a bitch! Bastard! Asshole!" he ranted. Mikoyan reported to Moscow that the Cuban leader was egocentric, "of a difficult character, expansive, emotional, nervous, high-strung, quick to explode in anger, and unhealthily apt to concentrate on trivialities."[121] Khrushchev threatened to cut off support if Castro remained recalcitrant. He didn't.

As for Cuba, it was to be the only Latin American nation in which a Communist regime managed to long maintain its control, and its fate was the social, cultural, and political retardation common to all Communist societies. Contrary to subsequent socialist mythology, Cuba at the time of the revolution had not been among the poorer or most class-riven nations in Latin America. It was in fact the second-wealthiest nation, behind oil-rich Venezuela. Prerevolutionary Cuba only came to seem poorer and poorer, retrospectively, in the intellectual imagination, as its hemispheric neighbors caught up and then surpassed it.

Like everywhere else it was tried, Communism in Cuba was a disaster. There were the inevitable symptoms: deprivation, rationing, pervasive indoctrination, a corrupt and inefficient bureaucracy; and everywhere, everywhere, government efforts to get workers to work harder and longer. Labor disillusion and absenteeism increased, the public grew disenchanted with the party's promises of the workers' paradise that was always just over the horizon. Cuba was being transformed into one of the poorest societies in the world. Eventually the government was forced to enact laws against "laziness," with sentences ranging from reindoctrination to years in a prison work camp.

The failure of Communism in Cuba did not prevent Castro—who had visions of an epic place for himself in history—from working aggressively to export it overseas. Supported by Moscow, he began sending thousands of Cubans abroad to help foster local Communist guerrilla movements in Africa and Latin America. The Kremlin praised Cuba as "the active vanguard of all the 200 million Latin Americans."[122] In 1964 the Organization of American States reported that the Cuban government was aggressively arming terrorist groups in the region, and voted to cut off diplomatic ties.

Che Guevara, a restless revolutionary, soon grew bored with building the totalitarian paradise in Cuba and set off abroad to foment "two, three, many Vietnams." He called for the "extremely useful hatred that turns men into effective, violent, merciless and cold killing machines," which was essential for establishing world socialism.[123] He planned to travel across South America, starting in Bolivia, with the strategy of organizing, in one country after another, Communist guerrilla movements of sufficient power that the governments would be forced to call on the United States for military assistance. Then the insurgencies could portray themselves as national liberation movements. He never got past Bolivia. He managed to organize only a tiny band of peasants there and was killed in a shootout with Bolivian soldiers in October 1967. He would be more successful in his next incarnation, as an icon for T-shirt radicals and a commodity for (capitalist) vendors.

Just as bands of political pilgrims once journeyed to Stalin's Russia to marvel at the social revolution under way there, groups of earnest Americans would henceforth make that same pilgrimage to the ersatz utopia in Cuba. At century's end, after forty years of Communist control, Cuba was the only major nation in Latin America that was *less* developed than it had been in the heady days of the revolution. In 2000 it had a per capita income (purchasing power parity) of only $1,700, among the lowest in the world, and far below neighbors such as Mexico ($9,100), Chile ($10,100), Venezuela ($6,200), or even Bolivia ($2,600), nations to which it had attempted to export its glorious revolution.

By century's end, over one hundred thousand Cubans had been incarcerated in the regime's gulag.[124] Armando Valladares, who spent twenty years in Castro's prisons for simply opposing the Communist philosophy, would write that, "Someday, when the history of all of [Castro's political prisons] is known in detail, mankind will feel the revulsion it felt when the crimes of Stalin were brought to light."[125]

Following the missile crisis, a hotline was installed between the White House and the Kremlin, and other measures were taken to prevent nuclear war. But, though there was an imperative to restrain the arms race, the fundamental American opposition to Communist tyranny had not diminished. On June 26, President Kennedy traveled to West Berlin, now a beacon of liberty amidst the gray pall of Soviet Eastern Europe. From the balcony of the city hall, he spoke to a crowd of over a quarter million cheering, weeping West Berliners. "There are many people in the world who really don't understand—or say they don't—what is the great issue between the free world and the Communist world. Let them come to Berlin. There are some who say that Communism is the wave of the future. Let them come to Berlin. . . . Freedom is indivisible, and when one man is enslaved, who are free . . . ? All free men, wherever they may live, are citizens of Berlin. And therefore, as a free man, I take pride in the words 'Ich bin ein Berliner.' "[126]

———◆———

Nikita Khrushchev had blustered into near-war in Berlin, then Cuba. By comparison, Stalin had almost seemed a diplomat. Khrushchev's rustic boorishness (including taking his shoe off and slamming it on the table at the United Nations) symbolized a rashness in international affairs that, worst of all, wasn't working. Abroad, China was emerging as a major competitor within the Communist world. At home, the soviet economy was floundering. Khrushchev's attempts to "reform" the economy without fundamentally altering the Communist system had been an abject failure. Russian per capita grain consumption was lower in 1962 than it had been in 1913, before the revolution.[127]

Khrushchev's own schemes had been part of the problem. Observing that the Americans had enjoyed enormous success in growing corn, during the 1950s he had ordered that Soviet collectives be turned to corn production, often replacing crops better suited to the soil and weather conditions. He also launched the "Virgin Lands Campaign," ordering that 35 million hectares of uncultivated land in Central Asia be put into production. As it turned out, there was good reason why the land had been uncultivated. Soil erosion and insufficient rainfall resulted in poor yields, after the expenditure of enormous resources. State control could dictate what crops were planted where, but could not compel them to grow. Most scientists who knew the absurdity of Khrushchev's schemes also knew enough not to criticize them. In 1962 the state was forced to double food prices. The following year the Soviet Union, with the greatest expanse of agricultural land in the world, was compelled to import grain.

In October, while vacationing in the Crimea, Khrushchev was removed from power by the party leadership, which referred to his "hairbrained schemes" when announcing his "retirement." The members of his bodyguard were changed, as was its function. He was effectively a prisoner. He survived, disregarded and depressed, until September 1971. His protégé, Leonid Brezhnev, who had played a central role in the coup, replaced him as head of the party.

Among the community of democratic nations there emerged a crack in the alliance, though not a schism. French president Charles de Gaulle held grand ambitions of a renewed international role for France, which in the previous century had seen a succession of blows to its national pride and international importance, most recently its losses in Southeast Asia and Algeria. De Gaulle believed that carving out a "policy of grandeur" for France on the international stage could only come by chipping at American power and prestige. He warned Europeans that the United States would not risk its own cities to defend Europe in a nuclear confrontation. Kennedy aide Theodore Sorensen later wrote that "De Gaulle cleverly played on European resentment of both the American nuclear monopoly and the influence in Europe's affairs of our massive military, economic and political presence. He also appealed to European pride . . . and to European suspicions that England and America wished to dominate."[128] The French president commonly referred to Britons and Americans coterminously as "the Anglo-Saxons," regarding both nations as obstacles to a French resurgence. In 1963, de Gaulle vetoed Britain's entry into the European Economic Community. (On a state visit to Canada in 1967, he cheered Quebec's French separatist movement, declaring to an ethnic French audience in Montreal, *"Vive le Quebec libre!"* He was asked by the Canadian prime minister to end his visit early and leave the country.)

In June 1963, President Kennedy made a successful tour of European capitals, assuring allies that the United States had no interest in dominating "the European councils of decision." If that had been the Americans' aim, he said, "We would prefer to see Europe divided and weak, enabling the United States to deal with each fragment individually." Instead, America was actively working for the establishment of a democratic Europe "united and strong, speaking with a common voice, acting with a common will, a world power capable of meeting world problems as a full and equal partner."[129]

France pursued its own nuclear weapons program and in 1966 withdrew from NATO's military command to pursue an "independent" foreign policy, with the purported doctrine of "defense in all directions." De Gaulle sought to enhance France's international position by establishing closer ties with the Soviet bloc, and working to position France as a "third force" between the Soviet Union and the United States. After removing France from the NATO command, he proclaimed that "The reappearance of a nation whose hands are free, as we have again become, obviously modifies the world interplay which, since Yalta, seemed to be limited to two powers."[130] He and his foreign minister traveled to European capitals, including to Warsaw, Prague, Bucharest, Budapest, and Sofia, hoping to establish a nonaligned movement within Europe, but were rebuffed on all sides. Plans for several more diplomatic forays into the Eastern bloc were in the works but, following a defeat in a national referendum on government reforms, de Gaulle resigned the presidency in 1969.[131] France's ostentatious withdrawal from the NATO military command was largely pretense: notwithstanding rhetoric of a "defense in all directions," in reality, Paris's strategic military doctrine continued to assume that there would be no attack from the West, and continued to depend heavily upon assistance from NATO nations, in the event of an attack from the East.

The departure of France from the NATO military structure, though, illustrated a key difference between the democratic and Soviet blocs. NATO, unlike its Soviet-bloc counterpart, the Warsaw Pact, was a strictly voluntary organization, resting upon popular opinion within its member nations. When France announced the withdrawal, there was never any consideration of forcing a reversal of the decision. Some Western diplomats were happy to have the vainglorious de Gaulle gone. When Hungary had attempted to withdraw from the Warsaw Pact, by contrast, it was invaded, and all opposition was violently crushed.

———•———

The American public had consistently opposed imperialism, American or foreign, and European decolonization was a salient political issue in the United States during the forties and fifties. "Liberation!" became a Republican slogan in the 1952 election. "Colonialism is on the way out as a relationship among peoples," President Eisenhower wrote to Winston Churchill in

1954.[132] The American involvement in Vietnam began as part of that ambitious project.

During the Second World War, France had given up Indochina—what was to become Cambodia, Laos, and Vietnam—to the Japanese in World War II, but attempted to reclaim it as a colony when the fighting was over. President Roosevelt opposed France (which he believed had a dismal record as an imperial power) recovering its Asian territories. "Indo-china should not go back to France," he wrote Secretary of State Hull in October 1944. "France has had that country for nearly one hundred years, and the people are worse off than they were at the beginning. . . . The people of Indo-China are entitled to something better than that."[133] He envisioned a UN trusteeship, followed by independence. But in the chaotic aftermath of the war, with the perceived need to assuage a key European ally, the imperative of restoring order in a chaotic region, and the prospect of looming conflict with the Soviet Union, the new Truman administration backed away from opposition.[134] The British, concerned about their own imperial interests, supported French claims.

United States policy came to be one of pressuring the French government to prepare Indochina for independence while helping it resist Communist subversion there. After the triumph of Mao in China in 1949 and the invasion by Communist North Korea of the South the following year, the importance attached to the latter, predictably, increased. "It would seem a case of 'Penny wise, pound foolish' to deny support for the French in Indochina," a State Department analysis concluded in 1950.[135] Washington continued to push Paris to prepare Indochina for sovereignty. This included calls, by 1951, for French development of a schedule for independence.[136]

Ho Chi Minh, born Nguyen Tat Thanh in central Vietnam in 1890, the son of a prosperous public official, became radicalized as a student in Paris and in 1920 joined the French Communist Party. He then moved to Moscow, where he was trained in revolutionary techniques and party organization. For a time Ho was assigned as a Comintern agent in China and Hong Kong, and then returned to Moscow for further training and indoctrination in the late 1930s.

When Japan was defeated by the United States in 1945, Ho declared himself head of a new independent Vietnamese state and waged a guerrilla war for independence from France. Supplied with weaponry and matériel by Moscow—and, after 1949, Beijing—his Viet Minh rebels took to the dense jungles, from whence they launched hit-and-run raids against French targets with the goal of wearing down the enemy's will. Public opinion in France grew weary of the long, costly struggle for an unprofitable colony.

When Viet Minh forces besieged and defeated a large French garrison, in March–May 1954, at the village of Dien Bien Phu, France lost the will to continue. At an international conference in Geneva that summer, Ho Chi Minh insisted on a united Vietnam, under his control, but ultimately agreed to a division of the country, similar to that in Korea, at the 17th Parallel. Laos and Cambodia became independent states.

Ngo Dinh Diem, a devout Catholic and a nationalist who had been living in exile during the occupation, was made prime minister of the new government established in the south by Emperor Bao Dai. Eisenhower told Diem that U.S. support would be contingent upon his "undertaking needed reforms" of the political system.

In the north, Ho followed the Stalinist model for consolidating power, brutally annihilating the landowning class, abolishing private property, collectivizing agriculture, and murdering ten to fifteen thousand political dissidents. A gulag labor camp system was established. When peasants revolted against the regime in November 1956, the rebellion was violently suppressed by Ho's troops. More than six thousand peasants were executed or imprisoned. The forced expropriation and collectivization of land resulted, as elsewhere, in diminished agricultural output and famines. Despite China's centuries of conflict with Vietnam, Chairman Mao pledged a massive $338 million aid package to the new Communist nation, insisting that the ideology which united the two regimes was more important that their history of conflict. In North Vietnam, no dissent was permitted. A political "reeducation" program on the Chinese model—and under the tutelage of thousands of advisers sent by Mao—was created. "Traitor elimination committees" were set up in urban neighborhoods and rural villages to root out political unorthodoxy.[137] (In later years the North Vietnamese government would insist that it had been pushed by "Chinese advisers" to use the brutal measures it did to consolidate power.)[138] A million refugees fled the Communist rule to South Vietnam.

As Kim Il-sung had done in Korea, once having secured power in the North, Ho Chi Minh began to aggressively support the Communist insurgency movement (derisively dubbed the 'Viet Cong' by South Vietnamese) around 1957, working to overthrow the government in the South. President Eisenhower increased military and economic support to South Vietnam and Laos, also sending a small number of military advisers to help rebuild the ineffectual and demoralized South Vietnamese army into a modern fighting force. Between 1955 and 1959 the United States provided South Vietnam with over $127 million in direct economic aid, $16 million in technical aid, and over $1 billion in trade.[139] By the late 1950s, South Vietnam was experiencing an economic revival. After a visit to the country in 1959, an American senator responsible for assuring that U.S. foreign aid funds were well spent suggested that South Vietnam could be made a "showcase" for demonstrating to aid recipients from other nations the salutary "effects of our efforts to help other peoples help themselves."[140] Eisenhower was determined, though, that U.S. forces would not be drawn into another land war in Asia. Under Eisenhower, the number of U.S. military advisers in Vietnam rose to only around eight hundred.

By 1961 the Viet Cong, armed and directed by Hanoi, were launching hundreds of terrorist attacks each month in an effort to subvert the Saigon government. Terror was employed against rural villages to establish VC control, and against urban areas to erode public support for the regime. In areas under their control, Viet Cong guerrillas levied taxes, expropriated food, and even conscripted young men into military service. The number of South Vietnamese officials murdered by Communist terrorists rose from 1,200 in 1959 to over 4,000 in 1961; in some vicinities the certain prospect of assassination by VC guerrillas made it impossible for the government to fill local leadership positions. To counter the growing Communist insurgency, President Kennedy increased economic and military aid to Diem. The South Vietnamese government was, indisputably, corrupt, but it at least contained within it the seeds of its own reform. America had come to the aid of democracy in Korea out of commitment to that principle, and did no less in Vietnam.

Diem used the wartime conditions to justify continued repression, and resisted U.S. pressures to hold promised elections in South Vietnam. In a military coup at least sanctioned by the Kennedy administration, Diem and his brother were ousted on November 1, and later executed by South Vietnamese army officers. A succession of bloodless coups resulted, by June 1965, in Gen. Nguyen Van Thieu becoming head of a military junta. Two years later Thieu was elected president of South Vietnam.

The United States did not enter into what became the quagmire of Vietnam in pursuit of economic gain: there was none there to be had. A strictly narrow, self-interested calculus would have kept America from going anywhere near Indochina. Involvement there represented the idealistic American notions that any society could become democratic, that every people have the right to live free, and that the United States had some international moral obligations to that end—even twelve thousand miles across the globe. In his inaugural address, Kennedy had pledged to maintain America's tradition of defense for liberty and democracy, and vowed not to "permit the slow undoing of those human rights to which this nation has always been committed, and to which we are committed today, at home and around the world. Let every nation know, whether it wishes us well or ill, that we shall pay any price, bear any burden, meet any hardship, support any friend, oppose any foe to assure the survival and success of liberty." During his presidency he made offhand remarks about wishing the United States could get out of Indochina as soon as possible, but always in the context of leaving a stable anti-Communist regime in the South. Robert McNamara, Kennedy's secretary of defense, would retrospectively say that Kennedy would have withdrawn U.S. troops from Vietnam if he had been reelected in 1964. McNamara's biographer wrote that this was not based on anything specific Kennedy had told him, but "was something that [McNamara] arrived at later when the war had become tragic and traumatic for him and the nation."[141] If Kennedy was planning, during his last days in office, on pulling U.S. forces out of Vietnam, he left no historical evidence of this. "I don't agree with those who say we should withdraw. That would be a great mistake," Kennedy told television newsman Walter Cronkite in September 1963. "This is a very important struggle, even though it is far away. We made this effort to defend Europe. Now Europe is quite secure. We also have to participate—we may not like it—in the defense of Asia."[142]

Vietnam was not an undertaking of one party or one president. It was carried on by five presidents, across three decades, reflecting the central principle of American foreign policy during the second half of the twentieth century: opposition to the spread of global Communism. A death creates a void, a blank slate upon which we are able to write our own yearnings. "What if Kennedy had lived?" The question is inevitable and contains its own implied answer. With apologies to certain writers and filmmakers, John F. Kennedy was a hawk, not a dove. When Kennedy was elected president in 1960, there were fewer than 800 American military advisers in Vietnam. When he died in 1963, there were 16,700.

On November 22, 1963, on a trip to Dallas, Texas, President Kennedy was assassinated by Lee Harvey Oswald, a disturbed Communist zealot who had defected to and lived in the Soviet Union for several years. In a speech to be delivered on the day of his death, the president was to acknowledge that commitments in Third World nations were "painful, risky and costly," but that "we dare not weary of the test."[143]

Lyndon Baines Johnson, a southern Protestant, had been picked to be Kennedy's vice presidential running mate to help the Northeastern Catholic win the general election. One of the most naturally gifted politicians of the century, Johnson, the son of an impoverished Texas hill country farmer and graduate of the undistinguished Southwest Texas State Teachers College, had risen to be master of the United States Senate before running against Kennedy in the Democratic primary. President Johnson shared the commitment to oppose the spread of Communism that had been the hallmark of his predecessors' foreign policies. Upon taking office, he pledged to "see things through in Vietnam," and to do so "not out of blind loyalty to Kennedy," but because he was "convinced that the broad lines of the policy in Southeast Asia . . . " had been right.[144]

———◆———

One of the central criticisms concerning American intervention in Vietnam was that the "Domino Principle" (the belief that the ascendance of Communism in Vietnam would make its neighbors vulnerable) was erroneous. The Kremlin leadership did not think so. In February 1950, Ho Chi Minh had met in Moscow with his mentor Joseph Stalin and Mao Zedong to negotiate treaties of support for Ho's regime and plan the spread of Communism across Southeast Asia. Communist-supported insurgencies were already raging in Indonesia, Burma, Malaya, the Philippines, and elsewhere. Documents revealed since the collapse of the Soviet Union show that Stalin believed that if a foothold was established in Vietnam, next Cambodia and Laos would be vulnerable, then onward. The Domino Principle was not only an American concern: it was an explicit Communist strategy.[145]

President Johnson concluded, as Harry Truman had in deciding upon intervention in an earlier war in a remote Asian country, that to abandon that nation to Communism would not only doom its own people to tyranny but facilitate its spread elsewhere. Kennedy had also believed this: asked whether he believed that the ascendance of Communism to power in South Vietnam would threaten its spread to neighboring nations, he replied, "I believe it. I believe it. China is so large . . . [the fall of Vietnam] would also give the impression that the wave of the future in Southeast Asia was China and the Communists. So I believe it."[146]

Mao believed it, too. "Because we will fight large-scale battles in the future," he told Ho while discussing construction of the Ho Chi Minh Trail, "it will be good if we also build roads to Thailand."[147] By 1963–64, Ho Chi Minh was waging a full-scale undeclared war against the South. Hanoi was now sending thousands of its best-trained and most ideologically dedicated soldiers southward to help lead the Viet Cong insurgency and pouring massive amounts of Soviet- and Chinese-made weaponry through the Ho Chi Minh "Trail," now six hundred miles long and up to 26 feet wide.

The Communists themselves, North and South, had high hopes of winning the war by 1965. These hopes were not unreasonable, and almost certainly would have been realized except for American action. After the war, officials in the Hanoi government acknowledged that, without American intervention in 1964–65, the fall of South Vietnam to the North was imminent. The cause was just. The problem, from the United States' strategic perspective, was that there had been no great decision taken, at any single point in time, weighing all the potential costs and benefits on whether to conduct an all-out war in Vietnam—and what it would take to decisively win one. Instead, a series of incremental escalations in the commitment had been made, like the frog in the pot of water in which the temperature is only gradually raised. Eisenhower had established the American policy of support for South Vietnam; Kennedy had expanded it; then Johnson.

On August 2, 1964, several North Vietnamese torpedo boats attacked the U.S. destroyer *Maddox*, on patrol in the Gulf of Tonkin. The *Maddox* returned fire, sinking one Vietnamese vessel and damaging others. Two days later the *Maddox* and the destroyer *Turner Joy* reported another attack. That evening Johnson made a national television address, announcing that "renewed hostile actions against United States ships on the high seas in the Gulf of Tonkin have today required me to order the military forces of the United States to take action in reply." U.S. bombers struck at several military targets in North Vietnam. On the fifth, Johnson asked Congress for powers to conduct the conflict in Vietnam. The Gulf of Tonkin Resolution passed unanimously in the House, and with only two opposing votes in the Senate.

The Resolution gave Johnson broad latitude in conducting the war. It was "like Grandma's nightshirt," he later said. "It covered everything."

Although some critics later charged the president with fabricating the *Maddox* affair, all evidence (including material in the so-called *Pentagon Papers* themselves) indicates that the attack did take place. There is no dispute that the first attack on the *Maddox* occurred, though limited visibility conditions subsequently raised questions about a second. But the Resolution, though precipitated by an incident, was necessitated and justified by a broader pattern of aggression. It accurately denounced "a deliberate and systematic campaign of aggression that the Communist regime in North Vietnam has been waging against its neighbors. . . . "

Yet Johnson declined to make Vietnam a central element of his *public* policy agenda, purposely downplaying its costs and effects, in order to maintain attention and support for his domestic "Great Society" agenda. The intensive and sustained effort that should have been made to rally a nation about to embark on war was never made.[148] Americans wanted to halt the spread of Communism in Asia and were willing to go to war to do it. But what would it take? A democratic nation, if it must go to war, cannot do so halfheartedly. At each subsequent stage of escalation, Johnson sought the minimum—of public attention and national resources—that would be required to prevail. Initially the war effort was sold as support for Vietnamese troops. "We don't want our boys to do the fighting for Asian boys," Johnson told voters during the 1964 presidential campaign. He promised that U.S. forces would not be put into direct conflict in Vietnam, even as he made plans for precisely that contingency. This proved to be a poor way to start a war.

———◆———

Mao viewed Vietnam as a means of striking at the Americans with little or no risk to China. The Hanoi leadership was suspicious of his motives, but took his support. Vietnam's prime minister later said that Mao was "always ready to fight to the last Vietnamese."[149]

General Westmoreland's strategy in South Vietnam was to eradicate Viet Cong units through "search and destroy" missions, to wear down the enemy through attrition—killing more soldiers than North Vietnam could replace. Within twenty-four months, he believed, Hanoi would be unable to sustain the losses and would enter peace negotiations.

The tactic of "search and destroy" in Vietnam has been widely regarded by military analysts as a failure. Most battles were initiated by hit-and-run raids on Americans, not the other way around, and the totalitarian government in Hanoi was able to endure an exponentially higher body count than the democratic government in Washington. Also, two hundred thousand North Vietnamese men reached conscription age yearly: attrition alone would be a long and agonizing process. The South Vietnamese army was in disarray, with an annual desertion rate of over 20 percent and a generally poor record of performance in combat. By late 1965, Secretary McNamara was expressing doubts about the strategy in Vietnam. In early 1966, hearings were held in the U.S. Senate on the conduct of the war, but support for it, both among the foreign policy establishment and the general public, remained high. *Newsweek* declared that "a U.S. failure [in Vietnam] could have far-reaching results."[150] Yet, prospects for a clear-cut victory seemed to be growing more remote. By 1967, Hanoi was infiltrating nearly 100,000 guerrilla fighters per year into the South, nearly three times the rate of 1965. A Marine Corps study issued in August concluded that North Vietnam could, at the present attrition rate, continue the war indefinitely.

To strike at Hanoi's sponsorship of the Communist insurgency in South Vietnam, President Johnson's military advisers, including all of the Joint Chiefs of Staff, advocated aggressive bombing of North Vietnam from the outset—large-scale aerial attacks against industrial and military sites—to force a surrender. Johnson's civilian advisers argued that, by beginning with modest initial air strikes, Hanoi would "get the signal" that the United States was serious, and Ho Chi Minh would back off from his support of the Viet Cong. Johnson chose the latter course and commenced a bombing campaign targeting supply routes to the south, in hopes of achieving a negotiated settlement. The enemy's power centers, in Hanoi and the vital port center of Haiphong, were off-limits to bombing. He personally selected the targets, with the aim to influence the Hanoi regime rather than crush it or destroy its material capability to provide support to the terrorists in the South.[151]

You can bomb a road, but unless you control the area with ground forces, it may be made passable the next day. Operation Rolling Thunder, the 1965–68 air campaign, taught the inadequacy of airpower alone to win a war, particularly against a largely preindustrial enemy. Half a million North Vietnamese women and young people were engaged full-time repairing damage to roads and bridges, and most of the important war material heading southward originated in Russia or China. Three years of strategic bombing did not diminish Hanoi's warmaking capacity, or its resolve, or its ability to supply men and material to the South. Every dollar's worth of damage inflicted on North Vietnam cost the United States ten dollars.[152]

Communist insurgents in the South established immense bases across the nearby borders of Laos and Cambodia, in the knowledge that the Americans would not target these. After the war, North Vietnamese officials said that if Johnson had granted Westmoreland's request to target bases in Laos and Cambodia, "Hanoi could not have won the war. It was the only way we could bring sufficient military power to bear on the fighting in the South."[153] A postwar survey of American soldiers who had been involved in heavy combat found that 82 percent believed that the war was lost because they were not allowed to fight to win.[154] Hanoi was waging a total war, meanwhile, including the use of women and children for espionage, terrorist bombings, and combat in the South.

President Johnson was also conscious of conducting the first television war, and conscious of the propaganda campaign that at times seemed to rival the military one in importance. Presumably for this reason, the effort to limit civilian casualties in North Vietnam was remarkable, perhaps unprecedented. "Taking the overall environment into account," wrote a British observer in 1967, "I personally have never seen airpower so discriminately applied, or so much care taken to avoid errors, often at great tactical disadvantage."[155] Soviet-supplied radar systems forewarned of every attack, and American pilots flew through some of the densest surface-to-air missile fire in history while making their bombing runs. By the end of 1967 over seven hundred American planes had been shot down by Russian-made anti-aircraft weaponry, and the fate of U.S. prisoners of war was becoming a major national issue.

For most U.S. combat soldiers in Vietnam, it was a small-unit war against an invisible and wily adversary; a war of rooting out concealed (often subterranean) guerrilla units and fighting one's way out of enemy ambushes. There was effectively no "front": an attack could come from any direction. And life in the field was brutally harsh, even aside from the enemy that was intent on killing them. There were two seasons: dry season, during which temperatures frequently averaged over 110 degrees, and monsoon season, when the ground was constantly soaked, and a soldier could go for weeks without ever being really dry. All manner of mosquitoes, fire ants, and other insects, snakes, and vermin were part of daily existence. Paths were strewn with land mines and punji sticks. Soldiers hacked their way through dense growth, vision limited in all directions, death by ambush or booby trap lying in wait at every blind turn. They patrolled for days or weeks through muggy jungles or fetid swamps, constantly soaked by the high humidity. Despite the treacherous conditions, most soldiers believed in the rightness of the cause and were proud to serve in Vietnam.

American forces were trained and equipped to fight conventional war against conventional armies. Instead, here they faced guerrilla units intent on *avoiding* major direct confrontations. In hit-and-run operations designed to inflict incessant, low-level losses on U.S. troops, they expected not to defeat the United States in great battles, but to erode America's will to continue. For the Americans, the usual standards for judging success in a conventional war, such as ground gained by an advancing army, were frustratingly inapplicable. Reliable measures of success were elusive. The government in Hanoi, certainly, was not measuring victory or defeat by classic military standards. Even wildly mismatched kill ratios—of as much as 10:1—were no indicator. If the war was still going on, Hanoi considered itself to be winning. As a military commander, Ho Chi Minh turned out to be a shrewd politician. He knew that, though the battles were fought in

Vietnam, the war could only be won in the United States. Eventually the Americans, like the French, would grow weary of the conflict and go home. "You will kill ten of our men, and we will kill one of yours, and in the end it will be you who tire of it," Ho told an American official. He was right.

———◆———

On January 30, 1968, during the Vietnamese holiday of Tet, Viet Cong and North Vietnamese regular army forces in South Vietnam commenced a major surprise offensive in the South. The Tet Offensive signaled the growing desperation of the Communist forces: effective VC control of areas in the South had slipped to a fraction of what it had been four years earlier, and momentum in the conflict was clearly shifting to the other side. The Communists yielded the natural advantages of a guerrilla force, organizing into large formations and attacking Southern strongholds, counting on a "general uprising" among the population (as Kim Il-sung had mistakenly done in Korea). It never materialized. And South Vietnamese soldiers did not desert or defect in large numbers, as Hanoi had expected.

Tet was a military catastrophe for the Communists. As one of the planners of the offensive later described, "We suffered heavy losses of manpower and matériel, especially of cadres . . . which caused a distinct decline in our strength."[156] U.S. forces lost around 1,100 casualties in Tet; the South Vietnamese army lost 2,300. Of the 80,000 North Vietnamese/Viet Cong involved in the offensive, 45,000 were killed, wounded, or captured. The Viet Cong, who had been close to victory in South Vietnam before American forces arrived in 1965, were essentially destroyed as a fighting force. After Tet, the North Vietnamese regular army troops dominated the misnamed "rebel insurgency" in the South. "Our forces in the South were nearly wiped out by all the fighting in 1968," recalled a North Vietnamese leader. If the American forces had not begun to withdraw in 1969, they could have punished us severely."[157] After Tet, the conflict waged by North Vietnam increasingly resembled a conventional war, in which U.S. forces had insuperable advantages. By February 1968 the outcome of the rebel insurgency in South Vietnam had been largely decided. Even with North Vietnamese regular army involvement, battalion-sized attacks in the South fell from 126 in 1968, to 34 in 1970, to 13 in 1971.[158] Never again would the guerrilla insurgency pose a threat to the survival of the Saigon regime, which by this time had held open elections, was preparing to implement land reform, and was steadily expanding effective administrative control. The proportion of the South Vietnamese population who lived in areas secure from Communist forces rose from 47 percent in 1968 to 71 percent in 1969, to 75 percent in 1970.[159]

On the ground, a turning point had been reached. But the Vietnam War was not only conducted in the jungles of Vietnam. Though Tet marked a military catastrophe for the Communists, it led to a shift in American public opinion that transformed the Communist military defeat into a political triumph, and another sort of turning point. The American media establishment had now largely written off the war as a lost, possibly immoral, effort. The media reported that Tet had been a disaster for U.S. and South Vietnamese forces, and disturbing nightly news images of dead American soldiers and widespread carnage, and an escalating tally of casualties, seemed to confirm this. Since the empirical facts of the situation were elusive, in the place of facts were interpretive "analyses," which Peter Braestrup, who covered the war for the *Washington Post*, later described as "the hasty reactions of the half-informed."[160] In his study of U.S. media coverage of Tet, historian David Culbert concluded that the American mass media portrayed a "North Vietnamese military and political disaster as a stunning victory contributing to a psychological victory within the United States."[161]

On February 27, respected CBS news anchor Walter Cronkite, after a brief trip to Vietnam in which he did no actual investigative journalism, announced on his broadcast that the United States should withdraw. That month, Secretary of Defense McNamara resigned in despair.

In some ways the war was going better in Vietnam than in the United States. American troops had won every major battle with the VC and North Vietnamese forces, had inflicted heavy losses, and demoralized the enemy in South Vietnam.[162] After a trip to Washington, the U.S. ambassador to Saigon, Ellsworth Bunker, said that he "was shocked to see the effect the Tet offensive had had at home."[163] A bumper sticker on a Vietnam veteran's car expressed the bewilderment experienced by many GIs who returned home to discover how much the public perception in America differed from their own experiences on the ground: "I Don't Know What Happened. We Were Winning When I Left."

During the Johnson years, there were over seventy peace overtures to Hanoi. The Communists had not accepted peace because they still expected to win the public opinion war. On March 12, Lyndon Johnson came close to losing the Democratic primary in New Hampshire to Sen. Eugene McCarthy (D-Minnesota), a proponent of withdrawal. On the thirty-first, Johnson made a national television address declaring that the United States would cease bombing North Vietnam. He also announced that he would not seek reelection.

Peace talks with North Vietnam got under way in Paris in May 1968. They would continue there, haltingly, for the next half decade. For Hanoi, still intent upon total victory, the negotiations were part of the political war. It rigidly held to the demand that the government in the South must be replaced by a coalition that included the Viet Cong, and insisted that ultimate unification of Vietnam under Communist rule was not negotiable.

The Kremlin leadership viewed Vietnam as an unmitigated success. At a cost of less than $1 billion annually, it had bogged the United States down in a debilitating conflict in Southeast Asia and diverted international attention away from its own internal and external predations.[164]

Even as its economy foundered, the Kremlin was diverting a growing share of its resources to dramatically expand both its strategic and conventional forces: military spending rose 40 percent between 1965 and 1970.[165] Notwithstanding the failures of Marxist policies at home, faith in the ascendance of world Communism had only grown, with the United States seemingly fettered by Vietnam and old European empires disintegrating, fodder for new revolutionary movements. Training camps for international revolutionaries were established in Bulgaria, East Germany, Russia, and Cuba. Communist parties from around the world sent aspiring insurgents for instruction in sabotage, guerrilla warfare, and Marxist indoctrination.

There were signs, though, that the Soviet empire was fraying at the edges. Uprisings in Eastern Europe were violently crushed. In August 1968, half a million Soviet troops invaded Czechoslovakia, a nation with a population of only 14 million. Pro-democratic reforms were quashed. In Moscow the Brezhnev Doctrine was announced, which held that no socialist nation would be permitted to deviate from correct socialist doctrine, and it would be Moscow which would determine what that doctrine was.

———◆———

Richard Nixon came into the presidency, in January 1969, intent on extricating the United States from Vietnam. "It is essential that we end this war, and end it quickly," he had said during the election campaign. "But it is essential that we end it in such a way that we can win the peace."[166] There was certainly no political benefit to be had from prolonging the war. All evidence is that Nixon was sincere in his belief—expressed in public statements and private conversations before and after the election—that a precipitate American withdrawal from Vietnam would weaken the United States' ability to oppose international Communism, and would leave the South Vietnamese regime vulnerable to being overrun by Hanoi. "I was aware that many Americans considered Thieu a petty and corrupt dictator unworthy of our respect," Nixon later wrote. "I was not personally attached to Thieu, but . . . the South Vietnamese needed a strong and stable government to carry on the fight against the efforts of the Viet Cong terrorists, who were supported by the North Vietnamese army in their efforts to impose a Communist dictatorship on the 17 million people of South Vietnam."[167]

In combat operations, small-unit actions increased, and there was growing coordination between U.S. forces and both South Vietnamese civilians and military. With increased training and equipment, the South Vietnamese army itself had become more proficient, more reliable in combat, and was inflicting more losses on the enemy. In 1969, U.S. battlefield commanders reported that the situation on the ground had improved dramatically in the year since Tet.[168] By 1971 the Communists had been largely expelled from the Mekong Delta, south of Saigon, huge swaths of which they had dominated until the late 1960s. Most units fled across the border to staging camps in Cambodia.[169]

Though most American opponents of the war simply hoped for an end to losses in a distant conflict, members of the self-described "New Left" believed that American withdrawal from Vietnam was to be only part of a larger retreat from activities around the world: the United States was a corrupt and arrogant hegemon, and it must quit interfering in other societies. For the United States to impose its values around the world was economic aggression, or "cultural imperialism." It was American belligerence that was the threat to world peace, not Communism. "If you understood what communism was, you would pray on your knees that we would someday be communist," as actress/antiwar activist Jane Fonda told cheering audiences.[170]

The New Left, at home and abroad, *wanted* to believe the worst reports from the battlefield. Thus, in one of the bizarre and recurring ironies of the age, they wildly exaggerated the misconduct of Americans involved in defending freedom while overlooking systematic atrocities of the totalitarian regime in Hanoi. They denounced GIs as "baby killers" and praised the Communist leadership for its compassion. After a visit to Mao's China, "Yippie" leader Jerry Rubin gushed over "the spirit of real love the people all have for each other. You can see it in their eyes."[171]

The Vietnam War, the first major war of the television age, became a battle of public relations: by the Communists in Hanoi and Beijing and Moscow, against Washington and Saigon. There was one crucial difference. Though advocates of the Communist position were free to organize, propagandize, and demonstrate in America, those who dared to speak against the Communist position in Communist nations were subject to imprisonment, political "reeducation," torture, execution. The Communists were using democratic public pressure to compel the United States to end the war. "The U.S. has a population of 200 million people, but it cannot stand wars," Mao told North Vietnamese leaders in late 1968.[172] On their return from Hanoi, antiwar activist and avowed Communist Tom Hayden and several fellow travelers stopped off in Beijing, where they were met by a member of the Chinese Communist Party's propaganda organ, the "Chinese Peace Committee." He presented the Americans with a copy of a *New York Times* article describing the journey, and congratulated them. "There's been a great deal of interest in your trip!"[173]

By 1968 there was a steady stream of political pilgrims to Hanoi, nearly all of them socialists or Communists, taking messages of solidarity to the regime in North Vietnam, making tours—arranged by the government's propaganda ministry—of villages where happy and fulfilled peasants lived in harmony and cooperation under Communism. As a generation of Western true believers had done for Stalin, they excused Ho Chi Minh's oppression of his own people (when they acknowledged it at all) and aggression against the South as necessitated by Western hostility. Socialist "peace activist"

A. J. Muste wrote during a visit to Hanoi, "We do not equate the violence employed in final desperation by people who have been subjugated, exploited and oppressed . . . with the violence against them by their oppressors or by foreign powers which intervene in their domestic affairs."[174] After an emotional visit to Hanoi, arts critic Susan Sontag wrote of the totalitarian government there that it "loves the people." North Vietnam was a place which "*deserves* to be idealized" (her italics). Hanoi treated captured U.S. prisoners well, Sontag explained, because "People in North Vietnam really do believe in the goodness of man . . . and in the perennial possibility of rehabilitating the morally fallen. . . . "[175]

Myths about Vietnam veterans were promulgated by the antiwar activists. They insisted that those who served and died in Vietnam were disproportionately from poor households, victims of a discriminating conscription. Certainly, some "fortunate sons" received favorable treatment in evading honorable service to their country; but in fact, young men from upper-income households were roughly 10 percent *more* likely to be killed in action than others. And most of those, in stark contrast to the subsequent mythology of the war, were . . . volunteers. Indeed, from 1964 to 1973, voluntary enlistment outstripped conscriptions by a ratio of four to one. Two-thirds of all U.S. soldiers who served in Vietnam were volunteers.[176]

Another allegation was that a disproportion of blacks were serving and dying in Vietnam. In fact, blacks, who constituted 13.5 percent of the American military-age population, never exceeded 12.5 percent of the force in Vietnam, and only 12.3 percent of all combat deaths.[177] Over 86 percent of combat deaths were Caucasians.

In its effort to contain Communism, the United States had become over-extended. Its commitments exceeded its capabilities. Nixon and Kissinger believed that America must extricate itself from Vietnam precisely because there were other struggles that must be waged in the contest against global Communism, and Vietnam was dissipating its capacity to act decisively elsewhere. At the same time, a sudden and unilateral retreat, abandoning South Vietnam, would have inevitably resulted in a total victory for the North. Most Americans opposed such a move. In a May 1969 Harris poll, only 9 percent favored accepting a peace agreement that would enable an eventual Communist victory.[178] Indeed, the Democrats had rejected it at their contentious 1968 convention in Chicago.

Instead, a policy was announced in June 1969 to phase out U.S. involvement, shifting responsibility for the conduct of the war over to the South Vietnamese government and people, and providing the increased matériel it needed to do so. In practice this meant gradually withdrawing U.S. troops while holding off the North Vietnamese army. U.S. airpower, less subject to large numbers of casualties, would still be used to support South Vietnamese ground forces.

In a speech on Guam in July 1969, the president enunciated what came to be known as the Nixon Doctrine. "We will keep our commitments to America's allies," Nixon repeated several times. But he added that "the United States is going to encourage and has a right to expect that this problem [of military defense] will be increasingly handled by, and the responsibility for it taken by, the Asian nations themselves."[179] There remained, however, the matter of getting out of Vietnam.

As the prospect of an American withdrawal loomed, the morale of U.S. troops became a vital issue. The South Vietnamese regime was manifestly corrupt and might not survive a U.S. pullout. At home, antiwar demonstrations were growing in size and ferocity, and returning vets were routinely subjected to verbal abuse by antiwar activists. Many of the young U.S. soldiers in Vietnam wondered what they were fighting for.

Nevertheless, contrary to one popular myth perpetuated by antiwar activists and media portrayals, the overwhelming majority of U.S. soldiers in Vietnam never used any illicit drugs, and there is no evidence that returning veterans had higher rates of alcoholism, drug abuse, divorce, unemployment, or other social pathologies than others of their age who remained behind in the United States. Nor did they have levels of post-traumatic stress higher than those among veterans of previous wars. Total psychiatric casualties were lower among veterans of Vietnam than of either Korea or World War II.[180] In the latter, 23 percent of all medical evacuations were for "combat fatigue" and other psychiatric symptoms; in Vietnam in 1968, the figure was under 6 percent.[181] Psychiatric symptoms increased in tandem with doubts back home about the war, so that, paradoxically, as engagements with the enemy declined, and inactivity grew, GIs had more and more free time to doubt. Thus, in stark contrast to past wars, historian Ronald Spector writes, "In Vietnam, as fighting and casualties grew *lighter*, the psychiatric casualty rate *increased*."

The Hanoi Politburo had already abandoned hope of getting a decisive military victory in the South. Instead, it adopted the strategy of waging a "protracted war" designed to wear down American will, which meant inflicting incessant low-level losses in small raids and playing to the antiwar movement in the West. When Ho Chi Minh died on September 3, 1969, North Vietnamese decision making fell to a committee of Communist leaders, making the country's policy process more opaque than ever. But the main tactical difficulties for American forces in South Vietnam remained the same. The most pressing of these was that VC and NVA forces had for years launched raids with impunity from bases in the border regions of Cambodia, attacking and then withdrawing back to sanctuaries behind the border, assured that American forces were not permitted to follow.

Cambodia's ruler, Prince Norodom Sihanouk, a playboy and self-conceived artist, had attached himself to Communism in 1963, shutting down the U.S. embassy and covertly supporting regional Communists. During the war he permitted his country to be used as a staging area for North Vietnam in exchange for foreign aid from Beijing and Hanoi, and because he wanted to be on what he believed to be the winning side of history. Over time, large areas of Cambodia had been effectively annexed by the NVA. In March 1969, following a major North Vietnamese offensive launched from camps in Cambodia, Nixon authorized an air campaign against the bases. Only a handful of sympathetic congressmen were informed, and the U.S. public not at all. The reason for the ill-advised secrecy was not the fear that the American public would oppose the actions against the North Vietnamese forces (most later supported it), but concern that a public announcement of the bombings might necessitate a face-saving repudiation of them by the Cambodian government. Kissinger later wrote that the secrecy had been a mistake.[182] The bombing was, in any case, of limited use without troops on the ground to follow up.

The following March, Sihanouk—away on a shopping trip to Paris at the time—was ousted by his own National Assembly, in a coup led by Gen. Lon Nol, head of a military junta that opposed the growing control by the Vietnamese over large swaths of Cambodia. Nixon and Kissinger were both surprised by this turn of events. In undertaking the coup, Lon Nol had acted without U.S. support, but on the reasonable assumption that, if successful, he would receive it. Upon taking power, he publicly requested U.S. assistance in pushing the Vietnamese Communist forces out of Cambodia.

On April 30, 1970, President Nixon made a televised national address to announce a planned U.S. ground offensive into Cambodia. "In cooperation with the armed forces of South Vietnam, attacks are being launched this week to clean out major enemy sanctuaries on the Cambodian-Vietnam border," he said.[183] He pledged that the ground troops would venture no farther than twenty-one miles into Cambodia, and the promise was kept. What came to be called an "invasion of Cambodia" by opponents of the war in fact consisted of attacks against Vietnamese strongholds within a narrow strip along the border. Once the sanctuaries had been cleared, U.S. and South Vietnamese forces withdrew, as promised.

Eleven thousand North Vietnamese soldiers were killed in the raid and 2,500 captured; 338 Americans and 638 South Vietnamese soldiers were killed.[184] Though it further energized the antiwar movement in the United States, the Cambodian incursion took a devastating toll upon Hanoi's supply efforts in the South: a vast stock of weaponry was captured, including a quarter million individual weapons and a year's supply of munitions.[185] U.S. and South Vietnamese casualties fell sharply as a result of the raids. Following the attacks in Cambodia, the number of American soldiers killed in action fell below one hundred per week for the first time in four years.[186]

———————◆———————

In the Paris Peace Talks, the Hanoi regime's strategy was to use negotiations, or the pretense thereof, to win international opinion to their side while buying time. In America, demonstrators complained that it was Nixon's intransigence that prevented an agreement and prolonged the war of aggression against the peace-loving Hanoi government.

During the presidential election campaign of 1972, Democratic challenger George McGovern made the war the central issue and promised an immediate withdrawal if he were elected. He made the election a referendum on how the nation would end the war. In one of the most lopsided votes in American history, Nixon won by 60.7 percent to 37.5 percent. Americans wanted out of Vietnam, but even now they didn't want to cut and run, leaving South Vietnam vulnerable and eroding America's credibility abroad.

Communist negotiators in Paris persisted in their delaying strategy. With negotiations again stalled, on December 18 Nixon ordered a resumption of bomber attacks on North Vietnam. During twelve days of raids, two thousand sorties were flown against targets in Haiphong and Hanoi. Industrial sites and power plants were destroyed, supply depots hit, and airfields and the railroad system ravaged. A great effort was made to minimize civilian casualties which, through the use of new laser-guided bombs, were remarkably kept to between 1,300 and 4,000.[187] Antiwar activists, of course, vehemently denounced the bombings. Columnist Anthony Lewis called the attacks "the most terrible destruction in the history of man." Other journalists compared the bombing to Hiroshima. The *Washington Post* alleged carpet bombing "across downtown Hanoi." George McGovern called the bombing campaign "the most murderous aerial bombardment in the history of the world." But the North Vietnamese government reported 1,318 killed in Hanoi and 305 in Haiphong—a total of 1,623. American antiwar activists covertly urged their allies in the North Vietnamese government to exaggerate the death toll—to claim 10,000 or more killed in the bombings.[188]

Telford Taylor, an opponent of the war who was in Hanoi during the December bombings, later wrote that "I rapidly became convinced that we were making no effort to destroy Hanoi. The city remained largely intact and it seemed quite apparent that if there were an effort to destroy Hanoi it could have been done very readily in two or three nights."[189] The death toll, wrote *The Economist* magazine, "is smaller than the number of civilians killed by the North Vietnamese in their artillery bombardment of An Loc in April or the toll of refugees ambushed when trying to escape from Quang Tri at the beginning of May."[190] A report on the aerial attacks subsequently revealed that the reason for the light civilian casualties despite the massive tonnage of bombs dropped, was that "B-52 pilots were ordered under threat of court-martial not to deviate from their prescribed bombing runs even when SAMs were coming at them, and as a result many Americans died for the purpose of avoiding unnecessary loss of life."[191]

The ferocious bombing campaign in the North achieved the desired goal: Hanoi finally agreed to a peace accord. The "Agreement on Ending the War and Restoring the Peace in Vietnam," called the Paris Peace Accords, was signed on January 27, 1973.

Desperate to extricate the United States from Vietnam, President Nixon had agreed to a settlement that permitted North Vietnamese troops (estimates ranged from 150,000 to 300,000) to remain where they had positions in South Vietnam. In blatant violation of the treaty, North Vietnam continued to infiltrate troops into the South—45,000 the first year.

By the end of March 1973 the last remaining units of U.S. combat troops had left Vietnam. Also, 566 American military POWs, and 25 civilian prisoners, were returned alive. Some had spent over eight years in North Vietnamese prisons, and included the longest-held American POWs in U.S. history. The bodies of 23 American prisoners who had died in captivity were also returned. Of the more than 1,200 men who were unaccounted for, and subsequently listed as missing, more than 50 had earlier been identified by North Vietnamese news media as having been captured alive. Eyewitness identifications of other POWs put the number of those killed in captivity—either through medical neglect, systematic malnutrition or torture—in the hundreds.[192] The longest war in American history was over. In June, Congress passed the Case-Church Amendment, cutting off all funding for U.S. forces anywhere in Indochina.

———◆———

Hanoi launched its invasion of the South in December 1974. Nixon was now gone. President Ford was in no position to rally U.S. support for Saigon, even had he wished to do so. Cut off from American support, forced to fight (as a North Vietnamese general put it) "a poor man's war"[193] against an adversary well supplied by the Kremlin with artillery, tanks, and ammunition, President Thieu fled the country, and the South Vietnamese defense. By late March the Communists were at the outskirts of Saigon.

It was a period of intense activity for the American embassy there. During those last days of the crumbling regime my father, who was District Director of the U.S. Immigration and Naturalization Service in Asia, flew to Saigon from our home in Hong Kong to help process the wave of applicants seeking emigration to the United States. He had had many experiences in Vietnam over the years, but as it turned out, it was my mother who was the last one in the family—and one of the last Americans—to be there before the fall of Saigon. As a nurse in the late 1960s, she had helped treat thousands of wounded GIs at the evacuation hospital at Camp Oji, in Japan. When I was growing up, she frequently spoke of the courage and grace of those young Americans, many of whom had lost limbs or suffered other permanent disability. Now, in early April 1975, South Vietnam was collapsing. On March 30, Da Nang, the country's second largest city, had fallen to North Vietnamese forces. Saigon would follow shortly. Harry Holt, head of Holt International, a nonprofit organization running orphanages in Asia (who had worked with my father many times in the past to help bring abandoned children from Korea, Vietnam, and elsewhere in Asia—many of them Amerasian children with GI fathers—to the United States), called to ask if my father could help arrange for an emergency evacuation of orphans from South Vietnam.

Holt had procured use of a 747 (donated by Pan-Am) to get the infants out. The flight left the Hong Kong airport on April 5, carrying a doctor from the local Seventh Day Adventist hospital, the plane's contingent of stewardesses, and eight American nurses living in Hong Kong who had volunteered to make the trip—employees at the Adventist hospital, or wives of embassy personnel, including my mother. For safety reasons the original plan had been to take the nurses to Guam, then fly to pick up the babies in Saigon, and then return to Guam. But there was no time. When they arrived at the Hong Kong airport, the women were told that the situation in Saigon was deteriorating rapidly: Communist forces on the outskirts of the city were preparing to move in—the plane would have to fly directly into Saigon. There was no air traffic control at the airport. The nurses were informed that the day before, a plane on a similar mission had crashed, killing most of those on board. They were given a chance to back out. None did.

The plane flew into Saigon and remained on the runway as Holt staff carried the orphans aboard. There were 409 in all, most of them under two years old. Their bassinets filled every seat, and the aisles. Except for the takeoff and landing, the women stood during the entire thirty-hour trip, caring for hundreds of infants, many of whom were ill, some with chickenpox. During the seventy-two-hour round trip to the United States and back, my mother lost seven pounds and her luggage, her toes turned purple, and her toenails fell off. She said it was one of the greatest experiences of her life.

A separate, massive U.S. government effort to evacuate homeless children, "Operation Babylift," managed to get some 14,000 orphans out of the country before it fell to the Communists. In America, radical activists complained that the evacuation of the orphans from Vietnam represented "cultural imperialism." Why should we be so arrogant as to assume that the children would be better off growing up in America rather than in Vietnam? A problem with activists is that, so often, they don't know what they are talking about. The single most propitious event in the lives of every one of those orphans was that they were rescued from Communist Vietnam, to be raised in America. Many of them were mixed-race and would have been social outcasts in Vietnam. If you think that there are racial problems in the United States, try growing up as a half-black child in Ho Chi Minh City. Many of the infants were brought to Saigon orphanages (or, in some cases, right to the airport) and left by their mothers, in the hope that they would be taken to America. Thousands of American families adopted and lovingly raised these Vietnamese orphans.

———————

Dominoes fell. In Laos, as U.S. support for the anti-Communist guerrillas (notably the members of the doughty Hmong mountain tribe) was cut off, the

Communist Pathet Lao forced its way into a coalition with the royal government in 1973, and then seized total control in August 1975. As many as a hundred thousand Hmong were slaughtered, and tens of thousands more were forced into "reeducation camps."[194]

In Cambodia, after the cutoff of U.S. support, government troops (some of whom fought literally until they ran out of ammunition)[195] were forced to surrender to Khmer Rouge forces. Pol Pot and the Communists seized power in Cambodia on April 17, 1975. Prince Sihanouk was brought from his retirement in China and held in virtual captivity in the royal palace, an anomalous monarchy in a Communist state, clinging to the last vestiges of power in exchange for bringing international credibility to the bloody regime. Sihanouk made a trip to the United Nations, where he was cheered by delegates of other Third World dictatorships and France when he said that powerful American imperialism had been thwarted by the Communist Khmer Rouge in tiny Cambodia. The following March, Sihanouk was ordered by Pol Pot to resign, which he did.

One of the most baffling and scurrilous arguments made by opponents of American policy in Indochina was that Pol Pot and his Khmer Rouge were moderate agrarian reformers, until resistance from U.S.-and U.S.-backed Cambodian forces compelled them to become vicious. Similar arguments had been used by Western socialists to justify the brutality of every Communist regime of the century. It was the ultimate act of ideological zeal, to blame Communism's horrors on the anti-Communists.

A leading American Marxist, Noam Chomsky, predicted in 1972 that a Khmer Rouge victory could lead to "a new era of economic development and social justice" in Cambodia. Chomsky later claimed that tales of Khmer Rouge atrocities were fabrications spun to retrospectively justify American intervention in the region. Finally, when the scope of the carnage became undeniable, he blamed it on *an American* plan to provoke the Khmer Rouge to become more violent and bloodthirsty, so that Cambodia's socialism would not appeal to other nations in the region.[196]

Not all proponents of the Communists chose to remain oblivious to the cataclysm that followed their taking power. Antiwar journalist Jean Lacouture later wrote of "my shame for having contributed to the installation of one of the most oppressive regimes history has ever known."[197] The Khmer Rouge were not pushed to embrace totalitarianism by American actions, as their apologists insisted. Their leaders had been dedicated Marxists, committed to violent revolution, since their college days in Paris. Indeed, the tempo of genocide escalated over the four years of Khmer Rouge rule and included a succession of bloody purges—as was typical of Communist regimes—within the party.

An egalitarian uniform—the native plain black pajamas—was decreed for the entire society. All educational institutions, public and private, were destroyed. Money was eliminated overnight. The state (meaning: the party; meaning: Pol Pot) controlled the allocation of all resources, and the dissemination of all ideas. The cities became ghost towns. In one of the most remarkable spectacles in history, Phnom Penh, a megalopolis of over 2 million, was emptied within a matter of days, as were the other urban centers. City dwellers were sent to farms to work at tasks for which they had no training. During the Khmer Rouge's first six months in power, a majority of the Cambodian population were uprooted from their homes, most of them herded onto collectives. Peasant laborers were assembled into work units, housed in communal huts or barracks. They dined in mass dining halls, often separated from their spouses and children. Within two years an entire nation was collectivized. Most commerce with foreign nations was cut off, worsening the effects of the famine that inevitably followed the Communist takeover.

In Pol Pot's new utopia there would be no need for schools, markets, or any civil institutions. Buddhist monks, regarded as potential competitors for the people's loyalty, were systematically slaughtered, their numbers falling from 60,000 to 1,000 in a few years.[198] Anyone caught in possession of anything written in English or French ("imperialistic languages") was subject to execution on the spot. Anyone wearing glasses was subject to execution. Execution centers were established around the country, and mass graves containing thousands of corpses were later discovered. Civilization ground to a halt. The once-vibrant city of Phnom Penh never topped 50,000 inhabitants during the era of Democratic Kampuchea—mostly government bureaucrats, soldiers, and workers held captive in barbed-wire-enclosed factories that more resembled prisons. Estimates of the Khmer Rouge's slaughter vary, but between 1975 and 1978 the country's population fell from 8 million to 6 million. Up to half of the 400,000 ethnic Chinese in the country were murdered, and an even greater proportion of ethnic Vietnamese.[199]

Beijing now found itself in a quagmire. By supporting the North Vietnamese against the Americans, it belatedly discovered that it had helped create a unified enemy on its border. Ideology aside, there were long-standing tensions between Vietnam and China, and these were exacerbated when Vietnam signed a mutual defense agreement with Moscow in November 1978. A month later Vietnam invaded Cambodia. Within two weeks the Pol Pot regime had been removed from power, its leaders fleeing back into the jungle whence they came. A new Communist government was set up in Cambodia, under substantial control of Vietnam.

China responded in February 1979 with an invasion of Vietnam, reportedly in retaliation for Hanoi's aggressions in the region, but after facing stiff resistance, a month after the invasion Beijing announced that Vietnam had been taught a lesson, declared victory, and withdrew. Vietnamese troops remained in Cambodia until 1991.

———

Pro-Hanoi activists in the West had said that the South Vietnamese *wanted* to live under Communism, but were prevented from doing so by the American imperialists and their puppet government in Saigon. In fact, by 1973 over 2 million Vietnamese had already fled from the regime in the North. The Viet-nam War had never been the guerrilla struggle of nationalist patriots against foreign imperialists, but a war of aggression by the Communist North, with support from Moscow and Beijing, against the South. After Tet, recruitment of South Vietnamese by the Viet Cong had all but dried up, and Hanoi's assault relied almost entirely on infiltrations by North Vietnamese regular army troops. The myth of the "people's war" became increasingly unsustain-able. In the great "guerrilla war" of the twentieth century, North Vietnam ultimately prevailed by using absolutely conventional warfare, with a con-ventional invasion by a conventional army. In their accounts of Hanoi's final offensive campaign, leading North Vietnamese generals scarcely mentioned the involvement of guerrilla forces at all.[200]

If the South Vietnamese Communists had imagined themselves to be fighting for either freedom or power, they were soon proven wrong. A million North Vietnamese party officials and their extended families moved south to take up the reins of power there. Party leaders fought amongst them-selves for the best houses, cars, and other wealth plundered from the citi-zens of Saigon—renamed Ho Chi Minh City. South Vietnam's gold reserves, sixteen tons, were shipped to the North. When a finance ministry official suggested that the wealth be invested, the idea was rejected as "capitalis-tic." Within two years the gold had vanished.

The Vietnamese people—and the world—would have been infinitely better off if the Communists had been defeated in the Vietnam War. Instead, the country lagged farther and farther behind its Asian neighbors—socially, economically, and politically. Immediately after their victory, the rulers in Hanoi set out to forcibly remake the political culture of the South. During the war the Communist leadership promised that under socialism the pris-ons would be made into schools: after the takeover, the schools became instruments of indoctrination, and prisons proliferated. All books except the handful expressly permitted by party authorities were banned. Compul-sory indoctrination sessions were held in each neighborhood, and in all workplaces. Neighborhood oversight committees were established, with neighbors encouraged to report on neighbors. Patriotic Youth teams, pat-terned after Mao's Red Guards, accosted citizens on the street whose hair-style or clothes reeked of capitalism. In the schools, children were instructed to report the potential counterrevolutionary activities of their parents; they were taught that "A good citizen is someone who turns you in."[201] Religious activity was repressed.

Hundreds of thousands of South Vietnamese were arrested by the new government, many of them tortured, as the Communist Party consolidated its power. In all, around half a million suspected opponents of the "social revolution," out of a population of 27 million, were rounded up and impris-oned in "reeducation" and forced labor camps.

Many former Viet Cong renounced Communism and fled the country, though most of Hanoi's defenders in the West, entrenched in their comfortable and insulated ideological strongholds, were never able to make such an admission. When antiwar activist Joan Baez wrote an open letter to the *New York Times* in May 1979, calling on the Vietnamese government to "end the imprisonment and torture" of political prisoners and "allow an international team of neutral observers to inspect your prisons and reeducation centers," she was publicly castigated by Jane Fonda and attacked in a letter to the *Times* signed by former antiwar activists, who praised the "remarkable spirit of moderation, restraint and clemency with which the reeducation program was conducted," and expressed envy toward the Vietnamese, who "receive, without cost, education, medicine and health care, human rights we in the United States have yet to achieve."[202]

Sociologist Peter Berger, a leader of the antiwar movement, was among the few activists to acknowledge that he had been wrong in supporting the Hanoi regime in the war. He wrote in 1980 that the transformation of Vietnamese society "now offers a crystal-clear difference between authoritarianism and totalitarianism, both in terms of political science and political morality"; and he marveled at "the persistent incapacity of even American professors to grasp a difference understood by every taxi driver in Prague." And French journalist Jean Lacouture, who had stayed after the war to cover the new Vietnam, expressed shame that he had advocated for the Communists during the war, becoming a "vehicle and intermediary for a lying and criminal propaganda, an ingenuous spokesman for tyranny in the name of liberty." As a former apologist for the Hanoi government, he had been allowed to visit one of the regime's reeducation camps. He called it "a prefabricated hell."[203]

Many antiwar militants, though—some of whose entire identities were rooted in opposition to the Vietnam War, and some of whom had made academic or journalistic careers of condemning American foreign policy—resolutely denied the human rights catastrophe under way in their New Vietnam. As former antiwar activist William Kunstler put it, "I don't believe in criticizing socialist governments publicly even if there are human rights violations."[204] Berger compared such individuals to those "who deny the facts of the holocaust," aptly describing them as "outside the boundaries of rational discourse."[205]

In Vietnam, at least, by the late 1970s the verdict on the Marxist experiment was unequivocal. "The fact is that today Communism has been rejected by the people and that even many Party members are questioning the faith," wrote former VC leader Truong Nhu Tang. "Members of the former resistance, and their sympathizers and those who supported the Viet Cong are disgusted and filled with bitterness. These innocent people swear openly that had they another chance their choice would be very different."[206]

During the Communist "liberation" of South Vietnam all private industry was abolished. Economic enterprises were coopted by the state. Millions of South Vietnamese citizens were herded into New Economic Zones (read: the jungle), where they were put to forced labor clearing land, building roads, digging ditches. At party-mandated rallies, workers were forced to make vows to increase production, take fewer breaks, turn in lazy coworkers. Like everywhere else, Marxism in Indochina was a disaster. By the mid-1980s the Hanoi regime, confronting a stagnant economy, the collapse of global Communism, and waves of fleeing refugees, began (much like Beijing) to enact social and economic reforms, working to attract foreign (i.e., capitalist) investment, and seeking closer relations with the United States.

———◆———

The more clearly that we are able to see the events of the Vietnam War and its aftermath with the passage of time, free from the political haze of the era, the more honorable the American effort seems, even notwithstanding the outcome. The war was, from the outset, a struggle between Moscow, Beijing, and Hanoi against the pro-Western government of Saigon and its American supporters. It cannot be understood in isolation. It can only be comprehended as part of the larger Cold War conflict between totalitarianism and democracy. On the twentieth anniversary of the fall of Saigon, a *Washington Post* editorial noted that "There was such a thing as communism on the march. It was not a misunderstanding. It was a threat to what deserved to be called the free world," and "for a reason—because it faced an armed takeover by an outside Communist regime—South Vietnam inevitably became a place where the confrontation was played out."[207]

A defeat retrospectively taints all that preceded it. It is seldom noted nowadays that U.S. forces in Vietnam were never defeated in a major engagement with the enemy. More than 2.5 million Americans served honorably in the fields and jungles of Vietnam. Fifty-eight thousand died there, giving their lives to oppose the spread of Communism at a critical juncture in history. The fight to stave off a totalitarian victory in Indochina was a just one: everywhere else that Communists had seized power they violently suppressed all opposition, garroted human rights, established brutal and dictatorial regimes. It was reasonable to expect that they would do the same if they took power in Indochina. In fact, they did. More people were killed in the year following the Communist takeover in Indochina than during the entire duration of the Vietnam war.

Was there never any possibility of success in defeating North Vietnam's invasion of the South? Might the outcome have differed, if policies had been tweaked this way or that? Like other totalitarian regimes, the leaders in Hanoi were willing to absorb enormous hardship—for their people—in pursuit of their aims. Political scientist John Mueller has written that "the military costs accepted by the Communists in Vietnam were virtually unprecedented in history."[208]

Was Korea an "unjust war"? Vietnam differed little from it, in fundamentals: a remote Asian nation divided between North and South, the Communist government in the North supported by Moscow and Beijing, dedicated to uniting the entire region, by force, under totalitarian rule; the government in the South was pro-Western but corrupt, protodemocratic but authoritarian. Where Korea and Vietnam differed was in their outcomes. Initial public support for Vietnam was at least as strong, and was as sustained, as it had been in Korea, which, after all, had been over in three years. Korea was the "forgotten war" long before Vietnam ever came along. Vietnam dragged on for over a decade. It was unreasonable to imagine that public support could be sustained for that long.

What did the American soldiers themselves believe about the war? Again, retrospective portrayals have often distorted the reality. In a poll taken a decade after the war, two-thirds of Vietnam veterans said that they would willingly serve again, even knowing the outcome.[209] Among the two-thirds of vets who were volunteers, 91 percent said that they were proud that they had served.[210]

A generation after the war, opinion polls showed that most Vietnamese felt positively toward the United States. Indeed, there was more positive feeling toward Americans among the Vietnamese, whom the U.S. had tried to defend from Communism but failed, than there was among the French, whom America had liberated from fascism. Why the goodwill? The Vietnamese knew that the Americans had never tried to colonize their country. Americans did not go to Indochina as conquerors. They struggled to help install a functioning democracy there but never attempted to subjugate the people, as previous waves of foreigners had done before. Americans sought no material gain from their involvement in Vietnam (the costs were, massively, in the opposite direction), only to limit an expanding sphere of totalitarian control there.

Idealistic Americans had believed that every good cause can be won. Was the effort made less valorous by the outcome? Would America—should it—have avoided the struggle, if it had known the ending? In every great venture there is the possibility of defeat. If the chance of loss precluded an undertaking, the United States would not have taken up arms against Hitler. American involvement in Vietnam was part of a broader policy of containment of Communism. It meant that where totalitarianism attempted to expand, it must not do so without resistance. The policy worked.

In the wake of Vietnam, America's leadership in the West, and its commitment to containing Communism, seemed to be faltering. The Kremlin had gained an ideological triumph, expanded control over Indochina, and won possession of the strategically vital (U.S.-built) port at Cam Ranh Bay, allowing it to powerfully project its naval forces in the Pacific. To Marxist ideologues it seemed that the prophecies of the collapse of capitalism might soon be fulfilled. "Inspired by its gains and by the decline of U.S. prestige resulting from Vietnam and the domestic upheaval," writes the Russian historian Ilya Gaiduk, "the Soviet leadership adopted a more aggressive and rigid foreign policy, particularly in the Third World."[211]

The cunning that made Richard Nixon odious in domestic politics made him artful at international affairs. Nixon exploited the growing rift between the Soviet Union and China, and worked to widen it, in order to achieve a detente, a "relaxation of tensions." It was a pragmatic recognition of the reality of the Kremlin's enormous military power, and a means for attempting to contain that power, at a time when the American public's spirit had grown fatigued by the seemingly endless struggle. Nixon and Kissinger believed that the divisions between the Communist giants could be exploited to help constrain each of them, and through a succession of diplomatic maneuvers they worked to exacerbate the divisions, which by the late 1960s had erupted into open gun battles along the border between the two nations.

With arms talks under way with the Soviet Union, Nixon made both public and back-channel overtures toward Beijing. In July 1971, Kissinger made a secret trip to Beijing, paving the way for the president's historic visit there the following February. Nixon calculated that a U.S. rapprochement with China would prompt the Kremlin toward greater reconciliation with Washington. In this belief he was vindicated. At a moment when the U.S. seemed paralyzed by Vietnam, and when some West European leaders were expressing doubts about American resolve and capabilities, and sought accommodation with Moscow, the breakthrough with China threw the entire international system into a new balance.

There were other, concrete benefits of detente, such as permission during 1972–73 for about 65,000 persecuted Jews to emigrate from Russia. It was a small portion of the total number seeking to leave, and even this process was marked by graft and political corruption, but it represented some progress: of the 80,000 Jews who had petitioned for exit permits during the preceding three years, only 18,000 had been allowed to leave.[212]

Detente, though, was a strategy, never an end in itself. "Detente does not mean the end of danger," as a Nixon administration foreign policy report stated. "Detente is not the same as lasting peace."[213] The Communists, with their dogma of historical inevitability, certainly did not regard detente as an end-state. After signing a succession of detente agreements in the first half of the 1970s, Brezhnev assured an international conference of Communist leaders in 1976 that "revolution, the class struggle, and liberation movements cannot be abolished by agreements. No power on earth is capable of reversing the inexorable process of the renovation of the life of society."[214] Anatoly Dobrynin, Soviet ambassador to Washington, wrote in his memoirs that Brezhnev viewed detente as a tactic in the "Marxist-Leninist approach to foreign affairs, which cast even peaceful relations into a mold of confrontation."[215] Soviet adventurism in Africa, the Middle East, Latin America, and elsewhere soon strained the new relationship.

———◆———

One of the more repellent episodes in the U.S. conduct of the Cold War was meanwhile unfolding in South America. In an election on September 4, 1970, Chilean Marxist Salvador Allende's coalition of socialists and Communists won 36.3 percent of the vote, ahead of former president Jorge Alessandri, who received 34.9 percent. The election was, by constitutional provision, thrown into a joint session of the Congress. During the interim, several large U.S. firms with business interests in the country—notably the International Telephone and Telegraph Corporation (ITT), and copper-producing companies—fearing nationalization of their assets in Chile, bribed members of the Chilean Congress to support Allende's opponents. To no avail. The CIA attempted to persuade leading opposition candidates to oppose Allende in a run-off, but this effort also failed. Agents also encouraged Chilean military leaders who were rallying around retired general Roberto Viaux, assuring them of U.S. government support during and following a coup.

By mid-October the CIA had withdrawn its support for what it deemed to be a poorly conceived plan, which was to include the kidnapping of the Chilean army chief of staff, Gen. Rene Schneider. Langley (CIA headquarters, in Virginia) ordered its agents in Santiago to try to prevent the "ill-considered action at this time," since "a failed coup would vitiate any further more serious action."[216] But on October 22 the coup went ahead, resulting in Schneider's death in a shootout, before it was aborted. Two days later the Chilean Congress elected Allende by a majority vote. He was inaugurated on November 3. Allende had become the first—and the last—Marxist ever to win a presidential election in Latin America.

The new regime, headed by Marxist intellectuals dismissive of practical politics, created for itself a rapidly expanding base of opponents. Foreign property was confiscated. Important Chilean corporations were "nationalized." Large landholdings were expropriated, not to be turned over to the peasantry, but to form the foundation of a new collectivized agriculture system. By mid-1972 the Communist newspaper *El Siglo* could boast that the government "has expropriated in only eighteen months 3,500 properties."[217] Fidel Castro made a monthlong visit to Chile in November–December 1971, congratulating Allende on his "road to socialism." Allende reciprocated with visits to Moscow and Havana the following year. By mid-1973, Chile's entire mining industry, the banking system, and much of its manufacturing sector had been nationalized. Agricultural output fell around 7 percent in 1972, and twice that in 1973.[218]

To win the support of workers, the government instituted large wage increases, even as productivity continued to fall. Government spending, sustained by simply printing more money, increased tenfold from 1970 to 1973.[219] Inflation soared to over 500 percent. Predictably, wealthy Chileans withdrew their money from the nation's banks. Physicians and other professionals went on strike. There were mass demonstrations by middle-class Chileans worried that the government was adopting authoritarian tactics (including placing growing restrictions on the press, and the arming of pro-government militias independent of the army) in order to carry out its collectivist agenda. In January 1972 the Chamber of Deputies approved the impeachment of Allende's minister of the interior for "continued, reiterated and serious infractions of the constitutional guarantees" involving freedom of the press, arbitrary arrests, and unwillingness to restrain the armed militias.[220] When the Chilean Supreme Court declared certain state seizures of private property and industries to be illegal, the regime ignored its rulings.

As civil war loomed, on August 20 the government's minister of defense resigned, and Allende replaced him with Gen. Augusto Pinochet. On September 11 the military launched its coup, bombarding and then storming the presidential palace. Allende's body was later found there, clutching a machine gun, apparently dead by his own hand. Statements by his wife and personal physician, and forensic examinations in later years, confirmed that it was a suicide.

During the next seventeen years of Pinochet's military rule, several thousand Chileans (estimates range from 3,000 to 10,000) were killed as the government violently suppressed the revolutionary movement. In October 1988, 55 percent of Chileans voted in a national plebiscite against Pinochet remaining in office after the end of his term in 1990, and the following month he promised to "depart quietly," which he did.[221]

American meddling in the internal affairs of any democratically elected government is to be reprehended and denounced, but we must be clear about what it is that we are denouncing. In fact, the CIA did spend $6-to-$7 million to support Allende's political opponents and funded groups opposed to him. A major Santiago daily newspaper critical of Allende received $2 million.[222] Opposition labor unions were subsidized. But it is giving too much credit or blame to ascribe Allende's downfall to the CIA. It was his policies, not the activities of a handful of American intelligence operatives, that were primarily responsible for actuating his nationwide opposition. While Chileans in contact with the CIA were among those who helped organize a strike of disaffected truckers' for example, it is a wild leap to conclude that the truckers' strike, which involved the participation of over half a million Chileans, was a "CIA operation."

The Chilean coup was a *Chilean* coup. It was neither initiated nor sponsored by the Central Intelligence Agency. Jonathan Goldberg, who has interviewed former American and Chilean officials and pored over declassified documents, concluded that U.S. interference in Chilean affairs is "worthy of retroactive condemnation," but that "it would be a mistake to exaggerate the U.S. role in the 1973 coup. In the final analysis, the coup was a Chilean affair, conceived and executed by Chileans."[223] After the coup, the Kremlin launched a massive international propaganda campaign to disseminate the idea that the CIA had been responsible for the death of Allende, whose purported martyrdom came to be employed by Communists worldwide as a symbol of American imperialism. The idea that the United States "overthrew Allende" became a matter of orthodoxy among the international left. A generation later, the facts of the history, even among the general public, are blurred by that ideological fog. In April 2003, when U.S. secretary of state Colin Powell was asked by a college student about the Chilean coup, he said that "it is not a part of American history that we are proud of."

That is so, but we must be clear about what it is that we are not proud of. The State Department quickly issued a clarifying statement, reiterating that the U.S. government "did not instigate the coup that ended Allende's government in 1973." William Rogers (who was undersecretary of state from 1975–76), said that he was concerned that Powell's remark reinforced "the legend" that the coup in Chile was the result of an American operation.

While condemning U.S. government actions in Chile as "deplorable and counterproductive," Robert Alexander has written in his comprehensive study entitled *Tragedy in Chile* that the CIA's activities "were of little or no importance in determining the ultimate fate of the Allende regime. They failed to prevent the election of Allende as president, they at most made only marginal contributions to the campaign against [Allende's] government, and they had nothing to do with the final decision of the military leaders to oust Allende."[224] It was a human tragedy, but it was a Chilean one.

The most pervasive and enduring propaganda tactic used by Communist regimes and their advocates in the West, from the very beginning of the Cold War to the bitter end, was to contend that the failure of socialist nations' economic policies, their social instability, and the Communist governments' need for repression resulted from Western (i.e., American) interference. The shorthand symbol for this interference came to be the CIA. Agents for the Central Intelligence Agency were indeed active in virtually all nations of security importance to the United States and the West, and often worked with opponents of regimes considered to be adversarial. But there had been an endless succession of coups and assassinations and instability in these nations long before there ever was a CIA. Part of the CIA's exaggerated reputation for influence in the domestic affairs of foreign nations came from the foreign leaders themselves, who found it convenient to label any political opponent as a CIA operative, any critical media as CIA-sponsored, any opposition group as CIA-backed, and any internal instability as a CIA plot.

There is little doubt that for a period of time the use of assassination was considered a legitimate instrument of policy, by at least some in the highest reaches of the intelligence community, though in 1975 the Senate's investigation into CIA activities, while deeply critical, concluded that the Agency had not directly assassinated any foreign leader. Its agents had, however, been linked to foreign "coup plots which resulted in the deaths of [Domini-can Republic's Rafael] Trujillo, [Vietnam's Ngo Dinh] Diem, and [Chile's Rene] Schneider." The CIA *had* actively backed attempts on Castro's life. The fact that he had not been assassinated, as William Colby (director of Central Intelligence from 1973 to 1976) later said, "wasn't for lack of trying."[225]

Due to its inexperience at it, the Agency simply had no institutional expertise with assassination, especially compared with the intelligence organizations of many other foreign governments. The only other instance where there is credible evidence of a direct CIA effort to assassinate a for-eign ruler, the case of the brutal African leader Patrice Lumumba, was also unsuccessful.[226] Lumumba, having fled the Congo after his failed coup attempt there, was killed on the orders of the ruler of breakaway Katanga Province, Moise Tshombe. In February 1976, President Ford issued an exec-utive order explicitly forbidding any government employee to "engage in, or conspire to engage in, political assassination."

A few relatively large-scale CIA covert operations attracted and con-tinue to attract the public's attention, and shaped conceptions of the Agency. But its role in human intelligence-gathering, conducted largely by individual agents at the retail level, while less sensational, was a far more fundamental task of the Agency, consuming the greater portion of its resources, personnel, and mission. As for covert operations, the vast major-ity were nonviolent political actions, supportive of democratic polity. Radio broadcasts that brought news of the outside world to isolated peoples helped undermine totalitarian control and create public pressure for change. The Kremlin's penetration of international youth, labor, and "peace" move-ments was opposed, as was its efforts to infiltrate foreign governments.[227] CIA agents and their local associates smuggled the works of dissidents (such as Solzhenitsyn's *Gulag Archipelago)* behind the Iron Curtain, and actively supported dissident groups there. It was the CIA that acquired and dissem-inated—with ramifying consequences that would only become apparent years later—copies of Khrushchev's 1956 speech condemning Stalin.

It was the CIA's remarkable U-2 spy plane reconnaissance program, capable of taking photographs from 80,000 feet, that assured President Eisenhower against the purported existence of a "missile gap" advantage for Moscow, and that alerted Kennedy of nuclear missiles in Cuba, and later justified his quarantine of Cuba to the United Nations. Planes were soon superseded by satellites, capable of rendering remarkable photographic clarity from a hundred miles up, but technology would never replace human intelligence. A photograph might show capabilities, but not intentions.

Both by the nature of its own activities and the personalities it requires to conduct them, any intelligence agency is mightily inclined toward excesses. It is a perpetual high-wire act: strict oversight and constraint are essential, yet oversight may produce dangerous leaks, and stifling limita-tions may hinder the agency's ability to protect the nation's security. The tension between the secrecy that people fear, and the security they demand, would never—could never—be fully resolved.

Years later, after the Cold War had ended, when the United States was subjected to a new type of threat (attacks launched not by governments, but by terrorist groups), there was a renewed public demand for a revitalization of covert capabilities, and even sanctioning of assassination. Now, members of Congress who had been crucial to gutting the Agency's intelligence-gathering capabilities condemned its unpreparedness. The fluctuation of public opinion, in tandem with perceptions of threat, reflected an observation once made by Gen. Vernon Walters, deputy director of the CIA from 1972 to 1976, one of the most turbulent periods in American history: "Americans have always had an ambivalent attitude toward intelligence. When they feel threatened they want a lot of it, and when they don't, they tend to regard the whole thing as somewhat immoral."[228]

For Communist rulers, the unfolding Watergate scandal was incomprehensible. They were bewildered by the drama of the most powerful man in the world being removed from office for what one Kremlin leader called "stealing some silly documents."[229] Richard Nixon resigned the presidency on August 8, 1974. He was succeeded by Gerald Ford, a former congressman from Michigan, a man of immense personal integrity who inherited a vast array of challenges abroad, and a public at home that had grown deeply cynical, distrustful of all politicians. President Ford, who supported Nixon's policy of detente, asked Kissinger to stay on as secretary of state.

In the SALT I (Strategic Arms Limitation Talks) agreement, the U.S. and USSR had pledged to continue negotiations toward further arms limitations. At a meeting between Ford and Brezhnev held at Vladivostok in November 1974, the two sides reached a framework for a second round of SALT talks. Those discussions proceeded, sporadically, for the next five years, buffeted by external events.

The high-water mark of detente, and the beginning of its end, came on August 1, 1975, when leaders of thirty-three European nations, plus the United States and Canada, met in Helsinki, Finland, to sign the Final Act of the Conference on Security and Cooperation in Europe—the so-called "Helsinki Accords," which pledged the signatory nations to respect the "territorial integrity" of the European states and permit the freer movement of people and information.

Some U.S. conservatives criticized the agreement for "legitimizing" the Soviet empire and accused President Ford of "selling out" the peoples of Eastern Europe—of participating in a second Yalta Conference.[230] But, while the treaty did indicate American acknowledgment of Soviet dominion, Ford responded that the United States was only conceding what had been a fact on the ground for a generation. The pragmatic recognition of the Beijing government had been no more of a sellout. He also pointed to the clauses on human rights as providing specific standards of conduct by which the Kremlin could be held accountable. By signing it, leaders in Moscow would tacitly acknowledge human rights as a legitimate international issue, and not only one of internal concern. In Moscow, Brezhnev assured concerned Politburo members that the Kremlin could ignore the provisions on human rights. "We are the masters in our own house, and we shall decide what we implement and what we ignore," he assured them."[231] Ford and Brezhnev had each perceived the agreement that they had wanted to perceive.

In retrospect it was Ford who was largely vindicated. Soviet control over Eastern Europe was not set into concrete by Helsinki, and Kremlin leaders, by agreeing to the human rights provisions, were to find themselves increasingly held accountable to those values. A Russian diplomat later said that the Helsinki Accords "gradually became a manifesto of the dissident and liberal movement, a development totally beyond the imagination of the Soviet leadership."[232]

The timing was critical. Despite Kremlin efforts to insulate the population, there was a growing awareness among Communist populations of the greater freedom and prosperity of the West, and the corruption and stagnation of the Soviet system. The populace was disillusioned and unwilling to work hard for the benefit of the party or state. Marxism might still hold some appeal among violent rebel groups in Third World countries and Western intellectuals, but among the masses who were actually living it, the sheen had long since worn off. In 1975, KGB chief Yuri Andropov sent the first of a series of secret reports to Brezhnev predicting difficult times ahead, and calling for reforms that would enable the state to elicit more labor from the people.[233]

Jimmy Carter, the former governor of Georgia who seemingly came from out of nowhere in 1976 to win the Democratic nomination and then the presidency, was the un-Nixon. He disdained the concessions to political pragmatism made by previous administrations: the compromises with national ideals that had been made in the name of national security—shady covert operations, support for corrupt regimes. "Our commitment to human rights must be absolute," he said in his inaugural address. President Carter regarded the regime in South Korea, for example, as corrupt and repressive, and within weeks after taking office he promised to withdraw the forty thousand U.S. troops stationed there. America would no longer support regimes that violated human rights, even if they were anti-Communist.

Leaders of the Communist world were feeling triumphant. Communism seemed to be on the offensive globally. The Kremlin was spending a huge amount on its military, and while it had not acquired clear strategic superiority, momentum was on its side: in the previous fifteen years, while the number of U.S. strategic missile launchers had been stable, the Soviets had increased theirs sevenfold; while U.S. ICBM warheads had doubled in number during that time—mainly through "MIR" Ving—the Soviets' arsenal had increased twentyfold.[234] CIA reports advised the president that the growing relative strategic power of the USSR would give the Kremlin "wider latitude" in the pursuit of its foreign policy goals, and warned that "these capabilities will discourage the U.S. and others from using force or the threat of force to influence Soviet actions."

President Carter believed that the United States must convince the Kremlin that America meant it no harm. Only then would Soviet leaders would feel secure enough to restrain their own global belligerency. He proposed a cut of over $6 billion in his first defense budget.[235] Americans, the president thought, had prudently overcome their "inordinate fear of Communism." Carter opposed the use of military force, spending increases for the Pentagon, clandestine operations, and other actions that he said might seem "provocative" to the leaders in the Kremlin. Secretary of State Vance told *Time* magazine that Carter and Brezhnev shared "similar dreams and aspirations" for mankind."[236]

Washington's stated policy of economically penalizing governments that violated human rights, while conducted with the best intentions, was applied unevenly: the most egregious transgressors were Communist regimes, and most of these were already not receiving U.S. assistance and were immune to its rhetoric.[237] As to the relationship with China (whose record on human rights was among the worst in the world, and where pro-democracy activists were pleading with Washington to highlight the widespread abuses in that country), it was regarded as too important to national security to be contingent upon human rights considerations, so they had little impact on the agenda with Beijing. In December 1978 the United States and China issued a joint communiqué announcing the normalization of full diplomatic relations. That left mainly regimes that were 1) U.S. allies, and 2) anti-Communist but not democratic (such as the Shah of Iran and Anastasio Somoza of Nicaragua) to be the targets of Carter's humanitarian aspirations. Administration critics complained that the president was harder on America's allies than on its avowed enemies. In a 1979 article entitled "Dictatorships and Double Standards," political scientist Jeane Kirkpatrick wrote that the Carter administration "actively collaborated in the replacement of moderate autocrats friendly to American interests with less friendly autocrats of extremist persuasion."[238]

In Nicaragua the rebellion against the corrupt and repressive regime of Anastasio Somoza had been led by the Sandinista National Liberation Front (FSLN) guerrilla movement, named after national hero Gen. Augusto Sandino. U.S. intelligence estimates put the total Sandinista force in 1976, when Carter took office, at fewer than one hundred. Policies in Washington and a badly timed Somoza heart attack galvanized the dictator's opponents, which included both moderate businessmen advocating constitutional government and the Sandinistas, with factions claiming ideological allegiance, variously, to Stalinism, Maoism, and Castro. As the civil war escalated, Castro recognized an opportunity and began funneling large shipments of weapons and other material to the Communist rebels. The *Washington Post* warned that Somoza might be ousted "not by centrist democrats but by elements politically and ideologically beholden to the guerrillas of the Sandinista National Liberation Front. A 'Second Cuba' in Central America? It is not out of the question."[239] In February 1979, Carter—who had already restricted military and economic assistance—cut off all support for the regime and called on Somoza to step down. Even at this time the Sandinistas still had fewer than 2,000 fighters, compared to the nearly 10,000 in the country's National Guard. Then, Carter imposed economic sanctions on Nicaragua. As the Somoza regime grew increasingly isolated, the power of the Sandinistas grew, supported by thousands of tons of Cuban and Soviet arms. On July 17, Somoza fled the country. The Sandinistas established a ruling junta, headed by Daniel Ortega. Shortly after the takeover, at a meeting in Managua of representatives of the Soviet, Czech, Bulgarian, and Cuban espionage services, Colonel Kolomyakov, head of the KGB section for Latin America, outlined a broad plan to use Nicaragua as the base for exporting Communist revolution throughout the region.[240]

For generations, leftist critics of American foreign policy had condemned U.S. anti-Communist policies for "forcing" would-be moderates like Stalin, Mao, Ho Chi Minh, and Castro into more extremist positions. Carter was determined not to make that mistake. Although since its inception the FSLN had been explicitly Marxist, anticapitalist, and anti-American, while expressing concerns about the Marxist rhetoric and Soviet affiliations of the FSLN, Carter began a program of aid to the new regime. Opposition to the new Communist government, Assistant Secretary of State Viron Vaky explained in congressional hearings in September 1979, would "surely drive the revolution into radicalization."[241] (Vaky resigned three months later.) There followed one of the most remarkable cases in history of a government funding an avowed enemy.

As the Communist Sandinistas consolidated their grip on power, Jimmy Carter increased aid to the regime, providing $118 million in direct aid the first year, with another $262 million from U.S.-backed international development banks, and debt refinancing of half a billion dollars. The United States was Communist Nicaragua's largest provider of foreign aid.[242] In its first year in power, the Sandinista regime received more U.S. funding than the Somoza regime had received in the previous four years.

There are many measures of a good foreign policy—strategic, humanitarian, and otherwise—but surely the first requirement is that, if you cannot defeat your enemies, at least you do not nurture them. The Sandinistas were surprised and delighted at Washington's beneficence and, even as they began to implement collectivist economic policies in the country, toned down the Marxist public rhetoric to keep the aid coming. "Our strategic allies [Moscow and Havana] tell us not to declare ourselves Marxist-Leninist," as one Sandinista leader put it. "[Nicaragua] will be the first experience of building socialism with the dollars of capitalism."[243] With the assistance of funding from Washington, the Sandinista regime launched the consolidation programs characteristic of all Communist revolutions. Its leaders worked to eradicate the "traitorous bourgeoisie," the "class interest" of middle-class private businessmen, and civic organizations that had the potential to oppose the revolution.[244] They quickly reversed their promise to hold open elections. Thousands of Cuban, Soviet, and East European troops were brought into the country, helping to make tiny Nicaragua the largest military power in the region. The regime began an aggressive program of support for Marxist rebels attempting to overthrow the government in neighboring El Salvador. By the early 1980s the Sandinistas were supporting guerrilla movements in Guatemala, El Salvador, and Honduras.

The Sandinistas banned opposition parties and restricted the press. In the late summer of 1979, Catholic bishops in the country issued a pastoral letter asking the government to restore freedom of expression and criticizing the "indoctrination process being carried out now in Nicaragua."[245] Centrist democrats who had also opposed Somoza and were given window-dressing appointments in the new government soon resigned in disillusion. Several fled the country in fear for their lives. A number of vocal opponents of the regime were assassinated. The government established neighborhood surveillance committees, along Cuban lines, and nationalized large landholdings and much of the industry, so that the state soon controlled most of the Nicaraguan economy.[246] Rural Indian tribes, fiercely independent and far removed from central control, were forcibly displaced. Tomas Borge, the minister of the interior, and an avowed Maoist, explained that "the revolution could tolerate no exceptions."[247]

The Sandinistas had turned out to be dedicated Marxists, after all. Presently there were thousands of political prisoners in Nicaragua, held in a penal system modeled on Cuba's and interrogated with techniques taught by East German and Cuban advisers.[248] Opposition to the new regime grew, unaided by Washington. It coalesced in a resistance movement composed of disparate groups of former soldiers, Indians, and armed peasants and farmers, which came to be called the *Contras*.

In the Middle East another crisis was brewing, with even broader ramifications. There was some truth to President Carter's statement in December 1977 that Iran was an "island of stability" in the troubled region, but Shah Reza Pahlavi increasingly maintained his control by force, including the SAVAK secret police, some of whose members had received training by the CIA. In January 1979, amidst a revolution led by fundamentalist Islamic clerics, the Shah fled the country, and the following month exiled religious leader Ayatollah Ruhollah Khomeini returned, further inflaming anti-American passions with his condemnation of the United States as the "Great Satan."

Like every other ruler in the Arab world, the Shah had been repressive and neglected human rights. What had most agitated the Islamic clergy was not repression of civil liberties, but the Shah's policies of modernization, including substantial progress in the emancipation of women, which was contrary to fundamentalist Islamic doctrine. Upon taking power, the theocrats reestablished the severe traditional Sharia Islamic law. On November 4, 1979, the American embassy in Teheran was overrun by Islamic militants incited to action by the Islamic clerics. Seventy Americans in the embassy were captured; 52 would remain captive through the entire duration of the ensuing hostage crisis.

As the presidential election campaign got under way, public approval ratings for the president were among the lowest ever recorded. Inflation was approaching 20 percent, the prime interest rate was over 14 percent, and the economy was torpid. Only 23 percent of Americans believed that the nation was headed in the right direction. Two-thirds thought that America's position in the world was "becoming weaker."[249]

———◆———

At Vienna on June 18, 1979, Carter and Brezhnev signed the SALT II treaty, which limited each side to 2,400 "strategic offensive arms," including ICBM launchers, submarine-based launchers, heavy bombers, and air-to-surface ballistic missiles. The president, though, had failed to cultivate the public support (and, more important, the Senate support) required for approval of the treaty. It was already stalled in the Senate when, on December 24, 1979, the Soviet Union invaded Afghanistan. Carter requested an increase in military spending, launched the creation of a rapid deployment military force, proceeded with planned installation of intermediate-range nuclear weapons in Western Europe, and announced an American boycott of the Olympic games slated for Moscow that summer.

By summer there were eighty thousand Soviet troops in the country, waging a violent war of occupation with MiG fighters, bombers, tanks, heavy artillery, and helicopter gunships against rebels (*mujahideen*) often armed only with World War I–era rifles. The invasion and ensuing war precipitated one of the great refugee crises of the century, sending millions of Afghans fleeing to Pakistan, Iran, and elsewhere.

Although the Brezhnev Doctrine had expressly stated that once a nation had become Communist, it must thereafter remain so, Jimmy Carter was caught entirely off guard by the Soviet action and publicly displayed his bewilderment. "This action of the Soviets made a more dramatic change in my opinion of what the Soviets' ultimate goals were more than anything they've done in the previous time in office," he said shortly after the invasion. Now, his foreign policy moved toward the realpolitik that the idealistic governor of Georgia had earnestly condemned four years earlier. Carter, who had run for president on a platform denouncing the Central Intelligence

Agency and early in his presidency had cut hundreds from its payroll, now called on the Agency to come up with more detailed intelligence on the interventions of the Kremlin and its satellites around the world, and initiated covert operations to counter Soviet activities in Afghanistan, the Arabian peninsula, and Central America. In the Horn of Africa, Central America, and Afghanistan, Carter's 1979 foreign policy more closely resembled that of Nixon-Kissinger than that of 1976 Jimmy Carter. The promise to withdraw U.S. troops from South Korea (whose government was indeed corrupt) had been quietly shelved when it was realized that plausible alternatives were likely to be worse. Carter also proposed substantial increases in defense spending—a total of $1.2 trillion in military expenditures over the following five years.

A military raid was launched on April 24 to rescue the Teheran hostages. The mission failed disastrously, resulting in the destruction in the Iranian desert of several helicopters, a C-130 transport plane, and the deaths of eight servicemen before it was finally aborted, without ever having confronted an opposing force. For many in the United States and abroad, the disaster seemed to signify a much broader collapse of American power.

Jimmy Carter was an irreproachably decent man with the noblest intentions, whose presidency demonstrated that decency and good intentions, in a dangerous world, were not nearly enough. He had made the job of the presidency seem exhausting, wearisome, and, ultimately, too much for one man. Political analysts were speaking of the "twilight of the presidency," and of America.

John Adams once said of George Washington that, "If he were not the greatest President, he was the best Actor of the Presidency we ever had." Every president is an acting president. Some know it. Under Carter the presidency had come to seem an "impossible burden," slowly whittling down the man who held the office, and the nation that observed him. The country was feeling exhausted. During the 1970s, America had sunk into a kind of national depression. It would fall to the oldest president in its history (Ronald Reagan was sixty-nine when he took office) to revive its spirit. In the election of 1980, Reagan, an actor, political orator, and former governor of California, received 50.7 percent of the vote, to Carter's 41 percent. (Independent candidate John Anderson received 6.6 percent.)

While many in the Western intelligentsia belabored the nation's cultural, economic, and political decline, Reagan conveyed a cheerful self-confidence in the fundamental goodness of the American democratic-capitalist civilization and the vital importance to humanity of sustaining it. While others decried the notion of "American exceptionalism" as triumphalist, provocative, and dangerously anachronistic, Ronald Reagan spoke of the United States as the "shining city on the hill."

Many intellectuals in the West believed that the Cold War would resolve itself as the two competing world systems, capitalism and Communism, thesis and antithesis, evolved toward some common synthesis. Many hoped so. Where critics demanded a return to detente and relaxation of tensions, Reagan insisted on applying greater pressure, with the expectation that the added stress would help Communism to "implode," hasten its demise.[250] The goal for the new president was not detente (which he called a "one-way street," favoring the USSR), nor even containment. The only practical policy, he said, and the only moral one was a *rollback* of world Communism. Reagan did not want to reform totalitarianism: he planned to eradicate it. The president called for a "forward strategy of freedom."

President Carter's own military advisers had worried about a military that was becoming "hollow." Reagan campaigned on a promise to "make America strong again." "It was obvious that if we were ever going to get anywhere with the Russians in persuading them to reduce armaments, we had to bargain with them from strength, not weakness," he later wrote.[251] Between 1981 and 1986, total U.S. defense spending more than doubled, from $171 billion to $376 billion.[252] "I intended to let the Soviets know," Reagan wrote in his memoirs, "that we were going to spend what it took to stay ahead of them in the arms race."

"The West will not contain communism, it will transcend communism," Reagan said in a speech at Notre Dame University on May 17, 1981. "We will not bother to renounce it, we'll dismiss it as a bizarre chapter in human history whose last pages are even now being written." AP reporter John Koehler was in Prague on the day the president gave the speech. He wrote to Reagan that "within hours, word had gotten round on your statements about communism and there were expressions of glee, and I detected some hope over your remarks that communism was a passing phenomenon."[253]

In July 1980, Polish workers went on strike against the government's repressive political and economic policies. They presented a list of twenty-one demands, including higher pay, acceptance of free trade unions, free speech and press, and a "halt in repression of the individual because of personal convictions." A banner that was hung over the main gate of one of the factories summed it up: PROLETARIANS OF ALL FACTORIES—UNITE![254] With the already faltering economy immobilized, the government of Prime Minister Edward Gierek was forced to permit the creation of independent trade unions. In September the nation's first independent union was established, *Solidarnosc* ("Solidarity"). Within months its membership had grown to over 10 million. Marx's goal of uniting workers was finally being realized.

Earlier workers' rebellions in Poland—in 1970 and 1976—had grown militant and were violently suppressed. This time, under the leadership of an articulate electrician, Lech Walesa, the unionists remained remarkably restrained in their civil disobedience, giving the state no pretext for the use of force.[255] Kremlin leaders drew up plans for an "intervention" in Poland that entailed the deployment of eighteen armored divisions, and commenced a massive military buildup along the border. Mired in Afghanistan and concerned about deteriorating relations with the West, Moscow ultimately decided against sending troops.[256] In February 1981, though, Gierek was removed and replaced with Gen. Wojciech Jaruzelski, who promised to get tough with the workers. On December 13 he declared a national "State of War" and outlawed Solidarity. Martial law was announced, and all public gatherings were banned.[257] By February as many as forty thousand suspected political opponents had been arrested.

"Something must be done," President Reagan told an aide. "We need to hit them hard, and save Solidarity."[258] Poland depended heavily on the West for both hard currency loans and trade. On December 29, Reagan announced that both would be curtailed. "The current struggle and travails of the people of Poland are of truly historic import to the entire world," he declared.[259] These actions proved to have immense impact: "Economic sanctions caused enormous losses," the Polish interior minister later said.[260] In addition, the sale of critical American oil and gas technologies to Moscow—which was a generation behind in them—was banned.

What was at stake was a natural gas pipeline, under construction, which would carry gas from the Soviet Union to Western Europe, providing tens of billions of dollars annually in vital hard currency revenue to the Kremlin. French and German corporations rushed in to fill contracts lost by American firms, but the administration expanded the sanctions to include foreign firms that licensed American technologies. A war of words ensued between the French government and Washington. Paris threatened a trade war and denounced the administration's "hostility" toward the Soviet Union. Reagan stood firm. In the end, access to U.S. technology and markets proved more important to the French than the Russian sale. Desperate for the hard currency the pipeline would provide, the Kremlin diverted a huge portion of its scarce capital and technical personnel to finish the pipeline. Engineers and scientists were pulled off of other important projects, with ramifications throughout the economy, but they were never able to accomplish the project.[261]

Reagan also launched a covert CIA campaign to support the struggling Solidarity movement: it secretly provided millions of dollars in funding annually, provided advanced communications equipment and training to help organize the Polish resistance movement, and shared critical CIA intelligence with Solidarity leaders.

To spread the message of democracy, Reagan revitalized the U.S. program of radio broadcasting to behind the Iron Curtain. The Kremlin Politburo feared the radio broadcasts "more than any other American weapon," recalled a ranking KGB agent.[262] Moscow spent over $1 billion yearly, which it could ill afford, to jam the broadcasts, but the administration counteracted the interference. By 1984 some 15 percent of the adult Soviet population was regularly listening to Voice of America, and another 8 to 12 percent listened to Radio Liberty. Rating in Eastern Europe were even higher.[263] VOA and Radio Liberty broadcast music, religious programs, news of the world, interviews with exiles, encoded messages, and encouragement to dissidents, and generally undermined one of the principle tactics by which the totalitarian regimes kept themselves in power: monopoly of information. "Under its influence people simply stopped being afraid, and this is always the beginning of the end of all sorts of tyrannies," said Henryk Piecuch, a senior Polish Interior Ministry official. "There wasn't a single coordinating meeting of the special services of the Soviet bloc which did not include consideration of matters relating to the radios."[264]

"We are approaching the end of a bloody century plagued by a terrible political invention—totalitarianism," Reagan said in an address to the British House of Commons on June 8. "Optimism comes less easily today, not because democracy is less vigorous, but because democracy's enemies have refined their instruments of oppression. Yet optimism is in order because day by day democracy is proving itself to be a not at all fragile flower." The West should wage a "crusade for freedom," Reagan declared. His message resounded across the globe. Prisoners in the Soviet gulag tapped out his speeches in code. Anatoly Sharansky, then a political prisoner being held at Permanent Labor Camp 35, deep in the Urals, later said, "I believe the most important step in the Cold War and the defeat of the Soviet empire was his words and his actions at the beginning of his presidency. There was fear in the West to deal with the Soviet Union. 'The Soviet empire is forever, whether we want to or not we will have to deal with it, and by the Soviet Union's rules.' But pragmatism led to our suffering! Reagan was one who understood that the Soviet Union was an evil empire and we could change it. And he believed that all the people of the world, Russians and Arabs and Jews, are as good for democracy as anyone. And he acted in accord with it."[265]

That November, Reagan issued a National Security Decision Directive, NSDD-66, which was, in essence, as its principle author in the NSC later said, a "secret declaration of war on the Soviet Union."[266] It stated that the United States and its allies in Western Europe and Japan had agreed to conduct their relations with the USSR and Eastern European nations "on the basis of a global and comprehensive policy designed to serve their common fundamental security interests." This included agreements with European allies to limit dependence on Soviet gas, restriction of Western technology transfers, and curtailment of crucial low-interest loan credits.

An invalid Leonid Brezhnev died on November 10, 1982. He was succeeded as party general secretary by the ailing former KGB chief, Yuri Andropov, whose main contribution to Soviet society had been his systematization of the practice of the psychiatric torture of political dissidents. The Kremlin leadership, weaned on and still deeply committed to Communist ideology, was now largely without the illusion that it could prevail by the merit of its own ideas and capabilities—certainly not in any foreseeable time frame. Russia's rulers no longer predicted the approximate date of the arrival of the Communist millennium, as Khrushchev had done. The system was, if anything, growing more corrupt, more inefficient, more dismal. Marx's New Man was an alcoholic who hated his job, disdained his government, accepted corruption as a part of everyday life, and did as little work as he could do without being punished.

In a speech to a group of American clergymen on March 8, 1983, Reagan warned against the inclination to "label both sides equally at fault" in the arms race, "to ignore the facts of history and the aggressive impulses of an evil empire . . . " The statement was scarcely refutable: Soviet Communism was undeniably in possession of an empire; and if there is such a thing as evil in the world, surely it was. But it provoked a furor, at least among Soviet leaders and the Western intelligentsia. *New York Times* columnist Anthony Lewis called Reagan what he said was the worst adjective that he could think of: "primitive."

The doctrine of rolling back Communism had been made explicit earlier in the year in a secret National Security Directive, NSDD-75, which Reagan signed in early 1983. "The United States does not accept the current Soviet sphere of influence beyond its borders, and the U.S. will seek to roll it back." To achieve this the U.S. must modernize its military forces "so that Soviet leaders perceive that the U.S. is determined never to accept a second place or a deteriorating military posture. . . . In Europe, the Soviets must be faced with a reinvigorated NATO. . . . " It also outlined cooperation among the Western democracies to limit Soviet economic, military, and political power.[267]

On March 23, President Reagan made an address to the country on the subject of national security. He urged citizens to "tell your Senators and Congressmen that you know that we must continue to restore our military strength. If we stop in midstream, we will send a signal of decline, of lessened will, to friends and adversaries alike. Free people must voluntarily, through open debate and democratic means, meet the challenge that totalitarians pose by compulsion."

He also proposed the development of technologies that would be capable of protecting the United States from ballistic missile attack. The president was calling for a program of research. "I know this is a formidable technical task, one that may not be accomplished before the end of this century," he said. It was not a project that would be accomplished soon, but which offered "a new hope for our children in the twenty-first century." It would take decades of effort in numerous fields, and there would be many obstacles and setbacks. "Yet, current technology has attained a level of sophistication where it's reasonable for us to begin this effort."[268]

The following year, after a visit to the White House, Prime Minister Thatcher announced her support for the Strategic Defense Initiative (SDI) program. Soon the leaders of most Western nations had embraced the project, and research was being conducted by scientists around the world. The

Kremlin, which had enormous faith in the innovative capabilities of American society, was genuinely concerned about breakthroughs in the field. Moscow's response to SDI was thus anomalous. The program was mocked as the unattainable delusion of an actor, and was condemned as threatening to disturb the entire strategic balance. "The intimidating and ultimately disabling impact made by the challenge of SDI on the Kremlin was incontrovertible," writes British historian Raymond Pearson. "Whether even the USA could have realized or afforded SDI still remains in doubt. What is certain is that the Soviet bloc had neither the military capability, the technological skills, nor the financial resources to counter SDI, a realization which delivered a devastating body-blow to the collective morale of the Soviet political and military establishment."[269]

Soviet dissident Alexander Solzhenitsyn later declared that "the Cold War was essentially won by Ronald Reagan when he embarked on the Star Wars program and the Soviet Union understood that it could not take this next step." Alexander Bessmertnykh, Soviet foreign minister under Gorbachev, said after the end of the Cold War that Reagan's SDI program had accelerated the collapse of the Soviet Union.[270]

———◆———

Later that month, on October 22, the government of the tiny Carribean island nation of Grenada was overthrown in a coup by Moscow-sponsored Marxist rebels, and its prime minister was executed. The Organization of Eastern Carribean States, fearing that the island would become a launching point for further insurrection in the region, requested American assistance in restoring democracy to Grenada. On the twenty-fifth, 1,500 soldiers from the U.S. 82nd Airborne Division, 400 Marines, and 500 troops from a half dozen Eastern Carribean nations landed in Grenada, and after three days of fighting against Cuban, North Korean, and Grenadan "People's Revolutionary Army" forces, dislodged the military junta. Though some later media portrayals lampooned the assault as a cakewalk, in fact there were pockets of intense resistance and fierce fighting.

President Reagan made a national address announcing that the Carribean island had become "a Soviet-Cuban colony being readied for use as a major military bastion to export terror."[271] The claim was ridiculed by the Kremlin, Havana, and the American intelligentsia, but documents uncovered after the invasion, and still other ones disclosed in previously closed archives after the collapse of the Soviet Union, confirmed that the Soviets did indeed have plans for using Grenada as a springboard for further adventurism in the region. The Grenadan ambassador to Moscow had reported to Bishop that, in order to receive continued Soviet assistance, "we have to be seen as influencing at least regional events. We have to establish ourselves as the sponsor of revolutionary activities in this region. . . . "[272] Soviet chief of staff Ogarkov had met with Grenadan military leaders in March, telling them that, while "two decades ago there was only Cuba in Latin America, today there are Nicaragua, Grenada and a serious battle is going on in El Salvador."[273]

U.S. troops were withdrawn by December, an open election was held, and democratic government was restored to Grenada. Though Castro railed against American imperialism and demanded Soviet intervention, in the face of a perceptibly renewed American will, Russian leaders declined to get involved so close to United States shores.[274]

The battle to liberate Grenada was not one of history's great battles. But the *decision* to liberate Grenada—against what was certain to be withering criticism—required political resolve and was of epic importance. It was the first time since 1917 that a Communist government had been removed by military force. Grenada was not just a place, or an event. It represented a renewed willingness of the United States to use force to halt the expansion of totalitarianism. The Soviet Union had suffered what the eminent British historian Brian Crozier called "its first strategic reversal."[275]

The planned deployment of INF missiles in Europe was, meanwhile, going forward. Prime Minister Thatcher staunchly defended the placement of the missiles on British soil, often in the face of intense criticism, and the first missiles were deployed there, as scheduled, at the Royal Air Base at Greenham Common in December. The previous month, the German Parliament voted to support the deployments there. Moscow had failed in its efforts to divide the Atlantic alliance over the issue.

Shortly after taking office, President Reagan authorized a robust program of assistance to the Nicaraguan Contras, whose potency grew alongside domestic resistance to the Sandinistas' collectivist economic policies. By the fall of 1987 over 60 percent of Nicaraguan territory was being contested by the Contras. Moscow (which was now preoccupied with its own problems) distanced itself from Managua, refusing requests for increases in fuel and other aid, and admonishing the Sandinistas to improve the efficiency of their economy. As Soviet support waned, the economy slipped further into disarray.

Under intense external and internal pressure, the Sandinistas finally agreed to the terms of a cease-fire with the Contras. The peace plan, negotiated by Costa Rican president Oscar Arias, included the release of political prisoners, the lifting of press censorship, and scheduling national elections in 1990. Ronald Reagan predicted that in free and fair elections the Sandinistas would be thrown out of power, though all the polls showed them decisively ahead. As it turned out, many Nicaraguans had been too fearful of retribution to give their true opinions. Opposition candidate Violeta Chamorro won 55 percent of the vote; Daniel Ortega received 41 percent. It was Nicaragua's first democratic transfer of power in its 160 years as an independent state.[276] It is implausible that the Sandinistas would have consented to the elections, except for the pressures applied by the United States and the Contras.

———————◆———————

When Yuri Andropov died on February 9, 1984, Politburo infighting could produce only an interim solution: Constantin Chernenko, another elderly and infirm old-guard stalwart, who was himself dying. Meanwhile, Soviet agents in the United States were assigned a new primary mission: work to defeat Ronald Reagan in the 1984 U.S. presidential election. The KGB issued to its operatives several themes which were to be hammered relentlessly in the Western press: Reagan was to be portrayed as militaristic, responsible for the arms race, and supportive of repressive regimes.[277]

In one of the most lopsided elections in American history, Reagan received 58.8 percent of the popular vote, winning every state but Minnesota, home of the challenger, Walter Mondale, who had been vice president under Jimmy Carter. During the campaign the president had declared that the United States would not accept "the permanent subjugation of the people of Eastern Europe." In his second inaugural address, on January 21, 1985, Reagan declared that "These will be the years when Americans have restored their confidence and tradition of progress, when Americans courageously supported the struggle for liberty, self-government, and free enterprise throughout the world, and turned the tide of history away from totalitarian darkness and into the warm sunlight of human freedom."

For many in the Western intelligentsia, Reagan's propensity to see the world in terms of stark black and white, good and evil, was passé and provocative. It had become commonplace to condemn U.S. opposition to Communism on the grounds that doing so was "cultural imperialism": that Americans were trying to dictate their values to other peoples. *Time* magazine writer Strobe Talbott derided the president as a political anachronism who had "the early fifties goal of rolling back Soviet domination of Eastern Europe."[278]

After a Kremlin-chaperoned trip to the USSR, economist John Kenneth Galbraith wrote in 1984 of the prosperity and well-being of Soviet citizens. "Partly, the Russian system succeeds because, in contrast with the Western industrial economies, it makes full use of its manpower."[279] [Years earlier Galbraith had displayed comparable insight into Communism's destiny in China, explaining, just after the disastrous Cultural Revolution, "There can be no serious doubt that China is devising a highly effective economic system."][280]

On his visit, historian Arthur Schlesinger found the USSR to be a prosperous and stable society. He derided Reagan's anti-Soviet policies, writing that "those in the U.S. who think the Soviet Union is on the verge of economic and social collapse, ready with one small push to go over the brink, are . . . only kidding themselves." Those who worked toward a defeat of Communism were comparable to Soviet officials who predicted an imminent collapse of democratic capitalism. There were "wishful thinkers" on both sides, Schlesinger said, who "always see other societies as more fragile than they are. Each superpower has economic troubles; neither is on the ropes."[281]

Princeton Sovietologist and perennial television commentator Stephen Cohen explained that the president suffered from "a potentially fatal form of Sovietphobia."[282]*New York Times* writer Flora Lewis dismissed Richard Pipes, who served on Reagan's National Security Council, as displaying "primitive anti-Bolshevism."[283] Harvard's Stanley Hoffman complained about Reagan's reflexive "ritualistic anti-Sovietism." Columbia University Sovietologist Seweryn Bialer wrote that "The Soviet Union is not now, nor will it be during the next decade, in the throes of a true systemic crisis, for it boasts enormous reserves of political and social stability that suffice to endure the deepest difficulties."[284]

Kremlin economists were not so optimistic. They reported that, for the Russian economy to have "normal development," labor productivity must be increased by 50 percent and state enterprises must become dramatically more efficient in their use of resources.[285] Around the world, Communist nations lagged farther and farther behind their neighbor nations that had embraced democratic capitalism. Liberal societies were more free, their cultures more vibrant; their economies were more technologically advanced, more productive, more prosperous; their citizens' lives were longer and, according to international surveys, happier. Western visitors to the Soviet Union (including myself as a young man) were inevitably struck by the overwhelming drabness, grayness, bleakness of the place. Waiting in line for needed staples was a central fact of existence in Soviet societies. Citizens spent their daily lives preoccupied with getting enough food, decent housing, clothing, a few consumer commodities. Communism, with its dream of abolishing the competitive capitalist culture had, by making the basic material necessities of life so scarce, made the people ravenously *materialistic.*

The Soviet Union's inept agricultural system (which possessed more arable land than any other nation in the world) was incapable of feeding the population. Only cheap vodka seemed available in abundance. Thus, while Russia lagged in innovation and productivity, it led the world in alcohol consumption and alcohol-related deaths. Around 85 percent of Soviet factory workers got drunk regularly.[286]

A Soviet economist estimated that, contrary to optimistic government reports, the economy had only grown a *total* of 5 percent from 1976 to 1980, and 3 percent from 1981 to 1985.[287] Mortality rates had actually risen, from 6.9 deaths per 1,000 people in 1964 to 10.3 in 1980, an occurrence unprecedented in the history of developed nations.[288]

It was not a question of whether there should be reforms of the totalitarian system. From the party boss to the man on the street, everybody knew that the status quo was unsustainable. On the very night of Constantin Chernenko's death, March 10, 1985, the Politburo unanimously selected fifty-four-year-old Mikhail Gorbachev as his successor. The choice reflected the recognition by even hard-liners in the party leadership that dramatic reforms were urgently needed to revive the system. At a party conference the previous December, Gorbachev had called for *perestroika* ("restructuring") and *glasnost* ("openness"). A devoted Marxist, he knew that Communism's ebbing fortunes could only be secured by reforming the party and the society.

Gorbachev was a great and vital leader at a critical moment, but he was not singular in his awareness of the need for reform: most Soviet citizens of his generation believed that Communism had failed to deliver on its promise. Government planners could not dictate a spirit of innovation or diligence. But what to do about it? Like Gorbachev, Yuri Andropov, the former KGB chief, had understood the box that the Soviet system was in: it could not flourish without reforms, but reforms threatened to undermine the very essence and stability of the system. A partial relaxation of restrictions on political liberties might open a floodgate that could not be closed again. "Too many groups have suffered repression in our country," Andropov had warned years earlier. "If we open up all the valves at once, and people start to express their grievances, there will be an avalanche and we will have no means of stopping it."[289] It was apparent that Communism was broken. Gorbachev's aim was to fix it, not replace it.

In his first year he quietly edged out of office many of the remaining old generation of party leaders who had cut their political teeth during the era of Stalinization and the hardships of the Second World War. He brought into his government party technocrats who had come of age in the postwar period. But Gorbachev's initial reforms were largely at the margins of the system. He repeatedly urged workers to "work an extra bit harder."[290] Vodka production was cut by one-third, which did not reduce alcohol consumption, but increased the medical and social pathologies associated with the proliferation of moonshine operations.[291]

Gorbachev knew that reforms at home would not be enough. In three decades as a party operative, he had come to the same conclusion that the leadership in Beijing had reached years earlier: economic progress in his socialist economy depended upon closer economic relations with the more productive capitalist nations. A summit meeting between Reagan and Gorbachev, held in Geneva on November 19, 1985, resulted in an agreement to expand bilateral cultural ties, but little of substance. Moscow increased its efforts to convince citizens of the Western nations that Reagan's arms buildup was a hazard to world peace, and a growing chorus of critics, inside the U.S. Congress and out, was calling for major cuts in defense spending. For Reagan this was precisely the moment to stand firm. He believed that U.S. defense spending increases were putting immense pressure on the Kremlin establishment. Military spending consumed 25 percent of the USSR's gross domestic product—compared to 6 percent for the United States.[292] The president knew from intelligence reports that Gorbachev desperately needed defense spending reductions to bolster his ailing economy. Gorbachev's adviser Anatoly Chernyaev later recalled that, in his effort to save Soviet Communism, the Soviet leader needed Reagan's cooperation on two issues: "the first was disarmament and the second was Afghanistan."[293] He was, instead, vigorously opposed on both.

In an address to the nation on February 26, 1986, President Reagan pointed to the "long history of Soviet brutality toward those who are weaker" and said that "Strength is the most persuasive argument we have to convince our adversaries to negotiate seriously and cease bullying other nations." He pledged continued American support for "freedom fighters" opposing Communism around the globe, and defended military expenditures. "The only guarantee of peace and freedom is our military strength and our national will," Reagan said. "Each generation has to live with the challenges history delivers. If we sustain our effort now, we have the best chance in decades of building a secure peace."[294] The American buildup continued.

———◆———

When Reagan took office, there was a major escalation of American support for the Afghan rebels fighting the Soviet occupation. Under Carter, the limited U.S. aid had been designed to "harass" Soviet forces in the country. Now the aim was nothing short of the defeat of the Red Army and its expulsion from Afghanistan. By 1984 the United States had provided the *mujahideen* with $400 million worth of military and other aid.[295] Fearing a propaganda blow to Communism from a defeat in Afghanistan, the new Soviet leader Gorbachev escalated the war there. He put a brash young commander, Gen. Mikhail Zaitsev, in charge and gave him almost unlimited resources to wage the war, including liquid gas explosives, *Spetsnaz* (special forces), and greatly increased airpower. It was under Gorbachev's tenure that most of the million Afghans who died during the Soviet invasion were killed.

"Do whatever you have to do to help the *mujahideen* not only to survive, but to win," Reagan instructed aides in 1985. There followed the largest covert operation in American history: that year the CIA delivered 10,000 rocket-propelled grenades and 200,000 rockets to the Afghan rebels. The first Stinger missile launchers began shooting down the feared Hind helicopters, with an accuracy rate of nearly 75 percent. They inflicted a terrible toll on the Soviet occupiers. By 1986, Soviet pilots were refusing to fly below 15,000 feet, the Stinger's range. The Red Army's airpower had been blunted, and its own casualties mounted. Equipped with high-tech U.S. communications equipment and satellite intelligence, and armed with sophisticated weaponry, the Afghan rebels now took the fight to the Soviets, who were increasingly confined to fortified strongholds. An estimated $100 billion, badly needed to bolster the flagging Soviet economy, was diverted to fund the Kremlin's war in Afghanistan. The Marxist Afghan puppet regime would outlast its Kremlin patrons by a few months.

———————

In administrative style Ronald Reagan was, depending upon whether one supported or opposed him, either a "delegator" or "detached." In the Iran-Contra affair, he would pay a price for this. The imbroglio entailed a combination of two disparate aims: to supply the Contras fighting against the Marxist regime in Nicaragua, and to secure the release of American hostages being held by radical Islamist groups in Lebanon. Both goals faced seemingly insuperable practical—and legal—obstacles. Congress had voted to curtail funding to the Contras, and the official policy of the U.S. government proscribed negotiating with terrorists or paying ransom for the release of hostages.

In 1985 the administration had received word from Israeli intelligence that the release of the American hostages might be secured if U.S. arms were supplied to "moderates" within the Iranian government. A tangled arrangement was devised by National Security Adviser Robert "Bud" McFarlane and his successor John Poindexter, and managed by his aide Oliver North, a Marine lieutenant colonel working as a White House staffer, with the knowledge and support of CIA director William Casey. In 1985 and 1986 several shipments of arms were made to Iran, and the profits from the sales were diverted to supply the Contras. In November 1986 a Lebanese newspaper published details of the activities in Iran. A congressional inquiry ensued, and the president appointed a special commission to investigate. McFarlane attempted suicide. Poindexter resigned. North was dismissed. Casey suffered a stroke and died a few months later. A special prosecutor won convictions of North and Poindexter, who received prison sentences.

The sale of arms to the Iranian "moderates" was ill advised, but legal, and in fact did help win the release of several hostages. President Reagan denied knowledge of the diversion of profits to the Contras, which circumvented the ban by Congress, though he had undoubtedly created an administrative environment that made it possible.

———————

General Secretary Gorbachev desperately needed to cut military spending in order to free up resources for the failing Soviet economy. To make matters worse, in late 1985 the Saudis, in cooperation with the administration's strategy, raised oil production dramatically, sending prices plummeting and slashing the Kremlin's main source of hard currency. So long as America was militarily resurgent, Gorbachev could not substantially cut military spending without weakening Moscow's grip over its empire. And, looming over it all was the ongoing prospect of developments in SDI, which had the potential to alter the strategic balance in a single stroke. In August 1986,

Gorbachev invited Reagan to meet for a low-key "pre-summit" in Reykjavik, Iceland, and in September the White House announced that a "planning session" would be held between the two leaders the following month.

On the first day of the meeting, Saturday, October 11, Gorbachev dramatically proposed a 50 percent reduction in both sides' nuclear arsenals. The talks proceeded even further, to the discussion of total abolition of nuclear weapons within a decade. Reports of the discussions alarmed hawks in Washington, but Reagan's commitment to reducing nuclear arms should have come as no surprise: he had long talked about the irrationality of the doctrine of Mutual Assured Destruction, and near the beginning of his presidency had proposed a "zero option" to the Soviets: the complete elimination of all intermediate range nuclear missiles in Europe. It had been rejected, dismissed as a propaganda ploy. Now, a new generation of Soviet leaders was ready to accept it.

The sticking point was the Strategic Defense Initiative. The president believed that the surest way to defend America and its allies against the possibility of missile attack was missile defense. He pledged that the development of SDI would be restricted to research and testing for the ten years, and that new technologies would be shared with the Soviets. Russian negotiators, though, could not return to Moscow with an accord that permitted the continued development of what they still publicly dismissed as an unworkable *Star Wars* program. In the end, an agreement could not be reached. Prime Minister Margaret Thatcher later wrote that "There was one vital factor in the ending of the Cold War. It was Ronald Reagan's decision to go ahead with the Strategic Defense Initiative."[296]

President Reagan, for his part, was undeterred by those who condemned him for destabilizing the international system with his strident anti-Communism. On June 12, 1987, on a trip to Europe, he spoke to an enthusiastic audience of tens of thousands of West Germans gathered at the Berlin Wall's Brandenburg Gate. From its beginnings and until the very end, the subjects of Communist nations—who were denied election ballots—regularly voted with their feet. Everywhere that Communism held power, fences and armed border guards were required to keep citizens *in* their socialist utopias. The Berlin Wall symbolized the glaring contrast between Marxism's pretensions and its practice. "General Secretary Gorbachev," the president proclaimed to the huge crowd, "if you seek peace, if you seek prosperity for the Soviet Union and Eastern Europe, if you seek liberalization: Come here to this gate! Mr. Gorbachev, open this gate! Mr Gorbachev, tear down this wall!" The crowd roared its approval. The speech reverberated behind the Iron Curtain. In the burgeoning pro-democracy movement, *samizdat* publications repeated the message. In the Soviet gulag, political prisoners tapped out Reagan's remarks.

The centralized Soviet economy continued to wane. The Kremlin desperately needed progress in arms talks. In February 1987, Gorbachev (now convinced that NATO's IMF deployment would not be derailed) unexpectedly announced that Moscow was willing to consider the reduction of intermedi-ate-range missiles in Europe. To the Kremlin's surprise, Washington responded with an even broader counterproposal, the "global zero option": the elimi-nation of all intermediate-range missiles, everywhere in the world.

Reagan and Gorbachev met at the White House on December 8 to sign the INF Treaty, the first Cold War accord to actually reduce nuclear arma-ments rather than simply establish limits on further expansion. Under it, the two nations agreed to eliminate all ground-based missiles with ranges of 500 to 5,500 kilometers—which included all U.S. Pershing missiles stationed in Europe, and Soviet SS-20s. Reagan's policy of building a stronger military in order to be in a position of strength at the bargaining table was being validated.

The summit also represented a personal public relations triumph for the energetic and charismatic Gorbachev who, with the charm of a demo-cratic politician campaigning for election, occasionally stopped his motor-cade to wade into crowds of well-wishing Americans. In his own country, though, Gorbachev could only maintain his precarious balancing act between conservation and reform by moving forward. To salvage Commu-nism he had attempted to wring greater efficiency from the rickety system, adopting policies to reduce absenteeism, negligence, alcoholism, and cor-ruption, all of which Andropov had made flailing attempts at. It had now become evident that these efforts would be inadequate. Wholesale reforms were required. Gorbachev went a step further: he acknowledged that eco-nomic and cultural progress required lifting the deadening hand of party and state control from society. The Kremlin could not continue to sequester its own people if it hoped to keep pace with the technological breakthroughs under way elsewhere. (It is noteworthy that, in an era of dramatic innova-tions in telecommunication technologies, not a single one of them occurred in Communist nations.) But the technologies essential to the free flow of ideas—and thus to productivity and creativity—also threatened state con-trol. The use of copy machines and personal computers was severely restricted, and the inefficiencies of authoritarianism were stifling. Soviet sci-entists required several days' notice to copy an article.[297] Critical develop-ments in promising new telecommunication technologies had bypassed the Communist world. Much of Gorbachev's "information revolution" was thus simply the sanctioning of the inevitable. International telephone communi-cations, the proliferation of video equipment, tape recorders, and even Xerox machines simply could not be sharply restricted in a society that hoped to sustain technological competitiveness. The state's desire to monopolize information was no longer tenable.[298]

What emerged from *glasnost* was not exactly a free press. The govern-ment continued to exercise enormous control. But the media was permitted to be more critical, and the result was the public airing of problems that everybody already knew existed, but had no idea of the scope: health care, social welfare, economic stasis, Afghanistan, state and party corruption. It had long been a Russian pastime to discuss grievances against the system—but in private. Under *glasnost*, discontent was going public.

Secretary Gorbachev made criticisms of corrupt local bureaucrats. He allowed criticisms to be made. The press was permitted to be more assertive. Isvestiya disclosed the official figure for total deaths caused by stalin's Great Terror: 50 million.[299] Yet Gorbachev was a Communist believer. "I will not stop, as long as I am able, to say and do everything to affirm [faith in Communism]," he said candidly. And, "do what you will to me, I shall not accept property in land. I will not." In late 1987 he reaffirmed that the forced collectivization of agriculture, notwithstanding some "excesses," was one of socialism's great achievements.[300] He continued to maintain that it was the prerogative of the party, and not the citizenry, to determine what were the interests of the people. To assist it in this, the KGB still had a half million personnel, a quarter million of whom were engaged in domestic surveillance—spying on ordinary citizens—abetted by tens of millions of informants.[301]

At the end of May 1988, Ronald Reagan, the man who had spent his adult life opposing Communism, traveled to Moscow for his fourth meeting with Gorbachev. At the American embassy on the thirtieth, he hosted a dinner for Russian political dissidents. The following day the president made a bold speech to students at Moscow State University, telling them that Communism had produced social and political aberrations that contrasted bleakly with social, economic, and political life in the democratic nations. "We do not know what the conclusion will be of this journey, but we're hopeful that the promise of reform will be fulfilled. In this Moscow spring, this May 1988, we may be allowed that hope: that freedom will blossom forth at last in the rich and fertile soil of your people and culture."[302]

Reagan was now not at the full vigor of his youth, but at diminished strength he was a more powerful speaker than most men at full capacity. This was not the political dinosaur of the Communists' propaganda. After the speech, the president was given a thunderous standing ovation by the students. "It was not the Reagan that we expected. There was nothing old-fashioned or stale about him," said a young Russian political science student. "He seemed to be so lively, active and thinking. This was a pleasant surprise."[303]

Communism had lost the war of ideas. Across Eastern Europe, Soviet control was weakening. Even in East Germany, one of the most repressive of the regimes, the *Stasi* reported that the public "openly express doubts" about state reports of economic progress, and in conversation bewailed the ineptness of socialist economies.[304]

History, as Reagan had said, was leaving the Communist nations behind. Not just Western Europe, but newly developing Asian nations that had adopted free markets, impoverished at midcentury, were now surpassing the Soviet Union and its ramshackle satellites in industrial production, longevity and health, and per capita income. Singapore, a tiny city-state with a population of only 2 million, exported more machinery than all Eastern Europe put together.[305]

Gorbachev was not the only one scrambling to make economic reforms to Communism in order to save it. Around the world, Communist dictatorships attempted to resuscitate bedraggled economies and cultures, and cling to power, by making socioeconomic reforms that were antithetical to the espoused tenets of Communism itself. The ideology was dead: only the residual tyranny survived. Party elites now described the virtue and inevitability of economic competition and inequality. In China, the state was in the process of adopting a mutant free market Communism: its only link to original Marxist ideology was the monopoly of the party over state power. In Moscow, the chief party ideologist explained that "instilling a sense of ownership was a good thing, for when a worker has a stake in something, a person will move mountains; if he does not, he will be indifferent."[306] Adam Smith couldn't have put it better. A month after Reagan's trip to Moscow, the Kremlin began its withdrawal from Afghanistan.

Ronald Reagan's policies did not, of themselves, topple Communism. But the intense pressure they applied were the coup de grace of fifty years of resolute American efforts, and those of other peoples fighting for liberal democracy and against totalitarianism. "Without claiming that the Reagan administration ran no risks or made no mistakes," writes the political scientist Tony Smith, "the mark of this presidency on the upsurge of democracy in the 1980s seems undeniable."[307]

Former KGB general Oleg Kalugin called Reagan's policies "a catalyst for the collapse of the Soviet Union."[308] "My opinion of his contribution toward ending the Cold War is very high," Gorbachev remarked after he left office.

"He inspired a nation and transformed a world," said former Canadian prime minister Brian Mulroney. Prime Minister Margaret Thatcher would say of him, "It is hard to deny that Ronald Reagan's life was providential. . . . Others prophesied the decline of the West; he inspired America and its allies with renewed faith in their mission of freedom. . . . Others hoped, at best, for an uneasy cohabitation with the Soviet Union; he won the Cold War—not only without firing a shot, but also by inviting enemies out of their fortresses and turning them into friends."[309]

———◆———

President Reagan's policy of peace through strength had been of decisive historical importance. The military buildup had affirmed American resolve, as he said it would. Massive United States assistance to the Afghan resistance had ultimately helped force a debilitating Soviet withdrawal there. Along with actions in Grenada, Nicaragua, and elsewhere, it had demonstrated the credibility of the Americans' pledge to resist Communism worldwide, had encouraged anti-Communist groups in Eastern Europe and the Soviet Union, and inflicted tremendous economic and political costs on the Kremlin.

The USSR, buckling under the weight of its own internal economic failures, was spending $40 billion annually to prop up satellite regimes in Cuba, Vietnam, Ethiopia, Nicaragua, and elsewhere.[310] Not a single Third World client state had managed to sustain economic growth comparable to that among the wave of developing capitalist nations. As if to certify the demise of Marxism as an ideology, General Secretary Gorbachev announced in early 1989 that Moscow would abandon its support for Communist rebel movements around the globe.

Economic development could not progress without increased interaction with the democratic world, and it grew increasingly difficult for the Communist regimes to hide from their people the huge disparity in living standards between East and West. Some of this was already proving to be beyond state control. The populations of the eastern parts of the empire were able to receive broadcasts from Europe. But even government-sanctioned interactions had unforeseeable consequences, such as when, in February 1988, a British television program was shown in Russia, including commercials that revealed to stunned Russian viewers that British cats routinely had access to more meat than they did.[311]

In Hungary in early 1989, under intense and growing public pressure the Parliament passed political reforms permitting freedom of speech, press, and assembly. In May, Hungary began to dismantle the barbed-wire fence along its border with Austria: the Iron Curtain was starting to come down. When, the following spring, Hungary held its first free parliamentary elections in forty-five years, Communist Party candidates received only 9 percent of the vote.

In Poland, the government of General Jaruzelski was forced to enter into talks with the banned Solidarity union, and then to agree to hold free parliamentary elections, scheduled for June 1989. Of the 161 candidates that the new Solidarity Party put up for election to the lower house, 160 won seats. Of the 100 seats it contested in the upper house, Solidarity won 99. President George Bush, Reagan's vice president and successor, traveled to Poland and Hungary in July to voice America's support for the reforms under way there.

In the spring and summer of 1989 the Baltic states of Estonia, Latvia, and Lithuania announced their sovereignty and moved toward independence from Moscow. In Russia, reforms only whetted the public's appetite for more liberty. In March 1989 elections were held for the new Soviet Congress of People's Deputies established by the constitutional reforms. They were the first open elections in the country since the Communists had come to power. Even some unopposed Communist candidates were defeated when more voters crossed their names out—signifying a vote against—than voted for them. When the first session of the Congress of People's Deputies met in May, a bloc of reformers quickly emerged and dominated proceedings—and the attention of a mass media over which the party was steadily losing its grip. On live television the reformers denounced repressive party policies, the KGB, the military, the ineffectual economy, and Gorbachev himself.

Mikhail Gorbachev knew that as soon as the party ceased to have a monopoly, the entire edifice would crumble. He was not willing to make that move. Instead, he waited until matters were taken out of his hands. Gorbachev, though, made a critical and positive contribution to history. The final stage of Communism, the endgame of the Cold War, might have been vastly more violent and destructive than it was. Gorbachev's decision to renounce the Brezhnev Doctrine, to allow the disintegration of the empire that Stalin had created, may not have altered the outcome, but it certainly spared the loss of countless lives.

In September, Hungary opened its border with Austria, signaling its willingness to permit free passage for East Germans wishing to emigrate to West Germany. Within weeks, 50,000 East Germans had fled to the West, in the largest migration since the construction of the Berlin Wall. It was a visible testament to the abject failure of the Communist experiment: there were no refugees going the other way. When dictator Erich Honecker, head of the brutal East German regime for the previous eighteen years, sealed the country's borders, thousands of demonstrators took to the streets to protest the government's repressive policies. Honecker ordered his internal security forces to fire on the crowds. Mindful of the recent bloodbath at Tiananmen, they refused. On October 18, with things slipping out of control, the East German Politburo removed Honecker from office, replacing him with its youngest member, Egon Krenz. The demonstrations continued to expand, drawing as many as half a million people at a time. Protesters who a few weeks earlier called for "reform" were now demanding "Democracy! Freedom!"

Krenz called Secretary Gorbachev. What should he do? Gorbachev suggested that opening up the borders would "let off steam" and avert an "explosion."[312] On the eighth, the East German government announced that all citizens wishing to "visit the West" would be granted visas. Hundreds of thousands of East Berliners gathered at the eight checkpoint gates that separated East from West. They began crossing over, a cautious few at first, and then in a torrent, heedless of the guards along the despised barrier. Around midnight, disconcerted border guards simply opened the gates and began letting people pass through. Later, the crowds were not content to cross over. They began chipping away at the Wall itself, tearing it down. Border guards, selected for being the most stalwart Communists, watched in confusion but did nothing—it was now evident which way history was flowing.

It was not only the Wall that was coming down. The Soviet system was being dismantled. In East Germany, where one in seven citizens was an informant for the feared secret police,[313] the government had not seen it coming. Erich Honecker fled to Moscow the following year and, once safely there, vociferously insisted that he had no regrets about what he had done to protect world socialism. Gorbachev rejected German efforts at extradition, but after the collapse of the Soviet Union, Honecker was taken back to Germany and put on trial for ordering border guards to shoot to kill. The trial was suspended after Honecker was diagnosed with terminal liver cancer. (He fled to Chile, where he died in 1994.)

On October 7, 1989, Hungary's Communist Party (the Hungarian Socialist Workers' Party), officially renounced Leninism. In November, hundreds of thousands of Czechs gathered in a series of mass demonstrations in in Prague. Finally, fearing for his life, on December 10 President Gustav Husak— leader of the Communist Party since 1968—resigned, clearing the way for democratic parliamentary elections. On the twenty-ninth, Vaclev Havel (a poet and playwright who had been jailed numerous times by the regime for his advocacy of human rights) was elected president of Czechoslovakia. "People," he declared to the jubilant nation, "your government has returned to you!" In January the Bulgarian Parliament, under intense public pressure, voted to revoke the constitution's requirement that the Communist Party control all the key institutions of the society and government.

In Romania, Communism did not go as quietly. After ten days of mass demonstrations and violent efforts to repress them, in late December 1989, the regime of the tyrant Nicolae Ceausescu was toppled. On the twenty-fifth, he and his wife were shot by a firing squad after being found guilty in a military tribunal of genocide and other crimes against the state.

The Kremlin had pressing problems closer to home. The Soviet State Planning Commission, Gosplan, issued a report declaring that centrally planned economics had been a failure and calling for moves toward a market economy. And the "restructuring" that Gorbachev had initiated to revive the economy and the culture (and the party) was now slipping out of his control. In early February 1990, millions of Russians took part in mass demonstrations protesting the slow pace of reform in their own country. As the protests grew, Gorbachev attempted to salvage what he could by proposing an amendment to the Soviet constitution, ending the Communist Party's monopoly on power. That May, the Russian Parliament elected reformer Boris Yeltsin president of the Russian Republic, spurning Gorbachev's candidate Alexander Vlasov. It also announced that its laws were supreme over Soviet laws. Though he and the other reformers had already distanced themselves from the Communist Party, at its Twenty-eighth Congress in July, Yeltsin quit the party entirely.

On December 8, 1991, the leaders of Russia, Ukraine, and Belarus announced the creation of the Commonwealth of Independent States. They informed President Bush of their agreement. Then, Gorbachev. He denounced the action as "illegal and dangerous," but by now nobody was listening. By the end of the month, eleven former Soviet republics had joined the Commonwealth. On Christmas day, Gorbachev resigned as head of a country that no longer existed. Around 7:30 that evening, the Soviet hammer-and-sickle flag flying over the Kremlin was unceremoniously taken down. The system that it symbolized, and the philosophy of totalitarian control that underlay it, had been relegated to the ash heap of history, as Reagan predicted. The long and bloody experiment with Communism was over. In Russia, which had suffered under Marx's dream for most of a century, the reform process was only beginning: it would require decades to repair the generations of cultural rot that Communism had inflicted. "We have made one important contribution," said Russian reformer Yuri Afanasyev. "We have taught the world what *not* to do."[314]

———————•———————

Only two tiny dictatorships seemed untouched by the tidal wave of liberty that was sweeping the globe. Not coincidentally, they were the ones in which power was most concentrated, liberty the most restricted, and cults of personality the most highly developed. In North Korea, despot Kim Jung-il deemed the collapse of the Soviet Union a "setback" for world Communism, but promised its eventual triumph and foreclosed the possibility of reforms in his own country. In Cuba, dictator Fidel Castro called the fall of Soviet Communism a "tragedy," making clear that his impoverished and increasingly isolated nation would give way to freedom only over his dead body. With Moscow embracing free market reforms, Castro denounced Russia's "betrayal of Marxism-Leninism" and insisted that Cuba would not adopt "any methods that reek of capitalism."[315] "Nobody should harbor any illusions that Cuba's socialism will make concessions . . . because we have one party, one single party!" he told Communist loyalists. "And there won't be a market economy. Our economy will be a programmed economy, a planned economy."[316] Dissidents continued to be imprisoned for holding unauthorized political meetings, printing without state permission, or expressing hostility toward Castro's rule. The party reiterated in 1992 that it "will not allow internal opposition."[317]

By the late 1980s, Communism's catastrophic failure was undeniable except to the most devout believers, mainly in academia, far removed from the real-life effects of Marx's notions. Others claimed that it was not Communism that had failed, but the imperfect application of it. Anne Applebaum, historian of the Soviet gulag system, has tried to understand why Western intellectuals have not had the same abhorrence of Communism's atrocities as of fascism's. She notes that the "founding philosophies of the Western left—Marx and Engels—were the same as those of the Soviet Union." They shared many of the same core values and shared the same rhetoric: "the masses, the struggle, the proletariat, the exploiters and exploited, the ownership of the means of production."[318] To acknowledge how badly the Soviet system was off track might require considering the possibility that the entire socialist program of several generations had been off track as well. "Thus," writes Harvey Klehr, the first American permitted to examine Comintern archives after the fall of the Soviet Union, "the nostalgic afterlife of communism in the United States has outlived most of the real Communist regimes around the world."[319]

Certainly the twentieth century refuted the excessive faith, prevalent in 1900, in the ability of technocrats and planners to engineer and then administer utopia. The century showed that the "soft sciences" are very soft indeed, and social "scientists" are as likely as the common man—or more—to propound ideological balderdash based on personal preferences rather than on anything resembling science.

And what, following the fall of Communism, was to become of the academics in the Soviet bloc who had specialized in the debunked Marxist philosophy? The head of one Soviet University's "Department of Scientific Socialism" explained that, of the department's thirty faculty members, ten could be fired, ten were old enough to be retired, and ten were retrainable.[320]

———————

Communism did not fall. It was pushed. Global totalitarianism collapsed because it existed in an intensely hostile international environment. America created and sustained that environment, at a vast expense in lives and resources. The United States confronted Soviet power resolutely and across an unprecedented span of the globe, across an unparalleled span of time, under many different leaders, across several generations. The United States had stood firm, and Soviet totalitarianism had been consigned to the ash heap of history. Many of the same intellectuals who had denounced the United States' resolute opposition to Communism (on the grounds that it was "cultural imperialism," or that it disturbed "world peace"), now insisted that totalitarianism would have toppled even without American resistance. In hindsight they say that Communism was a "flawed system," doomed to failure, though they never said so at the time. Well, Hitler's fascism was a flawed and doomed system: it was nevertheless necessary—and right—to resist it.

On a visit to newly liberated Central Europe a year after leaving office, former president Reagan was greeted by enormous audiences singing "The Ballad of Ronald Reagan," lauding "the man who made those pussyfooters and weaklings feel ashamed."[321] In Poland, Lech Walesa's parish priest gave a valuable antique sword to Reagan: "I am giving you this saber for helping us to chop off the head of communism," he said.[322] Czech leader Vaclav Havel frankly remarked that "the fact that we still exist" was the result of America's determined opposition to Communism.[323]

President Reagan was surely vital to that effort, but he was one of a long and honorable line of presidents, beginning with Harry Truman, who had led America's struggle against global totalitarianism. That struggle had received steadfast, largely bipartisan support from the Congress and, most essentially, it reflected the will of the American people. In 1947 diplomat George Kennan had argued that "the United States policy toward the Soviet Union must be that of a long-term, patient but firm and vigilant containment of Russian expansive tendencies." Ultimately, he said, this would lead "either to the breakup or the gradual mellowing of Soviet power."[324] The policy succeeded.

From 1946 to 1990 the United States gave a staggering $373 billion in economic and military aid to nations opposed to Soviet totalitarianism. Contrary to a widespread myth, most of the assistance was not military, but economic: only 38 percent of all aid given during the period was military; 62 percent was economic. Of this, over three-quarters consisted of outright grants.[325] It was the greatest act of philanthropy, and the largest transfer of wealth, in human history. More than one hundred thousand Americans died in that battle for freedom. The Cold War was a *war*.

The struggle against global totalitarianism was as great a challenge as destiny ever presented to a people. "Surely there was never a fairer test of national quality than this," Kennan had written in 1947, at the dawn of the great struggle. America met that test. All mankind is better off for it.

8

A World Safe for Democracy

THE AGE OF American preeminence has been a golden age of human progress. Individual well-being increased more during the twentieth century than in any previous epoch. At the dawn of the twenty-first century we live in a world that is, more than ever before, free and democratic. According to Freedom House's ongoing tally of global democracy, by the end of the twentieth century, 120 of the world's 192 nations (with 63 percent of its population) were democratic, up from only six nations just a hundred years earlier. "In a very real sense," it reports, "the twentieth century has become the 'democratic century.'"[1]

Consider what the last century of global affairs would have been like, and in what ways things would have turned out differently, if there had been no America in the world. The United States has played a vital role in the unfolding of the human potential. Here is a partial list of nations whose citizens live in more free and democratic societies today as a *direct* result of American action during the twentieth century:

Germany
France
Austria
Italy
Holland
Belgium
Netherlands
Russia
Belarus
Ukraine

Estonia
Latvia
Lithuania
Yugoslavia
Poland
Czechoslovakia
Hungary
Turkey
Greece
Israel
Kuwait
Philippines
Indonesia
Singapore
Malaysia
Nicaragua
El Salvador
Grenada
Japan
South Korea
Taiwan

It was not inevitable that freedom should triumph over tyranny in the twentieth century. Take America out of the picture, and the century would have turned out very differently than it did. The United States made many mistakes in its relations with foreign nations, but when the record is taken as a whole, and judged fairly, history will show that no nation could claim to have been so circumspect or just in the use of its power. No nation ever wielded such disproportionate capabilities, or used them to such worthy ends. Who would one prefer to have been predominant in the century: The Germans? The Russians? The Japanese? The Chinese?

The eminent British scholar Sir Alfred Zimmern wrote presciently in 1953 that, thanks to American leadership, "In fifty years time . . . the Soviet Union will be a historic memory, and the people now under Soviet rule will have achieved freedom and independence under the terms of the [UN] Charter. If the rest of the world could see the people of the United States as they truly are, the future of [international] leadership would be assured, and the peace of the world safeguarded for as far ahead as statesmen can see."[2]

At the dawn of the new millennium, there is no impending prospect of war between the leading nations. This is an almost unprecedented development in world affairs. Some political scientists even predict that authoritarian government may be virtually abolished within the next couple of generations. The forecast may be too optimistic, but the fact that people are talking about such things at all suggests how far the community of nations has come in the past age. A return to American isolationism would erode international stability far more than it would undermine U.S. material welfare, particularly in any short- to medium-term, but it is not in accord with either American interests or values. The oldest democracy in the world continues to be a vital force for freedom.

The United States is a great power of epic historic importance. It is with good reason that it has been compared to the Rome of the first and second centuries. But there are crucial differences. Ancient Rome was not interested in expanding freedom and democracy, but in domination. The American Age saw the end of imperialism; the defeat of European and Asian fascism; the transformation of key nations to liberal democracies; the defeat of global totalitarianism; the erosion of authoritarianism. The Pax Americana has seen, for the first time in human affairs, the establishment of truly global institutions for international political and economic cooperation. To call America the Rome of its day it to pay a tribute to Rome.

It has become popular to speak of the "American empire," even by those intending to commend U.S. power, but the term is ultimately not useful. It obfuscates more than it clarifies. The so-called "American empire" is in fact an anti-empire: it is a community of freedom-loving peoples, drawn together by common interests and values, not by force. Which it to say, it is no empire at all. It was America which, more than any other nation, hastened the end of the age of empire. America has offered leadership, not coercion. The so-called "American empire" is a commonwealth of ideas and ideals. It is the realm of liberty, a polity of citizens making free choices, in their social and economic and political lives; where power is obtained by giving the people what they want. Such a system is not without its problems: it remains to be seen what a world of free people *will* want. But those problems are preferable to tyranny. "Since the beginning of our American history, we have been engaged in change—in a perpetual peaceful revolution . . . " as President Franklin Roosevelt said in his Four Freedoms speech. "The world order we seek is the cooperation of free countries, working together in a friendly, civilized society."[3] America's greatest exports have been liberty and democracy.

This liberty has extended to economic as well as political life. America has been the leader in the drive to break down barriers between nations, one of the most important developments of the era. In this, too, it has led by example: before 1900, U.S. tariffs on imports averaged over 30 percent; by 2000, they had been reduced to just 5 percent. When asking Congress to ratify the Bretton Woods agreement in early 1945, President Roosevelt said that mankind was at a historic turning point. "The point in history at which we now stand is full of promise and danger," he said. "The world will either move toward unity and widely shared prosperity or it will move into necessarily competing economic blocs."[4] Though there have been the inevitable fits and starts along the way, that American vision of a global community of nations engaged in a harmonious and cooperative intercourse, is being realized. Massive American economic assistance helped to revive foreign economies following the Second World War, and open American markets enabled them to flourish. The establishment of the most stable and open international economic system in history has led to a period of unprecedented growth in living standards around the globe. The peoples of the world are increasingly interconnected. International conferences and negotiations are less and less about military arrangements, more and more about economic ones. Increasingly, it is commerce that determines a nation's place in the global order. That is a historic transformation.

For the first time in history, a nation championed a system of free and open international relations that assured its own relative decline and safeguarded the ascendance of its direct competitors. "Globalization" is anything *but* a mechanism for American hegemony. The only thing we know for sure about globalization is that it will reduce America's relative importance in the world. When in the early 1990s it appeared to many that Japan would supplant the United States in economic power, there was no talk in American foreign policy debates of military action against the Japanese challenge, or aggression against Japanese commercial interests, but, rather, what Americans needed to do to regain their competitive edge.

Thomas Jefferson wrote that "the natural progress of things is for liberty to yield and government to gain ground." That danger always exists, and populations must be on constant guard against the expansions of unaccountable power; but during the American Age the trend has been, almost across the entire globe, the other way. In 1900 just 12 percent of mankind lived in democratic polities; in 2000, 63 percent There will be new challenges ahead, and variations of the old challenges, but it is a splendid time to be alive. We should appreciate it, and the sacrifices that made it possible.

The American Age has been an age of creativity, discovery, and invention unmatched in history, an epoch of growing abundance and longevity. The establishment of a stable and open global economic system (the most stable and universal in history) has led to a period of unprecedented growth in standards of living across the globe. In the dialectics of its critics, globalization gets blamed for problems that have existed since the dawn of man— poverty, inequality, disease, malnutrition, oppression—but gets none of the credit for the spectacular advances that have been made across the world during the era of globalization: rising life expectancy; declining child mortality; increased caloric intake; enhanced worker safety; improved health care; increasing liberty for men and women. Human material welfare has expanded in conjunction with individual freedom. By virtually all standards of measurement (longevity, health, education, individual liberty, opportunity, etc.), there has never been a better time to be alive.

We are too consumptive, it is true, but only because there is more to consume than ever existed before, the fruits of an explosion of human knowledge and productive capability. No previous generation would have behaved more prudently in the face of such abundance. The daily life of the average man and woman today is an existence of freedoms and comforts scarcely dreamed of by most people in history. A short time ago our ancestors lived at the mercy of the elements: the rain and snow, the heat and cold. Most of mankind have scraped for a subsistence, living in oppressively rigid social structures, dying of malnutrition, disease, or violence at a young age. Today, obesity is a greater problem, *worldwide*, than starvation.

After surveying a mountain of empirical data on measures of human living conditions throughout history, statistician Julian Simon concluded that, "Over the course of the twentieth century, almost every measure of material human welfare—ranging from health, wealth, nutrition, education, speed of transportation and communications, leisure time, gains for women, minorities . . . has shown wonderful gains for Americans. Although the rest of the world lags behind the United States in most measures, almost everywhere the same trend of improvement is evident."[5] Economist Indur Goklany notes that, at the beginning of the twenty-first century, the average human "lives longer and is healthier, less hungry, and less likely to have children in the workforce" than just fifty years earlier. "Moreover, gaps in these critical measures of well-being between the rich countries and the middle- and low-income groups have generally shrunk dramatically since the mid-1900s."[6]

———•———

Amidst a morass in Iraq, a conflict of "preemption" ill conceived and deviating from long tradition, a growing number of Americans long to return to the relative quietude of isolationism. That would be a shame. The world is better off with America in it. Yet the empire of liberty will not be sustained by military might, but by the strength of ideas, well expressed, widely and consistently. The twentieth century has given propaganda a bad name, but it is a moral imperative. In domestic affairs, politicians know that they must seek influence in order to have power; increasingly, nations must do the same in international affairs. International opinion is more important today as a source of a nation's power than it was a generation ago, and will be more important yet a generation hence. Americans, as they have always done, must learn to master what's next.

Attending a conference following the American invasion of Iraq, Secretary of Defense Donald Rumsfeld was asked his view of the role of "soft power" in international affairs. "I don't know what it means," he replied, perhaps trying to be witty. It proved to be literally true. The greater the preponderance of military might, the greater the need for diplomatic skill. America will in any case be resented for its power, and will be despised by some for its principles; it need not fuel resentment by hubris, arrogance, or diplomatic ineptitude. Even the United States is not powerful enough to predominate in a world of nations hostile to it. The quickest way to lose power is to bring attention to it in a way that provokes resentment. Fortunately, the arena of international public opinion is one in which the United States possesses enormous advantages, including a diverse, multinational popula-tion; an attractive, enterprising, and innovative culture; long experience in marketing, and a vast reserve of international goodwill. Wendell Willkie described the pervasive goodwill toward the United states that he found while traveling the globe in the 1940s. "As I see it," he wrote, "the existence of this reservoir [of goodwill] is the biggest political fact of our time. Ours must be used to unify the peoples of the earth in the human quest for free-dom and justice. The preservation of this reservoir of good will is a sacred responsibility. . . . For the water in this reservoir is the clean, invigorating water of freedom."[7]

The United states was the undisputed leader of the free world in the twentieth century because of what it stood *for*, not only what it stood against. Its greatness has never rested mainly upon the power of its military (which just prior to the Second World War was among the weakest of all developed nations), but upon the power of its ideas. In addition to opposing hostile and antidemocratic regimes and movements, America must more actively wage a positive campaign on behalf of democratic ideals around the world, actively supporting international institutions that foster the values of democracy, individual freedom, and tolerance.

America spends more than $400 billion each year on defense. How much are we willing to spend in order to persuade hearts and minds? If we have learned anything from the past age, it is that as much attention must be paid to winning the peace as to prevailing in war. Economic development seems to be a basic prerequisite for stable, functioning democracy, and it is in the United States' interest—and consistent with its values—to assist in the economic progress of developing nations. America already does more of this than most people know. It is the world's largest international aid donor, giving $12 billion in Official Development Assistance (ODA) in 2002, and also the largest donor of food aid, providing twice as much of such assistance as all other nations combined. In addition, America is the largest source of private international charitable giving in the world; the largest donor to international development institutions; the largest contributor to AIDS and other global health projects; and the largest source of private capital to developing nations.

We can do even more. On the threshold of a new era, the time seems right for a bold new Marshall Plan. Imagine what could be accomplished with a foreign assistance budget that was *10 percent* of military spending. That is not an unreasonable figure. Also Washington can do more to disseminate the American perspective abroad, and to let people know the good that it is already doing: in 1991, at the end of the Cold War, the U.S. State Department had a paltry 2,500 "public diplomacy" officers around the world. By 2003 the figure had been slashed to half that number. Washington spent only about $1 billion annually on all public diplomacy and international broadcasting—roughly equal to the amount spent by Britain or France.[8] Private corporations already know that public relations is no place to scrimp; government must learn this, too.

Though American power attracts envy and resentment, that power has helped create a world in which freedom and democracy are more widespread than ever before. Woodrow Wilson said that American mothers who had lost sons in France would come to him and tearfully say "God bless you, Mr. President." Why should mothers bless the man who had ordered their sons to be sent overseas to fight and die in distant lands? "Why should they weep upon my hand and call down the blessings of God upon me? Because they believe that their boys died for something that vastly transcends any of the immediate and palpable objects of war. They believe, and they rightly believe, that their sons saved the liberty of the world."[9]

A review of the United States' role in the world becomes, implicitly, a brief for active involvement and against a return to isolation. Rooted in a notion of democratic polity and individual liberty, Americans have genuinely believed that certain rights are "inalienable," the legitimate prerogative of all people everywhere. That belief has indeed been a kind of civic religion, "our democratic faith," as President Roosevelt described it in rallying the nation against fascism. The American struggle to foster freedom in the twentieth century, to make the world safe for democracy, has not been an act of narrow self-interest, but a genuine effort to share the gift of liberty with mankind.

"There is a possibility I won't return," Gunnery Sergeant Carl Goldman wrote to his parents during the Second World War. "I was not forced to go to gunnery school and even after I arrived overseas I could have gotten off combat had I chosen to do so. If after this terrible war is over, the world emerges a saner place to live; if all nationalities are treated equal; pogroms and persecutions halted, then I'm glad I gave my efforts with thousands of others for such a cause."[10] Goldman was killed in that struggle.

The American struggle to advance liberty was, as British prime minister Herbert Asquith said of America's entry into the First World War, "one of the most disinterested acts in history." And in the twentieth century America really did make the world safe for democracy. It defeated global fascism and global communism, discredited authoritarianism, and put humanity on a path of unprecedented cooperation, prosperity, and liberty. The age of American paramountcy, now waning, has been an age of unprecedented human progress.

Notes

Introduction

1. "Report Says Schools Are Unfair to America," cnn.com. September 9, 2003.
2. "Democracy: Teach It," The Albert Shanker Institute, shankerinstitute .org., September 9, 2003.
3. "Losing America's Memory: Historical Illiteracy in the 21st Century," Washington, DC, American Council of Trustees and Alumni, 2000.

Chapter 1

1. James Stokesbury, *A Short History of World War I*. New York: William Morrow, 1981, p. 12.
2. Keith Robbin, *The First World War*. Oxford: Oxford University Press, 1993, p. 85.
3. Stokesbury, 1981, p. 34.
4. Robert L. O'Connell, *Of Arms and Men: A History of War, Weapons and Aggression*. Oxford: Oxford University Press, 1990, p. 246.
5. Charles Callan Tansill, *America Goes to War*. Boston: Little, Brown & Co., 1938, p. 464.
6. Alan Palmer, *Victory, 1918*. New York: Atlantic Monthly Press, 2000, p. 94.
7. Tansill, 1938, p. 643.
8. Stokesbury, 1981, p. 220.
9. John Keegan, *The First World War*. New York: Alfred A. Knopf, 1999, p. 372.
10. Woodrow Wilson, "War Message to Congress," April 2, 1917, in Richard Heffner (ed), *A Documentary History of the United States*. New York: Mentor, 1963, pp. 238–43.
11. Frederick S. Calhoun, *Power and Principle: Armed Intervention in Wilsonian Foreign Policy*. Kent, OH: Kent State University Press, 1986, p. 157.

12. John Bach McMaster, *The United States in the World War*. 2 vols. New York: D. Appleton, 1929, p. 360.

13. Ibid., pp. 360–61.

14. Ibid., p. 361.

15. Ibid., p. 22.

16. Ibid., vol. 2. pp. 76–84.

17. "Letters," from Lloyd Staley to Mary, July 18, 1918. http:www.u.arizona.edu/~rstaley/wwlettr1.htm

18. Woodrow Wilson, Speech Delivered to Joint Session of Congress, January 8, 1918, in Richard N. Currant et al., (eds), *Words That Made America*. Boston: Little, Brown & Co., 1972, pp. 345–48.

19. Jan Willem Nordholt, *Woodrow Wilson: A Life for Peace* (tr. Herbert Rowen). Berkeley and Los Angeles: University of California Press, 1991, p. 251.

20. Ibid., p. 262.

21. Palmer, 2000, p. 89.

22. Robert Asprey, *At Belleau Wood*. Denton, TX: University of North Texas Press, 1996, p. 347.

23. John Terraine, *The Great War, 1914–1918*. New York: Macmillan, 1965, p. 274.

24. Stokesbury, 1981, p. 222.

25. Ibid.

26. Terraine, 1965, p. 300.

27. Edward M. Coffman, *The War to End All Wars*. New York: Oxford University Press, 1968, p. 4.

28. McMaster, 1929, p. 432.

29. Ibid., p. 95.

30. Asprey, 1996, p. 97.

31. Ibid., p. 14.

32. Asprey, 1996, p. 224.

33. American Battle Monuments Commission, American Armies and Battlefields in Europe. Washington, DC: U.S. Govt. Printing Office, 1938, p. 31.

34. Laurence Stallings, *The Doughboys*. New York: Harper & Row, 1963, p. 160.

35. Keegan, 1999, p. 411.

36. Stallings, 1963, p. 38.

37. Palmer, 2000, pp. 251–52.

38. McMaster, 1929, vol. 2, p. 254.

39. Ibid., p. 262.

40. Michael Mandelbaum, *The Ideas That Conquered the World*. New York: Public Affairs, 2002, p. 17.

41. Ibid., p. 42.

42. Richard D. Heffner (ed), *A Documentary History of the United States*. New York: Mentor, 1963, pp. 243–48.

Chapter 2

1. Robert Leckie, *Delivered from Evil*. New York: Harper & Row, 1987, p. 359.

2. Charles Bracelon Flood, *Hitler: Path to Power*. Boston: Houghton Mifflin, 1989, p. 312.

3. Joachim C. Fest, *Hitler* (tr. Richard & Clara Winston). New York: Reynal & Hitchcock, 1973, p. 161.

4. William Shirer, *The Rise and Fall of the Third Reich*. New York: Simon & Schuster, 1960, p. 76.

5. Henry Ashby Turner, *Hitler's Thirty Days to Power*. Reading, MA: Addison Wesley, 1996, p. 9.

6. Paul Johnson, *Modern Times*. New York: HarperCollins, 1991, p. 285.

7. Ibid., p. 298.

8. Shirer, 1960, p. 208.

9. Ibid., pp. 233–34.

10. Norman Stone, *Hitler*. Boston: Little, Brown & Co., 1980, pp. 50–51.

11. Johnson, 1991, p. 321.

12. Shirer, 1960, p. 420.

13. Martin Gilbert, *The Second World War*. New York: Henry Holt, 1989, p. 91.

14. John Keegan, *The Second World War*. New York: Viking Press, 1990, p. 74.

15. Winston Churchill, *The Second World War*. Boston: Houghton Mifflin, 1949, p. 178.

16. Robert Aron, *The Vichy Regime*. New York: Macmillan, 1958, p. 116.

17. Ibid., p. 157.

18. John Lukacs, *The Last European War: September 1939–December 1941*. Garden City, NY: Anchor Press, 1976, p. 390.

19. Robert O. Paxton, *Vichy France*. New York: Alfred A. Knopf, 1972, pp. 38–39.

20. Gilbert, 1989, p. 129.

21. Michael Marrus & Robert O. Paxton, *Vichy France and the Jews*. New York: Basic Books, 1981, p. 3.

22. Paxton, 1972, p. 178.

23. Marrus & Paxton, 1981, p. 214.

24. Aron, 1958, p. 317.

25. Ibid., pp. 315–16.

26. Paxton, 1972, p. 144.

27. Aron, 1958, pp. 214–15.

28. Laurence Thompson, *1940*. New York: William Morrow, 1966, p. 178.

29. Fest, 1973, p. 648.

30. Lukacs, 1976, p. 141.

31. Ibid., p. 140.

32. Fest, 1973, p. 651.

33. Lukacs, 1976, p. 501.

34. Thompson, 1966, pp. 177–79.

35. Robert A. Divine, *Eisenhower and the Cold War*. Oxford: Oxford University Press, 1965, pp. 65–66.

36. Warren F. Kimball, *The Most Unsordid Act*. Baltimore: Johns Hopkins University Press, 1969, pp. 17–18.

37. Joseph P. Lash, *Roosevelt and Churchill, 1939–1941*. New York: W. W. Norton, 1976, p. 76.

38. Ibid., p. 85.

39. Kimball, 1969, pp. 28–29.

40. Divine, 1965, p. 73.

41. Philip Goodhart, *Fifty Ships that Saved the World*. New York: Doubleday, 1965, p. 27.

42. William L. Langer & S. Everett Gleason, *The Undeclared War: 1940–1941*. New York: Harper & Brothers, 1953, p. 194.

43. Geoffrey Perrett, *Days of Sadness, Years of Triumph*. New York: Coward, McMann & Geoghan, 1973, p. 40.

44. Goodhart, 1965, p. 26.

45. Lash, 1976, p. 198.

46. Churchill, 1949, p. 188.

47. Ibid., p. 401.

48. Divine, 1965, p. 88.

49. Kimball, 1969, pp. 57–58.

50. Ibid., p. 70.

51. Goodhart, 1965, pp. 181–83.

52. Churchill, 1949, pp. 408–9.

53. Perrett, 1973, p. 62.

54. A. Russell Buchanan, *The United States and World War II*. New York: Harper & Row, 1964, p. 15.

55. Divine, 1965, p. 101.

56. Langer & Gleason, 1953, p. 233.

57. Franklin Roosevelt, Message to Congress, January 6, 1941, *Congressional Record*, 77th Congress, 1st Session, lxxxvii, part 1, pp. 45–47.

58. Kimball, 1969, p. 150.

59. Ibid., p. 191.

60. Langer & Gleason, 1953, pp. 282–84.

61. Kimball, 1969, p. 229.

62. Divine, 1965, p. 143.

63. Lash, 1976, p. 418.

64. Ibid., p. 422.

65. Ibid., p. 492.

66. Adolf Hitler, *Mein Kampf* (tr. Alvin Johnson). New York: Reynal & Hitchcock, 1939, p. 399.

67. Leckie, 1987, p. 625.

68. Churchill, 1950, p. 608.

69. William L. O'Neill, *A Democracy At War*. Cambridge: Cambridge University Press, 1993, p. 106.

70. Shirer, 1960, p. 873.

71. Saul Friedlander, *Prelude to Downfall: Hitler and the United States, 1939–1941* (tr. Aline & Alexander Werth). New York: Alfred A. Knopf, 1967, p. 308.

72. Churchill, 1950, p. 608.

73. O'Neill, 1993, p. 106.

74. Buchanan, 1964, p. 125.

75. Leckie, 1987, p. 617.

76. Perrett, 1973, pp. 232–33.

77. O'Neill, 1993, pp. 130–31.

78. Ibid., pp. 136–37.

79. R. A. C. Parker, *The Second World War: A Short History*. Oxford: Oxford University Press, 1989, p. 131.

80. John Jeffries, *Wartime America*. Chicago: Ivan R. Dee, 1996, pp. 44–46.

81. O'Neill, 1993, p. 218.

82. Leckie, 1987, p. 623.

83. Jeffries, 1996, pp. 54–55.

84. D. Clayton James & Anne Sharp Wells, *From Pearl Harbor to V-J Day*. Chicago: Ivan R. Dee, 1998, p. 19.

85. Ibid.

86. Keegan, 1990, p. 218.

87. Hart, 1970, p. 384.

88. James & Wells, 1995, p. 49.

89. Buchanan, 1964, p. 148.

90. O'Neill, 1993, pp. 168–69.

91. Rick Atkinson, *An Army At Dawn*. New York: Henry Holt, 2002, pp. 74–77.

92. Ibid., p. 99.

93. George F. Howe, *Northwest Africa: Seizing the Initiative in the West*. Washington, DC: Center of Military History, United States Army, 1991, p. 277.

94. Charles Whiting, *Kasserine*. New York: Stein & Day, 1984, p. 117.

95. Ernie Pyle, *Here Is Your War*. New York: Henry Holt, 1943, p. 282.

96. Atkinson, 2002, p. 537.

97. Ibid., p. 1.

98. Albert N. Garland & Howard McGraw Smyth, *Sicily and the Surrender of Italy*. Washington, DC: Office of the Chief of Military History, Department of the Army, 1965, p. 52.

99. Stokesbury, 1980, p. 292.

100. Leckie, 1987, p. 535.

101. Fred Sheehan, *Anzio: Epic of Bravery*. Norman: University of Oklahoma Press, 1964, p. 217.

102. Parker, 1989, p. 195.

103. Andrew Carroll (ed.), *War Letters*. New York: Scribner, 2001, pp. 245–46.

104. Carlo D'Este, *Decision in Normandy*. New York: E. P. Dutton, 1983, pp. 108–9.

105. Ibid., p. 110.

106. John Toland, *The Last 100 Days*. New York: Random House, 1966, p. 45.

107. Carlo D'Este, *Patton: A Genius for War*. New York: HarperCollins, 1995, pp. 671–72.

108. Stephen Ambrose, *Citizen Soldiers*. New York: Simon & Schuster, 1997, p. 197.

109. Buchanan, 1964, p. 439.

110. Ibid., p. 497.

111. Toland, 1966, p. 60.

112. Ibid., p. 61.

113. D'Este, 1995, p. 720.

114. Patrick O'Donnell, *Beyond Valor*. New York: Free Press, 2001, p. 325.

115. John Ray, *The Second World War*. London: Cassell, 1999, p. 265.

116. Arthur Schlesinger Jr., "Did FDR Betray the Jews? Or Did He Do More Than Anyone Else to Save Them?" in Verne Newton (ed), *FDR and the Holocaust*. New York: St. Martin's Press, 1996, p. 161.

117. Marrus & Paxton, 1981, p. 348.

118. Martin Gilbert, *Never Again*. London: Universe, 2000, p. 77.

119. Michael Beschloss, *The Conquerors*. New York: Simon & Schuster, 2002, p. 59.

120. Ibid., p. 64.

121. Ibid., p. 66.

122. Richard Levy, "The Bombing of Auschwitz Revisited: A Critical Analysis," in Newton (ed), 1996, p. 262.

123. Ibid.

124. Ibid., p. 64.

125. John Wilhelm, "The Masters Buy Their Slaves," in Jack Stenbuck (ed), *Typewriter Battalion*. New York: William Morrow, 1995, p. 321.

126. Richard Courtney, *Normandy to the Bulge: An American GI in Europe During World War II*. Carbondale: Southern Illinois University Press, 1997, p. 123.

127. Ibid., p. 256.

128. Hitler, 1939, p. 123.

129. Stone, 1980, p. 130.

130. Louise Young, *Japan's Total Empire*. Berkeley and Los Angeles: University of California Press, 1998, pp. 29–30.

131. Ibid., p. 27.

132. Paul Manning, *Hirohito: The War Years*. New York: Dodd, Mead & Co., 1986, pp. 25–26.

133. Parker, 1989, p. 83.

134. Edwin P. Hoyt, *Japan's War*. New York: McGraw Hill, 1986, p. 197.

135. Manning, 1986, p. 28.

136. John Costello, *The Pacific War*. New York: Rawson Wade Publishers, 1981, p. 81.

137. Leckie, 1987, p. 311.

138. Saburo Ienaga, *The Pacific War*. New York: Pantheon Books, 1978, p. 141.

139. Ibid., pp. 263–67.

140. Ibid., p. 270.

141. Ibid., p. 211.

142. Dan van der Vat, *The Pacific Campaign*. New York: Simon & Schuster, 1991, p. 170.

143. Mitsuo Fuchida & Masatake Okumiya, *Midway*. Annapolis: U.S. Naval Institute, 1955, p. 178.

144. Eric Bergerud, *Touched with Fire*. New York: Penguin Books, 1996, p. 500.

145. Ronald Spector, *Eagle Against the Sun*. New York: Free Press, 1985, p. 264.

146. Ibid., p. 332.

147. John W. Dower, *Embracing Defeat*. New York: W. W. Norton, 1986, pp. 207–8.

148. Ibid., p. 290.

149. Ienaga, 1978, p. 155.

150. Ibid., p. 9.

151. Ibid.

152. Dower, 1986, p. 47.

153. Laurence Rees, *Horror in the East*. Cambridge: DaCapo Press, 2001, p. 76.

154. Edward Frederick Langley, Lord Russell, *The Knights of Bushido*. London: Military Book Club, 1958, p. 261.

155. Sheldon Harris, *Factories of Death*. London: Routledge, 1994, p. 70.

156. O'Neill, 1993, p. 293.

157. Spector, 1986, p. 495.

158. Bill D. Ross, *Iwo Jima*. New York: Vanguard Press, 1985, p. 150.

159. Ray, 1999, p. 294.

160. George Feifer, *The Battle of Okinawa*. Guilford, CT: Lyons Press, 2001, p. 411.

161. Ibid.

162. Ibid.

163. O'Neill, 1993, pp. 420–21.

164. Henry Berry, *Semper Fi, Mac*. New York: Berkeley Books, 1982, p. 348.

165. Carroll, (ed), 2001, p. 319.

166. Perrett, 1973, p. 196.

167. Wendell Willkie, "One World," in Currant et al. (eds), 1972, p. 451.

168. Ibid., p. 459.

Chapter 3

1. Paul Johnson, *A History of the American People*. New York: HarperCollins, 1999, p. 808.

2. Edgar McInnis et al., *The Shaping of Postwar Germany*. Toronto: J. M. Dent & Sons, 1960, p. 38.

3. Eugene Davidson, *The Death and Life of Germany*. New York: Alfred A. Knopf, 1961, p. 9.

4. Michael Beschloss, *The Conquerors*. New York: Simon & Schuster, 2002, p. 272.

5. Harold Zink, *The United States in Germany*. Princeton, NJ: Van Nostrand, 1957, pp. 326–27.

6. Ibid., p. 236.

7. Davidson, 1961, p. 274.

8. Beschloss, 2002, p. 277.

9. James Byrne, Speech delivered at Stuttgart, Germany, September 6, 1946; in Julia Johnsen (ed), *The Dilemma of Postwar Germany*. New York: H. W. Wilson, 1948, pp. 12–23.

10. Beschloss, 2002, p. 277.

11. Ibid.

12. Harry Bayard Price, *The Marshall Plan and its Meaning*. Ithaca: Cornell University Press, 1955, p. 34.

13. Robert Donovan, *The Second Victory*. New York: Madison Books, 1987, p. 31.

14. Price, 1955, p. 31.

15. Ibid., p. 30.

16. Daniel Yergin and Joseph Stanislaw, *The Commanding Heights*. New York: Touchstone, 1998, p. 15.

17. Charles Marshall, "The National Interest," in Robert A. Goldwin et al. (eds), *Readings in American Foreign Policy*. New York: Oxford University Press, 1959, p. 665.

18. Price, 1955, p. 38.

19. Charles L. Mee, *The Marshall Plan*. New York: Simon & Schuster, 1984, p. 140.

20. Price, 1955, p. 53.

21. Mee, 1984, p. 239.

22. Price, 1955, pp. 52–53.

23. "Ideas For Europe," editorial, *Life*, July 21, 1947, in Summers (ed), 1948, p. 219.

24. Price, 1955, p. 60.

25. Mee, 1984, p. 241.

26. Sen. Arthur Vandenberg, Speech on the Economic Assistance Act, *Congressional Record*, March 1, 1948, pp. 1981–86.

27. Price, 1955, p. 85.

28. John Orne, "The Original Megapolicy," in John D. Montgomery and Denis A. Rondinelli (eds), *Great Policies*. Westport: Praeger, 1995, pp. 15–16.

29. Price, 1955, pp. 116–17.

30. Ibid., p. 117.

31. Ibid., p. 399.

32. Ibid., p. 119.

33. Theodore Wilson, *The Marshall Plan, 1947–1951*. New York: Foreign Policy Association, 1977, p. 47.

34. Ibid., p. 47.

35. Donovan, 1987, p. 120.

36. Mee, 1984, p. 257.

37. Konrad Adenauer, "Germany Today and Tomorrow," in Grant S. McClellan (ed), *The Two Germanies*. New York: H. W. Wilson, 1959, p. 42.

38. Davidson, 1961, p. 217.

39. McInnis et al., 1960, p. 123.

40. Davidson, 1961, p. 221.

41. McInnis, 1960, p. 132.

42. Stephen E. Ambrose, *Citizen Soldiers*. New York: Simon & Schuster, 1997, p. 473.

43. Davidson, 1961, p. 270.

44. Price, 1955, p. 412.

45. John Curtis Perry, *Beneath the Eagle's Wings*. New York: Dodd, Mead & Co., 1980, p. 28.

46. Ibid.

47. Russell Brines, *MacArthur's Japan*. Philadelphia: J. B. Lippincott, 1948, p. 21.

48. Walt Sheldon, *The Honorable Conquerors*. New York: Macmillan, 1965, p. 39.

49. Kazuo Kawai, *Japan's American Interlude*. Chicago: University of Chicago Press, 1960, p. 1.

50. John W. Dower, *Embracing Defeat*. New York: W. W. Norton, 1999, pp. 485–86.

51. Kawai, 1960, p. 32.

52. Sheldon, 1965, p. 40.

53. Kawai, 1960, p. 11.

54. Theodore Cohen, *Remaking Japan*. New York: Free Press, 1987, p. 144.

55. Brines, 1948, p. 146.

56. Bowen C. Dees, *The Allied Occupation and Japan's Economic Miracle*. Surrey: Curzon Press, 1997, p. 285.

57. Arnold Brackman, *The Other Nuremberg*. New York: William Morrow, 1987, p. 99.

58. Kawai, 1960, p. 173.

59. Perry, 1980, p. 164.

60. Hugh Borton, "Past Limitations and the Future of Democracy in Japan," in Elizabeth Velen & Victor A. Velen (eds), *The New Japan*. New York: H. W. Wilson, 1958, p. 53.

61. Ray A. Moore & Donald Robinson, *Partners for Democracy*. Oxford: Oxford University Press, 2002, pp. 148–49.

62. Ibid., p. 149.

63. Ibid.

64. Dower, 1999, p. 225.

65. Cohen, 1987, p. 53.

66. Kawai, 1960, p. 14.

67. Sheldon, 1965, p. 127.

68. Rinjiro Sodei (ed), *Dear General MacArthur* (tr. Shizue Matsuda). Lanham, MD: Rowman & Littlefield, 2001, p. 22.

69. Ibid., p. 29.

70. Moore & Robinson, 2002, p. 51.

71. Ibid., p. 77.

72. Dower, 1999, p. 392.

73. Sheldon, 1965, p. 71.

74. Dower, 1999, pp. 403–4.

75. Ibid., p. 45.

76. Perry, 1980, p. 114.

77. Brines, 1948, p. 145.

78. Edwin O. Reischauer, *Japan: The Story of a Nation*. New York: McGraw Hill, 1990, p. 204.

79. Dower, 1999, pp. 90–91.

80. Kawai, 1960, p. 135.

81. Cohen, 1987, p. 145.

82. Dower, 1999, p. 94.

83. Cohen, 1987, p. 145.

84. Perry, 1980, p. 117.

85. Ibid., pp. 117–18.

86. Dower, 1999, pp. 533–34.

87. Ibid., p. 169.

88. Dees, 1997, p. 146.

89. Ibid., p. 197.

90. Ibid., pp. 230–35.

91. Cohen, 1987, p. 439.

92. Kawai, 1960, p. 179.

93. "Made In Japan: A New Record," *Business Week*, 1955, in Velen & Velen (eds), 1958, pp. 106–7.

94. Robert Trumbull, "Japan Regains Place as Industrial Giant," in Velen & Velen (eds), 1958, p. 95.

95. Reischauer, 1990, p. 225.

96. "Consider Japan," *The Economist*, September 1, 1962, p. 793.

97. Cohen, 1987, p. 464.

98. Sheldon, 1965, p. x.

99. Sodei (ed), 2001, p. 27.

100. Ibid., p. 220.

101. Ibid., p. 218.

102. Ibid., p. 225.

103. Dower, 1999, p. 231.

104. Ibid., p. 229.

105. Sheldon, 1965, p. 232.

106. Sodei (ed), 2001, p. 294.

107. Richard Finn, *Winners in Peace*. Berkeley: University of California Press, 1992, p. 316.

108. Dower, 1999, pp. 66–67.

Chapter 4

1. Alfred Zimmern, *The American Road to Peace*. New York: E. P. Dutton & Co., 1953, p. 31.

2. Alf Ross, *The United Nations: Peace and Progress*. Totowa, NJ: Bedminster Press, 1966, p. 22.

3. Zimmern, 1953, pp. 175–76.

4. Daniel Cheever & H. Field Haviland, *Organizing for Peace*. Cambridge, MA: Houghton Mifflin, 1954, p. 63.

5. Clark Eichelberger, *Organizing for Peace*. New York: Harper & Row, 1977, p. 251.

6. Ibid., p. 212.

7. Eichelberger, 1977, p. 2.

8. Raymond Betts, *Decolonization*. New York: Routledge, 1998, p. 11.

9. Ibid.

10. Gaddis Smith, "The British Government and the Disposition of the German Colonies in Africa, 1914–1918," in Prosser Gifford & William Roger Louis (eds), *Britain and Germany in Africa*. New Haven: Yale University Press, 1967, p. 299.

11. Daniel Schirmer and Stephen Shalom (eds), *The Philippines Reader*. Boston: South End Press, 1987, pp. 22–23.

12. Frank Gibney, *The Pacific Century*. New York: Charles Scribner's Sons, 1992, p. 463.

13. Frances B. Cogan, *Captured*. Athens, GA: University of Georgia Press, 2000, p. 22.

14. John Bastin and Harry Benda, *A History of Modern Southeast Asia*. Englewood Cliffs, NJ: Prentice-Hall, 1968, p. 171.

15. Gibney, 1992, p. 468.

16. Zimmern, 1953, p. 123.

17. Raymond Betts, *Europe Overseas*. New York: Basic Books, 1968, p. 118.

18. Denis Judd, *Empire: The British Imperial Experience from 1765 to the Present.* New York: Basic Books, 1997, p. 319.

19. A. N. Porter, *British Imperial Policy and Decolonization, 1938–64.* New York: St. Martin's Press, 1987, p. 26.

20. Wm. Roger Louis and Ronald Robinson, "The U.S. and the End of the British Empire in Tropical Africa," in Gifford and Louis (eds), 1982, p. 33.

21. William Roger Louis, *Imperialism at Bay.* New York: Oxford University Press, 1978, p. 134.

22. Paul Orders, "Adjusting to a New Period in World History: Franklin Roosevelt and European Colonialism," in David Ryan (ed), 2000, p. 69.

23. Judd, 1997, pp. 318–19.

24. Ibid.

25. Lloyd C. Gardner, *Economic Aspects of New Deal Diplomacy,* 1971, p. 177.

26. Louis and Robinson, 1982, p. 34.

27. Louis, 1978, p. 243.

28. "Note by Lord Hailey on 'Draft Declaration by the United Nations on National Independence,'" May 5, 1943, in Porter and Stockwell (eds), 1987, p. 155.

29. Henry Kissinger, *Diplomacy.* New York: Simon & Schuster, 1994, p. 408.

30. Orders, 2000, p. 72.

31. Louis, 1978, p. 27.

32. John Toland, *The Last 100 Days.* New York: Random House, 1966, p. 63.

33. Ibid., p. 51.

34. Robert Leckie, *Delivered from Evil.* New York: Harper & Row, 1987, pp. 842–43.

35. Raymond Betts, *Uncertain Dimensions.* Minneapolis: University of Minnesota Press, 1985, p. 191.

36. Betts, 1964, p. 129.

37. Raymond Betts, *Tricouleur.* London: Gordon & Cremonesi, 1978, p. 134.

38. John Springhall, *Decolonization Since 1945.* New York: Palgrave, 2001, p. 63.

39. Louis and Robinson, 1982, pp. 46–47.

40. Ibid., p. 47.

41. Betts, 1978, p. 17.

42. Ibid., p. 37.

43. Ibid., p. 41.

44. Springhall, 2001, p. 156.

45. D. A. Low, "The Asian Mirror to Tropical Africa's Independence," in Gifford and Louis (eds), 1982, p. 2.

46. David Wainhouse, *Remnants of Empire.* New York: Harper & Row, 1964, p. 14.

47. Ibid., p. 13.

48. Ibid., p. 10.

9. Alfred E. Eckes, *A Search for Solvency.* Austin: University of Texas Press, 1975, p. 7.

50. A. G. Kenwood and A. L. Lougheed, *The Growth of the International Economy.* London: George Allen & Unwin, 1983, p. 215.

51. Eckes, 1975, p. 19.

52. Brink Lindsey, *Against the Dead Hand.* New York: John Wiley & Sons, 2002, p. 63.

53. Eckes, 1975, p. 4.

54. Ibid., p. 39.

55. Ibid., p. 38.

56. Jim Bishop, *FDR's Last Year*. New York: William Morrow, 1974, p. 54.

57. James MacGregor Burns, *Roosevelt: The Soldier of Freedom*. New York: Harcourt Brace Jovanovich, 1970, p. 514.

58. Eckes, 1975, p. 167.

59. Ibid., p. 173.

60. Ibid., p. 174.

61. Ibid., p. 181.

62. Ibid.

63. Ibid., p. 201.

64. Gary Burtless et al., *Globaphobia*. Washington, DC: Brookings Institution Press, 1998, pp. 29–31.

65. Ibid., p. 4.

66. Ibid., p. 30.

67. Ibid., p. 68.

68. Ibid., p. 64.

69. President Harry S Truman, Inaugural Address, January 20, 1949, in Walter Daniels (ed), *The Point Four Program*. New York: H. W. Wilson, 1951, p. 10.

70. Ibid., p. 11.

71. Richard Fagley, October 15, 1949, in Daniels (ed), 1951, p. 45.

72. Paul Johnson, *A History of the American People*. New York: Harper Collins, 1999, p. 820.

73. "Report to the President by the International Development Advisory Board," March 1951, in Daniels (ed), 1951, p. 67.

74. Henry Hazlitt, "Foreign Investment versus Foreign Aid," 1970, in Joan Kennedy Taylor (ed), *Free Trade: Necessary Foundation for World Peace*. New York: Foundation for Economic Education, 1986, p. 127.

75. Ibid., p. 125.

76. Johnson, 1999, p. 821.

Chapter 5

1. Howard M. Sachar, *A History of Israel*. New York: Alfred A. Knopf, 2001, p. 167.

2. Mitchell G. Bard, *Myths and Facts*. Chevy Chase, MD: American Israeli Cooperative Enterprise, 2001, p. 44.

3. Baylis Thomas, *How Israel Was Won*. Lanham, MD: Lexington Books, 1999, p. 22.

4. Martin Gilbert, *Israel: A History*. New York: William Morrow, 1998, p. 23.

5. Michael Cohen, *Truman and Israel*. Berkeley: University of California Press, 1990, p. 112.

6. Michael T. Benson, *Harry S Truman and the Founding of Israel*. Westport, CT: Praeger, 1997, p. 187.

7. Cohen, 1990, pp. 84–86.

8. Ibid., p. 93.

9. Sachar, 2001, p. 289.

10. Benson, 1997, pp. 136–45.

11. Cohen, 1990, p. 170.

12. Ibid.

13. Ibid., p. 172.

14. Benson, 1990, p. 188.

15. Ibid., p. 167.

16. Sachar, 2001, p. 312.

17. Gilbert, 1998, p. 23.

18. Ibid., p. 155.

19. Paul Johnson, *A History of the Jews*. New York: HarperCollins, 1987, p. 530.

20. Michael Oren, *Six Days of War*. New York: Ballantine Books, 2003, p. 8.

21. Bard, 2001, p. 73.

22. Chester Cooper, *The Lion's Last Roar*. New York: Harper & Row, 1978, p. 80.

23. Paul Johnson, *The Suez War*. New York: Greenberg, 1957, pp. 43–46.

24. Ibid., pp. 55–56.

25. Cooper, 1978, p. 115.

26. Ibid., p. 124.

27. Anthony Eden, *The Suez Crisis of 1956*. Boston: Beacon Press, 1960, p. 185.

28. Johnson, 1957, pp. 80–82.

29. William Polk, *The United States and the Arab World*. Cambridge: Harvard University Press, 1969, p. 277.

30. Ibid., p. 276.

31. Herman Finer, *Dulles Over Suez*. Chicago: Quadrangle Books, 1964, p. 377.

32. Eden, 1960, p. 183.

33. Polk, 1969, p. 277.

34. Cooper, 1978, p. 189.

35. Johnson, 1957, p. 115.

36. Benny Morris, *Righteous Victims*. New York: Alfred A. Knopf, 1999, p. 297.

37. Ibid., pp. 298–99.

38. Morris, 1999, p. 299.

39. Cooper, 1978, p. 214.

40. Polk, 1969, p. 280.

41. Hal Kosut, *Israel and the Arabs: The June 1967 War*. New York: Facts on File, 1968, p. 10.

42. Oren, 2003, p. 16.

43. Ibid., p. 193.

44. Gilbert, 1998, p. 55.

45. Yossi Melman & Dan Raviv, *Friends in Deed: Inside the U.S.-Israel Alliance*. New York: Hyperion, 1994, pp. 110–11.

46. Ibid., p. 112.

47. Bard, 2001, p. 360.

48. Kosut, 1968, pp. 49–50.

49. Oren, 2003, p. 63.

50. Ibid., p. 137.

51. Oren, 2003, p. 100.

52. Kosut, 1968, p. 150.

53. Oren, 2003, p. 326.

54. Gilbert, 1998, p. 80.

55. William B. Quandt, *Decade of Decisions*. Berkeley: University of California Press, 1977, p. 83.

56. David Schoenbaum, *The United States and the State of Israel*. Oxford: Oxford University Press, 1993, p. 173.

57. Gilbert, 1998, p. 85.

58. Ibid., p. 85.

59. Gilbert, 1998, p. 82.

60. Walter J. Boyne, *The Two O'Clock War*. New York: St. Martin's Press, 2002, p. 58.

61. Ibid., p. 61.

62. Ibid., p. 105.

63. Lester A. Sobel (ed), *Israel and the Arabs: The October 1973 War*. New York: Facts On File, 1974, p. 104.

64. Morris, 1999, p. 429.

65. Ibid.

66. Nadav Safran, *Israel: The Embattled Ally*. Cambridge, MA: Belknap Press, 1978, p. 575.

67. Sobel (ed), 1974, p. 135.

68. Boyne, 2002, p. 167.

69. Jimmy Carter, *Keeping Faith*. New York: Bantam Books, 1982, p. 273.

70. Ibid., p. 223.

71. Ibid., p. 220.

72. Sachar, 2001, p. 859.

73. Thomas, 1999, p. 243.

74. Morris, 1999, p. 577.

75. William B. Quandt, *Peace Process*. Washington, DC: Brookings Institution Press, 2001, p. 275.

76. Ibid., p. 292.

77. Ibid., p. 119.

78. Arthur H. Blair, *At War in the Gulf*. College Station: Texas A&M University Press, 1992, p. 78.

79. Blair, 1992, p. 117.

80. Morris, 1999, p. 613.

81. Sachar, 2001, p. 1000.

82. Http://www.news.bbc.co.uk/2/hi/middle_east/2956424.stm

83. Claus Christian Malzahn, "Could George W. Bush Be Right?" *Der Spiegel*, http://service/spiegel.de/cache/international.

Chapter 6

1. Jonathan Spence, *The Search For Modern China*. New York: W. W. Norton, 1990, pp. 282, 382.

2. Michael Schaller, *The United States and China in the Twentieth Century*. Oxford: Oxford University Press, 1990, p. 53.

3. Ibid., p. 71.

4. Jonathan Spence, *Mao Zedong*. New York: Viking, 1999, p. 101.

5. Warren Cohen, *America's Response to China*. New York: John Wiley & Sons, 1971, p. 159.

6. Ernest May, *The Truman Administration and China*. New York: J. B. Lippincott, 1975, p. 10.

7. Ibid., p. 8.

8. Ibid., p. 20.

9. May, 1975, p. 21.

10. Richard Thornton, *China: A Political History*. Boulder, CO: Westview Press, 1982, p. 117.

11. Ross Terrill, *Mao: A Biography*. New York: Harper & Row, 1980, p. 191.

12. *Congressional Quarterly*, 1980, p. 84.

13. Ibid., p. 86.

14. Mao Zedong, "The Peasant Movement in Hunan," March 1927, in Franz Schurmann and Orville Schell, *Republican China*. New York: Random House, 1967, vol. 2, p. 131.

15. Gordon Chang, *Friends and Enemies*. Stanford: Stanford University Press, 1990, p. 13.

16. Schaller, 1990, p. 121.

17. Dean Acheson, "Letter of Transmittal Accompanying Report on United States Relations with China," July 30, 1949, in Schurmann and Schell, 1967, p. 370.

18. Chang, 1990, p. 13.

19. Terrill, 1980, p. 214.

20. Spence, 1990, p. 517.

21. Ibid., p. 121.

22. Kate Saunders, *Eighteen Layers of Hell*. London: Cassell, 1996, p. 2.

23. Robert Lifton, "Brainwashing in China," in Schurmann and Schell, vol. 3, 1957, p. 137.

24. Spence, 1990, p. 130.

25. William Stueck, *The Korean War*. Princeton: Princeton University Press, 1995, p. 20.

26. Max Hastings, *The Korean War*. New York: Touchstone, 1987, p. 41.

27. Joseph C. Goulden, *Korea: The Untold Story of the War*. New York: Times Books, 1982, p. 33.

28. Stueck, 1995, p. 31.

29. Jeremy Isaacs & Taylor Downing, *Cold War*. Boston: Little Brown, 1998, p. 87.

30. Stueck, 1995, pp. 10–11.

31. Robert J. Dvorchak, *Battle for Korea*. Pittsburgh: Combined Publishing, 1993, p. 9.

32. Clark Eichelberger, *UN: The First Twenty Years*. New York: Harper & Row, 1965, p. 21.

33. Hastings, 1987, p. 70.

34. Eichelberger, 1965, p. 59.

35. Hastings, 1987, p. 61.

36. Ibid.

37. Richard Whelan, *Drawing the Line*. Boston: Little, Brown, 1990, p. 149.

38. Callum MacDonald, *Korea: The War Before Vietnam*. New York: Free Press, 1986, p. 38.

39. Hastings, 1987, p. 83.

40. Ibid., p. 90.

41. Chong Suk Dickman, "Thank You," in Linda Granfield (ed), *I Remember Korea*. New York: Clarion Books, 2003, pp. 74–75.

42. Goulden, 1982, p. 165.

43. Hastings, 1987, pp. 95–96.

44. Shu Guang Zhang, *Mao's Military Romanticism.* Lawrence: University of Kansas Press, 1995, p. 63.

45. Ibid., p. 79.

46. Spence, 1999, p. 116.

47. Jian Chen, *China's Road to the Korean War*. New York: Columbia University Press, 1994, pp. 190–92.

48. Ibid., pp. 192–93.

49. Dvorchak, 1993, p. 122.

50. Clay Blair, *The Forgotten War*. New York: Anchor Books, 1987, p. 534.

51. Ibid., p. 164.

52. Stueck, 1995, pp. 145–46.

53. Ibid., p. 168.

54. Stueck, 1995, pp. 260–62.

55. Goulden, 1982, p. 622.

56. Harry Truman, *Years of Trial and Hope*. New York: Doubleday & Co., 1956, p. 488.

57. Whelan, 1990, p. 347.

58. Ibid., p. 357.

59. Stueck, 1995, p. 61.

60. Roderick MacFarquhar, *Sino-American Relations, 1949–71*. New York: Praeger, 1974, p. 188.

61. Ibid., p. 222.

62. Edward Rice, *Mao's Way*. Berkeley and Los Angeles: University of California Press, 1972, p. 147.

63. Spence, 1990, p. 579.

64. Rice, 1972, p. 164.

65. Jasper Becker, *Hungry Ghosts*. New York: Henry Holt, 1998, p. 113.

66. MacFarquhar, 1984, p. 330.

67. Becker, 1998, p. 262.

68. Ibid.

69. Isaacs & Downing, 1998, p. 258.

70. Rice, 1972, p. 324.

71. *Congressional Quarterly*, 1980, p. 180.

72. Rice, 1972, p. 349.

73. Chang, 1990, p. 274.

74. MacFarquhar (ed), 1972, p. 212.

75. Lyndon Johnson, Speech to the American Alumni Council, July 12, 1966, in MacFarquhar (ed), 1972, p. 230.

76. Chang, 1990, p. 274.

77. *Congressional Quarterly*, 1980, p. 173.

78. Richard Pipes, *Communism*. New York: Modern Library, 2001, p. 125.

79. Terrill, 2003, p. 264.

80. Schaller, 1990, p. 176.

81. Richard Nixon, Inaugural Address, January 20, 1969, in MacFarquhar (ed), 1972, p. 246.

82. Richard Nixon, "U.S. Foreign Policy for the 1970s, a Report to Congress," February 25, 1971, in MacFarquhar (ed), 1972, p. 253.

83. Richard Nixon, Television address, July 16, 1971, in MacFarquhar (ed), 1972, p. 257.

84. Schaller, 1990, p. 187.

85. Ibid., pp. 188–89.

86. Isaacs & Downing, 1998, p. 278.

87. Robert L. Suettinger, *Beyond Tiananmen.* Washington, DC: Brookings Institute Press, 2003, p. 14.

88. Jimmy Carter, Address, December 15, 1978, in *Congressional Quarterly*, 1980, p. 341.

89. Ibid., p. 207.

90. Isaacs & Downing, 1998, p. 319.

91. Samuel Huntington, *The Third Wave.* Norman: University of Oklahoma Press, 1986, p. 156.

92. *Congressional Quarterly*, 1980, p. 261.

93. Chang, 1990, pp. 144–45.

94. Ibid., p. 83.

95. Thomas B. Gold, *State and Society in the Taiwan Miracle.* Armonk, NY: M. E. Sharpe, 1986, p. 65.

96. Ibid., p. 73.

97. Ibid., p. 69.

98. Spence, 1990, p. 671.

99. Linda Chao & Ramon Myers, *The First Chinese Democracy.* Baltimore: Johns Hopkins University Press, 1998, p. 132.

100. Kongdan Oh & Ralph C. Hassig, *North Korea: Through the Looking Glass.* Washington, DC: Brookings Institution Press, 2000, p. 24.

101. Dan Oberdorfer, *The Two Koreas.* New York: Basic Books, 2001, p. 232.

102. Ibid., p. 337.

103. Oh & Hassig, 2000, p. 129.

104. Becker, 1998, p. 328.

105. Oh & Hassig, 2000, p. 25.

106. Oberdorfer, 2001, p. 361.

107. Granfield (ed), 2003, p. 76.

108. Ibid., p. 80.

109. Terrill, 2003, p. 337.

Chapter 7

1. Stephane Courtois et al., *The Black Book of Communism* (tr. Jonathan Murphy & Mark Kramer). Cambridge: Harvard University Press, 1999, p. 13.

2. Robert Conquest, *Stalin: Breaker of Nations.* New York: Penguin Books, 1991, p. 76.

3. Anne Applebaum, *Gulag.* New York: Doubleday, 2003, p. 9.

4. Alexander N. Yakovlev, *A Century of Violence in Soviet Russia* (tr. Anthony Austin). New Haven: Yale University Press, 2002, p. 20.

5. Sheila Fitzpatrick, *Everyday Stalinism*. New York: Oxford University Press, 1999, p. 29.

6. Richard Pipes, *Communism*. New York: Modern Library, 2001, pp. 46–47.

7. Ibid., p. 48.

8. Galina Ivanova, *Labor Camp Socialism* (tr. Carol Flath). Armonk, NY: M. E. Sharpe, 2000, p. 12.

9. Applebaum, 2003, pp. xvi–xx.

10. Vladislav Zubok and Constantine Pleshakov, *Inside the Kremlin's Cold War*. Cambridge: Harvard University Press, 1996, p. 25.

11. Martin McCauley, *Stalin and Stalinism*. London: Pearson, 2003, p. 104.

12. Robert C. Tucker, *Stalin in Power*. New York: W. W. Norton, 1990, p. 101.

13. Fitzpatrick, 1996, p. 48.

14. Yakovlev, 2002, p. 35.

15. McCauley, 2003, p. 39.

16. Miron Dolot, *Execution By Hunger*. New York: W. W. Norton, 1985, p. 169.

17. Edward Radzinsky, *Stalin* (tr. H. T. Willetts). New York, Anchor, 1997, p. 259.

18. Conquest, 1991, p. 163.

19. Tucker, 1990, p. 189.

20. Fitzpatrick, 1996, p. 75.

21. Robert Conquest, *The Great Terror: A Reassessment*. New York: Oxford University Press, 1990, p. 22.

22. Yakovlev, 2002, p. 20.

23. Davies, 1997, p. 38.

24. Tucker, 1990, pp. 111–12.

25. Ibid., 1990, p. 468.

26. Zbigniew Brzezinski, *The Grand Failure*. New York: Collier, 1990, p. 10.

27. McCauley, 2003, pp. 58–59.

28. Ibid., p. 59.

29. Applebaum, 2003, p. 123.

30. Conquest, 1990, p. 485.

31. Radzinsky, 1997, p. 261.

32. Nicolas Werth, "The Empire of the Camps," in Courtois et al, 1999, pp. 203–5.

33. Norman Friedman, *Conflict and Strategy in the Cold War*. Annapolis, MD: Naval Institute Press, 2000, p. 8.

34. Pipes, 2001, p. 67.

35. Brian Crozier, *The Rise and Fall of the Soviet Empire*. Roseville, CA: Prima Publishing, 1999, p. 65.

36. John Lewis Gaddis, *Strategies of Containment*. New York: Oxford University Press, 1982, p. 3.

37. Ronald E. Powaski, *The Cold War*. Oxford: Oxford University Press, 1998. pp. 60, 62,

38. John Lewis Gaddis, *We Now Know*. Oxford: Oxford University Press, 1997, p. 16.

39. Raymond Pearson, *The Rise and Fall of the Soviet Empire*. New York: Palgrave, 2002, pp. 40–41.

40. Pipes, 2001, p. 49.

41. Tucker, 1990, p. 47.

42. Gaddis, 1997, p. 21.

43. Michael Kort, *The Columbia Guide to the Cold War*. New York: Columbia University Press, 1993, p. 13.

44. Gaddis, 1997, p. 31.

45. Gaddis, 1997, p. 30.

46. Friedman, 2000, p. 52.

47. George Kennan, "The Sources of Soviet Conduct," July 1947, in Richard N. Currant et al., *Words that Made America*. Boston: Little, Brown & Co., 1972, pp. 479–89.

48. Ibid.

49. Kort, 1993, pp. 13–14.

50. Ibid., p. 14.

51. Walter LaFeber, *America, Russia and the Cold War, 1945–1992*. New York: McGraw Hill, 1993, p. 78.

52. Ibid.

53. Christopher Andrew, *For the President's Eyes Only*. New York: Harper-Collins, 1995, pp. 1–2.

54. John Ranelagh, *The Agency*. New York: Simon & Schuster, 1986, p. 27.

55. Ibid., p. 109.

56. Andrew, 1995, pp. 145–46.

57. Ranelagh, 1986, pp. 122–59.

58. Ibid., p. 144, 170.

59. Gregory Treverton, *Covert Action*. New York: Basic Books, 1987, p. 176.

60. Thomas Parrish, *Berlin in the Balance*. Reading, MA: Perseus Books, 1998, p. 331.

61. J. D. P. Dunbabin, *The Cold War: The Great Powers and Their Allies*. London: Longman, 1994, pp. 99–100.

62. Gaddis, 1997, p. 44.

63. Peter Duignan, *NATO: Its Past, Present and Future*. Stanford: Hoover Institution Press, 2000, p. 13.

64. Duignan, 2000, p. 17.

65. President Harry S. Truman, Inaugural Address, January 20, 1949, in Walter Daniels (ed), *The Point Four Program*. New York: H. W. Wilson, 1951, p. 11.

66. Powaski, 1998, p. 86.

67. Gaddis, 1997, p. 73.

68. NSC-68, Report to the President, April 7, 1950, in Edward H. Judge & John W. Langdon, *The Cold War: A History through Documents*. New York: Prentice Hall, 1999, pp. 66–67.

69. John Lukacs, *A History of the Cold War*. New York: Doubleday & Co., 1961, p. 166.

70. Courtois, 1999, p. 750.

71. Gaddis, 1997, p. 152.

72. Crozier, 1999, p. 75.

73. Harvey Klehr et al, *The Secret World of American Communism*. New Haven: Yale University Press, 1995, pp. 6–7.

74. Nikita Khrushchev, *Khrushchev Remembers*. Boston: Little, Brown, 1990, p. 194.

75. Christopher Andrew & Vasily Mitrokhin, *The Sword and the Shield*. New York: Basic Books, 2000, p. 164.

76. Conquest, 1990, p. 486.

77. Martin McCauley, *Russia, America and the Cold War*. London: Longman, 1998, p. 21.

78. Isaacs & Downing, 1998, p. 128.

79. John O. Koehler, *Stasi*. Boulder, CO: Westview Press, 1999, p. 59.

80. Christian F. Ostermann (ed), *Uprising in East Germany, 1953*. New York: Central European University Press, 2003, p. 180.

81. McCauley, 1998, p. 104.

82. Gaddis, 1982, p. 129.

83. Burton L. Kaufman, *Trade and Aid: Eisenhower's Foreign Economic Policy, 1953–1961*. Baltimore: Johns Hopkins University Press, 1982, p. 12.

84. Gaddis, 1982, p. 130.

85. Raymond Pearson, *The Rise and Fall of the Soviet Empire*. New York: Palgrave, 2002, pp. 52–53.

86. Yakovlev, 2002, p. 18.

87. Crozier, 1999, pp. 618–21.

88. Ibid.

89. Melvin J. Lasky (ed), *The Hungarian Revolution*. New York: Praeger, 1957, p. 62.

90. Department of State Bulletin, XXXVI, No. 917. January 21, 1957, pp. 83–87.

91. Brzezinski, 1990, p. 53.

92. David Painter, *The Cold War: An International History*. London: Routledge, 1999, pp. 43–44.

93. Friedman, 2000, pp. 237–38.

94. William Hyland, *The Cold War*. New York: Times Books, 1991, p. 121.

95. Gaddis, 1997, p. 183.

96. Zubok & Pleshakov, 1996, p. 208.

97. Ibid., p. 203.

98. Ibid., p. 205.

99. Theodore Sorensen, *Kennedy*. New York: Harper & Row, 1965, pp. 292–94.

100. Ibid., p. 530.

101. Gerard T. Rice, *The Bold Experiment*. Notre Dame: University of Notre Dame Press, 1985, p. 35.

102. Ibid., p. 35.

103. Ibid., p. 298.

104. Sorensen, 1965, p. 530.

105. www.usaid.gov/policy/budget/

106. Tony Smith, *America's Mission*. Princeton, NJ: Princeton University Press, 1994, p. 214.

107. Ibid., p. 217.

108. Painter, 1999, p. 63.

109. Robert M. Slusser, *The Berlin Crisis of 1961*. Baltimore: Johns Hopkins University Press , 1973, p. 20.

110. Isaacs & Downing, 1998, p. 170.

111. Slusser, 1973, p. 9.

112. Powaski, 1998, p. 140.

113. LaFeber, 1993, p. 211.

114. Ibid., p. 39.

115. Ibid., p. 652.

116. Julie Marie Bunck, *Fidel Castro and the Quest for a Revolutionary Culture in Cuba*. University Park, PA: Penn State University Press, 1994, p. 2.

117. William E. Ratliff, *Castroism and Communism in Latin America, 1959–1976*. Washington, DC: American Enterprise Institute, 1976, p. 38.

118. LaFeber, 1993, p. 212.

119. Mark White, *Missiles in Cuba*. Chicago: Ivan R. Dee, 1997, p. 40.

120. Ibid., pp. 125–26.

121. Alexander Fursenko & Timothy Naftali, "*One Hell of a Gamble*." New York: W. W. Norton, 1997, pp. 305–6.

122. Timothy Ashby, *The Bear in the Backyard*. Lexington, MA: Lexington Books, 1987, pp. 40–41.

123. Courtois et al, 1999, p. 652.

124. Ibid., p. 664.

125. Armando Valladares, *Against All Hope* (tr. Andrew Hurley). New York: Alfred A. Knopf, 1986, p. xiii.

126. Kennedy's Berlin Speech, June 26, 1963; in Judge & Langdon (eds), 1999, pp. 127–28.

127. Hyland, 1991, p. 124.

128. Sorensen, 1965, p. 570.

129. Ibid., pp. 574–75.

130. Coral Bell, *The Diplomacy of Detente*. New York: St. Martin's Press, 1977, p. 13.

131. Raymond Garthoff, *Detente and Confrontation*. Washington, DC: Brookings Institution, 1985, pp. 106–7.

132. Lloyd C. Gardner, *Approaching Vietnam*. New York: W. W. Norton, 1988, p. 14.

133. Maurice Isserman (ed), *Witness to Vietnam*. New York: Perigree, 1995, pp. 3–4.

134. George C. Herring, *America's Longest War*. Syracuse, NY: Syracuse University Press, 1996, p. 10.

135. Gardner, 1989, p. 92.

136. Ibid., p. 102.

137. Courtois, 1999, p. 567.

138. Harry G. Summers, *The Vietnam War Almanac*. Novarto, CA: Presidio Press, 1990, pp. 194–95.

139. Herring, 1996, pp. 64–5.

140. Ibid., p. 66.

141. Michael Lind, *Vietnam: The Necessary War*. New York: Touchstone, 1999, p. 195.

142. Ibid., p. 196.

143. Herring, 1996, p. 118.

144. Norman Podhoretz, *Why We Were in Vietnam*. New York: Simon & Schuster, 1982, p. 64.

145. Lind, 1999, p. 8.

146. Hyland, 1991, p. 136.

147. Ibid., p. 87.

148. Harry G. Summers, *On Strategy*. New York: Ballantine Books, 1995, p. 12.

149. Stanley Karnow, *Vietnam: A History*. New York: Viking Press, 1983, p. 329.

150. "U.S. in Asia: Is This the Dawn of a New Pacific Era?" *Newsweek*, October 31, 1966.

151. Philip B. Davidson, *Vietnam At War*. Oxford: Oxford University Press, 1991, pp. 339–41.

152. Mitchell Hall, *The Vietnam War*. London: Longman, 2000, p. 25.

153. Stephen Young, "How North Vietnam Won the War," *Wall Street Journal*, August 3, 1995, p. A, 10.

154. Karnow, 1983, p. 15.

155. Guenter Lewy, *America in Vietnam*. Oxford: Oxford University Press, 1978, p. 304.

156. Dunbabin, 1994, p. 255.

157. Young, 1995, p. A, 10.

158. Timothy J. Lomperis, *The War Everyone Lost—and Won*. Washington, DC: Congressional Quarterly, 1993, p. 82.

159. Lewy, 1978, p. 192.

160. Davidson, 1991, p. 485.

161. Ibid., p. 485.

162. Hyland, 1991, pp. 144–45.

163. Lewis Sorley, *A Better War*. San Diego: Harvest, 1999, p. 95.

164. Adam B. Ulam, *The Communists*. New York: Charles Scribner's Sons, 1992, p. 266.

165. Painter, 1999, p. 60.

166. Joan Hoff, *Nixon Reconsidered*. New York: Basic Books, 1994, p. 208.

167. Richard Nixon, *RN: The Memoirs of Richard Nixon*. New York: Grosset & Dunlap, 1978, p. 348.

168. Sorley, 1999, p. 104.

169. William Colby, *Lost Victory*. Chicago: Contemporary Books, 1989, pp. 309–11.

170. Henry Holzer & Erika Holzer, *Aid and Comfort*. Jefferson, NC: McFarland & Co., 2002, p. 21.

171. Fox Butterfield, *China: Alive in the Bitter Sea*. New York: Times Books, 1982, p. 6.

172. Lind, 1999, p. 47.

173. Mary Hershberger, *Traveling to Vietnam*. Syracuse, NY: Syracuse University Press, 1998, p. 49.

174. Ibid., p. xviii.

175. Podhoretz, 1982, pp. 90–91.

176. Sorley, 1999, p. 303.

177. Lewy, 1978, pp. 154–55.

178. Ronald Spector, *After Tet*. New York: Free Press, 1993, p. 315.

179. Ibid.

180. Lind, 1999, p. 175.

181. Spector, 1993, p. 63.

182. Henry Kissinger, *White House Years*. Boston: Little, Brown & Co., 1979, p. 253.

183. Hall, 2000, p. 103.

184. Davidson, 1991, p. 627.

185. Ibid., p. 627.

186. Kissinger, 1979, p. 508.

187. Lomperis, 1993, p. 93.

188. Karnow, 1983, p. 653.

189. Lind, 1999, p. 249.

190. Podhoretz, 1982, p. 122.

191. Ibid.

192. Lewy, 1978, p. 332.

193. Nghia M. Vo, *The Bamboo Gulag*. Jefferson, NC: McFarland & Co., 2004, p. 11.

194. Hall, 2000, p. 79.

195. Francois Ponchaud, *Cambodia: Year Zero* (tr. Nancy Amphoux). New York: Holt, Rinehart & Winston, 1978, p. 17.

196. Lind, 1999, p. 167.

197. Ibid.

198. Jean-Louis Margolin, "Cambodia: The Country of Disconcerting Crimes," in Courtois (ed), 1999, p. 591.

199. Margolin, 1999, p. 593.

200. Summers, 1995, p. 76.

201. Vo, 2004, p. 43.

202. Ibid., pp. 341–42.

203. Podhoretz, 1982, p. 199.

204. Doan Van Toai, "A Lament for Vietnam," *New York Times Magazine*, March 29, 1981.

205. Podhoretz, 1982, p. 205.

206. Ibid., p. 204.

207. Sorley, 1999, p. 386.

208. Spector, 1993, p. 315.

209. Karnow, 1983, p. 15.

210. Sorley, 1999, p. 303.

211. Lind, 1999, p. 48.

212. Ulam, 1983, p. 81.

213. Garthoff, 1985, p. 28.

214. Ibid., pp. 43–44.

215. Mona Charen, *Useful Idiots*. New York: HarperCollins, 2003, p. 133.

216. Paul E. Sigmund, *The Overthrow of Allende*. Pittsburgh: University of Pittsburgh Press, 1977, p. 121.

217. Robert J. Alexander, *The Tragedy of Chile*. Westport, CT: Greenwood Press, 1978, p. 161.

218. Ibid., pp. 178–79.

219. Ibid., pp. 187–89.

220. Sigmund, 1977, p. 164.

221. Crozier, 1999, p. 349.

222. C. L. Sulzberger, *The World and Richard Nixon*. New York: Prentice Hall, 1978, p. 69.

223. www.prospect.org/webfeatures/2003/09/goldberg-j-09-15-html.

224. Alexander, 1978, p. 231.

225. Ranelagh, 1986, p. 336.

226. Ray C. Cline, *Secrets, Spies and Scholars*. Washington, DC: Acropolis Books, 1976, p. 189.

227. Ibid., pp. 128–32.

228. Ranelagh, 1986, p. 584.

229. Isaacs & Downing, 1998, pp. 287–88.

230. Powaski, 1998, pp. 198–99.

231. Isaacs & Downing, 1998, p. 289.

232. LaFeber, 2004, p. 296.

233. Friedman, 2000, p. 344.

234. Robert M. Gates, *From the Shadows*. New York: Touchstone, 1997, pp. 170–71.

235. Ibid., pp. 108–9.

236. Charen, 2003, p. 78.

237. Gaddis Smith, *Morality, Reason and Power*. New York: Hill & Wang, 1986, pp. 51–52.

238. Smith, 1986, p. 55.

239. Robert Kagan, *A Twilight Struggle*. New York: Free Press, 1996, p. 55.

240. Peter Schweizer, *Reagan's War*. New York: Doubleday, 2002, p. 112.

241. Kagan, 1987, p. 124.

242. Charen, 2000, pp. 204–5.

243. Ibid., p. 206.

244. Kagan, 1996, p. 115.

245. Ibid., p. 117.

246. Pascal Fontaine, in Courtois et al., 1979, p. 668.

247. Ibid., p. 669.

248. Ibid., pp. 672–73.

249. Burton L. Kaufman, *The Presidency of James Earl Carter*. Lawrence: University of Kansas Press, 1993, p. 139.

250. Friedman, 2000, p. 453.

251. Peter J. Wallison, *Ronald Reagan*. Cambridge, MA: Westview Press, 2003, p. 64.

252. Dov Zakheim, "The Military Buildup," in Eric Schmertz (ed), *President Reagan and the World*. Westport, CT: Greenwood Press, 1997.

253. Ibid., p. 190.

254. Timothy Garton Ash, *The Polish Revolution*. New York: Vintage Books, 1985, p. 63.

255. Crozier, 1999, pp. 357–58.

256. Isaacs & Downing, 1998, p. 330.

257. General Jaruzelski's Radio Address, December 13, 1981, in Judge & Langdon (eds), 1999, pp. 211–12.

258. Schweizer, 2002, p. 165.

259. Smith, 1994, p. 300.

260. Schweizer, 2002, p. 167.

261. Ibid., p. 110.

262. Ibid., p. 193.

263. Ibid., p. 196.

264. Ibid., p. 198.

265. Peggy Noonan, *When Character Was King*. New York: Random House, 2001, pp. 353–54.

266. Ibid., p. 126.

267. www.fas.org/irp/offdocs/nsdd/nsdd-075.htm.

268. President Reagan, Speech to the Nation, March 23, 1983, in Judge & Langdon (eds), 1999, pp. 215–16.

269. Pearson, 2002, p. 112.

270. Dinesh D'Souza, *What's Right with America*. Washington, DC: Regnery Gateway, 1997, p. 173.

271. Crozier, 1999, p. 371.

272. Paul Seabury and Walter A. McDougal, *The Grenada Papers*. San Francisco: Institute for Contemporary Studies, 1984, p. 207.

273. Ibid., p. 190.

274. McCauley, 1998, p. 63.

275. Crozier, 1999, p. 371.

276. Fontaine, 1979, p. 675.

277. Christopher Andrew & Oleg Gordievsky, *KGB: The Inside Story*. New York: HarperCollins, 1990, pp. 589–90.

278. D'Souza, 1997, p. 3.

279. Schweizer, 2002, p. 143.

280. Becker, 1998, p. 299.

281. Schweizer, 1994, p. xiv.

282. Charen, 2003, p. 113.

283. Coulter, 2003, p. 149.

284. Schweizer, 2002, p. 143.

285. Ibid., p. 69.

286. Robert G. Kaiser, *Why Gorbachev Happened*. New York: Touchstone, 1992, p. 67.

287. Friedman, 2000, p. 344.

288. John Barron, *The KGB Today*. New York: Berkley Books, 1985, p. 10.

289. Pipes, 2001, p. 85.

290. Dunbabin, 1994, p. 27.

291. Pearson, 2002, p. 119.

292. Kort, 1993, p. 83.

293. Schweizer, 2002, p. 254.

294. www.reagan.utexas.edu/resource/speeches/1986/22686b.htm.

295. Mark Galeotti, *Afghanistan: The Soviet Union's Last War*. London: Frank Cass, 1995, p. 18.

296. D'Souza, 1997, p. 173.

297. LaFeber, 1993, pp. 319–20.

298. Pearson, 2002, p. 122,

299. Crozier, 1999, p. 408.

300. Ulam, 1992, pp. 444–5.

301. Pipes, 2001, p. 84.

302. Richard Powers, *Not Without Honor*. New York: Free Press, 1995, p. 418.

303. Schweizer, 2002, p. 276.

304. Charles S. Maier, *Dissolution*. Princeton: Princeton University Press, 1997, p. 106.

305. Brzezinski, 1990, p. 132.

306. Ibid., 1990, p. 11.

307. Smith, 1994, p. 305.

308. Peter Schweizer, *Victory*. New York: Atlantic Monthly Press, 1994, p. xi.

309. Margaret Thatcher, eulogy at Ronald Reagan's funeral, June 11, 2004.

310. McCauley, 1998, p. 66.

311. Pearson, 2002, p. 132.

312. Isaacs & Downing, 1998, p. 390.

313. Anna Funder, *Stasiland*. London: Granta, 1999, p. 5.

314. Kaiser, 1992, p. 228.

315. Julie Marie Bunck, *Fidel Castro and the Quest for a Revolutionary Culture in Cuba*. University Park, PA: Penn State University Press, 1994, p. 18.

316. Andres Oppenheimer, *Castro's Final Hour*. New York: Touchstone, 1992, p. 380.

317. Bunck, 1994, p. 79.

318. Applebaum, 2003, p. xxi.

319. John Earl Haynes & Harvey Klehr, *In Denial*. San Francisco: Encounter Books, 2003, p. 2.

320. Robert Conquest, *Reflections on a Ravaged Century*. New York: W. W. Norton, 2000, p. 43.

321. Schweizer, 2002, p. 149.

322. Ibid.

323. Powers, 1995, p. 428.

324. George Kennan, "The Sources of Soviet Conduct," *Foreign Affairs*, July 1947, pp. 575, 582.

325. Kort, 1993, p. 347.

Chapter 8

1. "Democracy's Century: A Survey of Global Political Change in the 20th Century," December 7, 1999, http://www.freedomhouse.org/reports/century .html.

2. Alfred Zimmern, *The American Road to World Peace*. New York: E. P. Dutton & Co., 1953, p. 267.

3. Franklin Roosevelt, "The Four Freedoms," speech, in Richard D. Heffner (ed), *A Documentary History of the United States*. New York: Mentor, 1963, pp. 288–89.

4. Tony Smith, *America's Mission*. Princeton, NJ: Princeton University Press, 1994, p. 115.

5. Ibid., p. 1.

6. Indur Goklany, "The Globalization of Human Well-Being," August 22, 2002, Cato Institute, Cato Policy Analysis No. 447.

7. Wendell Willkie, "One World," in Richard N. Currant et al. (eds), *Words That Made America*. Boston: Little, Brown & Co., 1972, pp. 456–57.

8. Joseph Nye, "A Dollop of Deeper American Values," *Washington Post*, March 30, 2004, p. A19.

9. Woodrow Wilson, speech at Pueblo, Colorado, September 25, 1919, in Heffner (ed), p. 247.

10. Jon E. Lewis (ed), *The Mammoth Book of War Diaries and Letters*. New York: Carroll & Graf, 1999, p. 412.

Select Bibliography

Adams, Henry H. *1942: The Year that Doomed the Axis*. New York: David McKay Co., 1967.

Adler, Bill (ed.) *Letters from Vietnam*. New York: Ballantine Books, 2003.

Alexander, Joseph H. *Utmost Savagery*. New York: Ivy Books, 1995.

Alexander, Robert J. *The Tragedy of Chile*. Westport, CT: Greenwood Press, 1978.

American Battle Monuments Commission, "American Armies and Battlefields in Europe." Washington, DC: U.S. Govt. Printing Office, 1938.

Ambrose, Stephen E. *Citizen Soldiers*. New York: Simon & Schuster, 1997.

———. *D-Day*. New York: Simon & Schuster, 1994.

———. *Nixon: Ruin and Recovery, 1973–1990*. New York: Simon & Schuster, 1991.

———. *Rise to Globalism*. New York: Penguin, 1985.

Ambrosius, Lloyd E. *Wilsonian Statecraft*. Wilmington, DE: SR Books, 1991.

Amis, Martin. *Koba the Dread*. New York: Vintage, 2002.

Andrew, Christopher. *For the President's Eyes Only*. New York: HarperCollins, 1995.

Andrew, Christopher, and Oleg Gordievsky. *KGB: The Inside Story*. New York: HarperCollins, 1990.

Andrew, Christopher, and Vasily Mitrokhin. *The Sword and the Shield*. New York: Basic Books, 2000.

Applebaum, Anne. *Gulag*. New York: Doubleday, 2003.

Appy, Christian G. *Patriots: The Vietnam War from All Sides*. New York: Viking, 2003.

Aron, Raymond. *The Opium of the Intellectuals* (tr. Terence Kilmartin). Garden City, NY: Doubleday & Co., 1957.

Aron, Robert. *The Vichy Regime*. New York: Macmillan, 1958.

Ascherson, Neal. *The Polish August*. New York: Penguin, 1982.

Ash, Timothy Garton. *The Magic Lantern*. New York: Vintage Books, 1999.

Ash, Timothy Garton. *The Polish Revolution*. New York: Vintage Books, 1985.

Ashabranner, Brent. *A Moment in History*. New York: Doubleday, 1971.

Ashby, Timothy. *The Bear in the Backyard*. Lexington, MA: Lexington Books, 1987.

Asprey, Robert B. *At Belleau Wood*. Denton, TX: University of North Texas Press, 1996.

Atkinson, Rick. *An Army at Dawn*. New York: Henry Holt, 2002.

Baker, Mark. *Nam*. New York: William Morrow, 1981.

Bard, Mitchell G. *Myths and Facts*. Chevy Chase, MD: American Israeli Cooperative Enterprise, 2001.

Bardach, Janusz, and Kathleen Gleeson. *Man in Wolf to Man*. Berkeley: University of California Press, 1999.

Barron, John. *The KGB Today*. New York: Berkley Books.

Bastin, John, and Harry Benda. *A History of Modern Southeast Asia*. Englewood Cliffs, NJ: Prentice-Hall, 1968.

Baylis, Thomas. *How Israel Was Won*. Lanham, MD: Lexington Books, 1999.

Bearden, Milt, and James Risen. *The Main Enemy*. New York: Random House, 2003.

Becker, Elizabeth. *When the War Was Over*. New York: Public Affairs, 1998.

Becker, Jasper. *Hungry Ghosts*. New York: Henry Holt, 1998.

Bell, Coral. *The Diplomacy of Detente*. New York: St. Martin's Press, 1977.

Benson, Michael T. *Harry S Truman and the Founding of Israel*. Westport, CT: Praeger, 1997.

Benz, Wolfgang. *The Holocaust* (tr. Jane Sydenham-Kwiet). New York: Columbia University Press, 1999.

Bergerud, Eric. *Touched with Fire*. New York: Penguin Books, 1996.

Berry, Henry. *Semper Fi, Mac*. New York: Berkley Books, 1982.

Beschloss, Michael. *The Conquerors*. New York: Simon & Schuster, 2002.

Betts, Raymond. *Decolonization*. New York: Routledge, 1998.

———. *Europe Overseas*. New York: Basic Books, 1968.

———. *Tricouleur*. London: Gordon & Cremonesi, 1978.

———. *Uncertain Dimensions*. Minneapolis: University of Minnesota Press, 1985.

Bhagwati, Jagdish. *Free Trade Today*. Princeton: Princeton University Press. 2002.

Bingham, Jonathan. *Shirt-Sleeve Diplomacy*. New York: The John Day Company, 1954.

Birmingham, David. *The Decolonization of Africa*. Athens, OH: Ohio University Press, 1995.

Bishop, Jim. *FDR's Last Year*. New York: William Morrow, 1974.

Black, Coit. *Hostage to Revolution*. New York: Council on Foreign Relations Press, 1993.

Blair, Arthur H. *At War in the Gulf*. College Station: Texas A&M University Press, 1992.

Blair, Clay. *The Forgotten War*. New York: Anchor Books, 1987.

Blond, Georges. *The Death of Hitler's Germany* (tr. Frances Frenaye). New York: Macmillan, 1954.

Blumenson, Martin. *Anzio: The Gamble That Failed*. Philadelphia: J. B. Lippincott, 1963.

———. *Patton*. New York: William Morrow & Co., 1985.

———. *Salerno to Cassino*. Washington, DC: Center of Military History, United States Army, 1969.

Boli, Zhang. *Escape from China* (tr. Kwee Kian Low). New York: Washington Square Press, 1998.

Bonachea, Rolando, and Nelson P. Valdes (eds.) *Cuba in Revolution.* New York: Anchor Books, 1972.

Bornet, Vaughn Davis. *The Presidency of Lyndon B. Johnson.* Lawrence University of Kansas Press, 1983.

Boyer, Paul (ed). *Reagan as President.* Chicago: Ivan R. Dee, 1990.

Boyne, Walter J. *The Two O'Clock War.* New York: St. Martin's Press, 2002.

Brackman, Arnold C. *The Other Nuremberg.* New York: William Morrow, 1987.

Bradley, Omar. *A Soldier's Story.* New York: Henry Holt, 1951.

Brady, James. *The Coldest War.* New York: Thomas Dunne, 2000.

Brines, Russell. *MacArthur's Japan.* Philadelphia: J. B. Lippincott, 1948.

Brittain, Vera. *Testament of Youth.* New York: Penguin, 1994.

Brook, Timothy. *Quelling the People.* Stanford: Stanford University Press, 1998.

Brooks, Jeffrey. *Thank You, Comrade Stalin!* Princeton: Princeton University Press, 2000.

Bryan, Lowell, and Diana Farrell. *Market Unbound.* New York: John Wiley & Sons, 1996.

Brzezinski, Zbigniew. *The Grand Failure.* New York: Collier, 1990.

Buchan, John. *A History of the Great War.* 4 vols. New York: Nelson, 1921–22.

Buchanan, A. Russell. *The United States and World War II.* New York: Harper & Row, 1964.

Buhle, Paul, and Dave Wagner. *Radical Hollywood.* New York: New Press, 2002.

Bullard, Robert Lee. *Personalities and Reminiscences of the War.* New York: Doubleday, Page & Co., 1925.

Bunck, Julie Marie. *Fidel Castro and the Quest for a Revolutionary Culture in Cuba.* University Park, PA: Penn State University Press, 1994.

Burns, James MacGregor. *Roosevelt: The Soldier of Freedom.* New York: Harcourt Brace Jovanovich, 1970.

Burrin, Philippe. *Hitler and the Jews* (tr. Patsy Southgate). London: Edward Arnold, 1994.

Burtless, Gary et al. *Globaphobia.* Washington, DC: The Brookings Institution Press, 1998.

Butterfield, Fox. *China: Alive in the Bitter Sea.* New York: Times Books, 1982.

Calhoun, Frederick S. *Power & Principle: Armed Intervention in Wilsonian Foreign Policy.* Kent, OH: Kent State University Press, 1986.

Cannon, Lou. *Reagan.* New York: G. P. Putnam's Sons, 1982.

Carbonell, Nestor T. *And the Russians Stayed.* New York: William Morrow & Co., 1989.

Carroll, Andrew (ed.) *War Letters.* New York: Scribner, 2001.

Carter, Gwendolyn. *Independence for Africa.* New York: Praeger, 1960.

Carter, Jimmy. *Keeping Faith.* New York: Bantam Books, 1982.

Cate, Curtis. *The Ides of August: The Berlin Wall Crisis, 1961.* New York: M. Evans & Co., 1978.

Center of Military History. *Anzio Beachhead.* Washington, DC: U.S. Army, 1990.

Chandler, David P. *Brother Number One.* Boulder, CO: Westview Press, 1999.

———. *Voices from S-21.* Berkeley: University of California Press, 1999.

Chang, Gordon G. *The Coming Collapse of China.* New York: Random House, 2001.

———. *Friends and Enemies.* Stanford: Stanford University Press, 1990.

Chang, Iris. *The Rape of Nanjing*. New York: Basic Books, 1997.

Chao, Linda, and Ramon Myers. *The First Chinese Democracy*. Baltimore: Johns Hopkins University Press, 1998.

Charen, Mona. *Useful Idiots*. New York: HarperCollins, 2003.

Cheever, Daniel, and H. Field Haviland. *Organizing for Peace*. Cambridge, MA: Houghton Mifflin, 1965.

Chen, Jian. *China's Road to the Korean War*. New York: Columbia University Press, 1994.

Churchill, Winston S. *The Great Republic*. New York: Random House, 1999.

———. *The Second World War*. 6 vols. Boston: Houghton Mifflin, 1948–53.

Clark, John Maurice. *The Costs of the World War to the American People*. New Haven: Yale University Press, 1931.

Clarke, George Herbert (ed.) *A Treasury of War Poetry: British and American Poems of the World War, 1914–1917*. New York: Houghton Mifflin, 1918.

Cline, Ray C. *Secrets, Spies and Scholars*. Washington, DC: Acropolis Books, 1976.

Coffman, Edward M. *The War to End All Wars*. New York: Oxford University Press, 1968.

Cogan, Frances B. *Captured*. Athens: University of Georgia Press, 2000.

Cohen, Michael. *Truman and Israel*. Berkeley: University of California Press, 1990.

Cohen, Theodore. *Remaking Japan*. New York: Free Press, 1987.

Cohen, Warren L. *America's Response to China*. New York: John Wiley & Sons, 1971.

Colby, William. *Lost Victory*. Chicago: Contemporary Books, 1989.

Cole, Hugh. *The Ardennes: Battle of the Bulge*. Washington, DC: United States Army, Center of Military History, 1994.

Coleman, John S. *Bataan and Beyond*. College Station: Texas A&M University Press, 1978.

Collier, Richard. *Bridge Across the Sky*. New York: McGraw Hill, 1978.

Congressional Budget Office. *The GATT Negotiations and U.S. Trade Policy*. Washington, DC: U.S. Govt. Printing Office, 1987.

Congressional Quarterly. *China: U.S. Policy Since 1945*. Washington, DC: CQ Press, 1980.

Conquest, Robert. *The Great Terror: A Reassessment*. New York: Oxford University Press, 1990.

———. *The Harvest of Terror*. New York: Oxford University Press, 1986.

———. *Reflections on a Ravaged Century*. New York: W. W. Norton, 2000.

———. *Stalin: Breaker of Nations*. New York: Penguin Books, 1991.

Cooper, Chester L. *The Lion's Last Roar*. New York: Harper & Row, 1978.

Cooper, Richard. *The Economics of Interdependence*. New York: Columbia University Press, 1980.

Cornell, Erik. *North Korea Under Communism* (tr. Rodney Bradbury) London: Routledge Curzon, 2002.

Costello, John. *The Pacific War*. New York: Rawson Wade Publishers, 1981.

Courtois, Stephane et al. *The Black Book of Communism* (tr. Jonathan Murphy & Mark Kramer). Cambridge: Harvard University Press, 1999.

Creel, George. *The War, the World and Wilson*. New York: Harper & Brothers, 1920.

Crozier, Brian. *The Rise and Fall of the Soviet Empire*. Roseville, CA: Prima Publishing, 1999.

Currant, Richard N. et al. (eds.) *Words That Made America*. Boston: Little, Brown & Co., 1972.

Czernin, Ferdinand. *Versailles 1919*. New York: G. P. Putnam's Sons, 1964.

Daniels, Walter (ed.) *The Point Four Program*. New York: H. W. Wilson, 1951.

Davidson, Eugene. *The Death and Life of Germany*. New York: Alfred A. Knopf, 1961.

Davidson, Phillip B. *Vietnam at War*. Oxford: Oxford University Press, 1991.

Davies, Sarah. *Popular Opinion in Stalin's Russia*. Cambridge: Cambridge University Press, 1997.

Davis, F. Hadland. *Myths and Legends of Japan*. New York: Dover, 1991.

Dawidowicz, Lucy. *The War Against the Jews, 1933–1945*. New York: Bantam, 1986.

Dawisha, Karen. *The Kremlin and the Prague Spring*. Berkeley: University of California Press, 1984.

Daws, Gavan. *Prisoners of the Japanese*. New York: Quill, 1994.

DeConde, Alexander. *A History of American Foreign Policy*. New York: Charles Scribner's Sons, 1963.

Dees, Bowen C. *The Allied Occupation and Japan's Economic Miracle*. Surrey: Curzon Press, 1997.

del Aguila, Juan M. *Cuba: Dilemmas of a Revolution*. Boulder, CO: Westview Press, 1994.

Deletant, Dennis. *Communist Terror in Romania*. New York: St. Martin's Press, 1999.

D'Este, Carlo. *Decision in Normandy*. New York: E. P. Dutton, 1983.

———. *Patton: A Genius for War*. New York: HarperCollins, 1995.

Divine, Robert A. *Eisenhower and the Cold War*. Oxford: Oxford University Press, 1981.

———. *The Reluctant Belligerent*. New York: John Wiley & Sons, 1965.

Doan Van Toai. *The Vietnamese Gulag*. New York: Simon & Schuster, 1986.

Dolot, Miron. *Execution by Hunger*. New York: W. W. Norton, 1985.

Donovan, Robert J. *The Second Victory*. New York: Madison Books, 1987.

Dower, John W. *Embracing Defeat*. New York: W. W. Norton, 1999.

———. *War Without Mercy*. New York: Pantheon, 1986.

Draper, Theodore. *Castroism: Theory and Practice*. New York: Praeger, 1965.

D'Souza, Dinesh. *What's Right with America*. Washington, DC: Regnery Gateway, 2002.

Dubcek, Alexander. *Hope Dies Last* (tr. Jiri Hochman). New York: Kodansha, 1993.

Dudley, William (ed.) *The Middle East: Opposing Viewpoints*. San Diego: Greenhaven Press, 1992.

Dudley, William, and Karin Swisher (eds.) *China: Opposing Viewpoints*. San Diego: Greenhaven Press, 1989.

Duignan, Peter. *NATO: Its Past, Present and Future*. Stanford: Hoover Institution Press, 2000.

Dunbabin, J. P. D. *The Cold War: The Great Powers and their Allies*. London: Longman, 1994.

Dunnigan, James F., and Albert A. Nofi. *The Pacific War Encyclopedia*. 2 vols. New York: Facts on File, 1998.

Dvorchak, Robert J. *Battle for Korea*. Pittsburgh, PA: Combined Publishing, 1993.

Eckes, Alfred E. *A Search for Solvency*. Austin: University of Texas Press, 1975.

Edelman, Bernard (ed.) *Dear America*. New York: W. W. Norton, 1985.

Eden, Anthony. *The Suez Crisis of 1956*. Boston: Beacon Press, 1960.

Edgerton, Robert D. *Warriors of the Rising Sun*. Boulder, CO: Westview Press, 1997.

Eichelberger, Clark. *Organizing for Peace*. New York: Harper & Row, 1977.

———. *UN: The First Twenty Years*. New York: Harper & Row, 1965.

Eisenhower, Dwight D. *Crusade in Europe*. Garden City, NY: Doubleday & Co., 1948.

———. *The White House Years*. New York: Doubleday & Co., 1965.

Ellis, John. *Cassino: The Hollow Victory*. New York: McGraw Hill, 1984.

Ellis, L. F. *Victory in the West*. 2 vols. London: Her Majesty's Stationery Office, 1968.

Ellwood, David W. *Rebuilding Europe*. London: Longman, 1992.

Eubank, Keith. *Summit at Teheran*. New York: William Morrow & Company, 1985.

Evans, Martin. *Retreat, Hell! We Just Got Here!* Oxford: Osprey Publishing, 1998.

Evans, Rowland, and Robert Novak. *Lyndon B. Johnson: The Exercise of Power*. New York: New American Library, 1966.

———. *Nixon in the White House*. New York: Random House, 1971.

Fairbank, John. *China: The People's Middle Kingdom and the USA*. Cambridge: Harvard University Press, 1967.

Feifer, George. *The Battle of Okinawa*. Guilford, CT: Lyons Press, 2001.

———. *The Red Files*. New York: TVBooks, 2000.

———. *Tennozan*. New York: Ticknor & Fields, 1992.

Fejto, Francois. *A History of the People's Democracies* (tr. Daniel Wessbort). New York: Praeger, 1971.

Fermi, Laura. *Mussolini*. Chicago: University of Chicago Press, 1961.

Ferrell, Robert H. *Woodrow Wilson and World War I*. New York: Harper & Row, 1985.

Fest, Joachim C. *Hitler* (tr. Richard & Clara Winston). New York: Harcourt Brace Jovanovich, 1973.

Finer, Herman. *Dulles over Suez*. Chicago: Quadrangle Books, 1964.

Finn, Richard. *Winners in Peace*. Berkeley: University of California Press, 1992.

Fisher, Ernest F. *Cassino to the Alps*. Washington, DC: Center of Military History, United States Army, 1993.

Fitzpatrick, Sheila. *Everyday Stalinism*. New York: Oxford University Press, 1999.

———. *Stalin's Peasants*. New York: Oxford University Press, 1996.

Flood, Charles Bracelen. *Hitler: The Path to Power*. Boston: Houghton Mifflin, 1989.

Flower, Desmond, and James Reeves (eds.) *The Taste of Courage*. New York: Harper & Brothers, 1960.

Flynn, Robert. *A Personal War in Vietnam*. College Station: Texas A&M University Press, 1989.

Foot, Rosemary. *Rights Beyond Borders*. Oxford: Oxford University Press, 2000.

Fossedal, Gregory A. *Our Finest Hour*. Stanford, CA: Hoover Institution Press, 1993.

Frank, Richard B. *Downfall: The End of the Imperial Japanese Empire*. New York: Penguin, 1999.

———. *Guadalcanal*. New York: Random House, 1990.

Friedlander, Saul. *Prelude to Downfall: Hitler and the United States, 1939–1941* (tr. Aline & Alexander Werth). New York: Alfred A. Knopf, 1967.

Friedman, Herbert J. *What America Did Right*. New York: University Press of America, 1996.

Friedman, Norman. *Conflict and Strategy in the Cold War*. Annapolis, MD: Naval Institute Press, 2000.

Friedman, Thomas L. *The Lexus and the Olive Tree*. New York: Anchor Books, 2000.

Fuchida, Mitsuo, and Masatake Okumiya. *Midway*. Annapolis: U.S. Naval Institute Press, 1955.

Funder, Anna. *Stasiland*. London: Granta, 2003.

Furet, Francois. *The Passing of an Illusion* (tr. Deborah Furet). Chicago: University of Chicago Press, 1995.

Fursenko, Alexander, and Timothy Naftali. *"One Hell of a Gamble."* New York: W. W. Norton, 1997.

Gaddis, John Lewis. *The Long Peace: Inquiries into the History of the Cold War*. Oxford: Oxford University Press, 1987.

———. *Strategies of Containment*. New York: Oxford University Press, 1982.

———. *The United States and the Origins of the Cold War, 1941–1947*. New York: Columbia University Press, 1972.

———. *The United States and the End of the Cold War*. Oxford: Oxford University Press, 1992.

———. *We Now Know*. Oxford: Oxford University Press, 1997.

Galeotti, Mark. *Afghanistan: The Soviet Union's Last War*. London: Frank Cass, 1995.

Gantter, Raymond. *Roll Me Over*. New York: Ivy Books, 1997.

Gao, Yuan. *Born Red: A Chronicle of the Cultural Revolution*. Stanford: Stanford University Press, 1987.

Gardner, Lloyd C. *Approaching Vietnam*. New York: W. W. Norton, 1989.

———. *Economic Aspects of New Deal Diplomacy*. Boston: Beacon Press, 1971.

Garland, Albert N., and Howard McGraw Smyth. *Sicily and the Surrender of Italy*. Washington, DC: Office of the Chief of Military History, Department of the Army, 1965.

Garraty, John A. *Woodrow Wilson*. New York: Alfred A. Knopf, 1956.

Garthoff, Raymond L. *Detente and Confrontation*. Washington, DC: Brookings Institution, 1985.

Garver, John W. *Face Off*. Seattle: University of Washington Press, 1997.

Gates, Robert M. *From the Shadows*. New York: Touchstone, 1997.

Gayn, Mark. *Japan Diary*. New York: William Sloane Associates, 1948.

Gelb, Norman. *The Berlin Wall*. New York: Times Books, 1987.

Getty, J. Arch, and Oleg V. Naumov. *The Road to Terror*. New Haven: Yale University Press, 1999.

Gibney, Frank. *The Pacific Century*. New York: Charles Scribner's Sons, 1992.

Gifford, Prosser, and William Roger Louis (eds.) *Britain and Germany in Africa*. New Haven: Yale University Press, 1967.

———. *France and Britain in Africa*. New Haven: Yale University Press, 1971.

———. *The Transfer of Power in Africa*. New Haven: Yale University Press, 1967.

Gilbert, Martin. *Israel: A History*. New York: William Morrow & Co., 1998.

———. *Never Again*. London: Universe, 2000.

Gilbert, Martin. *The Second World War.* New York: Henry Holt, 1989.

Gilpin, Robert. *The Challenge of Global Capitalism.* Princeton: Princeton University Press, 2000.

———. *The Political Economy of International Relations.* Princeton: Princeton University Press, 1987.

Gimbel, John. *The American Occupation of Germany.* Stanford: Stanford University Press, 1968.

———. *The Origins of the Marshall Plan.* Stanford: Stanford University Press, 1976,

Girardet, Edward. *Afghanistan: The Soviet War.* New York: St. Martin's Press, 1985.

Glynn, Patrick. *Closing Pandora's Box.* New York: Basic Books, 1992.

Gold, Hal. *Unit 731 Testimony.* Tokyo: Yen Books, 1996.

Gold, Thomas B. *State and Society in the Taiwan Miracle.* Armonk, NY: M. E. Sharpe, 1986.

Goldhagen, Daniel Jonah. *Hitler's Willing Executioners.* New York: Alfred A. Knopf, 1997.

Goldman, Merle. *Sowing the Seeds of Democracy in China.* Cambridge: Harvard University Press, 1994.

Goodhart, Philip. *Fifty Ships That Saved the World.* New York: Doubleday, 1965.

Goodrich, Leland M. *The United Nations.* New York: Thomas Crowell, 1959.

Goris, Jan-Albert. *Belgium in Bondage.* New York: L. B. Fischer, 1943.

Goulden, Joseph C. *Korea: The Untold Story of the War.* New York: Times Books, 1982.

Granfield, Linda (ed.) *I Remember Korea.* New York: Clarion Books, 2003.

Grant, Zalin. *Survivors.* New York: W. W. Norton, 1975.

Grayson, Cary T. *Woodrow Wilson.* New York: Holt, Rinehart & Winston, 1960.

Greene, Theodore P. (ed.) *Wilson at Versailles.* Boston: D. C. Heath, 1957.

Grose, Peter. *Operation Rollback.* Boston: Houghton Mifflin, 2000.

Grosser, Alfred. *Germany in Our Time* (tr. Paul Stephenson). New York: Praeger, 1970.

Gugeler, Russel A. *Combat Actions in Korea.* Washington, DC: U.S. Army Center of Military History, 1987.

Gunderson, Gerald. *The Wealth Creators.* New York: Truman Taley Books, 1989.

Gup, Ted. *The Book of Honor.* New York: Anchor Books, 2001.

Halebsky, Sander, and John M. Kirk (eds.) *Cuba: Twenty-Five Years of Revolution.* New York: Praeger, 1985.

Hall, Mitchell. *The Vietnam War.* London: Longman, 2000.

Hambro, C. J. *I Saw It Happen in Norway.* New York: D. Appleton & Co., 1940.

Hammel, Eric. *Chosin.* New York: Vanguard Press, 1981.

———. *Guadalcanal: Decision at Sea.* New York: Crown Publishers, 1988.

Hapgood, David, and David Richardson. *Monte Cassino.* New York: Congdon & Weed, 1984.

Hargreaves, J. D. *Decolonization in Africa.* London: Longman, 1990.

Harris, Sheldon H. *Factories of Death.* London: Routledge, 1994.

Hart, B. H. Liddell. *History of the Second World War.* New York: G. P. Putnam's Sons, 1971.

Hastings, Max. *The Korean War.* New York: Touchstone, 1987.

———. *Overlord: D-Day and the Battle for Normandy.* New York: Simon & Schuster, 1984.

————. *Victory in Europe*. Boston: Little, Brown & Co., 1985.

Haynes, John Earl, and Harvey Klehr. *In Denial*. San Francisco: Encounter Books, 2003.

Heffner, Richard D. (ed.) *A Documentary History of the United States*. New York: Mentor, 1963.

Heller, Andor. *No More Comrades*. Chicago: Henry Regnery, 1957.

Herring, George C. *America's Longest War*. New York: McGraw Hill, 1996.

Hershberger, Mary. *Traveling to Vietnam*. Syracuse, NY: Syracuse University Press, 1998.

Heydecker, Joe J. *The Nuremberg Trial*. Cleveland: World Publishing, 1962.

Hibbert, Christopher. *Il Duce: The Life of Benito Mussolini*. New York: Little, Brown & Co., 1962.

Hicks, George. *The Comfort Women*. New York: W. W. Norton, 1994.

Hitler, Adolf. *Mein Kampf* (tr. Alvin Johnson). New York: Reynal & Hitchcock, 1939.

Hoff, Joan. *Nixon Reconsidered*. New York: Basic Books, 1994.

Hoffman, Carl W. *Saipan*. Washington, DC: Historical Division, U.S. Marine Corps, 1950.

Hoge, James F., and Fareed Zakaria (eds.) *The American Encounter*. New York: Basic Books, 1997.

Hollander, Paul. *Political Pilgrims*. Oxford: Oxford University Press, 1981.

Holzer, Henry, and Erika Holzer. *Aid and Comfort*. Jefferson, NC: McFarland & Co., 2002.

Hook, Sidney et al. *Soviet Hypocrisy and Western Gullibility*. Lanham, MD: University Press of America, 1987.

House, Edward Mandell. *What Really Happened At Paris: The Story of the Peace Conference, 1918–1919*. New York: Charles E. Merrill, 1921.

Howe, George F. *Northwest Africa: Seizing the Initiative in the West*. Washington, DC: Center of Military History, United States Army, 1991.

Hoyt, Edwin P. *The Bloody Road to Panmunjon*. New York: Stein & Day, 1985.

————. *The Day the Chinese Attacked*. New York: McGraw Hill, 1990.

————. *Japan's War*. New York: McGraw Hill, 1986.

————. *To the Marianas*. New York: Van Nostrand Reinhold, 1980.

Hudec, Robert E. *The GATT Legal System and World Trade Diplomacy*. New York: Praeger, 1978.

Human Rights in China. *Children of the Dragon*. New York: Collier Books, 1990.

Human Rights Watch. *Punishment Season: Human Rights in China after Martial Law*. New York: Asia Human Rights Watch, 1990.

Huntington, Samuel. *The Third Wave*. Norman: University of Oklahoma Press, 1991.

Hyland, William. *The Cold War*. New York: Times Books, 1991.

Ienaga, Saburo. *The Pacific War*. New York: Pantheon Books, 1978.

Irwin, Douglas A. *Against the Tide*. Princeton: Princeton University Press, 1996.

Isaacs, Jeremy, and Taylor Downing. *Cold War: An Illustrated History*. Boston: Little, Brown, 1998.

Isserman, Maurice (ed). *Witness to Vietnam*. New York: Periree, 1995.

Ivanova, Galina. *Labor Camp Socialism* (tr. Carol Flath) Armonk, NY: M. E. Sharpe, 2000.

James, D. Clayton, and Anne Sharp Wells. *From Pearl Harbor to V-J Day*. Chicago: Ivan R. Dee, 1995.

Jeffreys-Jones, Rhodri. *American Espionage*. New York: Free Press, 1977.

Jeffries, John W. *Wartime America*. Chicago: Ivan R. Dee, 1996.

Jenkins, Roy. *Churchill*. New York: Farrar, Straus and Giroux, 2001.

Jiang, Ji Li. *Red Scarf Girl*. New York: Scholastic, 1997.

Johnsen, Julia E. (ed.) *The Dilemma of Postwar Germany*. New York: H. W. Wilson, 1948.

Johnson, Paul. *A History of the American People*. New York: HarperCollins, 1999.

———. *Modern Times*. New York: HarperCollins, 1991.

———. *The Suez War*. New York: Greenberg, 1957.

Johnson, Sam, and Jan Winebrenner. *Captive Warriors*. College Station: Texas A&M University Press, 1992.

Jones, F. C. *Japan's New Order in Asia*. London: Oxford University Press, 1954.

Judge, Edward H., and John W. Langdon. *A Hard and Bitter Peace*. New York: Prentice Hall, 1996.

———. *The Cold War: A History through Documents*. New York: Prentice Hall, 1999.

Kagan, Robert. *A Twilight Struggle*. New York: Free Press, 1996.

Kahler, Miles. *Decolonization in Britain and France*. Princeton: Princeton University Press, 1984.

Kaiser, Robert G. *Why Gorbachev Happened*. New York: Touchstone, 1992.

Kakar, M. Hassan. *Afghanistan: The Soviet Invasion and the Afghan Response, 1979–1982*. Berkeley: University of California Press, 1997.

Kang, Chol-hwan. *The Aquariums of Pyongyang* (tr. Yair Reiner). New York: Basic Books, 2000.

Karnow, Stanley. *Vietnam: A History*. New York: Viking Press, 1983.

Katsuichi, Honda. *The Nanjing Massacre*. Armonk, NY: M. E. Sharpe, 1999.

Kaufman, Burton L. *The Presidency of James Earl Carter*. Lawrence: University of Kansas Press, 1993.

———. *Trade and Aid: Eisenhower's Foreign Economic Policy, 1953–1961*. Baltimore: Johns Hopkins University Press, 1982.

Kawai, Kazuo. *Japan's American Interlude*. Chicago: University of Chicago Press, 1960.

Keegan, John. *The First World War*. New York: Alfred A. Knopf, 1999.

———. *The Second World War*. New York: Viking Press, 1990.

———. *Six Armies in Normandy*. New York: Viking Press, 1982.

Kelly, Brian, and Mark London. *The Four Little Dragons*. New York: Touchstone, 1989.

Kelly, Michael. *Martyr's Day*. New York: Vintage Books, 2001.

Kemp, Anthony. *The Unknown Battle*. New York: Stein & Day, 1981.

Kenwood, A. G., and A. L. Lougheed. *The Growth of the International Economy*. London: George Allen & Unwin, 1983.

Kessler, Ronald. *Inside the CIA*. New York: Pocket Books, 1992.

Kernan, Ben. *The Pol Pot Regime*. New Haven: Yale University Press, 2002.

Kimball, Warren F. *The Most Unsordid Act*. Baltimore: Johns Hopkins University Press, 1969.

Kissinger, Henry. *Diplomacy*. New York: Simon & Schuster, 1994.

———. *White House Years*. Boston: Little, Brown & Co., 1979.

Klehr, Harvey, and John Earl Haynes. *The Soviet World of American Communism*. New Haven: Yale University Press, 1998.

Klehr, Harvey et al. *The Secret World of American Communism*. New Haven: Yale University Press, 1995.

Knox, Donald. *Death March*. New York: Harcourt Brace Jovanovich, 1981.

Kort, Michael. *The Columbia Guide to the Cold War*. New York: Columbia University Press, 1993.

Koehler, John O. *Stasi*. Boulder, CO: Westview Press, 1999.

Kosut, Hal. *Israel and the Arabs: The June 1967 War*. New York: Facts on File, 1968.

Laber, Jeri. *The Courage of Strangers*. New York: Public Affairs, 2002.

LaFeber, Walter. *America, Russia and the Cold War, 1945–1992*. New York: McGraw Hill, 1993.

Lamb, Richard. *War In Italy, 1943–1945*. London: Penguin Books, 1993.

Langer, William L., and S. Everett Gleason. *The Undeclared War: 1940–1941*. New York: Harper & Brothers, 1953.

Langley, Michael. *Inchon Landing*. New York: Times Books, 1979.

Larson, Deborah Welch. *Origins of Containment*. Princeton: Princeton University Press, 1985.

Larsson, Tomas. *The Race to the Top*. Washington, DC: Cato Institute, 2001.

Lash, Joseph P. *Roosevelt and Churchill, 1939–1941*. New York: W. W. Norton, 1976.

Lasky, Melvin J. (ed) *The Hungarian Revolution*. New York: Praeger, 1957.

Leckie, Robert. *Delivered from Evil*. New York: Harper & Row, 1987.

———. *Okinawa*. New York: Penguin Books, 1995.

———. *Strong Men Armed*. New York: DaCapo Press, 1990.

Levine, Alan J. *The Strategic Bombing of Germany, 1940–1945*. Westport, CT: Praeger, 1992.

Lewis, Bernard. *Islam and the West*. Oxford: Oxford University Press, 1993.

———. *What Went Wrong?* Oxford: Oxford University Press, 2002.

Lewis, Jon E. (ed.) *The Mammoth Book of War Diaries and Letters*. New York: Carroll & Graf, 1999.

Lewy, Guenter. *America in Vietnam*. Oxford: Oxford University Press, 1978.

Li, Zhisui. *The Private Life of Chairman Mao*. New York: Random House, 1994.

Liggett, Hunter. *Commanding an American Army: Recollections of the World War*. New York: Houghton Mifflin, 1925.

Lilla, Mark. *The Reckless Mind*. New York: New York Review of Books, 2001.

Lind, Michael. *Vietnam: The Necessary War*. New York: Touchstone, 1999.

Lindsey, Brink. *Against the Dead Hand*. New York: John Wiley & Sons, 2002.

Lloyd George, David. *The Truth about the Peace Treaties*. London: V. Gollancz, 1938.

Loewenheim, Francis L. (ed.) *Roosevelt and Churchill: The Secret Wartime Correspondence*. London: Barrie & Jenkins, 1975.

Loewenstein, Karl. *Hitler's Germany*. New York: Macmillan, 1940.

Lomperis, Timothy J. *The War Everyone Lost—and Won*. Washington, DC: Congressional Quarterly, 1993.

Louis, William Roger. *Imperialism at Bay*. New York: Oxford University Press, 1978.

Lu, David J. *From Marco Polo Bridge to Pearl Harbor*. Washington, DC: Public Affairs Press, 1961.

Lukacs, John. *A History of the Cold War*. New York: Doubleday & Co., 1961.

Lukacs, John. *The Last European War: September 1939/December 1941.* Garden City, NY: Anchor Press, 1976.

MacDonald, Callum A. *Korea: The War before Vietnam.* New York: Free Press, 1986.

MacDonald, Charles B. *A Time for Trumpets.* New York: William Morrow, 1985.

MacFarquhar, Roderick. *The Hundred Flowers Campaign and the Chinese Intellectuals.* New York: Octagon Books, 1974.

———. *The Origins of the Cultural Revolution.* Vol. 1. New York: Columbia University Press, 1974.

———. *The Origins of the Cultural Revolution.* Vol. 2. New York: Columbia University Press, 1983.

———. *Sino-American Relations, 1949–71.* New York: Praeger, 1972.

Maddex, Robert L. *Constitutions of the World.* Washington, DC: CQ Press, 1995.

Maier, Charles S. *Dissolution.* Princeton: Princeton University Press, 1997.

Mandelbaum, Michael. *The Ideas That Conquered the World.* New York: Public Affairs, 2002.

Manning, Paul. *Hirohito: The War Years.* New York: Dodd, Mead & Co., 1986.

Manning, Stephen Neal. *The Courage of Common Men.* Plano, TX: Republic of Texas Press, 2001.

Marchal, Leon. *Vichy: Two Years of Deception.* New York: Macmillan, 1943.

Marrus, Michael R., and Robert O. Paxton. *Vichy France and the Jews.* New York: Basic Books, 1981.

May, Ernest. *The Truman Administration and China.* New York: J. B. Lippincott, 1975.

Mayer, Arno J. *Why Did the Heavens Not Darken?* New York: Pantheon Books, 1988.

McCauley, Martin. *The Origins of the Cold War.* London: Longman, 1995.

———. *Russia, America and the Cold War.* London: Longman, 1998.

———. *Stalin and Stalinism.* London: Pearson Education, 2003.

McClellan, Grant S. (ed.) *The Two Germanies.* New York: H. W. Wilson, 1959.

McInnis, Edgar. *The War: Fourth Year.* London: Oxford University Press, 1945.

McInnis, Edgar et al. *The Shaping of Postwar Germany.* Toronto: J. M. Dent & Sons, 1960.

McMahon, Robert J. *The Cold War.* Oxford: Oxford University Press, 2003.

McMaster, John Bach. *The United States in the World War.* 2 vols. New York: D. Appleton, 1929.

Mead, Walter Russell. *Special Providence.* New York: Alfred A. Knopf, 2001.

Mee, Charles L. *The Marshall Plan.* New York: Simon & Schuster, 1984.

Melman, Yossi, and Dan Raviv. *Friends in Deed: Inside the U.S.-Israel Alliance.* New York: Hyperion, 1994.

Mikaelian, Allen. *Medal of Honor.* New York: Hyperion, 2002.

Miller, Edward. *A Dark and Bloody Ground.* College Station: Texas A&M University Press, 2003.

Mills, Walter. *The Last Phase.* Boston: Houghton Mifflin, 1946.

Milosz, Czeslaw. *The Captive Mind.* New York: Vintage, 1990.

Milton, David, and Nancy Milton. *The Wind Will Not Subside.* New York: Pantheon Books, 1976.

Milton, David, Nancy Milton, and Franz Schurmann. *People's China.* New York: Random House, 1974.

Mitchell, Richard H. *Thought Control in Prewar Japan*. Ithaca: Cornell University Press, 1976.

Monahan, James, and Kenneth O. Gilmore. *The Great Deception*. New York: Farrar, Straus and Co., 1963.

Montgomery, John D., and Denis A. Rondinelli. *Great Policies*. Westport, CT: Praeger, 1995.

Moore, John Norton (ed.) *The Arab-Israeli Conflict: Readings and Documents*. Princeton: Princeton University Press, 1977.

Moore, Ray A., and Donald Robinson. *Partners for Democracy*. Oxford: Oxford University Press, 2002.

Moore, Stephen, and Julian Simon. *It's Getting Better All the Time*. Washington, DC: Cato Institute, 2000.

Moorehead, Alan. *Eclipse*. New York: Harper & Row, 1968.

Morgan, Ted. *FDR: A Biography*. New York: Simon & Schuster, 1985.

Morris, Benny. *Righteous Victims*. New York: Alfred A. Knopf, 1999.

Morris, Edmund. *Dutch*. New York: Random House, 1999.

Moses, Catherine. *Real Life in Castro's Cuba*. Wilmington, DE: Scholarly Resources, 2000.

Mu, Yi, and Mark Thompson. *Crisis at Tiananmen*. San Francisco: China Books and Periodicals, 1989.

Mulhall, John W. *America and the Founding of Israel*. Los Angeles: Deshon Press, 1995.

Nadav, Safran. *Israel: The Embattled Ally*. Cambridge: Harvard University Press, 1978.

Nathan, Andrew J. *China's Transition*. New York: Columbia University Press, 1997.

———. *Chinese Democracy*. Berkeley: University of California Press, 1985.

Natsios, Andrew. *The Great North Korean Famine*. Washington, DC: United States Institute of Peace Press, 2001.

Navratil, Jaromir. *The Prague Spring*. Budapest: Central European Press, 1998.

Newton, Verne W. (ed.) *FDR and the Holocaust*. New York: St. Martin's Press, 1996.

Nguyen, Van Canh. *Vietnam under Communism*. Stanford: Hoover Institution Press, 1985.

Nichols, Chas S., and Henry I. Shaw. *Okinawa*. Washington, DC: Historical Division, U.S. Marine Corps, 1955.

Nobecourt, Jacques. *Hitler's Last Gamble* (tr. R.H. Barry). New York: Schocken Books, 1967.

Nomberg-Przytyk, Sara. *Auschwitz*. Chapel Hill: University of North Carolina Press, 1985.

Noonan, Peggy. *When Character Was King*. New York: Random House, 2001.

Nordin, Carl S. *We Were Next to Nothing*. Jefferson, NC: McFarland & Co., 1997.

Norman, Elizabeth M. *We Band of Angels*. New York: Random House, 1999.

Oberdorfer, Dan. *The Two Koreas*. New York: Basic Books, 2001.

O'Connell, Robert L. *Of Arms and Men: A History of War, Weapons and Aggression*. Oxford: Oxford University Press, 1990.

O'Donnell, Patrick. *Beyond Valor*. New York: Free Press, 2001.

———. *Into the Rising Sun*. New York: Free Press, 2002.

Oh, Kongdan, and Ralph C. Hassig. *North Korea: Through the Looking Glass.* Washington, DC: Brookings Institution Press, 2000.

O'Neill, William L. *A Democracy at War.* Cambridge: Harvard University Press, 1993.

Oppenheimer, Andres. *Castro's Final Hour.* New York: Touchstone, 1992.

Oren, Michael B. *Six Days of War.* New York: Ballantine Books, 2003.

Osterman, Christian F. *Uprising in East Germany, 1953.* New York: Central European University Press, 2001.

Painter, David. *The Cold War: An International History.* London: Routledge, 1999.

Palmer, Alan. *Victory 1918.* New York: Atlantic Monthly Press, 2000.

Parker, James E. *Covert Ops.* New York: St. Martin's Press, 1995.

Parker, R. A. C. *The Second World War: A Short History.* Oxford: Oxford University Press, 1989.

Parmet, Herbert S. *Richard Nixon and His America.* Boston: Little, Brown & Co., 1990.

Parrish, Thomas. *Berlin in the Balance.* Reading, MA: Perseus Books, 1998.

Pastor, Robert A. (ed.) *A Century's Journey.* New York: Basic Books, 1999.

Paxton, Robert O. *Vichy France.* New York: Alfred A. Knopf, 1972.

Pearson, Raymond. *The Rise and Fall of the Soviet Empire.* New York: Palgrave, 2002.

Perkins, Dexter. *The American Approach to Foreign Policy.* Cambridge: Harvard University Press, 1962.

Perrett, Geoffrey. *Days of Sadness, Years of Triumph.* New York: Coward, McCann & Geoghegan, 1973.

Perry, John Curtis. *Beneath the Eagle's Wings.* New York: Dodd, Mead & Co., 1980.

Pershing, John J. *My Experiences in the World War.* New York: Frederick A. Stokes Co., 1931.

Piccigallo, Philip R. *The Japanese on Trial.* Austin: University of Texas Press, 1979.

Pierpaoli, Paul G. *Truman and Korea.* Columbia: University of Missouri Press, 1999.

Pipes, Richard. *Communism.* New York: Modern Library, 2001.

———. *Russia Under the Bolshevik Regime.* New York: Alfred A. Knopf, 1993.

Polk, William R. *The United States and the Arab World.* Cambridge: Harvard University Press, 1969.

Ponchaud, Francois. *Cambodia: Year Zero* (tr. Nancy Amphoux). New York: Holt, Rinehart & Winston, 1978.

Porter, A. N. *British Imperial Policy and Decolonization, 1938–64.* New York: St. Martin's Press, 1987.

Powaski, Ronald E. *The Cold War.* Oxford: Oxford University Press, 1998.

Powers, Richard. *Not without Honor.* New York: Free Press, 1995.

Prange, Gordon W. *At Dawn We Slept.* New York: McGraw Hill, 1981.

———. *Miracle at Midway.* New York: McGraw Hill, 1982.

Pratt, Fletcher. *The Marines' War.* New York: William Sloane, 1948.

Price, Harry Bayard. *The Marshall Plan and Its Meaning.* Ithaca, NY: Cornell University Press, 1955.

Pyle, Ernie. *Brave Men.* New York: Henry Holt, 1944.

———. *Here Is Your War.* New York: Henry Holt, 1943.

Quandt, William B. *Camp David*. Washington, DC: Brookings Institution Press, 1986.

———. *Decade of Decisions*. Berkeley: University of California Press, 1977.

———. *Peace Process*. Washington, DC: Brookings Institution Press, 2001.

Rabin, Yitzhak. *The Rabin Memoirs*. Berkeley: University of California Press, 1996.

Radzinsky, Edward. *Stalin* (tr. H. T. Willetts). New York: Anchor Books, 1997.

Ranelagh, John. *The Agency*. New York: Simon & Schuster, 1986.

Ratliff, William E. *Castroism and Communism in Latin America, 1959–1976*. Washington, DC: American Enterprise Institute, 1976.

Raviv, Dan and Melman, Yossi. *Friends in Deed*. New York: Hyperion, 1994.

Ray, John. *The Second World War*. London: Cassell, 1999.

Reagan, Ronald. *An American Life*. New York: Simon & Schuster, 1990.

Rees, David. *The Age of Containment*. New York: St. Martin's Press, 1967.

Rees, Laurence. *Horror in the East*. Cambridge, MA: DaCapo Press, 2001.

Reischauer, Edwin O. *Japan: The Story of a Nation*. New York: McGraw Hill, 1990.

Rigger, Shelley. *Politics in Taiwan*. London: Routledge, 1999.

Rice, Edward. *Mao's Way*. Berkeley: University of California Press, 1972.

Rice, Gerard T. *The Bold Experiment*. Notre Dame: University of Notre Dame Press, 1985.

Richelson, Jeffrey. *A Century of Spies*. Oxford: Oxford University Press, 1995.

Robbins, Keith. *The First World War*. Oxford: Oxford University Press, 1993.

Rochester, Stuart I., and Frederick Kiley. *Honor Bound: The History of American Prisoners of War in Southeast Asia, 1961–1973*. Washington, DC: Historical Office of the Secretary of Defense, 1998.

Rodinson, Maxime. *Israel and the Arabs*. New York: Pantheon Books, 1968.

Roosevelt, Theodore. *America and the World War*. New York: Charles Scribner's Sons, 1915.

Ross, Alf. *The United Nations: Peace and Progress*. Totowa, NJ: Bedminster Press, 1966.

Ross, Bill D. *Iwo Jima*. New York: Vanguard Press, 1985.

Russell, Edward Frederick Langley, Lord of Liverpool. *The Knights of Bushido*. London: Military Book Club, 1958.

Ryan, Cornelius. *The Longest Day*. New York: Simon & Schuster, 1959.

Ryan, David (ed.) *The United States and Decolonization*. New York: St. Martin's Press. 2000.

Sachar, Howard M. *A History of Israel*. New York: Alfred A. Knopf, 2001.

Safran, Nadav. *Israel: The Embattled Ally*. Cambridge, MA: Belknap Press, 1978.

Sandler, Stanley (ed.) *The Korean War*. New York: Garland Publishing, 1995.

Santoli, Al (ed.) *To Bear Any Burden*. Bloomington: Indiana University Press, 1985.

Saunders, Kate. *Eighteen Layers of Hell*. London: Cassell, 1996.

Schaller, Michael. *The United States and China in the Twentieth Century*. Oxford: Oxford University Press, 1990.

Schefter, James. *The Race*. New York: Anchor Books, 2000.

Schell, Orville. *Discos and Democracy*. New York: Anchor Books, 1989.

———. *Mandate of Heaven*. New York: Touchstone, 1994.

Schirmer, Daniel and Stephen Shalom. *The Philippines Reader*. Boston: South End Press, 1987.

Schlesinger, Arthur M. *A Thousand Days*. Boston: Houghton Mifflin, 1965.

Schmokel, Wolfe. *Dream of Empire*. New Haven: Yale University Press, 1964.

Schnabel, James F. *Policy and Direction: The First Year*. Washington DC: Office of Military History. 1972.

Schoenbaum, David. *The United States and the State of Israel*. Oxford: Oxford University Press, 1993.

Schoenhals, Michael (ed.) *China's Cultural Revolution*. Armonk, NY: M. E. Sharpe, 1996.

Schonberger, Howard B. *Aftermath of War*. Kent, OH: Kent State University Press, 1989.

Schurmann, Franz, and Orville Schell. *Communist China*. New York: Random House, 1967.

———. *Republican China*. New York: Random House, 1967.

Schwartz, Richard A. *Encyclopedia of the Persian GulfWar*. Jefferson, NC: McFarland & Co., 1998

Schweizer, Peter. *Reagan's War*. New York: Doubleday, 2002.

———. *Victory*. New York: Atlantic Monthly Press, 1994.

Scott, James. *Deciding to Intervene*. Durham, NC: Duke University Press, 1996.

Seaborg, Glenn T. *Kennedy, Khrushchev and the Test Ban*. Berkeley: University of California Press, 1981.

Seabury, Paul, and Walter A. McDougal. (eds.) *The Grenada Papers*. San Francisco: Institute for Contemporary Studies Press, 1984.

Seymour, Charles. *American Diplomacy during the World War*. Hamden, CT: Archon Books, 1964.

Shawcross, William. *Dubcek*. New York: Touchstone, 1990.

Sheehan, Fred. *Anzio: Epic of Bravery*. Norman: University of Oklahoma Press, 1964.

Sheldon, Walt. *The Honorable Conquerors*. New York: Macmillan, 1965.

Shirer, William L. *The Rise and Fall of the Third Reich*. New York: Simon & Schuster, 1960.

Shoichi, Koseki. *The Birth of Japan's Postwar Constitution*. Boulder, CO: Westview Press, 1997.

Sigmund, Paul E. *The Overthrow of Allende*. Pittsburgh: University of Pittsburgh Press, 1977.

Simonds, Frank H. *History of the World War*. New York: Doubleday, Page & Co., 1919.

Sledge, E. B. *With the Old Breed*. Oxford: Oxford University Press, 1981.

Slusser, Robert M. *The Berlin Crisis of 1961*. Baltimore: Johns Hopkins University Press, 1973.

Smith, E. D. *The Battles for Cassino*. New York: Charles Scribner's Sons, 1975.

Smith, Gaddis. *Morality, Reason and Power*. New York: Hill & Wang, 1986.

Smith, S. E. *The United States Marine Corps in World War II*. New York: Random House, 1969.

Smith, Tony. *America's Mission*. Princeton: Princeton University Press, 1994.

———. *The Pattern of Imperialism*. Cambridge: Cambridge University Press, 1981.

Snider, Delbert A. *Introduction to International Economics*. Homewood, IL: Irwin-Dorsey, 1975.

Snodgrass, Warren. *Swords to Plowshares*. Huntington, NY: New Science Publishers, 2000.

Sobel, Lester A. *Israel and the Arabs: The October 1973 War*. New York: Facts On File, 1974.

Sodei, Rinjiro (ed.) *Dear General MacArthur* (tr. Shizue Matsuda). Lanham, MD: Rowman & Littlefield, 2001.

Solzhenitsyn, Aleksandr I. *The Gulag Archipelago*. New York: Harper & Row, 1973.

Sorenson, Theodore C. *Kennedy*. New York: Harper & Row, 1965.

Sorley, Lewis. *A Better War*. San Diego: Harvest, 1999.

Spector, Ronald. *After Tet*. New York: Free Press, 1993.

———. *Eagle Against the Sun*. New York: Free Press, 1985.

Spence, Jonathan. *Mao Zedong*. New York: Viking, 1999.

———. *The Search for Modern China*. New York: W. W. Norton, 1990.

Spero, Joan. *The Politics of International Economic Relations*. New York: St. Martin's Press, 1990.

Springhall, John. *Decolonization Since 1945*. New York: Palgrave, 2001.

Stallings, Laurence. *The Doughboys*. New York: Harper & Row, 1963.

Stanik, Joseph. *El Dorado Canyon*. Annapolis: Naval Institute Press, 2003.

Stenbuck, Jack (ed.) *Typewriter Battalion*. New York: William Morrow & Co., 1995.

Stiglitz, Joseph E. *Globalization and its Discontents*. New York: W. W. Norton, 2003.

Stokesbury, James L. *A Short History of World War I*. New York: William Morrow, 1981.

———. *A Short History of World War II*. New York: William Morrow & Co., 1980.

Stone, Norman. *Hitler*. Boston: Little, Brown & Co., 1980.

Strawson, John. *The Battle for the North Atlantic*. New York: Charles Scribner's Sons, 1969.

Stueck, William. *The Korean War*. Princeton: Princeton University Press, 1995.

Suettinger, Robert L. *Beyond Tiananmen*. Washington, DC: Brookings Institution Press, 2003.

Sulzberger, C. L. *The World and Richard Nixon*. New York: Prentice Hall, 1987.

Summers, Harry G. *On Strategy*. New York: Ballantine Books, 1995.

———. *The Vietnam War Almanac*. Novato, CA: Presidio Press, 1990.

Summers, Robert E. (ed.) *Economic Aid to Europe*. New York: H. W. Wilson, 1948.

Talbott, Strobe. *The Russians and Reagan*. New York: Random House, 1984.

Tanaka, Yuki. *Hidden Horrors*. Boulder, CO: Westview Press, 1996.

Tang, Truong Nhu. *A Viet Cong Memoir*. New York: Vintage Books, 1985.

Tansill, Charles Callan. *America Goes to War*. Boston: Little, Brown & Co., 1938.

Terraine, John. *The Great War: 1914–1918*. New York: Macmillan, 1965.

Terrill, Ross. *Mao: A Biography*. New York: Harper & Row, 1980.

———. *The New Chinese Empire*. New York: Basic Books, 2003.

Thompson, Laurence. *1940*. New York: William Morrow & Co., 1966.

Thornton, Richard. *China: A Political History*. Boulder: Westview Press, 1982.

Tillman, Seth P. *The United States in the Middle East*. Bloomington: Indiana University Press, 1982.

Timperley, H. J. *Japanese Terror in China*. New York: Modern Age Books, 1938.

Tocqueville, Alexis de. *Democracy in America*. (J. P. Mayer ed.) New York: Doubleday, 1966.

Todorov, Tzvetan. *Voices From the Gulag* (tr. Robert Zaretsky). University Park, PA: Penn State University Press, 1999.

Toland, John. *The Last 100 Days*. New York: Random House, 1966.

———. *The Rising Sun*. New York: Random House, 1970.

Tompson, William J. *Khrushchev: A Political Life*. New York: St. Martin Griffin, 1997.

Tregaskis, Richard. *Guadalcanal Diary*. New York: Random House, 1955.

Triplet, William S. *A Youth in the Meuse-Argonne*. Columbia: University of Missouri Press, 2000.

Tuchman, Barbara W. *The Guns of August*. New York: Macmillan, 1962.

Tucker, Robert C. *Stalin in Power*. New York: W. W. Norton, 1990.

Turner, Henry Ashby. *Hitler's Thirty Days to Power*. Reading, MA: Addison Wesley, 1996.

Tyler, Patrick. *A Great Wall*. New York: Public Affairs, 1999.

Ulam, Adam B. *The Communists*. New York: Charles Scribner's Sons, 1992.

———. *Dangerous Relations*. New York: Oxford University Press, 1983.

Urquhart, Brian. *Decolonization and World Peace*. Austin: University of Texas Press, 1989.

U.S. News & World Report. *Triumph without Victory*. New York: Times Books, 1993.

Valladares, Armando. *Against All Hope* (tr. Andrew Hurley). New York: Alfred A. Knopf, 1986.

Van der Vat, Dan. *The Pacific Campaign*. New York: Simon & Schuster, 1991.

Van Dormael, Armand. *Bretton Woods*. New York: Holmes & Meir, 1978.

Vandiver, Frank E. *Black Jack: The Life and Times of John J. Pershing*. College Station: Texas A&M University Press, 1977.

Velen, Elizabeth, and Victor A. Velen. *The New Japan*. New York: H. W. Wilson Co., 1958.

Vo, Nghia M. *The Bamboo Gulag*. Jefferson, NC: McFarland & Co., 2004.

Wachman, Alan M. *Taiwan: National Identity and Democratization*. Armonk, NY: M. E. Sharpe, 1994.

Wainhouse, David. *Remnants of Empire*. New York: Harper & Row, 1964.

Wallison, Peter J. *Ronald Reagan*. Cambridge, MA: Westview Press, 2003.

Weinberg, Gerhard L. *A World At Arms*. Cambridge: Cambridge University Press, 1994.

Weinrod, W. Bruce (ed.) *The Heritage Foundation Arms Control Handbook*. Washington, DC: Heritage Foundation, 1987.

Weller, Nathan. *Spying for America*. New York: Paragon Books, 1989.

Weller, Robert P. *Alternate Civilities: Democracy and Culture in China and Taiwan*. Boulder, CO: Westview Press, 1999.

Westerfield, H. Bradford. *Inside the CIA's Private World*. New Haven: Yale University Press, 1995.

Whelan, Richard. *Drawing the Line*. Boston: Little, Brown & Co., 1990.

White, Mark. *Missiles in Cuba*. Chicago: Ivan R. Dee, 1997.

Whiting, Allen S. *China Crosses the Yalu*. Stanford: Stanford University Press, 1968.

Whiting, Charles. *The Battle of Hurtgen Forest*. New York: Orion Books, 1989.

———. *Death of a Division*. New York: Stein & Day, 1981.

———. *Kasserine*. New York: Stein & Day, 1984.

Willis, Clint (ed.) *The War*. New York: Adrenaline, 1999.

Wilson, Dick. *When Tigers Fight*. New York: Viking Press, 1982.

Wilson, George. *If You Survive*. New York: Ivy Books, 1987.

Wilson, Theodore. *The Marshall Plan, 1947–1951*. New York: Foreign Policy Association, 1977.

Winik, Jay. *On the Brink*. New York: Simon & Schuster, 1996.

Wolfe, Robert (ed.) *Americans As Proconsuls: The United States Military Government in Germany and Japan, 1944–1952*. Carbondale: Southern Illinois University Press, 1984.

Woodward, C. Vann. *The Battle for Leyte Gulf*. New York: Macmillan, 1947.

Wright, Robin. *Sacred Rage*. New York: Linden Press, 1985.

Wu, Harry, and Carolyn Wakeman. *Bitter Winds*. New York: John Wiley & Sons, 1994.

Yakovlev, Alexander N. *A Century of Violence in Soviet Russia* (tr. Anthony Austin). New Haven: Yale University Press, 2002.

Yergin, Daniel, and Joseph Stanislaw. *The Commanding Heights*. New York: Touchstone, 1998.

Yi, Zheng. *Scarlet Memorial* (tr. T. P. Sym). New York: Westview Press, 1996.

Young, Louise. *Japan's Total Empire*. Berkeley: University of California Press, 1998.

Yuan, Gao. *Born Red*. Stanford: Stanford University Press, 1987.

Zakaria, Fareed. *The Future of Freedom*. New York: W. W. Norton, 2003.

Zeman, Z. A. B. *Prague Spring*. New York: Hill and Wang, 1969.

Zhang, Shu Guang. *Mao's Military Romanticism*. Lawrence: University of Kansas Press, 1995.

Zimmern, Alfred. *The American Road to World Peace*. New York: E. P. Dutton & Co., 1953.

Zink, Harold. *The United States in Germany*. Princeton, NJ: Van Nostrand, 1957.

Zubok, Vladislav, and Constantine Pleshakov. *Inside the Kremlin's Cold War*. Cambridge: Harvard University Press, 1996.

Index

About the Author

MATTHEW C. PRICE is Assistant Professor of Political Science at Texas A&M University-Kingsville. He is the author of *Justice Between Generations: The Growing Power of the Elderly in America* (Praeger, 1997).